Proverbs: A Commentary from a Christian Counseling Perspective

Table of Contents

The Author's Preface

The Book of Proverbs is a treasure trove of both divine and universal wisdom, containing some of the most relevant wisdom and teaching in the Bible. It is not difficult for a child to read, yet it contains profound truths and insights in a simple and accessible way.

There are many commentaries and books on Proverbs that do a good job of explaining the profound truths and insights linguistically and theologically. However, I have been motivated for several years to write an exegesis of Proverbs from the perspective of a Christian counselor.

The research method I used is a phenomenological one: I read and interpreted the text from my own subjective perspective, writing down the thoughts that came to mind, and then relating the text to counseling only where there was a connection to Christian counseling. After doing the subjective writing, I checked my work against several trusted commentaries on Proverbs, cross-checking them against each other. These sources are primarily footnoted in the text, and I was greatly helped by Charles Bridges' commentary.

In commenting on some texts, I have quoted directly from my writings that have already been published through various channels, but I have not identified them in this book to avoid inconvenience. I am grateful to Elder Dae-yoon Chang, Editor of Daeseo Publisher, and Dr. Hee-kyung Moon, Editor of Head and Heart Publisher, for their willing permission for me to quote directly.

After finishing my writing on Proverbs, I have come to realize that the ultimate purpose of Proverbs is to help the reader of Proverbs live a God-fearing life. The fear of God, as Solomon so well pointed out, is the starting point and reference point for knowledge and wisdom. I hope you will read this book with that in mind. One of the characteristics of Proverbs is "repetitions." You may find some repetitions in my writing too. Through repetitions we are learned unconsciously.

I have written this book for pastors, seminarians, and Christian counselors and clients in mind, especially Korean-American Christians including adolescents and young people. I hope it also will be helpful for Christians scattered around the world who desire God's Word in the mission field. As a Korean author, I hope you will understand that the background of the Korean church and Korean culture is incorporated in the book. I especially wanted to help pastors and seminarians who are working in the field to understand the human heart and psychology while preaching on Proverbs. This book will help them apply the message of each text to real life. Christian counselors who are struggling with how to relate the Bible specifically to their counseling practice will also benefit from this book. Christian clients and members of the church who are wrestling with life's issues will find it helpful in understanding their inner lives and life problems in a more wise and discerning way. If you are a non-Christian reader, I pray that you may believe in God and Jesus Christ as your Savior through this book. Or if you happen to have lost your faith in Jesus Christ, I hope you can be recovered in your relationship and faith in him and to your church community.

This book was originally published in Korean in 2018 through Iktus Publisher. I immigrated to the United States December 2021 after my early retirement from

Chongshin Theological Seminary, where I had taught for many years. I was motivated to write this book in English to help English-speaking people in my much more relaxed life after retirement. This book is the fourth book in English after my retirement. I made some revisions to the previously published book. I omitted more than a half of footnotes for the convenience's sake for readers. I am grateful to Iktus Publisher for granting me the copyright to publish this book in English. The program DeepL was very helpful in the process of translating the Korean book into English. However, it took a lot of energy and time to read through and refine and edit it. The New International Version of the Bible (2011) is used. I wrote this commentary based on the 1984 version of NIV. In case of different translation I enclosed the 1984 version text in a parenthesis.

I am grateful to God who has strengthened me to focus on this work of translation that took over two months. During the period I had to fight with some symptoms of COVID-19 virus that lasted over two weeks. As I finish up this work, I still take Advil pills for pain relief of body aching. I am glad that I finish up this work now although there may be some minor errors or misspellings. Personally I experienced that God was speaking to myself through what I had already written. I pray that God may speak to you personally too as you read this book so that you may be encouraged, sustained, guided, challenged, confronted, healed, reconciled, and freed in your life journey. May God bless you.

Kwanjik Lee

Chapter 1 Fear God

The proverbs of Solomon son of David, king of Israel: for gaining wisdom and instruction; for understanding words of insight; for receiving instruction in prudent behaviors, doing what is right and just and fair; for giving prudence to those who are simple, knowledge and discretion to the young—let the wise listen and add to their learning, and let the discerning get guidance—for understanding proverbs and parables, the sayings and riddles of the wise (1:1-6).

This text, which serves as an introduction to the entire book of Proverbs, lays out the goals that Solomon aims for with his proverbs. First, to enable God's children to gain wisdom and instruction (2).

Second, it is to help God's children live a balanced life. Specifically, it is to urge them to develop and change the faculties of the intellect and emotions and the will. So that they can live a life that is wise, righteous, just, and fair (3b).

Third, to guide and direct God's children so that they may live prudent lives (4b).[1] These three goals align well with the direction of a God-fearing life mentioned in verse 7.

Counseling Application: It is important to set goals during the counseling process. It helps to objectively evaluate and review the effectiveness of counseling when the client and counselor have an agreed-upon goal in mind. Therefore, in short-term or problem-solving counseling, goals are often set together with the client.

It is important for Christian counselors to keep in mind the three key goals mentioned above. The approach should be to see the

---

[1] A prudent person is able to live a life of self-control, free from impulsive and immature behavior. Self-control is a fruit of the Holy Spirit that is beneficial in preventing the self-defeating behaviors that impulsive speech can lead to.

trees in the forest while keeping the big picture in mind. If a counselor's eyes are fixed on local and tentative goals without seeing the big picture, he or she lacks wisdom.

The fear of the LORD is the beginning of knowledge, but fools despise wisdom and instruction (1:7). See also 9.10.

After laying out the goals of Proverbs, Solomon makes it clear that the central purpose of Proverbs is to help us live in the fear of the LORD.[2] The final section of Proverbs, chapter 31:30, demonstrates that living in the fear of God is the central purpose of the entire book of Proverbs by stating, "Charm is deceptive, and beauty is fleeting; but a woman who fears the LORD is to be praised."

The text of verse 7 declares that the fear of God is the beginning and reference point of knowledge. True knowledge consists in "making associations" with God in all areas of life. So-called "knowledge" that is separate from God is not true knowledge; it can even be a hindrance to the fear of God.

Proper understanding of human beings and knowledge of the world must begin with God the Creator. It must begin with a "God-knowledge" of who God is, what God has done, what God is doing, and what God will do.

Human understanding without a Christian theological perspective is full of distortions and errors. It has a weak foundation. It is relative and variable according to the times. This is because the standard of value judgment is based on variable and subjective human beings or phenomena. In this subjective, relative, postmodern age, believers must never lose sight of the absolute

---

[2]   The importance of fearing the LORD is emphasized repeatedly in Proverbs: 2:5, 8:13, 9:10, 10:27, 14:27, 15:33, 19:23, 22:4. See Milton Horne, *Proverbs-Ecclesiastes*, Smith & Helwys Bible Commentary (Macon, GA: Smith & Helwys, 2003), 27. Solomon emphasized the importance of fearing the LORD in the final section of his Ecclesiastes: "Now all has been heard; here is the conclusion of the matter: Fear God and keep his commandments, for this is the duty of all mankind" (Eccl. 12:13).

standards and objective truths of the Bible.

As John Calvin made clear, true knowledge can only be gained by viewing the created world, including humans, through the glasses of the knowledge of God the Creator. Proverbs is part of the inerrant Word of God. As such, it provides true knowledge without error or distortion for understanding human beings.

Proverbs diagnoses as "foolish" anyone who fails to connect with God, differently from the world's standards. The foolish is "a fool." They think they are wise, but in reality they are foolish. The fool thinks, "There is no God" (see Ps. 14:1).

A fool hates to learn. A fool is "unteachable," no matter how much you teach him or her. All who have not been born again of the Spirit do not see, because their eyes cannot see, and their ears cannot hear.[3] They are spiritually unlearned. They are ignorant of their true condition. And they do not realize and do not admit that they are ignorant.

The second half of verse 7, "fools despise wisdom and instruction," captures the narcissistic personality disorder component of the fool (see 1:22).[4] A key symptom of this personality disorder is self-grandiosity. The persons with this personality disorder overestimate and idealize themselves, so they are unwilling to learn from others. They don't digest advice or admonishment from others. Instead, they get angry. Because they think so highly of themselves, they don't like people who point out their weaknesses. They misinterpret this as saying that they are problematic persons. They don't recognize or admit their own foolishness, weaknesses, and limitations.

It is wise to teach a person after understanding who he or she really is. As mentioned earlier, persons with narcissistic

---

[3] Spiritual fools do not recognize the light (John 1:10b). Rather, they actively dislike and even resent coming light. When the Pharisees and scribes heard the wise words of Jesus, they felt disgust and murderous rage. They thought they had wisdom, but in reality they were spiritually foolish and blind (John 9:39).

[4] Koptak notes that the wise possess the quality of humility, recognizing that they are not perfect, but they are in the process of change. Paul Koptak, *Proverbs: The NIV Application Commentary* (Grand Rapids, MI: Zondervan, 2003), 67. Those who despise wisdom and instruction are arrogant and have narcissistic personality disorder.

personality disorder will lash out when admonished or confronted. Even church members with that personality disorder resent preachers who make them realize their weaknesses. They turn a deaf ear. It is not surprising that the Pharisees and scribes who heard Jesus' wisdom-filled teaching were enraged and sought to kill him. It's no surprise that after hearing Stephen's brilliant sermon, the elders and scribes "covered their ears and, yelling at the top of their voices, they all rushed at him, dragged him out of the city and began to stone him" (Acts 7:57-58a).[5] They didn't think they were in trouble. They thought they were the leaders spiritually.

Counseling Application: To be an effective counselor, you need to add to the breadth and depth of your knowledge of human beings. Humanities, like psychology, psychiatry, and sociology, are general disciplines that explore knowledge of God's creation and human beings. Like other disciplines, they have their benefits for understanding human beings. But they cannot be the starting point for truth and knowledge.

Christian counseling must be grounded in knowledge and belief in the Triune God to be distinctly "Christian" in identity. Only then will it have a therapeutic effect that distinguishes it from other counseling. Counselors whose faith in God and the anthropology and worldview taught by God's Word, the Bible, are the reference point are wise and solid, like persons who build their house on a rock. On the other hand, if they use the humanistic anthropology as a reference point, they are as foolish as persons who build their house on sand.

Listen, my son, to your father's instruction and do not forsake your mother's teaching. They are a garland to grace your head and a chain to adorn your neck (1:8-9).

---

[5] Jesus said, "Do not give dogs what is sacred; do not throw your pearls to pigs" (Matt. 7:6a), and he gave the reason why, "If you do, they may trample them under their feet, and turn and tear you to pieces" (Matt. 7:6b).

The phrase "my son" indicates that the primary recipient of Solomon's proverbs was his son. His call to his son conveys the love and concern of a father.[6] However, another recipients of the proverbs are also the children of God. Through Solomon's lips, God still speaks to each believer who reads and meditates on these proverbs, calling him or her "my son" or "my daughter."

The counsel and laws of God are a crown on the head of God's children, a golden necklace around their neck. They are words of wisdom that make their face shine. They are not stumbling blocks to harass and annoy them, but stepping stones to transformation and salvation for them. When we recognize that Proverbs is a word of life, given by God for the benefit of his children, we will obey it voluntarily.

My son, if sinful men entice you, do not give in to them. If they say, "Come along with us; let's lie in wait for innocent blood, let's ambush some harmless soul; let's swallow them alive, like the grave, and whole, like those who go down to the pit; we will get all sorts of valuable things and fill our houses with plunder; cast lots with us; we will all share the loot"—my son, do not go along with them, do not set foot on their paths; for their feet rush into evil, they are swift to shed blood (1:10-16).

Notice the verbs in this passage that characterize the behaviors of the wicked.[7] Knowing the behavioral characteristics helps us to accurately identify and diagnose who the wicked are. First, the wicked "entice." They act like friends, but they secretly place

---

[6]   Koptak points out that both father and mother participate in the education of their sons, especially in the proverb of King Lemuel's mother in chapter 31, which indicates that mothers also took on the role of teacher to their children in the Old Testament days. Koptak, *Proverbs*, 72.

[7]   Fox comments that this description of the wicked seems to be a commentary on Proverbs 16:29: "A violent person entices their neighbor and leads them down a path that is not good." Michael Fox, *Proverbs 1-9* (New York: Doubleday, 2000), 85.

stumbling blocks to trip you up. They try to capture you with tempting bait. They have the mentality of a bird hunter trying to catch birds in a net with birdseed, as shown in verse 17, "How useless to spread a net where every bird can see it!" It is easy to be fooled by their outward appearance.

Second, the evil promote a sense of fellowship. They create a sense of "false intimacy" for those who don't have a sense of belonging or who have loneliness issues. They make you feel like you're part of a big family! They say, "Come with us," or "Let's just have a common purse." They invite you to partner with them. But these are scammers who want to take advantage of you. Worse, they make you an accomplice. It is a classic trick of the devil to get you to be an accomplice. The devil is always looking for partners to take to hell with him.

Third, the wicked kill the innocent without cause. They randomly attack or kill others. They take pleasure in doing evil (see 1 Cor. 13:6). They are persons with antisocial personality disorder and psychopaths in the modern sense. They cause harm to others in order to pursue their own interests. They have little capacity to empathize with others and feel no remorse.

Fourth, the wicked lie in wait and ambush. They are savage in that they attack while concealing their identity. It is unsportsmanlike and inhumane to ambush and attack in everyday life, not in a war situation. They wear masks to avoid revealing their identity. They are intelligent enough to be discreet to avoid leaving fingerprints. They belong to the devil. They are the children of darkness who dwell and walk in darkness.

Fifth, the wicked fill their houses with plunder. It is selfish and antisocial to fill their bellies with unearned, stolen, or tax evaded income.[8] Breaking the law is their daily behavior.[9]

---

[8] Paul exhorted believers to put an end to the evil behavior of stealing and instead practice the good behavior of giving with their labor: "Anyone who has been stealing must steal no longer, but must work, doing something useful with their own hands, that they may have something to share with those in need" (Eph. 4:28). It's not enough to avoid doing evil. Christians must live a life of actively doing good.

[9] Jezebel was an even worse psychopath than Ahab, who lay "on his bed sulking" and "refused to eat." She "wrote letters in Ahab's name, placed his seal on them, and sent them to the elders and nobles who lived in Naboth's city," setting up false witnesses

Sixth, the wicked have feet that rush into evil and "swift to shed blood." They are unable to control their impulsive aggression or sexual urges. They experience little of the conflict that normal people experience when they do evil. They rarely even feel remorse. So, after committing a crime, they walk around as if nothing happened. Even after being arrested, they nonchalantly reenact the crime scene. They are diagnosed as psychopaths or persons of antisocial personality disorder. But the Bible diagnoses them as "the wicked."

How useless to spread a net where every bird can see it! These men lie in wait for their own blood; they ambush [waylay] only themselves! Such are the paths [the end] of all who go after ill-gotten gain; it takes away the life of those who get it (1:17-19).[10]

It may seem temporarily prosperous for the wicked to seek gain through unrighteous ways and means. Some wicked people even live in good health and happiness until they die, even though they continue to do evil (see Ps. 73). But for these people, eternal destruction and judgment await (19b). God judges the wicked.

Even in this world, most wicked people don't last long. They repeat their self-defeating behaviors, and then one day their

that Naboth had cursed God and the king, and murderous instructions to stone him to death. Finally, they took the life of the righteous Naboth and stole his vineyard (see 1 Kings 21). Ahab and Jezebel were the wicked whose actions directly challenged the teachings of the Ten Commandments: "You shall not murder," "You shall not steal," "You shall not give false testimony against your neighbor," and "You shall not covet your neighbor's house." The writer of 1 Kings noted the influence of Jezebel, Ahab's companion: "There was never anyone like Ahab, who sold himself to do evil in the eyes of the LORD, *urged on by Jezebel his wife*" (1 Kings 21:25). Jezebel was the primary evil-doer, but Ahab was also a foolish wicked man who voluntarily joined her in her life. He was a foolish wicked man who "sold himself" and shed his own blood.

[10] Bridges cited Ahab, Haman, and Judas Iscariot as examples of men who secretly plotted evil and ultimately came to their own destruction. Charles Bridges, *Proverbs*, rpt. (Carslie, PA: The Banner of Truth Trust, 1977), 7.

accumulated crimes are suddenly exposed and they are shamed, punished, and destroyed.

In this respect, the wicked are foolish and stupid. They do not recognize that their evil actions are the shedding of their own blood (18a). They are obsessed with pursuing short-term gain and do not realize that they are causing long-term ruin for themselves.

Those who seek gain through fraud or illegal means are anti-social and demonic. Their final destination is prison and eternal hell.

Those who seek unrighteous gain "must" perish. The way of those who desire ill-gotten gain leads them to destruction and they will lose their own life (19). The word, "Then, after desire has conceived, it gives birth to sin; and sin, when it is full-grown, gives birth to death" (James 1:15) is an immutable biblical truth.[11]

Out in the open [in the street] wisdom calls aloud, she raises her voice in the public square; on top of the wall [at the head of noisy streets] she cries out, at the city gate she makes her speech; "How long will you who are simple love your simple ways? How long will mockers delight in mockery and fools hate knowledge? Repent at my rebuke! [If you had responded to my rebuke] Then I will pour out my thoughts [my heart] to you, I will make known to you my teachings [my thoughts]. But since you refuse to listen when I call and no one pays attention when I stretch out my hand, since you disregard all my advice and do not accept my rebuke, I in turn will laugh when disaster strikes you; I will mock when calamity overtakes you—when calamity overtakes you like a storm, when disaster sweeps over you like

---

[11] The first humans, Adam and Eve, were the foolish wicked who sinned against God because of their pride and greed and led all human beings to eternal condemnation, while the second Adam, Jesus Christ, was the righteous one who defeated the temptations of gluttony, greed, and pride in the wilderness with the Word of God.

a whirlwind, when distress and trouble overwhelm you. Then they will call to me but I will not answer; they will look for me but will not find me, since they hated knowledge and did not choose to fear the LORD. Since they would not accept my advice and spurned my rebuke (1:20-30).

In the text, Wisdom is personified as a woman. Solomon contrasts the prostitute, who leads to folly and foolishness, with the woman of wisdom, who leads to wisdom, understanding, and prudence. Spiritually, the harlot represents the devil, while wisdom represents God the Holy Spirit.

The Son of God, Jesus Christ, the greatest of wise men, came to earth and spoke about the kingdom of God. Most people heard but did not understand. They saw but did not see. This is because what the Holy Spirit says can only be heard by those whose ears are open and circumcised (see Rev. 2:11). Jesus came to earth and revealed himself, but those who were spiritually blind could not see and understand. Wisdom "cries out" and "stretch out" her hand, but it is meaningless noise to those whose ears are spiritually uncircumcised (20, 21).

In his novel *The Holy War,* John Bunyan described a scene in which the army of Jesus Christ arrives at a castle called "Mansoul," which has been taken over by the devil, and uses a megaphone to proclaim the gospel to the people living in the castle. Bunyan then described the unfortunate situation where the devil had his men put earplugs in the ears of all the people in the castle, so they couldn't hear the gospel message. Bunyan was well aware of the devil's work of spiritual deafness. In the parable of the sower, Jesus clearly pointed out the devil's involvement, saying that when seed falls by the wayside, "the evil one comes and snatches away what was sown in their heart" (Matt. 13:19).

Wisdom is shouting today in the plaza, in the workplace, on television, over the internet, and even through the natural world.[12]

---

[12] When our minds are filled with worldly sounds, we cannot hear God's whispering voice. As long as our interests are filled with worldly things, there is no interest in wisdom. It is characteristic that the voice of God begins to be heard clearly when we

But only those with open ears hear. God's chosen ones will surely have their ears opened at some point to hear the gospel.

During the time of the divided kingdoms, Israel and Judah, God sent prophets to communicate his will. Unfortunately, the people, uncircumcised in their hearts, did not heed the cries of the prophets and did not obey. So the historical events reminiscent of this proverbs passage (26-27) actually took place during the destruction of the kingdoms. In the face of the Babylonian army that stormed in from the north, people of Judah cried out to God, but God did not hear them, and they were killed or taken into captivity (28).

However, for those who meet with calamity and seek God and cry out, there is a chance and possibility to cut off their deep-rooted sins. Blessed are persons who can enter the kingdom of heaven by losing an eye or an arm or a leg. Those who suffer through a serious, unexpected crisis and shed the layers of foolishness one by one, become sincere seekers of God. And those who experience a transformation that gradually frees them from their narcissistic personality disorder are favored by God.

They will eat the fruit of their ways and be filled with the fruit of their schemes (1:31).

Those who disobey, trusting in their own thoughts and schemes, despite the wisdom's watchfulness, counsel, and admonition, will be punished (31a). Paul made this clear when he said, "Do not be deceived: God cannot be mocked. A man reaps what he sows. Whoever sows to please their flesh, from the flesh will reap destruction; whoever sows to please the Spirit, from the Spirit will reap eternal life" (Gal. 6:7-8). The wicked will reap the reward of their own schemes (31b). They will be caught in the snares they set for themselves. God is the one who makes sure that we reap what we sow.

drop everything and become silent. It's like how you can hardly see the stars in the night sky in a city where bright lights are on all night.

For the waywardness of the simple will kill them, and the complacency of fools will destroy them (1:32).

The simple and the fools are a hendiadys expression that emphasizes the same meaning by repeating it poetically. In a negative sense, simplicity is the same as foolishness. The foolish end up killing and destroying themselves. They lead not only to their own destruction, but also to the destruction of those connected to them.

Waywardness and complacency are also poetic expressions that repeat the same meaning. Waywardness or regression is an immature defense mechanism that can temporarily help one cope with anxiety. The same goes for complacency. Repeated use of anxiety-avoiding defense mechanisms prevents us from moving toward growth and change.[13]

Counseling Application: The foolish and simple are unaware of themselves. They are subject to the dynamics of the unconscious. They repeat self-defeating behaviors. They do not learn from their experiences of failure. By repeating self-defeating behaviors, they gradually bring their life to ruin. In this sense, the foolish and simple are ones who are slowly and unconsciously committing suicide.[14] Without realizing it, they end up in hell.

But whoever listens to me will live in safety and be at ease, without fear of harm (1:33).

Unexpected calamities may strike the lives of believers in God. Trouble also comes. Solomon doesn't say "without harm," but

---

[13] Infantile regression and complacency are well characterized in people with anxiety disorders. Using anxiety-avoidance behaviors provides temporary relief and complacency (secondary benefits). However, if one continues to use them, he or she cannot overcome anxiety disorder. Facing and overcoming anxiety itself are the path to healing and maturity.

[14] The foolish and the wicked have a common denominator, but they are also different. The wicked are those who are motivated to kill or destroy others, while the foolish are those who are motivated to kill or destroy themselves.

"without fear of harm." People of faith are not greatly frightened or agitated because they are good to live and good even to die. Those who are in God are assured of their ultimate safety—their eternal salvation.

Counseling Application: Distressing anxiety disorders are differentiated as phobias, panic disorders, obsessive-compulsive disorders, and generalized anxiety disorder. A faith-based approach to treating anxiety disorders is to thoroughly believe and acknowledge that God is in control of one's life. When you relinquish control of your life, anxiety and fear gradually lose their power. When you realize that it's okay to die, anxiety recedes. When you let go of things you are attached to, you have nothing to fear. But the harder you try to live, the more anxious you become. Those who struggle with anxiety and fear need to apply this paradoxical truth to their lives.

Chapter 2 Listen to Wisdom

My son, if you accept my words and store up my commands within you, turning your ear to wisdom and applying your heart to understanding—indeed, if you call out for insight and cry aloud for understanding, and if you look for it as for silver and search for it as for hidden treasure, then you will understand the fear of the LORD and find the knowledge of God (2:1-5).

Verses 1 through 4 are characterized by the use of conditional clauses, such as "if…." Verse 5 is a proverb that promises a reward for fulfilling the condition.

Fear of God does not happen on its own. It is a process of hearing, digesting, and applying the Word. In this passage, Solomon emphasizes the need for active human effort. It is true that Jesus promised to answer those who knock and seek him (Matt. 7:7-8). However, fearing the LORD and coming to know God, that is, having faith, is only possible by God's grace. Without the work of the Holy Spirit to open our spiritual eyes, we would be groping in darkness, no matter how much we seek and search.

The wise are receptive and internalize and remember the teachings (1). They are interested in wisdom and attempt to apply it to different situations (2). They take an active stance of seeking and exploring (3).

The wise have "Receptive Power" and open to new information and teachings. They have a habit of introspection and reflection, checking for truth. They take wise teachings and words into their hearts. They "internalize" what they hear and form a stable "self-structure." Digesting and embodying the words, commandments, and precepts of the wise "external object," they make them part of their "self."

Children of God are ones who have received and embraced in their heart the Triune God, the source of wisdom (John 1:12). They dwell in the Triune God and the Triune God dwells in him. The

Holy Spirit, the wise counselor, dwells in their heart. Thus, the Holy Spirit guides them and helps them to think and judge wisely.

Counseling Application: Christian counselors should always seek wisdom. In particular, they have to seek knowledge of God. They need to strive to experience more of the breadth, length, depth, and height of God's love (see Eph. 3:18-19). A counselor who has internalized God's wisdom and love can be a "good" "external object" for helping clients with wisdom and love.

For the LORD gives wisdom; from his mouth come knowledge and understanding. He holds success [victory] in store for the upright, he is a shield to those whose walk is blameless, for he guards the course of the just and protects the way of his faithful ones (2:6-8).

In this passage Solomon specifically mentions who God is and what he does. In other words, he teaches the knowledge of God.

Those who are honest and upright will eventually win (7). In the real world, it may seem like the honest are defeated. But that is only temporary. God is always on the side of the honest. He vindicates the upright, so the truthful are ultimately victorious.

Some believers may seem like failures in this world. In reality, they may live as losers. But ultimately, they are eternal victors in the kingdom of God. Lazarus the beggar is an example of such believers.

God protects those whose "walk is blameless" (7b). Daniel's life illustrates this. During the reign of King Darius, the administrators and the satraps, who were jealous of Daniel, tried to bring charges against him. But he was "blameless," as it says, "he was trustworthy and neither corrupt nor negligent" (Dan. 6:4). He knew about the decree that "anyone who prays to any god or human being during the next thirty days, except to you, Your Majesty, shall be thrown into the lions' den" (Dan. 6:7), but "three times a day he got down on his knees and prayed, giving thanks to his God, just as he had done before" (Dan. 6:10). He was not afraid of the king's threatening decree and had complete trust in God.

Finally, because of his faithful behavior, he was caught in a snare and thrown into the lions' den. But God became Daniel's shield in the lions' den: "My God sent his angel, and he shut the mouths of the lions. They have not hurt me, because I was found innocent in his sight" (Dan. 6:22).

Verse 8 is a proverb with poetic repetition of the same expression. God is the one who "guards" and "protects" "the just" and "his faithful ones." Children of God can live in this world when they remember that God watches over their paths and protects them from evil and destruction. In our modern world, with so many things to make us feel afraid, the spiritual resource that helps us overcome anxiety and fear is the protection of God. Not a single hair on our head can be harmed without God's permission.

Believers and spiritual leaders with impeccable behavior are indeed rare in this day. Of course, all human beings are sinners and flawed. Nevertheless, people of faith who strive diligently to reconcile faith and life are needed in our time. It is a reality in Korea that when a motion is made to appoint a minister or prime minister, many of them are rejected before they even have a chance to go through a personnel hearing. Especially those who would be leaders should pursue a life of integrity. At the same time, we should listen to Jesus' words, "Let one who is without sin be the first to cast the first stone." It would be normal for the world to see Christians as people of integrity. In a time when even pastors are being criticized, we desperately need Christians and leaders who are persons of integrity.

Then you will understand what is right and just and fair—every good path. For wisdom will enter your heart, and knowledge will be pleasant to your soul. Discretion will protect you, and understanding will guard you. Wisdom will save you from the ways of wicked men, from men whose words are perverse (2:9-12).

When wisdom and knowledge are internalized and become part

of who you are, you have the ability to know for yourself what is right, just, and honest in any situation (9). You have the ability to discern what is the good, pleasing, and perfect will of God, even if you don't remember all the Word of God or keep all the details of the law in mind (see Rom. 12:2). And you do not imitate this generation, but only renew your minds, continuing your psychological and spiritual development. You do not fall prey to the way of life lived by the wicked or to the temptations of those who speak contrary to God's Word (12).

There is a joy in the life of those who walk in the righteous path, the good path, that the world does not know (10). There is not only pain and loneliness for those who follow the narrow path. God gives great comfort and joy to those who give up the values of the world to obey his will. These Christians should take pride in walking the narrow way, knowing that they have joy, peace, and freedom that the world does not know.

One of the characteristics of the wicked is perverse speech (12). Perverse speech reveals a person's character and personality. Distorted speech, manipulative speech, hurtful speech, and poisonous speech are symptoms that indicate that the speaker's character is evil. "Seductive words" are also a symptom of the wicked (see 2:16).

Those who speak what is perverse insist on their own words and are not receptive to the correctness of the other person's words. They don't listen or try to understand what the other person is saying. Instead, they often use the defense mechanisms of rationalization and intellectualization. These people are self-centered and immature psychologically. They are incapable of basic communication. They communicate one-sidedly. Solomon describes them as "foolish."

Who have left the straight paths to walk in dark ways, who delight in doing wrong and rejoice in the perverseness of evil, whose paths are crooked and who are devious in their ways (2:13-15).

The wicked voluntarily follow a dark way (13). "Way" means a way of life, an attitude, and a philosophy. They love the night, and in the darkness they follow the desires of the flesh and do all kinds of sinful things. Furthermore, they actively forsake God and choose worldly values and religions.

Because the wicked are in darkness, they cannot properly recognize themselves and their life. Psychologically speaking, they are constantly being dragged along by unconscious dynamics and are unaware of their own issues; hence, they have no "insight." Even when they experience frustration, they don't realize it: "The way of the wicked is like deep darkness; they do not know what makes them stumble" (4:19). The Book of Proverbs diagnoses them as "wicked."

The "straight paths" are contrasted with "dark ways" and "crooked" paths. These paths are "bright paths" and lead to the city of heaven.

Persons whose words are perverse keep deviating from the right path because their perception is distorted. In their eyes, the "dark path" looks like the path of light.[15] So they walk in crooked and devious ways (15). They walk the way they want instead of the way God commands. Instead of the "norm-al" way, he walks in an "abnormal" way. To the drunkard, the straight way seems like a crooked path, and the crooked way seems like the straight way.[16] To the wicked, an abnormal life is considered normal. No matter how much they are taught, they don't listen. They insist on taking the crooked path.[17]

The wicked think they can cover up their dark deeds. They hide and conspire. They do evil in secret. They even try to destroy evidence.

---

[15] The wicked walk in the "dark way" because they are ignorant of the Word, which serves as a lamp. Even if they do know the Word, they do not obey it.

[16] Infidelity is a crooked path. The persons in infidelity perceive their adulterous life as normal and a more courageous way of life.

[17] Before we knew God, we too were wicked people, "we all, like sheep, have gone astray, each of us has turned to our own way" (Isa. 53:6). We were people who walked according to our own understanding (see Judg. 21:25). We have become righteous and walk on the right path because Jesus Christ, the way, the truth, and the life, "bore the sin of many and made intercession for the transgressors" (Isa. 53:12).

But the outcome for those who walk the dark path is clear. They will stumble and fall because they cannot see the stones. They will fall into a trap of their own making and be destroyed.

Another symptom of the wicked is that they delight in doing evil, taking pleasure in perversion (14).[18] The wicked revel in psychopathic behavior. They hate what they are told to do. They love to do what they are told not to do.[19]

Psychopaths are so evil that they get pleasure from killing people. They belong to the devil because the devil delights in lying, leading people into sin, and doing destructive behaviors.

The Bible explicitly prohibits homosexuality. There are biblical scholars and Christians who defend homosexuality, even to the point of distorting Bible texts about homosexuality. They take the "From Below" approach to interpreting the Bible instead of the "From Above" approach. They do not rely solely on the Bible as God's infallible revelation. Instead, they interpret the Bible with a focus on trying to understand social phenomena and human life.

Until recently, homosexuality was classified and diagnosed by psychiatry as a mental illness to be treated, but this is no longer the case. This is because proponents of homosexuality have lobbied the psychiatric community and it has been decided that homosexuality cannot be considered a mental illness. The reality is that homosexuality is becoming "politically correct" in many countries. But believers who follow the teachings of the Bible should clearly recognize that homosexuality is a sin that is contrary to the teachings of the Bible and insist that it is.

It is not in the spirit of the Bible to hate, ostracize, or treat homosexuals as less than human, but homosexuality itself is a distorted expression of human sexuality. Just because people who engage in homosexual behavior find joy and happiness in their relationships does not make it a measure of normalcy. Evil behavior is evil behavior, even when it is consensual. Sexual

---

[18] God hates the perverse: "The Lord detests the perverse" (Prov. 3:32).

[19] The characteristic of sin is that it gives the sinner a temporary taste of pleasure and gratification. If it were unpleasant, frightening, or too much guilt-provoking, we would not be tempted to sin. So most sins and vices have the characteristic of bringing pleasure. The characteristics of sin are also consistent with the characteristics of addiction.

misconduct in the form of sexual harassment, sexual assault, group sex, adultery, pornography, etc. is perverted and provides temporary pleasure to the perpetrator. That's why the people repeat the behavior.

It is not normal to feel joy and pleasure when doing wrong behavior. The way God wants us to be is to feel joy and pleasure when we do right and holy things. But the problem is that humans who are corrupted by sin get more pleasure and excitement from doing wrong and evil things. We find it hard to live right and holy.

Love does not rejoice in evil behavior (1 Cor. 13:6). It is demonic and antisocial to rejoice in destructive behavior. There are some people who kill a human being for a few dollars. Then they take pleasure in spending that money on entertainment. Their mental faculties are far below those of animals.

The devil's strategy is to make evil doers feel feelings of joy and pleasure so that they will repeat the behavior. He makes them learn to do evil. Drivers who speed recklessly on the highway enjoy the thrill. Motorcycle bikers get more pleasure from a possibility of being stopped by police. People who dabble in drugs are well aware that drug use is a legally prohibited behavior that carries severe penalties. The greater the punishment, the greater the sense of adventure and the pleasure that accompanies it.

Those who rejoice when they do evil are those whose sin has become a personality disorder, so they repeat it predictably. It is very difficult for them to change unless they recognize and acknowledge their problem. Even if they do recognize it, they are likely to repeat the evil behavior without some effort and determination.

All humans are prone to evil. It is difficult to do good. Living a life of good requires constant effort. It also requires God's compassion and grace.

Psychologically immature people take the easy way out. They avoid the hard path, and when they do choose it, they give up easily. People with antisocial personality disorder, in particular, delight in unearned income, such as profiting from fraud. They seek to benefit themselves by taking what belongs to others. They like to steal other people's money and spend it lavishly. They don't care about other people's losses or suffering.

Wisdom will save you also from the adulterous woman, from the wayward woman [wife] with her seductive words, who has left the partner of her youth and ignored the covenant she made before God (2:16-17).

In this text, the adulteress or wayward wife refers to a woman who practices adultery.[20] The English word translated "wayward" is an adjective that means "fickle" or "unstable." The Hebrew word means "foreign (alien)" or "exotic."[21] If interpreted as "foreign," it could be seen as a warning against foreign women based on Solomon's own experience of spiritual degradation from marrying numerous foreign women.

However, if we consider that these prostitutes or heathen women were also those who were once in a marriage covenant before God (17b), then the harlot or heathen woman in the text refers to a sexually degraded woman, i.e., a married woman who is having an affair. Although this proverb is expressed from a male-centered perspective, it is God's word of warning to both men and women. It is wisdom and blessing for both men and women to obey the seventh commandment, "You shall not commit adultery." And it is God's will that married people remain faithful to their spouses.

The phrase "the wayward woman with her seductive words," also applies to both men and women (16). In general, women are susceptible to "seductive words" or "auditory" seduction. They are easily swayed by men who compliment them on their beauty or promise to be responsible for them. Men, on the other hand, are more susceptible to "visual" seduction, such as a woman's flirtatious behavior or attractive appearance. However, it's important to keep in mind that married people, both men and women, are more likely to be seduced by people who "can talk to them." The risk of crossing sexual boundaries increases when you feel like you're having conversations with someone else that don't

---

[20] Koptak notes that the "foreign woman" or "prostitute" appears four times in Proverbs 1 through 9: 2:16-22, 5:1-23, 6:20-35, and 7:1-27. Koptak, *Proverbs*, 102.

[21] Michael Coogan (ed.), *The New Oxford Annotated Bible*, 3rd Edition (Oxford University Press, 2001), 907.

work in your marriage. When you hear words of praise, recognition, attention, and care that you don't hear from your spouse, it's very tempting. It makes you lose control.

It's no exaggeration to say that much of what we say on social media today is designed to satisfy our need for validation. When we express our thoughts and post them on social media, many of us compulsively give short, positive feedback. This feedback makes people with low self-esteem feel alive, albeit temporarily. As a result, people who post for recognition often become depressed or angry when others don't respond to their posts or are slow to respond. In the modern world, where many people are psychologically immature, social media has both positive and negative functions. Married people who are inarticulate and unable to express intimacy in real life, but who use funny or fancy words in the virtual world to relieve their loneliness by gaining attention and recognition from others, are at risk of emotional infidelity.

Against "seductive words," Solomon warns in similar terms in Proverbs 6 and 7: "Correction and instruction are the way to life, keeping you from your neighbor's wife from the *smooth talk* of a wayward woman" (6:23b-24); "With *persuasive words* she led him astray; she *seduced* him with her *smooth talk*" (7:21). Listening to what sounds good to you first will lead to the same result as being deceived by the "smooth talk."

The NIV Bible (1984) translates "woman" as "wife" in verse 16. Married persons are more aware of the vulnerable parts of the opposite sex than single people, so they are better able to express empathy and say understanding words than single men or women. This is very tempting to the opposite sex. When you express yourself as if you understand them, as if you are accepting of them, they experience a fulfillment of their childhood experiences of not being understood. Therefore, there is a great risk that they will perceive you as a "good object" or even an "idealized object" and easily cross the forbidden boundary.

A Korean four character phrase "a wife as his old life partner"(糟糠之妻) is connected to the expression, "the partner of her youth" (17).[22] If you fall in love with another man or woman,

---

[22]   Anders connects the text of verse 17 with Malachi 2:14-15: "You ask, 'why?' It is because the LORD is the witness between you and the wife of your youth. You have

you are very likely to abandon your spouse like an old shoe. You make the wrong choice because the new one looks much better than your first mate.[23]

The people of Israel were God's bride, but they worshiped lewdly, following pagan gods that seemed more awesome than God. Jeremiah diagnosed Judah as follows: "You are a swift she-camel running here and there, a wild donkey accustomed to the desert, sniffing the wind in her craving—in her heat who can restrain her? Any males that pursue her need not tire themselves; at mating time they will find her" (Jer. 2:23b-24); "Do not run until your feet are bare and your throat is dry. But you said, 'It's no use! I love foreign gods, and I must go after them.'" (Jer. 2:25).

The second half of verse 17, "ignored the covenant she made before God," captures the meaning and importance of remembering the promises you made in your wedding before God and before your spouse. It is wisdom to recall that you laid your hands on the Bible, in the presence of God, and in the presence of many witnesses and vowed to love your spouse for life, under all circumstances, and to maintain conjugal fidelity. This wisdom can prevent you from falling into the deadly trap of infidelity (16). The

---

been unfaithful to her, though she is your partner, the wife of your marriage covenant. Has not the one God made you? You belong to him in body and spirit. And what does the one God seek? Godly offspring. So be on your guard, and do not be unfaithful to the wife of your youth." Max Anders, *Proverbs: The Holman Old Testament Commentary* (Nashville, TN: Broadman & Holman Publishers, 2005), 28.

[23] Young children have a weak ability to see the whole picture and make judgments. So if something new looks good, they are likely to put down what they already have and choose something new. This dynamic is seen in the symptoms of borderline personality disorder. In interpersonal relationships, people with that disorder like someone enough to "idealize" them, and then they are disappointed by the same person and "devalue" him or her. When a new partner comes along, the new person is immediately idealized. The person they liked before is experienced relatively worthless, so they devalue him or her. The problem is that they repeat this behavior. These people cannot maintain "object constancy" in relationships. They have "unstable" object relations. People who abandon their partner of youth are very likely to have dynamics of borderline personality disorder. They devalue their old spouse. Instead, they are seduced by another man or woman's appearance or flirtatious words and give up what is important to them.

adulterous woman in the text is one who has failed to remember her marriage vows and the Seventh Commandment.

Jesus taught us the prayer, "Lead us not into temptation, but deliver us from evil." This is because even Christians are vulnerable to temptations and can fall into the path of death. Sexual temptation, in particular, is stronger and more dynamic than any other temptation, and it is difficult to overcome with any amount of ego power. We must keep in mind that the more we convince ourselves that we are an exception, the more prone we are to fall in temptation.

Surely her house leads down to death and her paths to the spirits of the dead. None who go to her return or attain the paths of life (2:18-19).

This proverb contains a strong warning: "None who go to her return or attain the paths of life!."[24] Unlike other sins, adultery (infidelity) is the sin of becoming one with another person. A relational attachment is made, and an addictive relationship is formed, which is often difficult to extricate oneself from.[25] As the parable of the prodigal son illustrates, adulterers lose everything, and it's hard to come to their senses until they're empty-handed. Even when they do, it's not easy to make the decision to return to their own family. And the devil, the force behind sexual sin, rarely lets go of his captives once he has them. The addictive dynamic of sexual sin is illustrated by the fact that Pharaoh of Egypt promised Israel nine times that he would release them from captivity, but he repeatedly reneged.

This proverb warns us that the end result of fornication is death and hell. When fornication is repeated and adultery continues to progress, the two persons involved are alienated from God.

---

[24] Fox notes that in Hebrew usage, "go to" a woman is a euphemism for intercourse. Fox, *Proverbs 1-9*, 122.

[25] Paul well pointed out the dynamic of adultery when he said, "Do you not know that he who unites himself with a prostitute is one with her in body? For it is said, 'The two will become one flesh.'" (1 Cor. 6:16).

Without repentance, they will be judged for failing to give up their "temporary" relationship of adultery in this world and suffer in the fires of hell for eternity. Therefore, those who commit adultery or fornication repeatedly are very foolish.[26]

In the text, "her house" (18) is the house of the adulterous woman. Solomon warns that the household of the adulterous woman is also inclined toward death and destruction. A household with infidelity issues suffers psychological death as the marriage suffers. This is because infidelity is the psychological murder of the other spouse. Children growing up in homes where there is infidelity also experience psychological trauma that is comparable to death. They lose a sense of trust and security in their father or mother. They experience anxiety, anger, confusion, shock, and depression when their parents argue and fight over the affair. Divorce is like a death sentence for children, especially when the affair leads to divorce. They experience rejection and abandonment physically and emotionally, from their parents. They may also experience spiritual abandonment from God. During this process, children go through a painful grieving process.

God, well aware of this dynamic, gave us the commandment "You shall not commit adultery" in the Ten Commandments because he wants all his children to enjoy the benefits of a healthy family life. The explicit commandment against adultery was not given to be sexually suppressive. It is to protect the families of believers from sin and misery.

Thus you will walk in the ways of the good and keep to the paths of the righteous. For the upright will live in the land and the blameless will remain in it; but the wicked will be cut off from the land, and the unfaithful will be torn from it (2:20-22).

This proverb summarizes the entirety of chapter 2. The good and the righteous, and the upright all know and fear the LORD (5).

---

[26] When Paul mentioned the obvious works of the flesh, he pointed out "sexual immorality, impurity and debauchery" first of all in the list and made it clear that "those who live like this will not inherit the kingdom of God" (see Gal. 5:19-21).

Verse 20 emphasizes the "ways" and verses 21-22 emphasize the "land. God protects the "way" of his faithful ones (8). The upright and the blameless will inherit the "land" and enjoy long life to their descendants (21). But the way of the wicked is dark and crooked and it is a path that leads to Sheol (13, 15, 18). In the end, the wicked will perish, and the unfaithful cannot not live long on the "land" (22).

The rule of the kingdom of God comes upon both the righteous and the wicked. God rewards the righteous and punishes the wicked, so those who fear God and walk in the ways of the righteous are wise.

Chapter 3 Keep the Law of Wisdom

My son, do not forget my teaching, but keep my commands in your heart, for they will prolong your life many years and bring you peace and prosperity (3:1-2)

Koptak points out that chapter 3 is a three-part teaching. He divides it into three parts based on the "my son" call to attention in verses 1, 11, and 21. He sees the first part as consisting of five admonishments, the second part as dealing with the blessings that wisdom will bring, and the third part as consisting of five prohibitions.[27]

We can understand this passage by focusing on two verbs: First, "do not forget" "my laws," that is, "remember" the proverbs.[28] Remembering is related to the ability to learn. If you remember your previous mistakes and don't repeat them, you have learned. People with poor learning ability will quickly forget and not make connections no matter how much you teach them.

Second, "keep" (cherish) "my commands." To keep the laws and commands in one's heart means to digest them well, to personalize them. When a good teaching is internalized as a good "external

---

[27] Koptak, *Proverbs*, 117. Koptak understands that the theme of the first part is "Do not forget my law" (v. 1) and the one of the second part is "Do not despise the discipline of the LORD's discipline" (v. 11), and the theme of the third part is "Do not let wisdom and understanding out of your sight" (v. 21).

[28] Koptak comments that the proverbs in chapter 3 are more concerned with remembering and keeping the LORD's precepts and wisdom than with merely remembering and keeping Solomon's own personal precepts and teachings. Koptak, *Proverbs*, 118. Solomon's concern was to ensure that his son would be a man who feared the Lord: "Trust in the LORD with all your heart" (5); "in all your ways submit to him" (6); "fear the LORD" (7), "honor the LORD" (9); "do not despise the LORD's discipline" (11); the LORD made the heavens and the earth (19-20); "the LORD will be at your side" (26); "the LORD detests the perverse" (32); "The LORD's curse is on the house of the wicked" (33); "He mocks proud mockers but shows favor to the humble and oppressed" (34).

object," it becomes part of the "good self."[29] When good teachings are well digested, the superego, or conscience, is developed, and one becomes a healthy human being who can live with others. Furthermore, he or she can develop as a person who fears God.

There are promises for those who remember, treasure, and obey the words of Proverbs. There is also a reward for those who obey. The reward is long life and prosperity (2).

Let love and faithfulness never leave you; bind them around your neck, write them on the tablet of your heart. Then you will win favor and a good name in the sight of God and man (3:3-4).

Verses 1-2 and 3-4 are largely a poetic structure of A-B-A'-B'. "My teaching" and "my commands" are linked to "love" and "faithfulness." "Do not forget" and "keep my commands in your heart" in verse 1 are linked to "let love and faithfulness never leave you" and "write them on the tablet of your heart" in verse 3. The "for" in verse 2 is connected to the "then" in verse 4. While verse 2 promises blessings on the earth, verse 4 promises blessings specifically in our relationship with God.

Persons who digest and obey the words of Proverbs are ones who make "love and faithfulness" part of their "self-structure" (3). With love and faithfulness engraved on the tablets of their hearts, they are naturally loving and faithful in their interpersonal relationships without much effort. Such persons live in good object relations with God and with others. As a result, they receive favor and a good name from God and their neighbors (4b).

Counseling Application: Counselors who are equipped with

---

[29] Conversely, when a parent's teaching is obsessive-compulsive or pathological, children who contain it in their heart develop "bad self" and suffer from neurotic guilt. They become persons with low self-esteem and an excessive sense of shame. Therefore, when teaching God's Word, the psychological and spiritual maturity of the person teaching the Word is very important and necessary. If God's Word is distorted, exaggerated, diminished, or only partially emphasized, children or believers who receive it will be filled with neurotic fear and anxiety.

capacity to love and trustworthiness can be a good object for clients. Counselors with these qualities can facilitate their clients to develop into ones who love God and their neighbors and are able to keep faithful relationships.

God recognizes counselors who are both loving and faithful. He will give them a reputation as "excellent" counselors. Clients will like and respect their counselors with these qualities. And they will actively refer them to others in need.

Trust in the LORD with all your heart and lean not on your own understanding; in all your ways submit to him, and he will make your paths straight (3:5-6).

The essence of "my teaching" and "my commands"(1) is to trust in the LORD wholeheartedly and to acknowledge him in all things.[30] The structure of these two verses is similar to the previous passage, with an active and passive command followed by a promise of reward. "Trust in the LORD with all your heart" (5a) is linked to "in all your ways submit to him" (6a). Passively speaking, it is to "lean not on your own understanding" (5b). Then God will "make your paths straight."

"Lean not on your own understanding" (5b) can be interpreted to mean "do not follow your emotions" or "do not trust the judgment of distorted reason." The worldly truths are "live spontaneously," "be true to your feelings," and "trust yourself." But the truths that come from God are, "What is natural can be corrupted," "Emotions are variable, and following them can lead to deception," and "Trust in God." In this sense, the teaching of Proverbs is strongly opposed to the trends of modern society, which is dominated by postmodernism.

Counseling Application: Christian counselors must recognize the danger of relying on their own counseling theories, clinical experience, and life experience. Loving God wholeheartedly and relying on him in all things is an attitude that Christian counselors

---

[30] Bridges noted that trust in God must be not only "whole" but also "exclusive," i.e., trusting in God "alone." Bridges, *Proverbs*, 23.

must maintain throughout their counseling practice.

Do not be wise in your own eyes; fear the LORD and shun evil. This will bring health to your body and nourishment to your bones (3:7-8).

Verse 7 can be understood as a proverb that emphasizes verse 5 and the first half of the proverb in verse 6. In verse 7, "shun evil" is added. The sentence structure of verses 7 and 8 is the same as that of verses 1-2, 3-4, and 5-6. The addition of the conjunction "then" is not out of place in the context.

The truth of the world is to "be wise in your own eyes" (7). Those who are wise in their own eyes do not feel the need to fear God at all. This is evil (7b). But those who fear God are promised long life and riches (2). They are also promised good health (8). The phrase "nourishment to your bones" can be understood literally.

Honor the LORD with your wealth, with the firstfruits of all your crops; then your barns will be filled to overflowing, and your vats will brim over with new wine (3:9-10).

Verses 9 and 10 are also connected by the conjunction "then." Therefore, the proverbs up to verse 10 are characterized by the same sentence structure of two verses.

The passive way to fear God is to depart from evil (7b). The active way is to keep God's word (1), to engrave love and faithfulness on the tablet of your heart (3), to trust in God and acknowledge him in all things (5, 6), and to set apart the firstfruits of your labor and give them to God (9). It is to recognize that everything is a gift from God and be grateful for it. This is wisdom.

But those who are wise in their own eyes (7) mistakenly believe that their wealth and income are the result of their own efforts and labor. They don't feel any need to be grateful to God. They are foolish.

Nabal, a foolish man, made a great feast on the day of shearing and enjoyed himself. But he despised and rejected the request of David's men who came to him on the day of the feast. He thought that he had shepherded the sheep well by his own skill and wisdom. He was ungrateful that David and his men had been a fence for the shepherds of his flock. Finally, he was struck down by God, and he "became like a stone" and he died (see 1 Sam. 25). People who think they live by their own strength and power are like Nabal. They are fools, just as Nabal's name implies (1 Sam. 25:25).

In the modern world, which is no longer an agrarian society, the firstfruits are the most precious things Christians have from their economic endeavors and offerings in many forms. Tithing and other offerings are the vaccine that prevents God's children from falling into the deadly sin of greed. Jesus said that where your treasure is, there your heart is also, and that you cannot serve mammon and God at the same time (see Matt. 6:24).

Ones who grasp the wealth and possessions that God has graciously given them, thinking that they are their own, are foolish. Such persons are unable to have compassion on and relieve the poor. They use their possessions only for themselves or are excessively stingy.

The life of faith is a paradox. If you try to hold on to what you have, you lose it. People who endeavor only to accumulate riches become misers. Eventually, they end their lives at the expense of their own health, unable to live to their full lifespan. In Jesus' parable, the foolish rich man laid up enough food for many years in his storehouses and said to himself, "Take life easy; eat, drink and be merry." But he didn't expect his life to end that night (see Luke 12:16-21). Jesus said, "This is how it will be with whoever stores up things for themselves but is not rich toward God" (Luke 12:21).

The Word of God promises that if you give God your firstfruits with distinction, he will bless you with an overflowing storehouse (10). In contrast, even when you are frugal with your food, suppose that you fall seriously ill, then you will suffer hardship and your savings will fly away as if they had wings. No matter how hard you farm, if God does not send rain at the right time but hail, you will be in debt. If God does not protect you, your poultry business may be destroyed by the bird flu virus. Foot-and-mouth disease can destroy your pig business. The wise are ones who do not forget that the things they take for granted are God's grace and blessing.

My son, do not despise the LORD's discipline, and do not resent his rebuke, because the LORD disciplines those he loves, as a father the son he delights in (3:11-12).

Solomon continues his teaching by calling him "my son" again. He asks his son not to disregard God's discipline and rebuke of his children who do not obey his laws and commands. God's discipline, he says, is like that of a father to his beloved children.

Believers should not ignore or resent God's discipline and rebuke, for God disciplines and rebukes his beloved children.[31] He will not discipline or rebuke ones whom he does not love.

Counseling Application: Discipline or rebuke can be associated to the confrontation required in the counseling process. Counseling is a process of care and concern, but it also involves confronting the client about areas that need to be recognized.

Confrontation is effective when the client feels that the counselor is confronting him or her out of love. It can be a burden for the counselor to say something unpleasant to the client. But it must be done lovingly, wisely, and sensitively. Confronting the client without love may be linked to the counselor's own anger or dynamics of countertransference. The Christian counselor must face the client with the heart of God and the heart of a parent.

---

[31] Erickson has a funny way of explaining this. God is not our "heavenly grandfather," but rather our "heavenly father." God is not like a grandfather who just lets you do whatever you want. Millard Erickson, *Christian Theology*, 2nd ed. (Grand Rapids, MI: Baker Books, 1998), 977. Fox points out that verse 12 is similar to Deuteronomy 8:5: "Know then in your heart that as a man disciplines his son, so the LORD your God disciplines you." Fox, *Proverbs 1-9*, 152.

Blessed are those who find wisdom, those who gain understanding, for she is more profitable than silver and yields better returns than gold. She is more precious than rubies; nothing you desire can compare with her (3:13-15).

One of the fundamental concepts in math is the notion of equality (=) and inequality (≠, <, >). There are things that are equal and things that are not equal. A<B means that B is greater than A. A<B<C means that B is greater than A but C is greater than both B and A. Solomon uses this concept repeatedly in the book of Proverbs.

This passage of proverb can be summarized as "silver < wisdom, gold < wisdom, rubies < wisdom, and everything you desire < wisdom." Using the concept of fractions, if you divide the sum of wisdom and understanding, the numerator, by the sum of silver, gold, rubies, and all that is desired, the denominator, the result would be infinity (∞).

The wisdom and understanding that help us live in this world are only valid for this world. However, the wisdom and understanding that lead to eternal life are incomparably more beneficial than worldly wisdom and knowledge. Therefore, it can be labeled as "worldly wisdom < God's wisdom." God's wisdom is God himself and Jesus Christ.

Blessed and wise are ones who possess things of core and lasting value. On the other hand, those who lose things of eternal value in pursuit of things of incidental and temporary value, are foolish. Unfortunately, the people of the world pursue things of temporary value and hold to temporal values. They are not interested in the value of a life of salvation and eternal life through Jesus Christ. They are fools!

Long life is in her right hand; in her left hand are riches and honor. Her ways are pleasant ways, and all her paths are peace. She is a tree of life to those who take hold of her; those who hold her fast will be blessed (3:16-18).

In verse 2, Solomon mentioned long life, peace and prosperity as blessings for those who have gained wisdom and understanding. He reiterates these blessings in the first half of verse 16. Instead of "peace and prosperity," he poetically uses "riches and honor." Additional blessings are "pleasure and peace" (17).

Living long is something every human being wants. The same is true for wealth. But long life and riches are valuable when they are given to the wise. If long life and riches are given to the foolish or the wicked, they only serve to enrage the poor and the weak (see Ps. 73). Such is the case in reality. Nevertheless, the wise have hope, for they know that just as a fresh vegetable soon withers, so the long life and riches of the wicked are a prelude to eternal destruction.

Christians who obey God's Word can maintain holistic health and are therefore more likely to live long lives. If they do not swerve to the left or right, do not suffer from excessive stress, and do not overeat or be greedy, they are likely to live until their God-given lives reach their full span.

Those who have the wisdom and understanding to know God and believe in Jesus Christ have found the tree of life (18a). Those who live in the noble knowledge and wisdom of Jesus Christ has already eaten of the fruit of the tree of life. They eat of it now and will eat of it forever. Blessed are the ones who have found the tree of life (18b).

By wisdom the LORD laid the earth's foundations, by understanding he set the heavens in place; by his knowledge the watery depths were divided, and the clouds let drop the dew (3:19-20).

Solomon urges his son to lift his eyes to the heavens, to the LORD God, the creator of the earth, sky, deep sea, and air, because fearing God is the "big picture." It's easy for us to get caught up in the details of Proverbs and lose sight of the big picture. Standing before our Creator brings clarity to our self-perception and understanding of the world.

Solomon explicitly reveals that the wisdom and understanding that he personified in 1:20 is the LORD God in this text. He means that this wisdom, understanding, and knowledge are not earthly but "divine," coming "from above."

God's wisdom is amazing. By his wisdom, God created all things in the universe, and by his word of wisdom, he separated light from darkness. Finally, he created humans in his image. In his wisdom, he parted the deep sea. In the face of imminent crisis, he made a way for the Israelites to cross the Red Sea as if it were land. God's wisdom is hard to measure as he faithfully provided manna from the dew as daily food for forty years for about two millions in the wilderness where grain could not grow.

God is the Creator. He made the earth firmly grounded (19a). He designed the mechanisms of the universe so that the water in a teacup doesn't move in the slightest despite the speedy rotation of the earth. He created the solar system so that humans and animals don't feel dizzy at all despite the speed at which it spins.

God made and still sustains all the space surrounding the earth as a "holding environment. He preserves the earth by running the sun, moon, and countless stars in outer space (19b). Although it suffers from air pollution, God still, by his grace, faithfully provides air for all living things, including the wicked, to breathe. He provides "breath" (*sum* in Korean) and "rest" (*suim* in Korean) for humans and animals. He carries out his wisdom to purify the air with wind and rain, thunder and lightning.[32] He causes plants and animals to reproduce and perpetuate life. He gives the "gentle grace" that causes dew to fall from the sky so that vegetation can be moisturized and grow (20b). He provides "secret sunshine" so that photosynthesis can take place and all plants and animals can

---

[32] Among God's questions to Job, the following one can be connected with Prov. 3:19-20: "Who cuts a channel for the torrents of rain, and a path for the thunderstorm, to water a land where no one lives, an uninhabited desert, to satisfy a desolate wasteland and make it sprout with grass? Does the rain have a father? Who fathers the drops of dew? From whose womb comes the ice? Who gives birth to the frost from the heavens when the waters become hard as stone, when the surface of the deep is frozen?" (Job 38:25-30). Bridges brilliantly commented that God's creation makes the universe a parable and mirror of the gospel. Bridges, *Proverbs*, 36.

maintain their lives.

My son, do not let wisdom and understanding out of your sight, preserve sound judgment and discretion [My son, preserve sound judgment, do not let them out of your sight]; they will be life for you, an ornament to grace your neck. Then you will go on your way in safety, and your foot will not stumble. When you lie down, you will not be afraid; when you lie down, your sleep will be sweet (3:21-24).

In verse 21 Solomon calls attention back to "my son," reiterating and emphasizing the key commands of verses 1 and 3: "Keep my commands in your heart," and "write them on the tablet of your heart." Verses 22 through 24 contain specific promises that are connected by the conjunction "then." Solomon promised the blessings of long life and prosperity (2) and now promises safety (23a, 24a), and "a good night's sleep" (24b) for those who keep wisdom.

Solomon exhorts us to "preserve" "sound judgment and discernment" (21a) and not to lose them (21b). Sound judgment and discernment are essential capacities and qualities in our social life. They are also essential gifts and qualities in our spiritual life. Judgment that is not biased to the left or right, and discernment that differentiates right from wrong, good from evil, are qualities and virtues that should be developed into the character of each believer.

Misjudgment or lack of discernment can cause serious problems in interpersonal relationships. If you make impulsive decisions without thinking things through, you are at risk of getting things wrong. As verse 23 puts it, your foot will stumble.

Counseling Application 1: Christian counselors must have well-balanced judgment and discernment, including biblical and faith-based judgment and discernment. A healthy and balanced understanding of human beings is also necessary. Discernment is also required in the counseling process. Counselors may lose their judgment and discernment when they become emotionally involved in their relationship with a client or when they are caught up in the dynamics of negative countertransference.

Counseling Application 2: This proverb can be applied to sleep. Many people today suffer from insomnia. In some cases, insomnia is a symptom of depression. It can be a consequence of a decrease in sex hormones during middle age. In the case of insomnia related to biochemical changes, sleeping pills or antidepressants can help.

However, there is also insomnia linked to stress or anxiety. When the mind is in a state of tension, the brain is aroused, which makes it difficult for people to sleep. For those who have trouble in sleeping due to these environmental factors, counseling can help. It's a therapeutic experience for them to be able to verbalize their stress and anxiety that they experience. Receiving empathy and support from a counselor reduces anxiety and stress. When you feel at peace, your perception of your environment becomes more positive. Then the symptoms of insomnia are alleviated. Deep breathing to relax your muscles can also help with insomnia. Hot baths are also beneficial. However, the most fundamental remedy is to pray and surrender control of your life to God. Verbalizing to the Lord in your prayer about the stress and anxiety that arises in your mind can can be an experience of "talking cure." When you bring any problem situation to God, who is in control of your life and death, he will guard your heart with "the peace of God, which transcends all understanding" (Phil. 4:6-7). When you experience peace in your heart, you can sleep (23, 24).

Have no fear of sudden disaster or of the ruin that overtakes the wicked, for the LORD will be at your side [be your confidence] and will keep your foot from being snared (3:25-26).

This proverb expands on the preceding verses 23 and 24. After promising in verse 24 that "you will not be afraid when you lie down," Solomon exhorts in verse 25, "Have no fear of sudden disaster or of the ruin," "for" God will "keep your foot from being snared" (26b) and "Your foot will not" (23b). Because God, who is in control of your life and death, is "your confidence" (26a).

Most disasters are characterized by happening when you least expect them. So "sudden disaster" may shock you with fear. Anxiety and fear are often psychological experiences that occur when we worry in advance about "what if..." disasters. Anxiety and fear are functional in that they allow us to prepare for a sudden disaster. However, in many cases, anxiety and fear are dysfunctional because they cause unnecessary distress in our lives by alarming us to experience anxiety and fear excessively or sensitively.

Solomon counsels us not to fear even sudden calamities (25). This counsel is both comforting and challenging to people who are so afraid of disaster that they are unable to function in their daily lives. God is the one in whom we can put our confidence. Disasters have frightening consequences for unbelievers, but we Christians live with a basic sense of trust that not even disaster can separate them from the love of God (see Rom. 8:39). So even in a world of disasters, we are ultimately not overcome with fear. We can leave it to God and sleep peacefully (24b).

When you don't want to die, you feel anxiety and fear. But when we realize that it is okay to die, anxiety and fear lose their power. Having resolved the issue of death and dying, we can live boldly in this world, where disaster can strike suddenly, without being overwhelmed by anxiety. Christians are the ones who are assured of their resurrection and eternal life.

Counseling Application: In my counseling practice, I sometimes come across with clients who complain of anxiety disorders. Some suffer from symptoms of generalized anxiety disorder, where they feel anxious in all aspects of their lives for vague reasons. Others struggle with obsessive-compulsive disorder, which is characterized by obsessive thoughts and compulsive behaviors. Some clients struggle with phobias, which are characterized by a fear of certain objects and an avoidance response. A growing number of people suffer from panic attacks, which are recurring episodes of sudden heart palpitations and shortness of breath. Some clients suffer from post-traumatic stress disorder (PTSD). PTSD is not categorized under the umbrella of anxiety disorder any longer but has its own diagnostic category, which is characterized by nightmares and flashbacks.

People who suffer from anxiety disorders have one thing in common: they are caught in the "snare" of anxiety and fear. As they try to control their anxiety, they become more anxious and their radius of activity shrinks. Their energy and vitality diminish. In severe cases, they can't leave the house. They are locked themselves in a prison without bars, and you're stuck with anxiety and fear. It's not easy for them to get out of this trap.

A deep-seated issue that all people have in common is the fear of death. Once the fear of death is overcome, anxiety disorders slowly recede. Those who will die will live, and those who will live will die. In other words, if you are willing to die, you can overcome your anxiety disorder, but if you want to live, it's hard to escape it.

Effective for most anxiety disorder symptoms, behavioral therapy involves encouraging the client to gradually approach the nature of the anxiety, helping them to confront the anxiety experience and exposing them to the situation with a technique of "systematic desensitization." Instead of taking the easy route of avoidance, the hard route of confrontation is used to reduce the intensity and frequency of anxiety.

Do not withhold good from those to whom it is due [those who deserve it], when it is in your power to act. Do not say to your neighbor, "Come back tomorrow and I'll give it to you"— when you already [now] have it with you. Do not plot harm against your neighbor, who lives trustfully near you. Do not accuse anyone for no reason—when they have done you no harm. Do not envy the violent or choose any of their ways (3:27-31).

This proverb deals with how to use the sound judgment and discernment mentioned in verse 21 in interpersonal relationships. It is characteristic for this passage to have "Do not..." structure for each verse. Lucas categorizes these interpersonal proverbs into three categories: the first is for people with whom we are in debt (27-28), the second is for people who are getting along (29-30). Lucas categorized these interpersonal proverbs into three groups: first, those with whom one is in a debt relationship (27-28); second, those with whom one gets along well (29-30); and third, those who are wicked (31).[33]

First proverb is about debt relationships (27-28). Depending on how you interpret it, it can be seen as an attitude that a borrower should have toward a lender. Conversely, it can also be interpreted as an attitude that a lender should have toward someone who wants to borrow money. I interpreted it in the latter sense. If you say, "I'll give it to you tomorrow," despite having money, you are actually expressing that you don't want to lend it. In this case, the borrower will intuitively recognize the difference between what you say and what you mean. As a result, he or she will not come back to borrow again. "Come back and I will give you tomorrow" is actually a euphemistic refusal by the lender to save face. Solomon cautions against this kind of refusal when you can afford to lend.

On the other hand, there are some people who take advantage of the other person's position and situation to ask him or her to lend them money. There are even debtors who don't think about repaying after they borrow. This is the behavior of the wicked.

The next proverb is about neighbors who live faithfully (29-30). Solomon teaches us not to first hurt or plot to hurt our faithful neighbor. To plot means to intentionally attack.[34] Those who gossip secretly, create rumors for social burial, and attack others with malicious comments should realize that God is watching them and hates them (32).

We humans live in society. Just as you want others not to attack or harm you, so do others. At the very least, it's a passive form of neighborly love to try not to hurt or harm others. To sue or attack a

---

[33] Ernest Lucas, *Proverbs* (Grand Rapids, MI: William B. Eerdmans Publishing Company, 2015), 65.

[34] In his commentary on this text, Phillips associates to the fact that David took Bathsheba and taught Joab to have Uriah, her husband and David's loyal commander, killed on the battlefield to cover up his transgression. John Phillips, *Exploring Proverbs: An Expository Commentary*, Vol. 1 (Grand Rapids, MI: Kregel Publications, 1995), 103.

neighbor when he or she has done no harm to you is psychopathological and demonic. The devil is the one who sues without cause.

The third proverb is about evil neighbors (31). Solomon sternly commands, "Do not envy the violent, or choose any of their ways." The reality is, we don't often envy the "violent." Most people dislike people who are abusive verbally or physically. However, you may consciously or subconsciously envy the power that the violent has enough to abuse others. You may have ambivalent feelings about them who are able to control and overpower others.

This dynamic is seen in people who grew up in homes where verbal abuse or physical assault was commonplace. As they grew up traumatized by the image of an abusive father or mother, they envisioned themselves in the future retaliating against their abusive parent by being abusive themselves. As a result, they are at risk of unconsciously taking on the role of the abuser in their family and social life as adults. They may become abusive toward those weaker than themselves. Eventually, they "choose" to follow the behavior of their abuser (31). This dynamic is called the "parallel process."[35]

For the LORD detests the perverse but takes the upright into his confidence. The LORD's curse is on the house of the wicked, but he blesses the home of the righteous. He mocks proud mockers but shows favor [gives grace] to the humble and oppressed [the humble]. The wise inherit honor, but fools get only shame [fools he holds up to shame] (3:32-35).

The text is composed of many elements of contrast: The rebellious vs. the upright, the LORD detests vs. the LORD takes into his confidence, the house of the wicked vs. the home of the

[35] Parallel processes means that the dynamics of one process are the same or similar to the dynamics of another. This term is often used in supervision theory, where the relationship between a supervisee and a supervisor is often the same or similar to the relationship between a client and the supervisee. This is called a parallel process.

righteous, curse vs. bless, mock vs. show favor, proud mockers vs. the humble and oppressed, the wise vs. fools, inherit honor vs. get only shame. In verses 27 through 31, those who fear the LORD are the upright, the righteous, the humble, and the wise. Those who disobey the LORD are the perverse, the wicked, proud mothers, and fools.

Both blessings and curses come from God (33). God curses the disobedient and their houses.[36] On the other hand, he blesses those who obey him and their homes. The devil does not have the power to curse at will. God builds up and tears down. Indeed, God is the sovereign King of kings.

---

[36] Fox makes a good point that while theologically the responsibility for sin is individual and not collective, as Ezekiel 18 suggests, in practice it is common for the consequences of sin to fall on the entire family to which the individual is related. Fox cites the case of Achan (Josh. 7:24-25), Haman and his followers (Esth. 8:11), and Korah (Num. 16:32) as examples. Fox, *Proverbs 1-9*, 168. The reverse is also true. Examples include the case of Rahab, the Philippian jailer, and Cornelius the centurion.

Chapter 4 Gain Wisdom

Listen, my sons, to a father's instruction; pay attention and gain understanding. I give you sound learning, so do not forsake my teaching. For I too was a son to my father, still tender, and cherished by my mother [an only child of my mother]. Then he taught me, and he said to me, "Take hold of my words with all your heart; keep my commands, and you will live" (4:1-4).

Chapter 4 also can be divided into three main sections. The three sections begin with verse 1, "My sons," verse 10, "My son," and verse 20, "My son." Notice that verses 1, 10, and 20 all begin with the imperative verb "listen." This verb doesn't just mean to listen, but to hear, take to heart, and obey.

Solomon's words of wisdom to his sons were, after all, words he had heard from his father David (3). David's lessons are summarized in verses 4 through 9. The importance of the mental and spiritual legacy from one generation to the next is evident in this text. Solomon himself was a king of wisdom, but his wisdom was the wisdom he had heard and digested from David, the father of faith. He was once "still tender, and cherished" in his mother's sight. But when he digested his parents' teachings and pursued wisdom and understanding, he became a wise king.[37] When God

---

[37] From the perspective of self psychology of Heinz Kohut, Solomon was a son who had a "mirroring" experience of having been tenderly loved by his mother Bathsheba and an "idealizing" experience of his father David. It can be said that his psychological, spiritual self-structure was cohesively formed with the combination of his father's specific religious education and his life education. Solomon is characterized by qualities that set him apart from David's other sons. Amnon, Absalom, and Adonijah were not men of wisdom, although they might have had the same fatherly experience. It's unfortunate that many modern children who lack stable object relations with their fathers are growing up with a lack of idealizing their fathers, both psychologically and spiritually. The growing lack of respect for proper authorities can be interpreted from the perspective of self psychology as being linked

told him to ask for anything, he asked for wisdom because he had already internalized the teachings of his father David.

Get wisdom, get understanding; do not forget my words or turn away [swerve] from them. Do not forsake wisdom, and she will protect you; love her, and she will watch over you. The beginning of wisdom is this: Get wisdom [Wisdom is supreme; therefore, get wisdom]. Though it cost all you have, get understanding. Cherish [Esteem] her, and she will exalt you; embrace her, and she will honor you. She will give you a garland to grace your head [set a garland of grace on your head] and present you with a glorious crown [a crown of splendor] (4:5-9).

David's instruction to Solomon continues from verse 4 to verse 9. Solomon repeats his father's instruction to his sons. In this passage, wisdom and understanding are personifications of God. The verbs "get," "love," and "cherish/esteem" refer to an ongoing relationship with God. The teaching, "Though it cost all you have, get understanding" (7b), indicates that putting God and his kingdom first is wisdom and understanding (see 2:15). When we "worship" (worth+ship) God as the most worthy, he will protect, keep, exalt, and glorify us. Jesus said that whoever acknowledges him before others, he will also acknowledge before his Father in heaven (see Matth. 10:32).

Listen, my son, accept what I say, and the years of your life will be many. I instruct [guide] you in the way of wisdom and lead you along straight paths. When you walk, your steps will not be hampered; when you run, you will not stumble (4:10-13).

to a lack of good fatherly experiences.

Solomon's desire to guide his children in life and faith is evident in this passage. Just as David taught him with compassion and regret, so he teaches his sons with the same attitude and mind.

Those who follow the wise path and the upright way will live a life in which they will not grow weary when they walk and will not be overwhelmed when they run (12a). They will not stumble (12b). And even if they fall, God's strong right arm will uphold them and lift them up.

God, on the other hand, stands in the way of those who rely on their own thoughts and wisdom. The angel who appeared to the prophet Balaam, who was on his way to curse Israel for his greed, drew his sword and blocked Balaam's path. Lot's life is also an example to this. He followed what he saw and ended up barely escaping Sodom empty-handed. The wise are those who obey God's Word, recognizing that their lives are not their own and "it is not for them to direct their steps" (Jer. 10:23).

Do not set foot on the path of the wicked or walk in the way of evildoers. Avoid it, do not travel on it; turn from it and go on your way (4:14-15).

Solomon reiterates his admonition from chapter 1: "Do not go along with them, do not set foot on their paths" (1:15). The strong imperative verb "do not" is repeated three times in this passage. The message is one of strong warning.

To avoid crossing an explicitly prohibited "boundary" requires the activation of functional anxiety and fear. A person who disobeys a prohibitive command after hearing it repeatedly is a person who does not feel fear. Anxiety and fear are necessary to feel in danger.

In this text, "the path" or "the way" refers to lifestyle, attitudes, and behavior. If you associate with the wicked, you are bound to be influenced by their judgment. It is very difficult to be a good influence on a wicked person, but it is very easy to be influenced by a wicked person. And the way of the wicked is addictive, and it is hard to get out of it once you have entered it.[38] If you happened to enter it, your must quickly realize it and "turn from it" (15), even at great cost. That is the way to live.

For they cannot rest [sleep] until they do evil; they are robbed of sleep [slumber] till they make someone stumble [fall]. They eat the bread of wickedness and drink the wine of violence (4:16-17).

The righteous can go to bed without fear and sleep soundly (see 3:24). But the wicked sleeps only when he does evil (16a). For them, what makes someone fall is a sleeping pill.[39] The bread and wine they eat and drink are deprived by injustice and violence (17).

The evil live by the drive of *thanatos*, what Freud named it, that is, death (destruction) instinct. They are not at peace until the destructive instinct's needs are satisfied. Their anxiety is so heightened that they cannot sleep. If their sexual needs are not satisfied, they are restless and crave sexual objects until their drives are gratified.[40]

We have seen in the past in Germany and Japan that not only individuals, but also groups and countries can become this evil. And we can see it in the political system of North Korea. Hitler

---

[38] Lucas insightfully comments that the path of the wicked is an easy one to be tempted by because it is "at least sometimes" close to the path of righteousness. Lucas, *Proverbs*, 67.

[39] Lucas notes on this text in an interesting way. He describes doing evil, making someone stumble, eating the bread of wickedness, and drinking the wine of violence as the sleeping pills of the wicked. Lucas, *Proverbs*, 67.

[40] The father of evil, the devil, is characterized as the wicked in this text. The devil doesn't sleep until he finds someone to devour. He does not rest. And no matter how many he swallows, he's never satisfied: "The leech has two daughters. 'Give! Give!' they cry. There are three thing that are never satisfied, four that never say, 'Enough!': the grace, the barren womb, land, which is never satisfied with water, and fire, which never says, 'Enough!'" (Prov. 30:15-16). Peter warns us: "Be alert and of sober mind. Your enemy the devil prowls around like a roaring lion looking for someone to devour" (1 Pet. 5:8).

and his followers rejoiced and celebrated while committing atrocities such as the Holocaust, which no human being in good conscience could ever do. Invading other nations by force, taking away their sovereignty, and oppressing them are evil. Japan's unrepentance for its past misdeeds of eating "the bread of wickedness" and drinking "the wine of violence" is exemplified by its behavior in claiming sovereignty over Dokdo (an island in South Korea). This is a symptom of the collectively evil system with the psychology of evil. Christian psychiatrist Scott Peck proposed a new diagnosis for the psychiatric community: "the psychology of evil." This is because there are real people in the world who feel no remorse, who don't see their problems, and who enjoy their destructive behaviors. These are the sadists who "take pleasure in doing evil." They are the ones who enjoy the bread of wickedness and the wine of violence (17).

The path of the righteous is like the morning sun [the first gleam of dawn], shining ever brighter till the full light of day. But the way of the wicked is like deep darkness; they do not know what makes them stumble (4:18-19).

The lives of the wicked are like "deep darkness." They do not recognize sin for what it is. They don't realize that living apart from God is sin itself. They are completely unaware that he is on a path to destruction.

Solomon's description of the wicked in this proverb is similar to that of person with personality disorders who are unaware of themselves and their own issues. They are unaware of the unconscious dynamics of their life and repeat the same mistakes or wrongdoings. They do so without realizing why they failed, what they are responsible for, how others have affected them, or how dysfunctional the family system they were part of was. They blame their environment or others, not realizing that the problem may be within themselves. Psychiatrists and psychologists diagnose these persons as having personality disorders, but the Bible diagnoses them as "the wicked."

If we understand the expression "the way of the wicked is like deep darkness" in a psychological sense, we can say that the behavior of the wicked is mostly governed by the unconscious.[41] The wicked have little insight into the causes and dynamics of their problematic behavior. When negative consequences arise from their actions in darkness, that is, from their unconsciousness, they don't understand why. So they don't learn, realize, and grow from their mistakes or errors. Still driven by unconscious dynamics, they repeat the same mistakes and misdeeds.

But the path of the righteous is like the morning sun that grows brighter and brighter (18). The righteous may be frustrated and suffer because the darkness does not completely recede in the immediate future. But they gradually move closer to the light that enables them to clearly perceive themselves, others, their environment, and God. All Christians now understand and grasp dimly, as in a mirror, but in the kingdom of God to come they will perceive clearly, as in seeing face to face (see 1 Cor. 13:12).

Counseling Application: Christian counselors need to help their clients who may wander in deep darkness have "insights" on their issues. By illuminating their darkness, counselors facilitates them to gradually become more aware of themselves and others.

There are many people of faith who profess the Christian faith, but live without much sense of their "true self." Like the Pharisees and scribes, there are many believers who live in self-righteousness or who mistake their obsessive-compulsive life for godliness. These people will not seek counseling unless they are in crisis. And when they are in crisis, they usually don't seek counselors. They may not even seek God. They are more likely to use familiar methods of self-help and defense mechanisms over and over again. But if they do seek God or a counselor, they will have an opportunity to look at themselves objectively. They will be able to expand their awareness of the causes of their repeated stumbling. Furthermore, through healing and transformation, they can become people who love God and their neighbors authentically.

---

[41] Clifford comments that the Hebrew word for "darkness" in the text, *apelah*, is always used in a negative sense, and in this context it symbolizes "ignorance and danger." Ignorance and unconsciousness are related. Richard Clifford, *Proverbs* (Louisville, KY: Westminster John Knox Press, 1999), 64.

My son, pay attention to what I say; turn your ear [listen closely] to my words. Do not let them out of your sight, keep them within you heart; for they are life to those who find them and health to one's whole body. Above all else, guard your heart, for everything you do flows from it [for it is the wellspring of life] (4:20-23).

Solomon calls "my son" again and then continues to teach. This paragraph are composed of several imperative verbs: "pay attention," "turn your ear," "do not let," "keep," and "guard." Verse 22 and the second half of verse 23 are made up of the conjunction "for." Using the conjunction "then" instead of "for" should be no problem in the context.

Specifically, the "them"s of verse 21 refer to Solomon's words of exhortation to his sons, especially his son Rehoboam. However, in a broader sense, it is the Word of God. The Word of God has life-giving power that leads to eternal life (22a). And because it ripples through the whole person, it also contributes to one's physical health (22b).[42]

Solomon describes the human heart as "the wellspring of life" (23b).[43] It is no exaggeration to say that our lives depend on our minds. A wrong thinking can lead to suicide, so you must guard your heart, where thoughts, feelings, will, and desires spring from (23a). A gatekeeper must be alert at the entrance to the heart so

---

[42] Lucas notes that there is no word for body in Hebrew, so "body" in the text refers to each organ in context. He means that when the ears in verse 20, the eyes in verse 21, the heart in verse 23, the mouth and lips in verse 24, the eyes and eyelids in verse 25, and the feet in verses 26 and 27 function well, then the whole body is healthy. Lucas, *Proverbs*, 68.

[43] Lucas points out that the Hebrew word *leb*, translated "heart," either refers to the heart, an actual bodily organ or is used as a metaphor and does not refer to the "center of emotion" as used in English, but rather to the "inner person" or "inner self" in which the functions of intellect and emotion and will are done intricately. Lucas, *Proverbs*, 68.

that evil may not impulsively come out of your heart. Recognizing that your corrupted heart is always "vulnerable" to evil, you must always put on the spiritual full armor and carry the sword of the Word. Furthermore, you must strive to restore and reform your inner world that bears the image of God. Counseling and psychotherapy can be beneficial in this regard.

Counseling Application: The wisdom and understanding that can be gained from God's Word has the ability to heal clients to regain vigor and vitality in their life. It teaches them to realize their worth as human beings, their identity, and their sense of purpose in life. Once they realize the will of God who created them, they will be able to live a life that is pleasing to God.

The Bible is the Word of God, written with the full inspiration of the Holy Spirit. Therefore, the Holy Spirit is a God of power who works in the human heart through his written Word. As clients read the written Word as they explore his inner world, the Holy Spirit shines a light into their darkened mind, helping them to perceive and realize anew. The Spirit also enables them to realize their own dynamics, where before they have been acting unconsciously in the dark, expending much energy unnecessarily.

Therefore, Christian counselors need to help their clients internalize the Bible, including Proverbs, in the counseling process. To do this, counselors themselves will need to be continually transformed by the Bible. They will also need to be equipped with abilities to skillfully use the Bible in the counseling process.

Keep your mouth free of perversity; keep corrupt talk far from your lips. Let your eyes look straight ahead; fix your gaze directly before. Give careful thought to the paths for your feet and be steadfast in all your way [Make level paths for your feet and take only ways that are firm]. Do not turn [swerve] to the right or the left; keep your foot from evil (4:24-27).

Solomon emphasizes his proverbs with similar wording

poetically: "keep your mouth free of perversity" and "keep corrupt talk far from your lips"; "let your eyes look straight ahead" and "fix your gaze directly before"; "be steadfast in all your ways" and "make level paths for your feet" and "take only ways that are firm."

Words come from the heart. If the words of life are in the heart, words of life will come out of the mouth. But if the heart is evil, crooked and corrupt words will come out of it. Therefore, the heart must be restored and healed in order to keep crooked and perverse speech away. When your heart is right, you see right and speak right. When the heart is crooked, you see crookedly and speak crookedly.

In order to walk the path without swerving to the left or right, your eyes must look straight ahead, and "fix your gaze directly before you" (25).[44] Is it possible for us to keep walking through life looking straight ahead? How many people will be able to walk without turning to the left or right? It's not easy to answer.

God does not swerve to the right or left. He is not partial neither with the rich nor with the poor. He doesn't like partiality. There is absolute balance in him. This is seen in the divinity and humanity of Jesus Christ. The Chalcedon Creed is a statement of faith that affirms that Jesus Christ is one hundred percent divine and one hundred percent human, differentiated yet inseparable. Jesus Christ is a balanced being of divinity and humanity, neither lacking nor skewed. So overemphasizing divinity or overemphasizing humanity is not a balanced Christology.

Counseling Application: Swerving to the right or left come from immaturity psychologically and spiritually. There are many clients who struggle due to the consequences of their living with deviation to the right or left.

Therefore, Christian counselors need to use God's Word as a guide to help their clients regain a balanced life psychologically and spiritually. For example, if a client is living too worldly or too detached from the world, the counselor will need to help him or her live a life that is in the world but not of the world.

---

[44] Bridges observed that Lot's wife would not have become a pillar of salt if she had kept her eyes straight ahead. Bridges, *Proverbs*, 54. Looking backward is more dangerous than looking to the left or right.

Deviating to the right or left means one's inability to integrate the left and right. Or, it means that they are not able to distinguish between the left and the right. This is related to a defense mechanism called "splitting," which is seen in borderline personality disorder. In elementary school, when we were divided into blue and white teams at sports games, we were not able to perceive the fact that both blue and white teams were friends in the same class and same school. So we saw the other team as enemies to be defeated. This dynamic took place as a temporary experience of "splitting". Only after the sports day is over we could return to being friends again.

It is a counselor's responsibility and privilege to help his or her clients with deviations in thinking, emotions, willpower, and interpersonal relationships to develop and grow enough to live a balanced life psychologically and spiritually. To do so requires maturity and integrity on the part of the counselor. If a counselor has simplistic attitudes and perceptions on the left or the right or good or bad, he or she will not be able to lead the client to a life of maturity and transformation in a complex and diverse world. Rather, like a cult leader, he or she will have the effect of perpetuating and reinforcing the client's immaturity.

Chapter 5 Pay Attention to Wisdom

My son, pay attention to my wisdom, turn your ear [listen well] to my words of insight, that you may maintain discretion and your lips may preserve knowledge. For the lips of the adulterous woman [an adulteress] drip honey, and her speech is smoother than oil; but in the end she is bitter as gall, sharp as a double-edged sword. Her feet go down to death; her steps lead straight to the grave. She gives no thought to the way of life; her paths wander aimlessly [are crooked], but she does not know it (5:1-6).

Chapter 5 again calls attention to readers, using the phrase "my son" three times (1, 7, 20). In verse 7, it is pluralized as "my sons." From verse 1 to verse 6, it is characterized by the repetitive wording poetically in each verse: "pay attention to my wisdom" and "turn your ear to my words of insight"; "maintain discretion" and "preserve knowledge"; "the lips of the adulterous woman drip honey" and "her speech is smoother than oil"; "she is bitter as gall" and "sharp as a double-edged sword"; "her feet go down to death" and "her steps lead straight to the grave"; "she give no thought to the way of life" and "she does not know it."

The prevalence of extramarital affairs among unbelievers and believers alike today is not a new phenomenon. The fact that affairs occurred in Solomon's day with the same dynamics as they do today shows that humans have been struggling with the same sin since the beginning of creation. Therefore, the lessons on sex and infidelity that Solomon wrestled with, that his father David stumbled with, and that Solomon himself taught his son, offer the same insight and wisdom to believers of today.[45]

---

[45] Bridges noted that Solomon's own experience of suffering might have given him wisdom and clarity about infidelity. Bridges, *Proverbs*, 56. He cited Eccl. 7:26 as evidence: "I find more bitter than death the woman who is a snare, whose heart is a

The "lips of the adulterous woman" are so seductive enough to drip honey (3a). Solomon rightly points out that "her speech is smoother than oil" (3b). But her lips and mouth are deceptive (4).[46] Therefore, once attached to the adulterous man or woman, it is not easy for one to get out without God's grace and help.

Solomon is well aware that the consequences of a brief fling with a prostitute will be bitter as gall (4a). It is wise to expect that the fruits fornication will be bitter like wormwood. Infidelity may be experienced as sweet as honey right away, but it will soon give you the bitterest taste in your life.

The words of a whore are sharp as a two-edged sword, and with it she drags the life of her adulterers to the place of death, to the grave (4b, 5). The Word of God is a two-edged sword that saves life, but the words of the adulterous person are a two-edged sword that takes life. The prostitute is a "representative" of the devil. Satan works in her, so the words that flow from her lips are actually words of the devil. The words of the serpent that tempted Eve in the Garden of Eden were the words of the devil.

Adulterers and those who engage in sexually inappropriate relationships are very likely to have distorted perceptions of themselves, their partners, others, and even God. They have a self-centered understanding of God. Instead of obeying God's will and commandments, they distort and rationalize their own will as if it were God's will. They do not well recognize that their attitudes, perspectives, emotions, and relationships are distorted. Therefore, they do not understand and accept the objective feedback and confrontation of those around them. "Her paths wander aimlessly, but she does not know it" (6) sums it up well.

Counseling Application: We need to understand the cognitive

---

trap and whose hands are chains. The man who pleases God will escape her, but the sinner she will ensnare."

[46] Kim insightfully points out that the prostitute has no face, but is represented only by her lips and feet. Jung-woo Kim, *Bible Commentary: Proverbs* (Seoul: Korean Christian Books Publishers), 208-209. Those who fall in love with a harlot do not have the wisdom to see the "whole object" of the harlot. They only see the "part object," her eyes, lips and breasts. The part objects are tempting, but they are only a small part of her. When they recognize the rest of her characteristics and dangers, the seductive parts object will be less tempting.

distortions of a person who is involved in an affair. Infidelity is a process of "madness." Those who have crossed the forbidden boundary do not recognize that they have a problem for themselves. So it is important to understand that their ability in reality testing is fairly impaired. You need to realize that it may take a significant period of time for their distorted cognitive ability to return to normal. This will help you pray continually and persevere, even if you don't see changes right away.

Now then, my sons, listen to me; do not turn aside from what I say. Keep to a path far from her, do not go near the door of her house, lest you lose your honor [give your best strength] to others and your dignity [your years] to one who is cruel, lest strangers feast on your wealth and your toil enrich the house of another. At the end of your life you will groan, when your flesh and body are spent. You will say, "How I hated discipline! How my heart spurned correction! I would not obey my teachers or turn my ear [listen] to my instructors. And I was soon in serious trouble in the assembly of God's people [I have come to the brink of utter ruin in the midst of the whole assembly]" (5:7-14).

The "her house" in verse 8 is the house of the adulterous woman, so she can be seen as a woman with her husband. And while the prostitute in the text refers to a woman, in many cases of infidelity and adultery, a man is the perpetrator of adultery.

The consequences of sexual sins are evident. The consequences of adultery with an adulterous person could lead to material loss (10). You may be sued by the other's spouse and pay back a significant amount of money. You will be disgraced in your relationships with you family, relatives, friends, and coworkers (9).

Adulterous relationships don't last long. Boredom sets in after the temporary idealized experience. And in many cases, the affair will be exposed and the parties and their families will be humiliated.

Even if the affair is undisclosed, there will come a time when sexual desire diminishes, sex hormones decrease, and sexual pleasure is no longer experienced in the same way. Therefore, there will "surely" be a day of regret for those who have risked everything for the pleasure of a temporary affair. As Solomon so aptly put it, there will come a day of remorse and mourning (12-14).

Furthermore, the Bible is clear that eternal judgment awaits those who live this way. Only by realizing that today's pleasure will turn into tomorrow's weeping and lamentation we can avoid falling into fornication and adultery. All those who live in the pursuit of worldly values, including infidelity, will finally spend eternity in lamentation, sorrow, and regret.

Adultery devastates not only both parties, but also their spouses and children, if they have, causing PTSD in the spouse and shame and anger in the children. It can destroy one's own family and even the other family involved.[47] We all must clearly be warned that the lips of an adulterous person are bitter as gall and will pierce us as sharply as a two-edged sword.

Drink water from your own cistern, running water from your own well. Should your springs overflow in the streets, your streams of water in the public squares? Let them be yours alone, never to be shared with strangers. May your fountain be blessed, and may you rejoice in the wife of your youth. A loving doe, a graceful deer—may her breasts satisfy you always, may you ever be intoxicated with [captivated by] her love. Why, my son, be intoxicated [captivated] with another man's wife [by an adulteress]? Why embrace the bosom of a wayward woman

[47] There is a high risk of devastating consequences such as shame and low self-esteem for children, depression and possible suicide for the spouse, risk of suicide for the offender himself or herself, homicide or co-suicide, litigation between the parties, or separation and divorce. Thinking about these deadly results in advance can be an important prevention against committing the sin of adultery (infidelity).

[another man's wife]? (5:15-20).

In this passage, Solomon suggests an active way to prevent the dangers of infidelity with an adulterous woman or another man's wife: to delight in only a wife of one's youth, and to be satisfied with her breasts always and "to ever be captivated by her love" (19b). This is life wisdom that applies to believers and unbelievers alike.

In a marriage relationship, the spring that is shared by the husband and wife is the exclusive cistern that cannot and should not be shared by others. This boundary is not a flexible boundary. It's a boundary that must be clearly honored and kept.

An active way to protect this boundary is to be self-sufficient in one's own spring of water (15).[48] "Your own cistern" and "your own well" are the springs of water in the relationship with your spouse, who has been given to you in marriage. Each spouse is responsible for keeping the marriage relationship healthy so that this spring does not run dry. This is because when it is depleted, you may feel thirsty to drink from other springs. And when this spring overflows out of the house or flows into the street, it is polluted and can no longer be a fountain of joy and thankfulness (16).

The metaphors used in conjunction with the metaphors of "cistern," "well," "springs," and "streams" are "a doe" and "a graceful deer" (19).[49] It is only when the husband feels self-sufficient and grateful for his marriage relationship before God that he can still see his wife of his youth as lovely and beautiful. It is the order of creation and the will of God that the husband is captivated only by his wife's breast. The same is true of how the

---

[48] Bridges noted that the dissatisfied marriage increases the risk of a spouse's distraction. Bridges, *Proverbs*, 58. Wisdom of living a contented life, even in the face of dissatisfaction, can provide one with the strength to prevent infidelity.

[49] Fox rightly points out that Solomon used these metaphors in the Song of Songs: "My beloved is like a gazelle or a young stag" (Song. 2:9); "Turn, my beloved, and be like a gazelle or like a young stag on the rugged hills" (Song. 2:17); "Your breasts are like to fawns, like two fawns of a gazelle that browse among the lilies" (Song. 4:5); "Come away, my beloved, and be like a gazelle or like a young stag on the spice-laden mountains" (Song. 8:14). Fox, *Proverbs 1-9*, 202.

wife should look at her husband. Being satisfied with the bosom of one's spouse "at all times" is an active way of prevention against infidelity (19b).

For your ways are in full view of the LORD, and he examines all your paths. The evil deeds of the wicked ensnare them; the cords of their sins hold them fast. For lack of discipline they will die, led astray by their own great folly (5:21-23).

There is not a single life that escapes God's eye. God knows and sees every human being's path, that is, ahead, behind, to the right and left, past, present, and future.[50]

The wicked are destroyed by their own wickedness and sin (23). They invite judgment because they are not admonished and because they reject God's Word. The wicked will find that the way they walked, thinking it was right, was wrong (23b).

During the flood, all humans except Noah's family were judged by God for their overflowing sins. None of them heeded Noah's admonition (23a). History proved them to be fools. The same is true today. All who refuse to listen to God's Word and reject the gospel are foolish. The wages of foolishness is eternal death and judgment.

---

[50] Bridges insightfully commented on the question of whether the idea that God knows and watches over the path of life might stop sinners' steps. He observed that one can be a practical atheist who is careful and cautious about the eyes of others, or even the eyes of a child, but does not care that an omniscient God is watching over his or her life. Bridges, *Proverbs*, 59. It is a sad reality that many believers are more anxious to the eyes of men than in the eyes of God. We need to be awakened. The words of the prophet Hanani as he confronted Asa, king of Judah, are very pertinent with this proverb: "For the eyes of the LORD range through the earth to strengthen those whose hearts are fully committed to him" (2 Chron. 16:9a).

Chapter 6 Depart from Folly and Adultery

My son, if you have put up security for your neighbor, if you have shaken hands in pledge for a stranger [struck hands in pledge for another], you have been trapped by what you said, ensnared by the words of your mouth. So do this, my son, to free yourself, since you have fallen into your neighbor's hands; Go—to the point of exhaustion—[Go and humble yourself] and give your neighbor no rest [press you plea with your neighbor]! Allow no sleep to your eyes, no slumber to your eyelids. Free yourself, like a gazelle from the hand of the hunter, like a bird from the snare of the fowler (6:1-5).

In chapter 6, the phrase "my son" appears in verses 1 and 3 and again in verse 20. Notice that in verses 6 and 9, instead of "my son," Solomon addresses his son as "you sluggard." Several instances of the use of repetitive poetic wording are also found in this passage.

There will be few occasions when a king's son is required to vouch for a neighbor or a stranger. If there is, it will be in royal matters, in-law matters, or treaties between nations. But in the life of an ordinary individual, this counsel is just as applicable. It is not uncommon for a guarantee or security to go awry, bringing suffering not only to the individual but also to the entire family. Therefore, it is wise to say "No" to a request for a guarantee or security, even if it is difficult to do so at first.

Solomon gives his son specific instructions on what to do when he finds himself in a double bind, a situation where he cannot do this or that, like being caught in a snare. First, address it as soon as possible and don't put it off or avoid it. It's easy to avoid, but it's a recipe for bigger problems. Just as the Bible teaches us not to hold onto a grudge until the sun goes down, but to settle it (see Eph. 4:26), Solomon advises us to visit the party in person and plead with them before going to bed.

Second, humble yourself and ask your neighbor for consideration and understanding. If you don't talk about it and put it off because you're saving your pride, you'll not save yourself with nine stitches for a stitch in time. Therefore, you must recognize the seriousness of the problem and have the courage to face it. And you need to be committed to doing your best until the problem is solved. It's not wise to let a rejection or two hurt your pride and not to humble yourself further. It is foolish to suffer some major losses because of the minor issues.

In verse 5, the metaphors of "a gazelle" and "the hand of the hunter," and "a bird" and "the snare of the fowler" are used. It is practically impossible for a gazelle caught in a snare or a bird caught in a net to escape. Nevertheless, if they strain desperately enough, they may miraculously escape from the hunter's hand just as the hunter's hand is about to remove the snare. In the same way, when faced with a crisis, it is wise not to despair, but to stay up all night thinking of ways to escape, and to make every effort to do so. It goes without saying that it is wise to be vigilant and alert not to be caught in a net or snare at all.

Counseling Application: People who have a hard time being rejected tend to be unable to say no when they need to. Those with low self-esteem are not good at expressing their true feelings and thoughts, so they are more likely to put up security for others, even though they don't want to, and even with some awareness of being manipulated. Saying "yes for yes" or "no for no" is living truthfully. Truth ultimately sets you free in relationships.

It's important to remember that saying no can be also helpful to the other person who asks security from you as well. For clients who are unable to say no, it is beneficial to give them a task that involves saying no and encourage them to practice so that they can learn a new lesson that saying no is not life-threatening. In the long run, rebuilding self-esteem is essential for these clients. Once they recognize that they have the power to say no, they will not be stumbled by guarantees.

Go to the ant, you sluggard; consider its ways and be wise! It has no commander, no overseer or ruler, yet it stores its provisions in summer and gathers its food at harvest. How long will you lie there, you sluggard? When will you get up from your sleep? A little sleep, a little slumber, a little folding of the hands to rest—and poverty will come on you like a thief [bandit] and scarcity like an armed man (6:6-11).

Twice Solomon confronts his son with the label "you sluggard."[51] This is a label that he confronts not only his own son, but God confronts those who have issues with laziness in general.[52] In verse 5, a gazelle and a bird are used as analogies, but in verse 6, one of the smallest animals, an ant, is used as an analogy. Solomon urges his son to see for himself what he can learn from the behavior of ants. But the lazy and foolish do not learn from the behavior of ants. And even if they did, it wouldn't change their lives.

Solomon points out two characteristics of ants. First, ants have no commander, overseer, or ruler.[53] Nevertheless, they work voluntarily, preparing their own food (7-8). In contrast, the lazy person is very lacking in spontaneity and motivation. They rarely do things voluntarily. Second, ants discern timing (8). They have the ability to recognize when it's time to work and when it's time to rest.[54] Sluggards, on the other hand, don't know when to work and when to rest: "How long will you lie there, you sluggard? When will you get up from your sleep?" (9).

---

[51] Koptak notes that the Hebrew word for "sluggard," *asel*, occurs 14 times in Proverbs alone and is not found anywhere else in the Old Testament. Koptak, *Proverbs*, 187.

[52] Fox notes that Solomon's reference to "the sluggard" refers to anyone who hears the words of this proverb, regardless of whether the listener is actually sluggish. Fox, *Proverbs 1-9*, 216. It is wise for everyone to hear the words of this proverb and examine himself or herself.

[53] Bridges asks how thankful we are that unlike ants, we have overseers of our souls. At least we have "conscience," "Scripture," and "pastors. Bridges, *Proverbs*, 62.

[54] Kim pointed out that "summer" and "harvest time" are practically interchangeable. In Israel, the harvest season was not the fall, which is our usual time for harvesting, but the summer season, from April, when barley harvesting begins, to the end of May, when wheat harvesting begins. Kim, *Proverbs*, 233.

It's human to want to sleep a little longer, to rest a little longer. However, when this attitude becomes a habit, it becomes a personality, which means that if laziness becomes a personality, it is not possible to live life sincerely.

Solomon warns the sluggard that poverty and scarcity will come suddenly, like robbers or enemies attacking (11). It may not be immediately apparent. But it is very likely that the lazy will soon experience economic and relational difficulties from which they will have difficulty recovering. Furthermore, their sloth has a devastating effect on their spiritual life. The soul of the lazy can suffer consequences that can lead to death and eternal judgment.

If a person sleeps until the sun is in the middle of the sky when he or she should be up and active in the morning, he or she is a lazy person. It is normal for people who have to work at night to sleep until late in the morning. But if there is a teenager or young person who does not sleep but is engrossed in games until dawn and does not get up until the afternoon, he or she is definitely lazy. Those who play games when they should be sleeping and stay up late when they should be working are "wicked, lazy servants" in God's eyes (see Matt. 25:26).

A trouble maker and a villain [A scoundrel and villain], who goes about with a corrupt mouth, who winks maliciously with his eye, signals with his feet and motions with his fingers, who plots evil with deceit in his heart—he always stirs up conflict [dissension]. Therefore disaster will overtake him in an instant; he will suddenly be destroyed—without remedy (6:12-15).

Verses 1-5 were a lesson on the surety, and verses 6-11 were a lesson on the sluggard. Verses 12-15 are proverbs about the characteristics of the wicked and the consequences that will befall them.

Solomon characterizes "a scoundrel and villain" by using bodily organs: Mouth, eyes, feet, fingers, and mind (heart). First, the mouth. The wicked walk around and make mischief. They create rumors and speak corrupt words. They use their mouths antisocially.

Second, eyes, fingers, and feet. The wicked communicate using a body language that only they know, and they use it to accomplish their evil deeds. They are clever at signaling with winks, hand gestures, and foot gestures to do evil without others noticing.[55] They use passwords and code words. In modern language, they know how to communicate without leaving any evidence behind. They use burner phones to do evil. They gesture with their eyes or hands secretly. They even conspire by communicating with their feet under the desk.

Third, the heart and head. The wicked devise and harbor lies and evil from their hearts. They are, as Jesus said, depraved and wicked in their hearts (see Matt. 15:19-20). Their minds do not work to think about good things. But when it comes to evil thoughts, they are inventive and quick to think.

A community with bad and wicked people in it is always full of strife, quarrels, and conflicts. These wicked people have a destructive influence, just as a single loach can muddy a stream.

You should still not lose heart in the midst of the environment set up by the wicked. For disaster will suddenly come upon the wicked (15). They will be irretrievably destroyed. For there is a righteous judgment of God upon them. However, it is wise to discern the characteristics of the wicked and not to associate with them.

There are six things the LORD hates, seven that are detestable to him: haughty eyes, a lying tongue, hands that shed innocent blood, a heart that devises wicked schemes, feet that are quick to rush into evil, a false witness who pours out lies and a

---

[55] Koptak insightfully comments on the striking similarity between the physical descriptions of a troublemaker and a villain and the behaviors listed in the six or seven sins God hates in verses 16-19. Koptak, *Proverbs*, 189. He also well points out what God detests in the whole book of Proverbs: dishonest scales (11:1, 20:10, 23), lying lips (12:22, 26:25), the sacrifice of the wicked (15:8-9, 21:27), the thoughts of the wicked (15:26), all the proud of heart (16:5), and acquitting the guilty and condemning the innocent (17:15), Koptak, *Proverbs*, 190.

person who stirs up conflict in the community [dissension among brothers] (6:16-19).

Solomon articulates the things that God abhors.[56] These are behaviors that the devil delights in. This proverb is a more specific description of the sins that the wicked do with their bodily parts that were discussed in the previous passage. In this proverb, Solomon uses bodily parts to illustrate the behaviors of the wicked: eyes, tongue, hands, heart, and feet.

First, God hates "proud eyes."[57] The eyes are the windows to the heart. The eyes of people with a proud heart are filled with pride. Their eyes reflect their attitude of disrespect for those weaker than them. Empathy and compassion for those in need are rarely seen in his eyes. Prideful eyes are typically found in the eyes of a person with narcissistic personality disorder.

Second, God hates a "lying tongue."[58] One with a lying tongue is "a false witness who pours out lies" and "who stirs up conflict in the community" (19). In the ninth commandment, God explicitly commands, "You shall not give false testimony against your neighbor." To testify against a person falsely in a court of law, where a his or her life could be on the line, is a deadly sin akin to

---

[56] Kim points out that the physical actions that God abhors are characterized by starting from the top and moving downward: eyes --> tongue --> hand --> feet. Kim, *Proverbs*, 239.

[57] In verse 13 of the same chapter, the troublemaker and villain is one who "winks maliciously with his eye." He makes eye contact to communicate his evil intentions.

[58] A scoundrel and villain is one who "goes about with a corrupt mouth" (12). He or she has the tongue that the serpent had in the Garden of Eden. This is the tongue that perverted the Word of God and tempted Eve. This tongue is used to produce bitter water and curses (see James 3:9-12). Verse 13 refers to the act of signaling with the hand or foot to promote evil, but the sign with the lips was used by Judas Iscariot when he sold Jesus: "Now the betrayer had arranged a signal with them: 'The one I kiss is the man; arrest him and lead him away under guard'" (Mark 14:44). This was an abuse of the beautiful greeting of a kiss between Jesus and his disciples. This contrasts with the "holy kiss," a beautiful greeting among the members of the Corinthian church (see 2 Cor. 13:11). Bridges cites Gehazi (see 2 Kings 5:25-27) and Ananias and Sapphira (see Acts 5:1-10) as examples of lying tongues. Bridges, *Proverbs*, 63.

murder. Those with a lying tongue have an undeveloped superego. They belong to the devil, the "father of lies." They are a servant of the devil, especially when they speak words that stir up strife in the community. In the Garden of Eden, the devil lied to divide God, Eve, and Adam. Anyone who speaks distorted words against one another to cause distrust is evil. They are like foxes that tear apart a church community or a family of believers. They delight in and promote division in the church or family. God detests them.

Third, God abhors the hand that sheds the blood of an innocent person. God created the hands to be skillful in doing good works. But Cain's hands shed the blood of his innocent brother Abel. Likewise, the hands of the wicked are skillful in doing evil.

Fourth, God hates the heart that devises evil plans. The mind that plots evil plans has wisdom in sinning. In general, people with antisocial personality disorder have above-average intelligence quotients. Those who commit fraud are especially skilled at deception. It is truly evil to use one's God-given intelligence and brain to devise antisocial behavior.

Fifth, God is averse to the feet that run fast toward evil. He hates the feet that do not brake when the urge (drives) arise but rather help one's doing evil behavior impulsively. Jeremiah likened the people of Judah's rush to idolatry to a camel and a wild ass:

> How can you say, "I am not defiled; I have not run after the Baals"? See how you behaved in the valley; consider what you have done. You are a *swift* she-camel *running here and there*, a wild donkey accustomed to the desert, sniffing the wind in her craving—*in her heat* who can restrain her? Any males that pursue her need not tire themselves; at mating time they will find her. Do not *run* until your feet are bare and your throat is dry. But you said, "It's no use! I love foreign gods, and I must go after them" (Jer. 2:23-25).

Those who sin impulsively in the practice of idolatry and other sins, despite the warnings and restraints of God's Word, conscience, and superego, are wicked and foolish.

Counseling Application: Christian counselors need to assess and diagnose their clients' repeated sins against God. In order for them to change to a life pleasing to God, counselors encourage them to become more aware of their sinful "old selves" and help them to put off their old selves day by day and to put on new self in Jesus Christ.

Christian counselors also need to discern if their client is a liar. Persons who lie enough to be a false witness are psychopaths. These are very difficult people to help in counseling. They generally have high IQs, which means they are good at manipulation and deception. Even counselors are likely to be deceived.

My son, keep your father's command [commands] and do not forsake your mother's teaching. Bind them always on your heart [your heart forever]; fasten them around your neck. When you walk, they will guide you; when you sleep, they will watch over you; when you awake, they will speak to you. For this command is a lamp, this teaching is a light, and correction and instruction [the corrections of instruction] are the way to life, (6:20-23).

Father and mother are representations of the Wise. The commands and teachings of the Wise are a lamp and a light on the journey of life (23).[59] They are a lighthouse that shows the way. They are the path that leads to life (23b).

keeping you from your neighbor's wife [the immoral woman], from the smooth talk of a wayward woman [the wayward wife]. Do not lust in your heart after her beauty or let her captivate

---

[59] Bridges comments that these lamps and lights are especially beneficial for avoiding lustful temptations. Bridges, *Proverbs*, 65. Teachings in Proverbs reveal the reality of the seductive words and face of a harlot. They disclose that the face that looks so attractive is actually the face of the devil, and that the lips that seem to flow honey are a sword that kills the soul.

71

you with her eyes (6:24-25).

Solomon raises the level of warning against the immoral woman. He has already warned against the prostitute in 2:16-19, and 5:3-20. And here he again emphasizes the need to be wary of adultery in a relatively lengthy section, from verses 24 through 35. In the next chapter, chapter 7, he warns against a wayward woman for almost the entire chapter, specifically verses 5 through 27. If we were to number the assigned verses, it would be 4 --> 18 --> 12 --> 23.

Solomon uses both active and passive voice to repeat the same warning. Actively, he warns us against lusting after outward beauty (25a). Passively, he warns us not to be captivated to tempting "eyelids," that is, to a seductive look in her eyes (25b).

The "seductive look" can be better understood in terms of psychodynamic theory. The "look" is an "external object image." The process of seduction is when this external object image awakens an "internal object image" that has been unconscious for a long time. The beautiful external object, the seductive gaze, and the "gentle words" (24) are experiences that are identified with the "real mother" object image or "fantasy mother" object image that one had experienced as an infant early in his or her life. The beautiful object's gaze is linked to the "mirroring" that the mother gave to the baby. The experience of the mother's gaze satisfying and "mirroring" the baby's "narcissistic" needs that has been latent in the unconscious is awakened by the seductive woman's gaze. This means that a transference occurs. This unconscious dynamic can lead to the destruction of an immature person's life, because the foolish person cannot distinguish between the look of the seductive woman and the look of the mother he experienced as a baby.

For a prostitute can be had for a loaf of bread [for the prostitute reduces you to a loaf of bread], but another man's wife [the adulteress] preys on your very life. Can a man scoop fire into his lap without his clothes being burned? Can a man walk on hot coals without his feet being scorched? So is he who sleeps with another man's wife; no one who touches her will go unpunished. People do not despise a thief if he steals to satisfy his hunger when he is starving. Yet if he is caught, he must pay sevenfold, though it costs him all the wealth of his house (6:26-31).

The beauty of a prostitute and the attraction of her eyelids are a lure that leads to predictable destruction. It is wisdom to know in advance that what is wrapped up in a pretty package will lead to ruin. The harlot leads her captive to destruction as easily as she takes her prey, or as she eats a piece of cake (26b). She reduces him to the miserable condition of having to beg for a loaf of bread (26a). Especially, those who commit adultery with another man's wife suffers consequences incomparably worse than those who are caught stealing (31). Anticipating the potentially devastating consequences that can take over one's entire life can deter the sin of adultery.

Solomon says that embracing an adulterous woman is like trying to embrace fire and is like the foolish act of trying to walk barefoot over hot charcoals (27, 28). If you embrace fire, your clothes will quickly burn. You will even get burned all over your chest. If you stand on hot charcoals, your feet are bound to be burned.[60] Such are the sure and predictable consequences of adultery. So Solomon affirms, "So is he who sleeps with another man's wife; *no one* who touches her *will go unpunished*" (29b). This warning is related to Paul's command to "reject every kind of evil" (1 Thess. 5:22).

In a modern sense, this passage of proverbs can be applied as a warning against pornographic materials.[61] The women and men

---

[60] In the text, "foot" refers to a man's genitals, and "his genitals will be tormented and judged as if they were being burned with hot charcoals," Kim comments. Kim, *Proverbs*, 249.

[61] Anders emphasizes that it is important for Christians to apply Proverbs as God's Word for their modern lives. He sees Proverbs as still beneficial and valid for our day

who appear in easily accessible pornography on the internet are modern-day prostitutes. They abound in all kinds of pornography that corrupts the eyes and defiles the heart. These are wicked people who prey on the souls and homes of the believers. To draw near to these prostitutes is like trying to embrace fire. It will eventually lead to the same result as stepping on hot charcoals. The shame of being discovered to have had contact with these people in pornography is unspeakable. In addition to the "sevenfold loss" if you are found out, the shame from people is not easily removed. The consequences can be devastating, especially for ministers who are expected to have high moral standards. A few years ago, an American pastor who was a member of an Internet site that allowed married men to have sexual relationships with married women committed suicide because of the shame he felt when his identity was exposed when his membership information was hacked. Don't think it's someone else's business.

The problem is that we predict these outcomes to a certain extent, and yet we venture out using the defense mechanism of denial. The reality of today's world is that too many people turn to pornographic videos and photos to temporarily alleviate or anesthetize negative emotions such as anxiety, anger, sadness, and loneliness. Christians are no exception. We must foresee the deadly consequences and boldly break the vicious cycle of addiction of accessing pornography. We must live a life of vigilance to avoid shame and destruction.

But a man who commits adultery has no sense [lacks judgment]; whoever does so destroys himself. Blows and disgrace are his lot, and his shame will never be wiped away. For jealousy arouses a husband's fury, and he will show no mercy when he takes revenge. He will not accept any compensation; he will refuse a bribe [the bribe], however great it is (6:32-35).

and age. Anders, *Proverbs*, 52.

Adulterers lack judgment to recognize that they are engaging in self-destructive, self-defeating behaviors. They are the foolish who sell their lives for a pittance, not to mention the hurt, humiliation, and shame they suffer in the world (32b, 33).

Jesus said that those who look at a woman with lustful eyes have already committed adultery with her in their hearts (Matt. 5:28). How many of us are not guilty of adultery in the eyes of the Lord, who is more concerned with our inner motives and actions than our outward behaviors? It is necessary for us to have the discernment to examine our own inner world before pointing fingers at others who are accused of outward adultery. When we are aware of the sexual dynamics that take place in our hearts, we can avoid committing adultery, at least outwardly.

Adulterers are unable to make association between their temporary pleasure of the affairs and their permanent pain and suffering that follow the affairs.[62] Because of their cognitive distortions that occur during the affairs, they voluntarily choose short-term gratification over long-term satisfaction. They fail to foresee the ruin of their souls, the hurt and humiliation, and the irreparable shame (33).[63] Furthermore, they fail to recognize that they are not only destroying their own lives, but also their families.

Counseling Application: In case of counseling to infidelity, counselors must help clients confront their dynamics of borderline personality disorder and the long-term destructiveness of the affair.

---

[62] The dynamics of infidelity are very similar to those of borderline personality disorder, which is characterized by idealization vs. devaluation. This is because adulterers idealize the object of the affair while simultaneously devaluing their own spouse. This happens because their ego functioning is immature or regressed, which means that their ability to make association and differentiation is very poor. When an affair occurs, their ability to differentiate between the value of one's spouse and the value of the object of the affair is not functioning properly. They don't have a holistic, integrated view of how their relationship with their spouse has been. They devalue their spouse because they only remember and connect with negative experiences in their previous relationships.

[63] Kim insightfully comments on adultery as a "suicidal act," saying, "Adulterers do not die immediately, but as long as they live, they are wounded, humiliated, and shamed. Kim, *Proverbs*, 251.

Before confrontation, however, it is necessary to understand and empathize with their attachment to and obsession with short-term gratification. When you empathize with their childlike state of mind, they will be more likely to open up honestly and hear your confrontation.

Chapter 7 Do Not Be Misled by the Way of the Prostitute

My son, keep my words and store up my commands within you. Keep my commands and you will live; guard my teachings as the apple of your eye. Bind them on your fingers; write them on the tablet of your heart. Say to wisdom, "You are my sister," and to insight, "You are my relative." They will keep you from the adulterous woman, from the wayward woman [wife] with her seductive words (7:1-5).

Solomon repeatedly urges his son to heed and keep the words of Proverbs, using different phrasing. In verses 1 and 2, the imperative verbs "keep," "store up," and "guard" are used and emphasized.

Solomon exhorts us to treat wisdom and insight like our own sister and relative (4), which means not to treat them like enemies or strangers. He challenges us to accept them as if they are part of us, and cherish them as the apple of our eye (2). He promises that if we do it, wisdom and understanding will protect us, especially for from the adulterous person and from his or her seductive words (5).[64]

The active way to avoid fornication is to live before God, the source of wisdom. This means staying close to his Word and actively obeying it. When you are close to God, you can face one of the key emotions that contributes to fornication head-on: loneliness. Even if you are unhappy in your relationship with your spouse, you can find comfort and strength in God's Word. You can then avoid the foolish behavior of trying to solve your loneliness

---

[64] Koptak notes that Solomon's most vivid description and warning of the harlot is in the following verses, 6-23. He notes that Solomon has already warned against sexual immorality three times leading up to this text (2:16-19; 5:3-20; 6:20-36), and this fourth warning is the longest and most narrative in length. Koptak, *Proverbs*, 204.

with temporary, addictive relationships.

At the windows of my house I looked down through the lattice, I saw among the simple, I noticed among the young man, a youth who had no sense [who lacked judgment]. He was going down the street near her corner, walking along in the direction of her house at twilight, as the day was fading, as the dark of night set in. Then out came a woman to meet him, dressed like a prostitute and with crafty intent. (She is unruly [loud] and defiant, her feet never stay at home; now in the street, now in the squares, at every corner she lurks.)[65] She took hold of him and kissed him and with a brazen face[66] she said: "Today I fulfilled my vows, and I have food from my fellowship offering at home [I have fellowship offerings at home]. So I came out to meet you; I looked for you and have found you! I have covered my bed with colored linens from Egypt. I have perfumed my bed with myrrh, aloes and cinnamon.[67] Come, let's drink deeply

---

[65] Fox insightfully comments that the figuration of the adulterous woman as "unruly and defiant, her feet never stay at home; now in the street, now in the squares, at every corner she lurks" contrasts with the figuration of the Shulammite woman wandering the streets in search of her beloved (cf. Song. 3:2). Fox, *Proverbs 1-9*, 244. He translated it as "[she is] in ambush." He also comments that her behavior is like that of a hunter, lion, army, or robber in ambush. Fox, *Proverbs 1-9*, 245.

[66] Fox connects the facial features of the harlot's lack of moral conflict or shame to the words of Jeremiah 3:3, which says "Yet you have the brazen look of a prostitute; you refuse to blush with shame." Fox, *Proverbs 1-9*, 245.

[67] The prostitute stimulates the young man's sexual impulses by giving him visual and olfactory descriptions. A young man with weak ego-strength has little control over his sexual urges. Even if he had the strength, he would find it difficult to escape the temptation of the seductive woman. The young man has already crossed the "boundary" of the warning signs of danger and is disarmed.

[deep] of love till morning; let's enjoy ourselves with love! My husband is not at home; he has gone on a long journey. He took his purse filled with money and will not be home till full moon." With persuasive words she led him astray; she seduced him with her smooth talk. All at once he followed her like an ox going to the slaughter, like a deer stepping into a noose till an arrow pierces his liver, like a bird darting into a snare, little knowing it will cost him his life (7:6-23).

Solomon describes the seductive words and demeanor of the prostitute in this passage as if it were a scene from a movie. She disarms the young man by making a religious statement, "Today I have fulfilled my vows, and I have food from my fellowship offerings at home" (14). Thereby she allays any guilt he might feel and weakens the voice of his superego. We can infer from her religious wording that she is not necessarily a secular, unbelieving person. We don't know if she actually made a fellowship offering, because the prostitute is a deceitful person who can lie to deceive him. However, even if she did offer her fellowship offering to God, she is an adulterous wife who lives an unbelieving life in real life. There are many so-called Christians who live with a huge gap between their worship and their daily life. The wording of the prostitute in this passage suggests that there may be people of faith who repeatedly commit sexual sins. In particular, there is a phrase in verse 15 that can be linked to the religious rationalizations that some Christians use when engaging in their extramarital affairs: "So I came out to meet you; I looked for you and have found you!" (15). In this expression, the prostitute expresses her interest in the young man, "with persuasive words" of recognition and praise and "with her smooth talk." She then distorts this "wrong encounter" as God's "providential encounter."

The adulterous woman actively engages in sexual seduction: "I have covered my bed with colored linens from Egypt. I have perfumed my bed with myrrh, aloes and and cinnamon" (16-17).[68]

---

[68] Kim insightfully notes that both the bed and the perfumes in verses 16-17 symbolize

She stimulates hims with visual and olfactory descriptions to seduce the young man. Then she continues, "Come, let us drink deeply of love till morning; let's enjoy ourselves with love!" (18). It is "not good" even when people love and enjoy in each other. Although one may be happy in extramarital relationships, it is not "the way" to go for Christians.

The seductive woman reveals herself as a married woman and as an available woman for sex to the young man: "My husband is not at home; he *has gone on a long journey*. He took his purse filled with money and *will not be home* till full moon" (20). It is not clear from the text whether the young man is married or unmarried. It is likely that he is single. If he is unmarried, the seduction of the married woman could be interpreted psychoanalytically as stimulating the dynamics of the young man's unresolved "Oedipus complex." For an unmarried young man, a married woman is an object that provides motherly comfort. A married woman's breasts unconsciously remind him of his long-lost mother's breasts. Solomon describes the prostitute's behavior as seducing "with persuasive words" and "with her smooth talk" (21).[69]

Solomon gives a good metaphorical description of the consequences of the young man who is sexually tempted and follows the adulterous woman: "All at once he followed her like *an ox* going to the slaughter, like *a deer* stepping into a noose till an arrow pierces his liver, like *a bird* darting into a snare, little knowing it will cost him his life" (22-23).[70]

---

death. He notes that the young man could not have imagined that the bed he is lying on would become a coffin for his body and that the myrrh, spicy incense, and cinnamon would make fragrance to disperse the odor of his body. Kim, *Proverbs*, 270.

[69] Kim excellently comments: "This woman is not a mere prostitute, but a master with her own perspective, values, and worldview." Kim, *Proverbs*, 273.

[70] This truth does not apply only to sexual desires. Those who live their lives unconnected to Jesus Christ and driven by the needs and desires of this world are, without exception, like an ox going to the slaughter. "After desire has conceived, it gives birth to sin; and sin, when it is full-grown, gives birth to death" (James 1:15) is a statement of truth that well points to this process. James warns those who live by their desires that there will be "the day of slaughter" for those who "have lived on earth in luxury and self-indulgence" and "have fattened" themselves (James 5:5).

It is irrational to choose long-term ruin for short-term gratification. No pleasure in this world can satisfy us forever. No human relationship can provide true joy and satisfaction in the long run. Only those who thoroughly recognize this basic truth can avoid falling into the sins of adultery and sexual immorality. Sadly, many people repeat trial and error, despite the fact that they can learn from the second-hand experience of others. This is because they have "stubbornness" and a "stiff neck."

Solomon's strong warnings and admonitions against prostitutes in Proverbs can be understood psychoanalytically as a twofold dynamic. Based on his own experience of being seduced by numerous heathen women and being sexually promiscuous, it can be interpreted that he experienced "projective identification" with his son, with the issue of "countertransference." When there seemed to be a risk of his son experiencing what he himself had experienced, he could identify with his son who might be vulnerable to sexual issues through his own experience. In that sense, we can see the dynamic of countertransference. Solomon is a "wounded wise man" who warns all later believers through the trials and tribulations of his own life.

Now then, my sons, listen to me; pay attention to what I say. Do not let your heart turn to her ways or stray into her paths. Many are the victims she has brought down; her slain are a mighty throng. Her house is a highway to the grave, leading down to the chambers of death (7:24-27).

Solomon points out that because of fornication, many have been broken and fallen, and many have been slain (26). The house of the adulterous person is the way to the grave, the chambers of death. The way is a way "down" (27b). It is a pitfall from which it is difficult to climb back up.

It's a reality that many people suffer from infidelity and adultery. Nonetheless, there are still many people who fall into the snare of infidelity. Cheaters are relationship addicts in that they deny that they will suffer eventually.[71] Believing they are the exception and refusing to acknowledge reality is a common symptom of addiction.

[71] Bridges also commented beautifully that we need to fear the first step and not to think that we are able to stop ourselves when we want to, for familiarity with sin will weaken our aversion to it. Bridges, *Proverbs*, 71.

Chapter 8 Wisdom Is Better Than Pearls

Does not wisdom call out? Does not understanding raise her voice? At the highest point [on the heights] along the way, where the paths meet, she takes her stand; beside the gate [gates] leading into the city, at the entrance [entrances], she cries aloud: "To you, O people, I call out; I raise my voice to all mankind. You who are simple, gain prudence; you who are foolish, set your hearts on it [gain understanding]. Listen, for I have trustworthy [worthy] things to say; I open my lips to speak what is right. My mouth speaks what is true, for my lips detest wickedness. All the words of my mouth are just; none of them is crooked or perverse. To the discerning all of them are right; they are upright [faultless] to those who have found knowledge [have knowledge] (8:1-9).

In verse 1, wisdom and understanding are personified. In this context, wisdom and understanding are attributes and works of the Triune God, so much so that they can be understood interchangeably as God, Jesus Christ, or the Holy Spirit.

This wisdom and understanding shouts and raises her voice on the scene of people's life to awaken them (4).[72] Likewise, God speaks today, sometimes loudly, sometimes with a still, small voice, on the hillsides, in the streets, by the city gates, along the roads where people come and go.[73] Those whose ears are open to hear can hear

---

[72]   Clifford points out that Proverbs 8 is the longest discourse by Wisdom in the entire book of Proverbs. In his view, it is the most majestic and beautifully poetic portrayal of Wisdom personified. Clifford, *Proverbs*, 93. He also contrasts the wisdom's crying out at the city gate with Absalom's judging at the city entrance to steal people's favor from David. Clifford, *Proverbs*, 94. Lucas and Koptak also relate it with Absalom's behavior. Lucas, *Proverbs*, 78; Koptak, *Proverbs*, 227.

it. But the foolish have uncircumcised ears, so no matter how loudly God speaks, they do not hear it at all.

God wants even the foolish and the simple to listen to him and become prudent and instructed (5). This is one of the goals of the book of Proverbs. However, there is a problem that foolishness and folly are very hard to get rid of: "Though you grind a fool in a mortar, grinding them like grain with a pestle, you will not remove their folly from them" (27:22), because they cannot hear and are not inclined to listen. They do not heed the teaching and admonition of wisdom because they think themselves wise and they delight to dwell in darkness.

God actively hates evil (7b). Truth is incompatible with evil. Evil cannot dwell with truth. The Word of truth is righteous and it cannot tolerate crookedness and perversity (8).

Every word that Jesus, who is the way, the truth, and the life, spoke when he came to earth is truthful: "All the words of my mouth are just, none of them is crooked or perverse" (8). He did not pervert or twist the will of God the Father in the least. His lips were used righteously to hate evil and to defeat falsehood.

Choose my instruction instead of silver, knowledge rather than choice gold, for wisdom is more precious than rubies, and nothing you desire can compare with her. "I, wisdom, dwell together with prudence; I possess knowledge and discretion. To fear the Lord is to hate evil; I hate pride and arrogance, evil behavior and perverse speech" (8:10-13).

The counsel and knowledge of God are far more valuable than

[73] Kim comments that the time and place chosen by Wisdom is bright daylight as opposed to "at twilight," "as the dark of night set in," and "at the highest point along the way," "beside the grate leading into the city," and "at the entrance" as opposed to "now in the street, now in the squares, at every corner" in 7:8-11. "The harlot speaks privately and secretly in the dark of night for her own sexual gratification, but the woman wisdom invites all to come in the bright light of day," he notes. Kim, *Proverbs*, 282-83.

any treasure, including money represented by gold, silver, or rubies that the world values (10, 11). People in the world rejoice and are pleased when they earn or receive money that is visible. But they do not know how to rejoice and be glad because of the invisible God. They do not know the true joy that comes from incorporating and practicing the knowledge and counsel of God into their lives.

The active way to fear God is to rejoice and glorify him forever and ever. The passive way is to hate evil (13a). To fear God is to hate what God hates. The things God hates are "pride, arrogance, evil behavior, and perverse speech" (13b). Furthermore, to fear the LORD, you must not only abhor evil in others, but also hate the evil that remains within yourself. Unless evil is abhorred, pride, evil deeds, or perverse speech will not depart from your life. The process by which the old self, held together by narcissism, dies over and over again on the cross, day after day, is the process of abhorring and putting off the evil within.

Counsel and sound judgment are mine; I have insight [understanding], I have power. By me kings reign and rulers issue decrees [make laws] that are just; by me princes govern, and nobles—all [all nobles] who rule on earth (8:14-16).

The Triune God gives wisdom and authority to those who rule on earth to dispense justice and to govern. This is God's will.[74] So kings, presidents, prime ministers, judges, and police officers are responsible for upholding God's justice and for using their authority justly so that God's will is done on earth as it is in

[74] Paul recognized this fact: "Let everyone be subject to the governing authorities, for there is no authority except that which God has established. The authorities that exist have been established by God. Consequently, whoever rebels against the authority is rebelling against what God has instituted, and those who do so will bring judgment on themselves" (Rom. 13:1-2). However, earthly authorities cannot demand unconditional obedience. Peter and John refused to accept the Sanhedrin's threats against their preaching the gospel in Jesus' name, responding, "Which is right in God's eyes: to listen to you, or to him? You be the judges!. As for us, we cannot help speaking about what we have seen and heard" (Acts 4:19-20).

heaven.

Counseling Application: Skillful ability to counsel and sound judgment are essential qualities of an effective counselor. However, it is important to realize that the power to heal does not come from counselors themselves. They are only a channel and a midwife for the power of God from above to reach the client. Counseling should always be done with the awareness that therapeutic power comes "from above," that is, from God the Almighty.

I love those who love me, and those who seek me find me. With me are riches and honor, enduring wealth and prosperity. My fruit is better than fine gold; what I yield surpasses choice silver. I walk in the way of righteousness, along the paths of justice, bestowing a rich inheritance on those who love me and making their treasuries full (8:17-21).

Wisdom and knowledge are given from above. At the same time, they are also something that humans must actively seek and find. Jesus said that the door will be opened to him who knocks (Matt. 7:7). The descent of the Holy Spirit at Pentecost was promised, but it also came to those who gathered with eager anticipation and prayer.

Humans are "seekers." It matters what we seek and what we desire. Those who seek God and eagerly find Jesus Christ will not be disappointed, for they will find understanding and wisdom more precious than gold (19).

The wealth of those who love God, who walk in the paths of justice and righteousness, is "enduring" (18) and their treasuries are full (21b). Their grain is not eaten by worms, and their treasuries become storerooms for others. They don't live a foolish life, like the foolish rich man, who filled his barns with grain to satisfy himself, but only had his soul called away that night (see Luke 12:16-21).

"The LORD brought me forth as the first of his works, before his deeds of old; I was formed long ages ago [appointed from eternity], at the very beginning, when the world came to be [from the beginning, before the world began]. When there were no watery depths [no oceans], I was given birth, when there were no springs overflowing [abounding] with water; before the mountains were settled in place, before the hills, I was given birth, before he made the world [the earth] or its fields or any of the dust of the earth [the world]. I was there when he set the heavens in place, when he marked out the horizon on the face of the deep, when he established the clouds above and fixed securely the fountains of the deep, when he gave the sea its boundary so the waters would not overstep his command, and when he marked out the foundations of the earth. Then I was constantly [was the craftsman] at his side. I was filled with delight day after day, rejoicing always in his presence, rejoicing in his whole world and delighting in mankind" (8:22-31).

This passage presents Solomon as a prophet who clearly revealed the attributes and work of Jesus Christ. This proverb clearly reveals the deity and pre-existence of Jesus Christ, the Son of God, who, along with God the Creator, accomplished the work of creation through his Word. Solomon reveals that the wisdom of Proverbs is the cosmic, transcendent, spiritual wisdom that goes far beyond earthly and secular wisdom. This Wisdom had existed long before all phenomenal things existed. This Wisdom is God the Father and Jesus Christ the Son of God and the Holy Spirit.

This proverb can be connected to Genesis 1, where it is written that each day of the creation of the world was "good in the sight of God." During that creation process, Jesus Christ the Son was the delight of God the Father every day. The Son Wisdom rejoiced with God and was pleased with the human beings they created: "And God said, 'Let *us* make mankind in *our* image, in *our* likeness" (Gen. 1:26a). Solomon leads us in a flashback of the Triune God rejoicing in the creation of the heavens and the earth.

There is a feast in heaven when one person repents and becomes a child of God in Jesus Christ. Blessed are those who have spiritual eyes to see God's rejoicing over the saved and spiritual ears to hear God's laughter. There are a surprising number of Christians who are not convinced, questioning, "How can the glorious God be pleased with and love a lowly person like me?" The Psalmist expresses this sentiment well: "What is mankind that you are mindful of them, human beings that you care for them" (Ps. 8:4). But the fact that God love us with his grace in Jesus Christ is a biblical truth.

"Now then, my children, listen to me; blessed are those who keep my ways. Listen to my instruction and be wise; do not disregard [ignore] it. Blessed are those who listen to me, watching daily at my doors, waiting at my doorway. For those who find me find life and receive favor from the LORD. But those who fail to find me harm themselves; all who hate me love death" (8:32-36).

Blessed are those who have attained true wisdom and have encountered God personally. For they who have seen God and listen to him personally has found life (34) and received his favor (35b). But those who don't listen to God, the source of wisdom, are self-defeating, leading their souls to ruin (36a). Furthermore, they who hate God and the gospel are lovers of death and of the devil (36b). These people are subject to eternal judgment.

Chapter 9 The Fear of the LORD Is Wisdom and Knowledge

Wisdom has built her house; she has set up [hewn out] its seven pillars. She has prepared her meat and mixed her wine; she has also set her table. She has sent out her servants, and she calls from the highest point of the city, "Let all who are simple come to my house [come in here]!" To those who have no sense [lack judgment] she says, "Come, eat my food and drink the wine I have mixed. Leave your simple ways and you will live; walk in the way of insight [understanding]" (9:1-6).

In the first half of chapter 8, wisdom and insight were described as shouting at the highest point along the way, beside the gate leading into the city, and at the entrance to awaken people. In this chapter, wisdom calls again in the highest point of the city (3). She invites the foolish and the simple to come to the feast she has prepared in her house, to eat and drink and leave their simple ways (6a). Because wisdom cries out at the highest point of the city, no one can excuse himself or herself for not hearing.

The feast of wisdom is connected to the parable of the king's banquet, where even the uninvited were invited to the feast (Matt. 22:1-4). Those who were invited to the feast did not come, citing various reasons. The king was furious with those who rejected his invitation, and he commanded his servants to go out and bring even the lame, the blind, and the maimed to the feast and fill the seats. The reversal of the parable was that the uninvited were invited and the invited were rejected to the feast.

Isaiah described this feast of God as follows "Come, all you who thirsty, come to the waters; and you who have no money, come, buy and eat! Come, buy wine and milk without money and without cost" (Isa. 55:1). If we associate the passage of Isiah with the proverb above, the foolish and the simple are "thirsty" people and "poor" people. They are thirsty, but they don't recognize it. They are poor in spirit, but they don't sense it! They don't know why they are thirsty. They don't know what they are thirsty for. Wisdom invites them to come to her.

If you are invited to the feast, eat the delicious food and drink the sweet wine of the wisdom, your hunger and thirst will be quenched. You will have life (6a). The food and wine foreshadow Jesus' body and blood shed for sinners on the cross. Those who eat his body and drink his blood will have eternal life: "But here is the bread that comes down from heaven, which anyone may eat and not die. I am the living bread that came down from heaven. Whoever eats this bread will live forever. This bread is my flesh, which I will give for the life of the world" (John 6:50-51).

Whoever corrects a mocker invites insults; whoever rebukes the wicked incurs abuse. Do not rebuke mockers or they will hate you; rebuke the wise and they will love you. Instruct the wise and they will be wiser still; teach the righteous and they will add to their learning (9:7-9).

The mocker and the wicked are contrasted with the wise and the righteous. They have a cynical view of life and make a boast of themselves. These people have no desire or attitude to learn.[75] If you correct or advise them, they will respond cynically, saying, "You should mind your own business." If you rebuke or confront them, they will humiliate you with counterattack (8a).

But the wise and the righteous are humble and mature. They receive your confrontation humbly and thankfully (8b). They use your rebuke as an opportunity for change and growth. They learn with humility when there is something to learn, even from someone younger than them. They admit that there are still many areas they need to grow. This is what makes good leaders, because

---

[75] Bridges interpreted the arrogant and the wicked as those who do not respond to the invitation to the feast of wisdom, connecting it to the previous verses. He understood that the arrogant and the wicked are not naively ignorant, but deliberately and consciously rejecting the grace of salvation. Bridges, *Proverbs*, 86.

they are open to confrontation enough to hear it without anger or shame even after they become a leader.

The symptoms of narcissistic personality disorder and paranoid personality disorder are similar to the characteristics of the mockers and the wicked. People with narcissistic personality disorder sufferers are arrogant and haughty. They have grandiose self images. As a result, they deny that they may do wrong and that there may be problems within themselves. They can't tolerate negative feedback from others. Uncomfortable feedback causes narcissistic wounds and makes them very angry.

People with paranoid personality disorder interpret the other person's innocent remarks as malicious and attacking and become angry. They cannot tolerate even the slightest insult but counterattack. They are unforgiving and hold on to the idea of retaliation for a long time.

It is wise to know the person you are reprimanding before you confront him or her. Rebuke and discipline are ineffective with vulnerable people, aggressive people, and people who are not self-aware. This is something to consider for us in disciplines in the church. Disciplining someone with any of the above characteristics can cause narcissistic wounds, so they are unwilling to repent of their wrongdoing and instead project their anger onto the church and its leaders.

Counseling Application: Discipline and rebuke in the text are linked to confrontation in counseling. When confronting a client, it is wise to assess his or her condition and level of understanding. As this proverbs well points out, the arrogant or the simple are not good candidates for confrontation. Confrontation is especially at risk of being ineffective if the client is characterized by narcissistic personality disorder, paranoid personality disorder, anti-social personality disorder, or borderline personality disorder. These clients are more likely to express aggression and threats toward the counselor and abuse verbally or physically.

The fear of the LORD is the beginning of wisdom, and knowledge of the Holy One is understanding. For through wisdom your days will be many, and years will be added to your life. If you are wise, your wisdom will reward you; if you are a mocker, you alone will suffer (9:10-12).

Verse 10 is related to 1:7, "The fear of the LORD is the beginning of knowledge." So we see that "wisdom" and "knowledge" are interchangeable. And "fearing God" and "knowing God" are linked (10).

God blesses those who fear him, promising them the blessing of a long life (11). But mockers will suffer and be harmed "alone" (12), because God hates the proud and haughty. However, he wants even the arrogant to be saved. He allows suffering for them so that they may finally be humbled and granted grace for salvation. Nevertheless, there are many arrogant people who go on to destruction. Years of life will be added to the wise, but be shortened to the proud.

Folly is an unruly woman [The woman Folly is loud]; she is simple and knows nothing [is undisciplined and without knowledge]. She sits at the door of her house, on a seat at the highest point of the city, calling out to those who pass by, who go straight on their way, "Let all who are simple come to my house!" To those who have no sense [lack judgment] she says, "Stolen water is sweet; food eaten in secret is delicious!" But little do they know that the dead are there, that her guests are deep in the realm of the dead [in the depths of the grave] (9:13-18).

At the beginning of this chapter, wisdom, expressed in the feminine form, has built her house, making feasts, and inviting people to come and turn from their foolish ways. But at the end of this chapter, the foolish, simple woman sits at the door of her house, on a seat at the highest point of the city, inviting passersby to come to her house! (16a).[76] This is a clear contrast to the beginning of chapter 8, where Wisdom calls out at the highest point along the way, beside the gate leading into the city, and at the entrance to the city. The foolish woman is actually more elevated than Wisdom, as she plausibly presents herself in a higher position.

Solomon characterizes the foolish woman as "unruly" and "simple [undisciplined]" and "without knowledge." She is Folly who doesn't realize the impact of her words or even what she is saying. She is also a wicked woman who leads people to the grave. Her words sound correct in the world: "Stolen water is sweet, food eaten in secret is delicious!" (17). Her statement is seductive but deceptive. In fact, stolen food actually tastes better. This is because the chemicals released in the brain at the moment of stealing promote feelings of relief and pleasure. But it's a vice and sin.

Some people steal from department stores or shops not because they don't have the money, but because they enjoy the intense pleasure of getting away with it undetected.[77] These people are foolish. They are foolish because one day they will be caught and humiliated. The reason infidelity makes you feel happier than a normal marriage is because it's secret. The brain is more stimulated when you do something forbidden.[78]

---

[76] In his commentary on this text, Kim notes that while there are similarities in form between the actions of Wisdom and the foolish woman, they are all fundamentally different in content: "She 'has her house,' but she has not built her house; she invites to a feast, but she has not prepared a feast; she calls out, but she is not speaking the truth. Above all, the foolish do not know that her house is the house of the dead." Kim, *Proverbs*, 332.

[77] Bridges commented on the text by referring to an episode in which Augustine stole pears from a pear tree. Augustine threw away most of the pears he stole because he did not steal them because he was hungry, but just to taste the joy he felt when he sinned. Bridges, *Proverbs*, 89.

[78] Kim explains that "stealing" in this text refers to sexual gratification, and he cited relevant passages in Proverbs (2:17, 5:9, 6:30-35, 7:19). He suggests that "food eaten in secret" also refers to a sexual relationship and provided Proverbs 30:20 as a supporting text: "This is the way of an adulterous woman: She eats and wipes her

The foolish woman seduces even those who "go straight on their way" (15). It is as if the devil tempts even believers. It is very dangerous for you to listen to this temptation.

This foolish woman seduces and deceives the poor in judgment and the simple. She promises them sweet and delicious things. But anyone who is attracted to a bait that is sweet, savory, or fragrant and bites into it is a fool. A foolish one does not know that those who have already fallen for the bait are trapped in a deep pit, like Sheol, and cannot get out (18). Those who are deceived by the words of Folly will be in the same situation as a fish being lured in by the bait, not realizing that there are many of his fellow fish already in the fisherman's net, and only end up on the chopping board.

mouth and says, 'I've done nothing wrong.'" He continues, "The reason forbidden sex is 'sweet' is because it is 'forbidden,'" making a good point about the enhanced pleasure that comes from the anxiety of doing something forbidden. Kim, *Proverbs*, 335.

Chapter 10 The Tongue of the Righteous and the Lips of the Wicked

The proverbs of Solomon: A wise son brings joy to his father, but a foolish son brings grief to his mother (10:1).[79]

Chapters 1 through 9 are characterized by a series of proverbs that are linked together like a short sermon. However, chapters 10 through 29 are mostly stand-alone proverbs, although there are occasional contextual connections.[80] The fact that chapter 10 begins with "The proverbs of Solomon:" and chapter 25 begins again with "These are more proverbs of Solomon" helps us to understand them as a larger group. So we can understand chapters 10 through 24 as one group and chapters 25 through 29 as another group of Solomon's proverbs.

Wise children please their parents because they are mature relatively well for their age, and so their parents don't have to worry about them. Rather their parents are grateful and proud for them. Foolish children, on the other hand, cause their parents to worry, because they are psychologically and spiritually immature. They are unable to think independently. They are often deceived by people, are not confident in interpersonal relationships, and have a poor social life. Having a foolish adult child makes his or her parents feel uneasy. Moreover, if the child does not fear God and does not live by faith in God, believing parents cannot help but feel anxious and stressed.

---

[79] Fox notes that in the case of chapter 10, fourteen of the thirty-two total verses of the proverbs take the chiastic form (A-B-B'-A' or A-B-A'-B'). Fox, *Proverbs 10-31*, 477.

[80] Fox points out that the proverbs of Solomon, chapters 10 through 29, are characterized by the fact that they consist of stand-alone proverbs, as opposed to the format of chapters 1 through 9. With a few exceptional passages that must be interpreted in context, he believes it is necessary to interpret each proverb with the understanding that each proverb stands alone, with no connection to other proverbs. Fox, *Proverbs 10-31*, 477-78.

Ill-gotten treasures have no lasting value [are of no value], but righteousness delivers from death. The LORD does not let the righteous go hungry, but he thwarts the craving of the wicked (10:2-3).

"Ill-gotten treasure" is connected to "the craving of the wicked." "Righteousness" is connected to "the righteous." God hates those who take the riches of unrighteousness. Riches, even if they are not unrighteous, have no value or power in themselves to justify us before God (2a). Riches have no power to save a person from death. Ill-gotten money has no lasting value even in this world. It has only temporary power.

The righteous, whom God approves of, are delivered from the brink of their death (2b). God does not let them go hungry (3a). As Jesus argued, the God who clothes the wild lilies and feeds the birds of the air, will provide his children with food, drink, and clothing (see Matt. 6:30).[81]

The wealth of unrighteousness is of no value (2a). Rather, it destroys the souls of the wicked.[82] It bring God's judgment upon them. But righteous wealth is used to save people. God sees in secret, recognizes, and praises the hand of the one who scatters riches to help people in need (see Matt. 6:3-4).

God rejects the cravings of the wicked (3b). He also abhors the prayers of those whose hands are full of blood: "Even when you offer many prayers, I am not listening. Your hands are full of blood" (Isa. 1:15).

Lazy hands make for poverty, but diligent hands bring wealth.

---

[81] Fox connects this proverb with Ps. 37:25-26, "I was young and now I am old, yet I have never seen the righteous forsaken or their children begging bread. They are always generous and lend freely; their children will be a blessing" Fox, *Proverbs 10-31*, 512.

[82] Bridges pointed out that Judas Iscariot's act of selling Jesus for thirty pieces of silver was a foolish act that was both futile for him and led to his eternal death. Bridges, *Proverbs*, 67.

He who gathers crops in summer is a prudent [wise] son, but he who sleeps during harvest is a disgraceful son (10:4-5).[83]

"Lazy hands" and "diligent hands" are contrasted to each other. "He who gathers crops in summer" is compared to "he who sleeps during harvest." "Poverty" and "a disgraceful son" differ from "wealth" and "a prudent son."

Masters have incredibly skillful hands. They have gotten good at what they do through trial and error and hard work. People recognize and respect them. As a result, people flock to their businesses. It's like the proverb says, "diligent hands bring wealth." However, there are some people who are so lazy that they are ashamed to have their hands on their bodies. lazy people are slow to play with his hands and less professional. Their business is doomed to failure (4a). It is incorrect to say that all poor people are lazy. But it is true that lazy people become poor.

Sloth is one of the seven deadly sins. A sluggard's life is spiritually counted for nothing before God. In Jesus' parable, the servant who was given one talent and buried it, and then brought it back, was condemned to be wicked and lazy.[84]

Adult children who are diligently working their hands in the time of harvest don't cause their parents to worry. But if they don't work enough to support their families, they are a disgrace and a burden to their parents (5b). If a husband is idle and idle at work when he should be working, he is a disgrace and a burden to his family. If a high school child is late for school almost every day because of his or her oversleep, he or she would be burdensome to his or her parents.

---

[83] Koptak well notes that this proverb against laziness also reappears in verse 26, "As vinegar to the teeth and smoke to the eyes, as are sluggards to those who send them." Koptak, *Proverbs*, 289.

[84] Koptak makes a good point that the general truth about the value of hard work should not be interpreted as a promise that God will surely bless. He sees the emphasis of this proverb as teaching a truth that has general application in life. Koptak, *Proverbs*, 289.

Blessings crown the head of the righteous, but violence overwhelms the mouth of the wicked (10:6). See 10:11.

Reckless speech, inconsiderate speech, cursing, and swearing are examples of "verbal abuse or violence." Aggressive words spoken without consideration for the other person penetrate deeply into the hearts of those who hear them and wound painfully because they are "poisonous."

When parents often verbally abuse their children, the children become victims of domestic violence. Such children develop aggression in their minds and grow up with a strong sense of inferiority. Later in life, unable to cope with minor crisis experiences, they may commit suicide or become perpetrators against their own spouse or children.

Verbal abuse is as much an assault as physical violence. Verbal abuse is a sin and a vice. People with borderline personality disorder are especially likely to use physical or verbal violence to express their extreme anger. As such, violence is both a symptom of a personality disorder and a sin.

Counseling Application: Wise counselors who understand the power of negative words, know how to speak healing words to wounded clients. If verbal abuse belongs to the devil, then healing words belong to the Holy Spirit, the Spirit of life. Wise counselors search for and identify the abusive words that have entered their client's psyche and neutralize or expel them. By speaking words of empowerment, blessing, encouragement, and support, they fill the client's inner world with the language of life. Furthermore, they fill the client's mind and heart with the therapeutic Word of God. Mind and heart filled with the Word of God is also filled with the Holy Spirit.

The name [memory] of the righteous is used in blessings, but the name of the wicked will rot (10:7).

When the righteous leave this world, people honor them and

mourn them for a long time. When faithful pastors leave their pastorate, the remaining members of the congregation do not forget them for a long time. There is a Korean proverbs, "Tigers die and leave their hides, but people die and leave their names." We don't have to leave behind a distinguished name. Blessed are those who are remembered by an honorable name. We are not to be remembered with a stigma.

The wise in heart accept commands, but a chattering fool comes to ruin (10:8).

"The wise in heart" is contrasted with "a chattering fool." Those who are wise in heart are wise in mouth. They don't talk too much. They don't spend much time making idle talk. They don't get caught talking about useless things. Instead of speaking, they accept and digest commands and teachings (8a). They don't grumble about teachings and admonitions. As James exhorts, they are "quick to listen, slow to speak" (James 1:19).

Conversely, chattering fools have foolish lips and a foolish heart. They come to ruin because of their chatter. The foolish chatters also vomit up what they are taught and commanded. They excuse and rationalize for why they don't follow commands. They often use "Yes, but..." language. When told to take the narrow path, they disobey, questioning why they should take the narrow path when many people take the broad path. Repeating disobedience and rebellion, the foolish eventually come to destruction (8b).

God's commandments are always right and good. God's thoughts are different from our human thoughts, and therefore cannot be obeyed on the level of reason. Without faith, it is impossible to obey God's command and to please him. If you believe and obey God's truthfulness and faithfulness, even if you cannot understand it with your mind, you can live a blessed life. And you can live a life of eternal life. As the Bible says, "For God so loved the world that he gave his one and only Son, that whoever believes in him shall not perish but have eternal life" (John 3:16), so if you believe in and receive Jesus as your Savior, you will have eternal life.

Living wisely is not complicated or difficult.

Whoever walks in integrity walks securely, but whoever takes crooked paths will be found out (10:9).

Those who walk in integrity are not perfect persons. But they are "relatively" truthful and whole in thought, behavior, and relationships. They don't stray too far to the left or right in the path of life (9a). Greed and other temptations can't change the direction of their lives. They live a life characterized by consistency, predictability, and faithfulness. Even when hardships come, they can't stumble them to despair. They may fall down, but they get back up and continue on their journey of life. The immature and foolish, on the other hand, go on crooked paths (9b), because to them the crooked path does not seem crooked; what is distorted seems normal to them.

From a biblical perspective, those who have departed from God are, without exception, people who walk crooked paths. The crooked road and the broad path look easy to them. It looks normal because many people are walking these paths. But they are paths that lead to destruction and eternal condemnation. They have nothing to do with Jesus. Those who walk these roads will finally be found out (9b). At the end of these roads, there are no more exits, no more turns. There will be only eternal destruction.

Whoever winks maliciously causes grief, and a chattering fool comes to ruin (10:10).

The second half of this proverb is the same as the second half of verse 8: "a chattering fool comes to ruin." In verse 8, the heart was connected to the mouth; here, the eyes are connected to the mouth.

Destruction awaits those who are careless with their words and those who misuse their eyes (10). There are many other proverbs that warn of the dangers of speech, so I will focus here on the warning against those who misuse their eyes. Those who conspire and signal with their eyes to do evil will be destroyed. They wink in secret, but their malice will finally be disclosed.

When the eyes, the God-given window of the heart to the world, are misused, they cause grief and worry to others. Those who see things they shouldn't come to ruin. David was tempted to see Bathsheba's nakedness and had to pay off the serious results from his sins.

Today's high-speed internet networks are bringing pornography into our homes. Even among believers, there are many who see things they shouldn't through pornographic sites. Viewing pornography is a big problem in itself. What's worse is being caught, which can be traumatizing and devastating to one's spouse or children. For pastors, being caught hurts their congregation and dishonors God.

The mouth of the righteous is a fountain of life, but the mouth of the wicked conceals violence [violence overwhelms the mouth of the wicked] (10:11). See 10:6.

Hatred stirs up conflict [dissension], but love covers over all wrongs (10:12).

Hatred, animosity, dissension, and envy cause quarrels and conflict (12a). Unless reconciliation or forgiveness occurs, conflict and strife will repeat in a vicious cycle.

When hatred grows in marriage, husband and wife become estranged and eventually divorce. When misunderstandings and resentment lead to hatred between siblings, they stop communicating with each other. This is because they see each other's faults alone and blame each other. Then, they are unable to forgive.[85]

---

[85]   Lucas interprets the love that covers all transgressions as the meaning of forgiveness expressed in Ps. 85:2: "You forgave the iniquity of your people and covered all their

But love has incredible power. It has power to cover the wrongs of the other person (12b).[86] Love "keeps no record of wrongs" (1 Cor. 13:5). Love has power to make trespasses invisible. It has the power to keep us from getting angry even when we see them. In a relationship where faults are covered, there is no longer resentment, conflict, or strife. Anger and bitterness disappear. Reconciliation and peace reign. The source of this love is the cross of Jesus Christ.

Wisdom is found on the lips of the discerning, but a rod is for the back of one who has no sense [lacks judgment] (10:13).

The lips are contrasted to the back as bodily parts. In verse 11, Solomon described that the mouth of the righteous is a fountain of life, while the mouth of the wicked conceals violence. This proverb in verse 13 views the mouth from a different angle: the mouth of the discerning is wise (13a). Solomon connotes that there is praise and recognition instead of a disciplinary action for those with discerning lips (13b).

Those who lack discernment and judgment invite ruin, that is, "a rod for the back" (13b). They speak impulsively and recklessly because they don't have a discerning heart and sound judgment. They lose all because of their mistake of a word. A single impulsive word can cause a person to be removed from his or her position of power.

The wise store up knowledge, but the mouth of a fool invites ruin (10:14).

sins." Lucas, *Proverbs*, 92. Forgiveness in this proverb text refers to the horizontal dimension of forgiveness in human relationships rather than the vertical dimension of God's forgiveness.

[86] Koptak connects this proverb to James 5:20, "Remember this: Whoever turns a sinner from the error of their way will save them from death and cover over a multitude of sins." Koptak, *Proverbs*, 293.

The second half of this proverb, "the mouth of a fool invites ruin," is paired with "a chattering fool comes to ruin" in the second half of verses 8 and 10. "The wise in heart accept commands" in the first half of verse 8 is paired with "the wise store up knowledge" in the first half of this proverb. Taken together, to "store up knowledge" can be interpreted to mean to take in and internalize teachings, commandments, and admonitions. Thus, the wise are ones who digest the teachings of parents or teachers, who are meaningful "external objects," and who make them a part of their "self." Such persons have a strong foundation of faith in God. So even in the midst of difficult trials, they ruminate on the internalized words and do not despair.

The foolish, however, by refusing to accept admonition, have "fragile self" psychologically and spiritually. Therefore, they are vulnerable to break down in the face of crisis or trial (14b). Such persons cannot speak wise words because they don't have much internalized wisdom. So they tend to say foolish things. They often don't know what they are talking about. Even if they pray, they babble incoherently and pray foolishly, not knowing what they really need.

The wealth of the rich is their fortified city, but poverty is the ruin of the poor (10:15).

This proverb contrasts "the rich" with "the poor," "wealth" with "poverty," and "fortified city" with "ruin." The Bible does not condemn wealth per se. Rather Proverbs admits the importance of wealth in this world. It warns against accumulating wealth through unrighteous means, but it praises those who become wealthy through the labor of diligent hands. Solomon spoke positively about wealth in verse 4 of this chapter when he said, "Lazy hands make for poverty, but diligent hands bring wealth." So it is necessary to understand Solomon's positive view of wealth in this context.

Solomon says that for the rich, wealth is a "fortified city" (15a).

Rich people are rarely strained financially when hard times come. Similarly, wealthy nations can weather an economic crisis like a fortified city.

Being economically vulnerable increases the risk of separation and divorce (15b). This is because people who are stressed financially may not be able to overcome conflicts that they would normally have been able to cope with. Especially, the more psychologically or spiritually immature a couple is, the higher the risk of divorce.

The wages of the righteous is life [bring them life], but the earnings [income] of the wicked are sin and death [brings them punishment] (10:16).

Solomon contrasts the wages of the righteous with the earnings of the wicked. Even though they may earn the same amount of money, their income has different roles and different outcomes. The righteous humbly acknowledge and appreciate that God is the giver of their wages. The wicked, on the other hand, think they earned their income in their own strength, and so they use it as they please.

The income of the righteous is also the harvest of their own labor and sweat. But they regard their earnings as a favor and grace from God. They believe that God has given them health, skills, wisdom, and all the conditions to work. Therefore, they spend their income on things that are pleasing to God. They use it on good works. They live a life of storing up their treasure in heaven (16a). They are good servants as citizens of God's kingdom. They use their income to serve others. And they also bring joy and thankfulness to their families.

The income of the wicked may be the harvest of their own labor and sweat too. But their earnings do not acknowledge God: that is sin (16b). For everything that is not done by faith is sin (see Rom. 14:23). Furthermore, for the active wicked, their earnings are unearned. They are the harvest of threatening or defrauding others.[87]

The income of the wicked harms their life (16b), because greed leads to death (James 1:15). Those who take a bribe to fill their belly will eventually be exposed and arrested. Furthermore, they will face eternal judgment because they have lived a life that is not pleasing to God.

Whoever heeds discipline shows the way to life, but whoever ignores correction leads others astray (10:17).

Those who listen to and obey admonition and exhortation walk the way of life (17a). On the other hand, those who ignore counsel, disobey it, and do their own walk the way of destruction for themselves and lead others astray (17b).[88] There are only two paths in our lives. There are no other paths. It is each person's choice whether to go the way of life or the way of destruction.

God made two covenants with Israel about to enter the land of Canaan: the covenant at Ebal hill and the covenant at Grishim hill. They were the covenant of blessing and the covenant of curse. God promised to bless them if they obeyed Gods' laws and he also promised to curse them if they disobeyed them. The history of Israel after the book of Judges was the fulfillment of these two promises.

Counseling Application: Counselors-in-training benefit their clients when they receive feedback from their supervisors and incorporate it into their counseling process. They are trained by supervisors to acquire the skills and qualities necessary to become professional counselors. Trainees who listen carefully to their

[87] Kim comments that the income of the wicked is "earned for one's own selfish desires, at the expense of others, and through antisocial behavior." Kim, *Proverbs*, 356. In this sense, we can say that the income of the wicked is the income that antisocial personality disordered people take from others through criminal behaviors, such as stealing, tax evasion, fraud, and so forth. These people are usually more intelligent than the average people. They are wicked people who use their good intellectual abilities to do evil things.

[88] Fox notes that this proverb implies that those who ignore discipline not only go astray themselves, but lead others to go astray as well. Fox, *Proverbs 10-31*, 520.

supervisors' supervision and feedback and take them to heart can guide their clients on a path of change and growth. On the other hand, trainees who do not heed their supervisor's feedback and corrections or are not unwilling to become more aware of themselves, they will not be able to benefit their clients. They will lead their clients astray.

From the client's perspective, clients who practice the counselor's feedback and admonitions in their lives will progress toward change. On the other hand, those who ignore their counselor's feedback and confrontation will revert to the familiar path they have been walking.

Whoever conceals hatred with lying lips and spreads slander is a fool (10:18).

The first half of this proverb is connected to the second half of 16:30, "Whoever purses their lips is bent on evil."[89] There are many reasons for hiding hatred, or closing the lips. In this proverb, it is to hide anger and aggression. For example, to hide aggression with lying lips, one might speak as if he or she likes the other person or speaks with an inappropriate smile.

Psychologically immature people often use this defense mechanism of suppression or repression: they suppress or repress hatred in order to avoid avoidance or conflict; they conceal aggression. The problem is that they continue to use these mechanism, their interpersonal relationships will suffer. In a relationship where true emotions aren't shared, they can't experience intimacy. They will only experience anxiety and tension.

Lying lips are lips that are inconsistent on the outside and inside. Speaking truthfully gives us freedom in relationships. When you

[89] Bridges pointed out that since the fall in the Garden of Eden, there are numerous examples of people in the Bible who demonstrated this proverb, including Cain, who killed his brother Abel (Gen. 4:8), Saul, who tried to kill David (1 Sam. 18:21, 22, 29), Joab, who killed Abner and Amasa (2 Sam. 3:27; 2 Sam. 20:9-10), and Judas Iscariot (Matt. 26:48-49). Bridges, *Proverbs*, 101.

are angry, you are being truthful if you at least look angry. In communication, a frequent inconsistency between the outside and inside means deceiving the other person.

It is a reality that inconsistency on the outside speech and inside is present in the lives of Christians at times. We are to live with at least the awareness that we sometimes speak with lying lips.

Those who conceal hatred with lying lips "and" spread slander are "passive-aggressive." David well describes his experience with these people: "My enemy say of me in malice, 'When will he die and his name perish?' When one of them comes to see me, he speaks falsely, while his heart gathers slander: then he goes out and spreads it around" (Ps. 41:5-6).

Sin is not ended by multiplying words [When words are many, sin is not absent], but the prudent hold their tongues (10:19).

Proper holding of the tongue means one's ability to control impulses. The immature are likely to make mistakes in their speeches. But the prudent know what to say and what not to say, when to speak and when not to speak, and how to speak. So they make fewer mistakes and cause less hurt in their interpersonal relationships.

Talking at the right amount is a key to maintaining healthy relationships with others. Talking too much increases the risk of saying unnecessary or hurtful things. On the other hand, especially in marriage relationship, being too reserved and silent makes one's spouse uneasy to experience intimacy and leads to communication problems to each other. Avoiding talking altogether to avoid making any mistakes is a sign of immaturity.

Counseling Application: To become an effective counselor, you need to speak therapeutically: you say empathically, clearly, briefly, and appropriately. There are reasons why some counselors talk more. First, counselors talk more than clients when their anxiety levels are high. The more novice counselors are, the more they talk during counseling sessions.[90] This is because they are

---

90   Bridges insightfully commented on the sin of "vain babbling" saying that people talk

anxious. Counselors who cannot handle their anxiety, especially when their client is silent, avoid the anxiety of silence by bringing up new topics or talking themselves. Second, counselor-centered counseling makes counselors to talk a lot. This is because they are trying to teach their client. This can lead to a one-way communication. Third, when counselors experience countertransference with their client, they tend to talk a lot. When a counselor is connected to an issue, either positively or negatively, that is brought up dynamically in the counseling process, he or she may overreact and talk too much.

A good way for counselors to check in with themselves in their training is to write a verbatim or listen to recordings. Noticing where and why they are talking a lot is a very important way to self-supervise. If a counselor talks more than his or her client does, it is almost certainly an ineffective session.

It is very important for counselors to provide a safe and secure environment where their client can talk. This is why counseling or psychotherapy is often called "talking cure." When you talk, and someone listens, empathizes, and connects with you, you can have an opportunity to rewrite your narrative. When you speak in therapy, pent-up emotions may be connected and expressed in unexpected moments, expanding your horizons of awareness. Speaking allows the client' inner world to be revealed, helping the counselor to understand, assess, and diagnose the client's state of mind and to help him or her effectively.

The counselor's primary purpose is to facilitate the client's ability to speak with ease and clarity. The counselor can facilitate his or her client to talk without distraction with his or her good listening skills. When the counselor is brief and to the point, the client can experience that he or she is understood and empathized.

The tongue of the righteous is choice silver, but the heart of the wicked is of little value. The lips of the righteous nourish many, but fools die for lack of sense [judgment] (10:20-21).

a lot because they are empty inside, not because they are full. Bridges, *Proverbs*, 72.

The righteous are those who are not foolish, not wicked. They encourage and empower many with their lips. The wicked are fools who lack judgment and sensitivity. They devalue many with their aggressive words. They destroy others including themselves.

The tongue of the foolish or wicked is not just of little value, but almost useless. But the tongue of the righteous is like a valuable silver. It "nourishes" and saves many people. It is worth enough to "pay one's debt in a word."

Many people live with their tongues that are not functioning as God intended. They don't speak up when they need to speak up. They don't speak up because they are unsafe, insecure, afraid, or unconfident. They don't speak because they feel powerless and helpless. Like the servant who received the one talent in Jesus' parable, there are many who do not use their God-given tongue well and simply remain silent, avoiding, and closed-mouthed. Such people are like those who seem to be alive but are actually dead (21b): "fools die."

On the other hand, there are people who say things they shouldn't because they lack judgment. They say hurtful things impulsively. They say all kinds of destructive things because they can't control their anger and their mouth.

Counseling Application 1: Christian counselors can help the foolish or the wicked grow and change into the righteous and wise. They provide a "speech therapy" to help them say the right thing for the right occasion. This is not a speech therapy that corrects pronunciation, but a speech therapy that helps them speak appropriately and sensitively.

For a therapy of "talking cure" to work, therapists must empathize with their client. They are to express verbally and non-verbally well to the client what they are empathizing with. When their empathic words and behaviors are internalized, digested, and become a part of his or her "self," the client unconsciously begins to mimic the counselor's empathic words and behaviors in his or her life with others. He or she begins to empathize with the other person's story a little more, and begins to express it in a way that fits the situation. The client, who used say things inappropriately or unconfidently, is changed gradually to speak clearly and wisely. The change may even be noticeable to those around him or her.

Nurturing methods that a good enough mother uses with her baby can be used in counseling process. When the counselor is "mirroring" clients who babble, they gradually begin to speak their own words. They begin to speak understandably and enjoy speaking. When the counselor responds them with warmth, listening with interest, responding empathically, recognizing, praising and idealizing, clarifying, and even blessing, it can do wonders for the client's inner world.

Clients' change from speaking without discernment to speaking wisely and appropriately can take place because they have been "re-cognized" by their counselor. Clients who are recognized by their counselor become intellectually smarter. Their "cognitive" abilities are empowered. So they say less hurtful things to others. They are less likely to act like fools. When this happens, the clients' tongue becomes that of the servants who received two talents or five talents. They can live a life of value, pleasing God their master and experiencing a sense of accomplishment and joy in their lives. Especially, Christian clients can experience through their empathic counselor that God accepts, approves, and blesses them. Then the counselor can be used as a healing instrument of God.

The prophet Isaiah described that God gave him "a well-instructed tongue" to help people in need: "The Sovereign LORD has given me a well-instructed tongue, to know the word that sustains the weary" (Isa. 50:4). His tongue was not a tongue that spoke for itself; it was a tongue that spoke what he had learned from God who wakened his ear to listen morning by morning.

Christian counselors should seek to have a "well-instructed tongue" as the prophet Isaiah did. Pastoral counselors, including Christian counselors, should be bilingual. The Christian theological language must be their mother language. At the same time, they must be able to speak the psychological language well enough as their second language. When a pastoral counselor speaks both languages fluently and confidently, they can be very effective in their help with their clients. Therefore, pastoral counselors must learn theological language morning by morning and day by day, as Isaiah did. They are to read diligently, meditate, and study the Bible. They need to make it a habit to read theological articles and books on a regular basis. They also need to read and study books and journals related to psychology so that they have a good command of psychological language. Counseling will be as effective as they study, listen, learn, and pray.

The blessing of the LORD brings wealth, without painful toil for it [he adds no trouble to it] (10:22).

This proverb is linked with verse 15, "The wealth of the rich is their fortified city, but poverty is the ruin of the poor." God's blessings include wealth. God is a wealthy God. When he gives, he gives generously.

However, those who are blessed by God are not attached to wealth. They have the faith to confess, as Job did, "The LORD gave and the LORD has taken away; my the name of the LORD be praised" (Job 1:21). Material wealth does not cause them anxiety (22b). This is because, as Paul confessed, they can confess, "I know what it is to be in need, and I know what is is to have plenty. I have learned the secret of being content in any and every situation, whether well fed or hungry, whether living in plenty or in want" (Phil. 4:12).

A fool finds pleasure in wicked schemes [evil conduct], but a person of understanding delights in wisdom (10:23).

It is foolish and wicked to delight in doing evil (23a). Doing evil may be pleasing temporarily. This is because sin and evil always provide temporary pleasure. "Stolen water is sweet, food eaten in secret is delicious!" (9:17). It feels that way. But these tastes, smells, and pleasures are short-lived. The joy and pleasure are also addictive. They eventually lead the wrongdoer and those around him to ruin. Therefore, those who seek these evil, temporary pleasures are foolish and wicked.

Love "does not delight in evil but rejoices with the truth" (1 Cor. 13:6). A person of love, a person of God, and a person of wisdom and understanding does not delight in "wicked schemes" (23b).

111

They rejoice with truth and wisdom. They also rejoice with truth-tellers. And they rejoice in God, the source of truth and wisdom. The joy of knowing God, the joy of knowing Jesus Christ more deeply, and the joy of walking with the Holy Spirit cannot be overstated (23b). This joy makes Christians wise and insightful.

What the wicked dread will overtake them; what the righteous desire will be granted. When the storm has swept by, the wicked are gone, but the righteous stand firm forever (10:24-25).[91]

Deep in the heart of most people is the anxiety of fearing their own mortality. Unbelievers, in particular, have a fear of death. They just don't recognize it because they repress it through defense mechanisms. For some, this fear of death is experienced as an anxiety disorder. Others become superstitious and engage in obsessive-compulsive behaviors related to death. But no matter how much they try to avoid it, death comes when they least expect it. It comes like a whirlwind and sweeps away everything in life (24a, 25a).

The wicked are delightful in doing evil (23a), but they also experience dread (24a). They are happy when they are not exposed, but they are also afraid that their evil deeds will be exposed. Of course, there are those who suppress this fear and don't feel it.

God's justice is sure to be carried out, because God is watching over. At some point, God discloses the wicked people's evil deeds so that they can no longer do them.

God's children sin, too. When they sin repeatedly, sometimes God takes the rod of love and exposes their sins, letting them suffer shame. Those who stop sinning by being shamed are shamed but

---

[91] Murphy connects this proverb with Jesus' statement at the end of the Sermon on the Mount about the foolish who built their house on the sand and the wise who built their house on the rock. Roland Murphy, *Proverbs: A Word Biblical Commentary* (Nelson Reference & Electronic, 1998), 76.

saved. It is better that way to enter the kingdom of heaven. So God disciplines his children. It is much better for them to enter the heavenly place with one eye or one hand or one foot than to go to hell with their intact body.

Death comes even to the righteous. The righteous get sick and die without exception. The wind may blow and the waters may rise in the life of the righteous. But the house of the righteous will never fall (25b). Even when the tent of the flesh is torn down, they have an eternal house in heaven (see 2 Cor. 5:1), because they have lived in obedience to Jesus' words (see Matt. 7:24-25).

The desires of the righteous are fulfilled (24b), because what they desire and pray for, God the Father hears. If you believe Jesus' words, "Ask, seek, and knock," you will receive what you ask for. If you want and ask for what pleases God, it will be given to you. When you pray, "Thy kingdom come, thy will be done on earth as it is in heaven," God fulfills his will. The words and prayers of God's children have power. Not every word that comes out of their mouths falls to the ground but bears fruit. God surely answers in his time and in his way. Unless you ask according to your greed, God is sure to answer (see James 4:3).

As vinegar to the teeth and smoke to the eyes, so are sluggards to those who send them (10:26).

When you light a fire, the smoke wafts toward you, stinging your eyes and making them water. When the sour taste of vinegar irritates your teeth and tongue, you will reflexly spit out the vinegar. Like this lazy servants cause displeasure and anger to their master. They cannot be sold to others. If they are sold as diligent, it would be deceiving the buyer.

It is not clear who the people who send sluggards are. However, if we apply this proverb to the relationship between God and his workers, we should keep in mind that lazy workers grieve God's heart and provoke him to anger.

Lazy servants who don't empathize with their master may not experience much stress for themselves. Only the master will be frustrated and angry. Similarly, lazy Christians and leaders who do not empathize with God's heart do not realize that their sloth is like smoke in God's eyes.

This proverb implies that diligent or conscientious workers please those who send them. They work voluntarily, actively, creatively, and gratefully. They work as if it were their own job. Even when their master is not watching, they supervise themselves and work faithfully and dependably. Both God and other people will recognize them.

The fear of the LORD adds length to life, but the years of the wicked are cut short. The prospect of the righteous is joy, but the hopes of the wicked come to nothing (10:27-28).

There are many studies that try to explain longevity from a scientific perspective. These studies take into account variables such as what people ate, their lifestyle, and where they live, and suggest ways to improve their longevity. Generally speaking, if you take good care of yourself, have low stress, don't overeat, and don't get greedy, you're more likely to live a long life.

God promises a long life to adult children who honor their parents. He also tells us through Solomon in this proverb that the righteous who fear the LORD will live a long life. It is a reality that those who fear God are more likely to live a long life. By avoiding a sinful life, Christians' bodies are generally less susceptible to stress and diseases than non-Christians who may smoke or drink. Their attitude of being thankful in every circumstance in their life journey with God is also a contributing factor for their longevity.

Christians who fear God have a positive outlook on the future. They have faith and hope. They are not overly worried, anxious, or fretful because they know that God will work together for good in all situation (see Rom. 8:28). They are immune to generalized anxiety disorder. They "know" that they can rejoice in the midst of trials and stressful situations because they have hope and hope never disappoints them (Rom. 5:3-4).

Even among the wicked, there are some people who live long lives. The Bible tells us that there are such people. They are strong and healthy, living a life of well-being until death. They may suffer a day or two and die painlessly and peacefully (see Ps. 73:4-5). But their life can be equated to the life of pigs that live a happy life and go to the slaughter. Their life of well-being is a stumbling block for their possible repentance and eternal salvation. If there were sufferings in their life, there would be a hope that come from suffering, patience and character change (see Rom. 5:3-4). Anyway, the life span of the wicked is generally shorter than the average life span. This is because God, who is sovereign in their life and death, judges them even in this world and shortens their lives (27b).

The desires of the wicked, the things they seek, are like a mirage, even though they may be actualized (28b). When the day comes when all things in this world are cut off from them, the things the wicked desire will vanish away.

The way of the LORD is a refuge for the blameless [righteous], but it is the ruin of those who do evil. The righteous will never be uprooted, but the wicked will not remain in the land (10:29-30).

The way of the LORD is a fortified city and a fortress for the righteous (29a). The way of the LORD refers to the "life of fearing the LORD" of verse 27. God protects those who fear him like a invincible fortress, providing refuge, especially in times of tribulation. The righteous "stand firm forever"(25b) and "will never be uprooted" (30a) by any circumstance because their trust in God is deeply rooted. God provides them with an unwavering "object constancy" and "holding environment." God upholds and leads the righteous to the end.

The way of the LORD also means judgment and destruction for the wicked (29b). The way of the LORD is like a double-edged sword. For the upright it is a sword that protects their lives, but for the wicked it is a sword that destroys their lives. Therefore, the

115

wicked do not live long on this earth (30b). They are like the grass that is cut and soon withers (Ps. 37:2). James' brother Jude well depicts the life of the wicked with the following words:

> Yet these people slander whatever they do not understand, and the very thing they do understand by instinct—as irrational animals do—will destroy them. Woe to them! They have taken the way of Cain; they have rushed for profit into Balaam's error; they have been destroyed in Korah's rebellion. These people are blemishes at your love feasts, eating with you without the slightest qualm—shepherds who feed only themselves. They are clouds without rain, blown along by the wind; autumn trees, *without fruit and uprooted*—twice dead. They are wild waves of the sea, forming up their shame; wandering stars, for whom blackest darkness has been reserved forever....These people are grumblers and faultfinders; they follow their own evil desires; they boast about themselves and flatter others for their own advantage (Jude 1:10-16).

From the mouth of the righteous comes the fruit of wisdom [The mouth of the righteous brings forth wisdom], but a perverse tongue will be silenced [cut out]. The lips of the righteous know what finds favor [what is fitting], but the mouth of the wicked only what is perverse (10:31-32).

This proverb is structured in the chiastic form of A-B-A'-B'. The mouth of the righteous and the lips of the righteous reveal wisdom (31a). Wisdom is found in their words. The righteous open their mouths knowing well what they are going to say. Moreover, they speak "what finds favor" and "what is fitting" (32a). They speak what is appropriate to the situation, what is in touch with reality, and what hits the bull's-eye.

Jesus, the truly righteous, had power and authority when he opened his mouth. He spoke neither too much nor too little. The multitudes who heard him were amazed: "The crowds were amazed at his teaching, because he taught as one who had authority, and not as their teachers of the law" (Matt. 7:28b-29).

The mouth of the wicked pours out perverse words (32b). They say things that don't fit the occasion because they don't listen attentively. They speak unilaterally without listening to the other person. They speak falsely and untruthfully. It is better not to have a tongue that says these things. These words have no authority and power. Those words have only destructive power.

The destructive, deceptive tongues of the wicked will be cut out and silenced (31b). In particular, those who speak rebellious words and blaspheme against God will be judged on the last day without being able to speak a word before the judgment seat of God. Jesus warned that "everyone will have to give account on the day of judgment for every empty word they have spoken" (Matt. 12:36), referring to those who speak rebelliously as "brood of vipers." He said,

> You brood of vipers, how can you who are evil say anything good? For the mouth speaks what the heart is full of. A good man brings good things out of the good stored up in him, and an evil man brings evil things out of the evil stored up in him....For by your words you will be acquitted, and by your words you will be condemned (Matt. 12:34-37).

Chapter 11 The Fruit of the Righteous Is the Tree of Life

The LORD detests [abhors] dishonest scales, but accurate weights find favor with him [are his delight] (11:1).

This proverb is a reminder of the attributes and works of God, who watches over in secret, and is omniscient and omnipresent. God sees and detests those who use deceitful scales without anyone knowing (1a).[92] He also sees and favors the actions of those who use accurate scales (1b).[93]

In Bunyan's devotional novel, *Journey to Hell*, he described a character named "Badman" who was on his way to hell.[94] One of Badman's evil behaviors was his unrighteous business. Badman was described as follows:

> Again, I will begin with his fraudulent dealings. Just as I have shown how dishonest he was with his creditors, now I will tell you how unfairly he treated his customers. He used deceitful weights and measures. He kept weights to buy by and weights to sell by, measures to buy by and measures to sell by. Those he bought by were too big, and those he sold by were too little....Moreover, he had the ability to miscalculate accounts, whether by weight, measure, or money, and would often do it to his advantage and his customers' losses. And if he was questioned about his accuracy, he had his servants ready to vouch and swear to his books or his word. This was Mr. Badman's practice.[95]

---

[92] This proverb states that God hates those who use dishonest scales. Those who deceive others with false scales and measures belong to the devil, the father of lies.

[93] Bridges noted that this proverb is already explicitly mentioned in the law given in Deut. 25:13-16: "You must have accurate and honest weights and measures, so that you may live long in the land the LORD is giving you. For the LORD you God detests anyone who does these things, anyone who deals dishonestly" (Deut. 25:15-16). Bridges, *Proverbs,* 77.

[94] John Bunyan, *Journey to Hell* (Whitaker, 1999).

Bunyan warned against those who acquire wealth dishonestly: "God will then repay their evil upon their own heads, when He shuts them out of His presence, favor, and kingdom forever and ever."[96]

Pastors need to confront their church members wisely who do dishonest economic activities. Teaching and exhorting through their preaching can be beneficial to all members preventively. For those with whom they have basic trust, it would be pastoral to meet them individually and confront them gently. They need to adjust the level and method of their confrontation depending on levels of psychological and spiritual maturity of the members. It is also true that this is a risky approach of pastoral care which needs sensitivity and integrity of a pastor.

When pride comes, then comes disgrace, but with humility comes wisdom. The integrity of the upright guides them, but the unfaithful are destroyed by their duplicity (11:2-3).

The result of pride is shame and disgrace (2a).[97] This is because God humbles the proud. Jesus said that to avoid the humiliation of sitting at the head of the table at a banquet and then being forced to sit in a lower place when someone higher comes it is better to humble ourselves and to take the lowest place (see Luke 14:7-11).

The proud have no one around to help them in times of trouble because they have not been truly interpersonal. Therefore, the proud have no one to advocate for them in their reproach and

---

[95]   Bunyan, *Journey to Hell*, 159-60.

[96]   Bunyan, *Journey to Hell*, 165.

[97]   Noting that pride was a key issue that led to Adam and Eve's fall in the Garden of Eden, Bridges connected this text to their shame, which came first as a result of the fall. Bridges, *Proverbs*, 112-13. He gave specific examples of biblical characters who had been humiliated by their pride: The builders of the tower of Babel (Gen. 11:4), Miriam (Num. 12:2, 10), Uzziah (2 Chron. 26:16-21), Haman (Esth. 5:11; 7:10), Nebuchadnezzar (Dan. 4:29-32), and Herod (Acts 12:22-23). Bridges, *Proverbs*, 113.

shame.

The wise man, on the other hand, are humble (2b). Humble persons rarely fall, and they are well-liked in interpersonal relationships. Therefore, they get help and empathy from others even when they fall. Even when they do fall, they are not broken and not humiliated. God delights in the humble and raise them up again. King David is a good biblical example. Humble persons' character and integrity don't change, even in their high places. They are not much attached to their high positions.

Even in the secular world, people with duplicity cannot be not respected. People are well aware of those deceptive people. Even in business, such people will never succeed because they cannot be trusted.

The problem is that the unreliable don't recognize the severity of their own problems, which is why they repeatedly fail in work, business, or interpersonal relationship (3b). Because they don't realize that the problem is within themselves, they often blame other people or circumstances. These are typical symptoms of people with personality disorders. When their blaming doesn't work, they rationalize that they are unlucky. They don't learn from their repeated mistakes, so they are eventually destroyed completely (3b).

Wealth is worthless in the day of wrath, but righteousness delivers from death. The righteousness of the blameless makes their paths straight, but the wicked are brought down by their own wickedness. The righteousness of the upright delivers them, but the unfaithful are trapped by evil desires. Hope placed in mortals die with them [When a wicked man dies, his hope perishes]; all the promise of their power [all he expected from his power] comes to nothing. The righteous person is rescued from trouble, and it falls [comes] on the wicked instead (11:4-8).

"The day of wrath" in verse 4 is the day of the end. On the days of the personal end and the universal end, riches have no value at all (4a). Riches are only "temporary objects" that are beneficial in this world. No amount of riches can redeem even one person' life before God. Gold, silver, jewelry, and money, which are considered to be of the highest value, are of no value on the day of death. We came to this world empty-handed and depart from this world empty-handed. Not only riches, but also power, honor, and health are temporary. But the righteous are saved from death and eternal condemnation (4b). Their righteousness has eternal value. It is a righteousness that is given by grace through Jesus Christ.

The blameless are delivered from God's judgment. Their paths are straight (5b). Christians, counted blameless by the righteousness of Jesus Christ, walk their paths in obedience to the end, and finally will enjoy eternal life. But the wicked and the unfaithful who live only by their own wicked nature and do not fear God, and live independently of Jesus Christ, fall and are destroyed, never to rise again (6b, 7a).[98]

The unfaithful who do not have faith in the LORD live their lives that are "trapped" in the pursuit of their own evil desires and sensual cravings (6b). They are attached and addicted to their sins and cannot break free from their sinful addictions. Eventually they perish.

The wicked and the unfaithful are not necessarily wicked and evil morally. They are wicked in the sense that they do not acknowledge and rely on God's righteousness in their lives. Such people have no hope (7a). They pursue worldly things, and they are destroyed forever.

Those who don't obey the Word of God, the source of all power, but who rely on their intellect, physical strength, wealth, and personal connections, deny the undeniable fact that all things end suddenly. No matter how much they have in this world, if their

---

[98]   Bridges cited the contrasting events of Israel's deliverance from the Red Sea while the Egyptians drowned, and Mordecai being saved from hanging on a pole while Haman was hanged instead. He also mentioned Daniel being delivered from the lion's den and his accusers being fed to the lions instead. Bridges, *Proverbs,* 114.

121

heart stops beating or their breathing stops for even a few minutes, they become vegetative or unable to rise again. After death, they fall into eternal death and hell. Those who do not know this truth are, without exception, foolish and stupid.

With their mouths the godless destroy their neighbors, but through knowledge the righteous escape (11:9).

It is a marvelous, thankful grace of God to have given us a mouth and tongue that can speak a multitude of words, but it is also an uneasy grace of God. The mouth is an important tool for praising God, expressing our thoughts and feelings in words, and sharing the gospel. But it is our reality that it can also be used to hurt our closest neighbors, that is, our family, and cause pain to relatives, friends, and others. Especially the godless destroy their neighbors with their mouths (9a). They wound people with their words. They plunge dagger to the hearts of neighbors by bearing false witness, gossiping, and swearing. The wicked of the worst kind do not even realize or acknowledge that they are hurting their neighbors by speaking such offensive words. But those who have knowledge, that is, knowledge of God, are saved, and they save others with their words (9b). By preaching the gospel, by comforting people with words, they save them.

When the righteous prosper, the city rejoices; when the wicked perish, there are shouts of joy. Through the blessing of the upright a city is exalted, but by the mouth of the wicked it is destroyed (11:10-11).

In this proverb, the righteous and the wicked are leaders, including kings. When a good, wise king rises, loyalists flock to the king, and the people rejoice. But when a wicked, foolish king rises, disloyal subjects flock to the king, and the people grieve and rage.

In denominational politics, when the unwise or the wicked rise, the hearts of pastors, elders, and members in the denomination are filled with sighs and tears. But when they are removed, shouts of joy and thanksgiving overflow (10a).[99]

Righteous and wise leaders are like trees by the water that are evergreen and yield fruits in all seasons: a city, a church, or a nation is exalted (11a). They provide shade and rest for many people. But unrighteous, foolish, and greedy leaders are like trees in the wilderness, unable to provide shade and fruits. Rather, they are like thorns, piercing those who are close to them.

Communities with good leaders have shalom and joy. A church that has a faithful senior pastor thrives and its members are happy. Children and families with good enough parents are happy and thankful. Employees whose boss is good enough and wise, are happy and fulfilled in their work.

Whoever derides their neighbor has no sense [lacks judgment], but the one who has understanding holds their tongue (11:12).

Disregard and contempt for one's neighbors is a typical sign of narcissistic personality disorder. In that sense, people with narcissistic personality disorder have a poor judgment. They are psychologically immature. If a neighbor is smart or wealthy, they like to hang out with him or her. They brag to others about how well they are associated with their neighbor In contrast, if their neighbor is below their expectation economically, intellectually, or socially, they don't show little interest or empathy to him or her.[100]

---

[99] Bridges noted that this shout of joy does not arise from selfish vindictiveness, nor from a heartless and hardened hear for the destruction of the wicked, but from the execution of God's justice against sin and the deliverance of his people from evil. Bridges, *Proverbs*, 116. Although God allowed the kingdom of Judah to be destroyed by Babylon for her idolatrous sins, he pointed out the sin of Edom, that rejoiced in her destruction, as "the violence against your brother Jacob" (Obad. 1:10): "You should not gloat over your brother in the day of his misfortune, nor rejoice over the people of Judah in the day of their destruction" (Obad. 1:12).

But those who are experienced in life and know human reality hold their tongue (12b). They don't judge or devalue their neighbors easily. They don't say hurtful or dismissive things about their neighbors. Even when their neighbor does something contemptible, they know how to keep silent (12b). They have the ability to distinguish between what is appropriate to say and what is not.

A gossip betrays a confidence, but a trustworthy person keeps a secret (11:13).

"Betrays a confidence" is contrasted with "keeps a secret." There is also a contrast between "a gossip" and "a trustworthy person." **Application to counseling**: Southard defined Christian counseling as "the wisdom of God in the context of friendship."[101] To divulge a client's story shared in this environment of trustful friendship is breaking the friendship and promise to keep confidentiality and is an act of betrayal. A basic quality of a counselor is to adhere to the counseling ethics of keeping confidentiality, with a few exceptions such as a case in which a client's story involves his or her crimes against the law.

For lack of guidance a nation falls, but victory is won through many advisers [many advisors make victory sure] (11:14).

Strategy is crucial to winning a war. The phrase, "Know your

---

[100] People with narcissistic personality disorder don't relate with people who are lesser or weaker than them. They like to socialize with people who are smart and powerful and rich. These are actually immature persons who lack the judgment to see people for who they really are. They are foolish to judge people by their appearance or education. They lack the ability to empathize with people. They don't listen attentively.

[101] Samuel Southard, *Theology & Therapy: The Wisdom of God in a Context of Friendship* (Dallas, TX: Word Publishing, 1989).

enemy and know yourself, and you will never be defeated" is also related to strategy. A president or king must have smart and wise advisors to help him or her lead the country well. A country or company that has many wise people who can properly analyze the situation and propose alternatives creatively will be stable and secure (14b). But when unqualified persons occupy positions of leadership, families, churches, communities, corporations, or nations will be unstable. Their existence may be jeopardized (14a).

If a nation is going to fight a war, it has to fight a winning war. It's very foolish to wage war in hopes of getting lucky. In our life journey, it's wise to have a specific plan and methodology. It is recklessness and laziness that increase the risk of failure.

Counseling Application: When an individual or family is faced with a difficult situation, a person or family who has a trustful counselor they can go to does not fall apart. This is because counseling provides comfort and wisdom. People who have many supportive friends to whom they can turn to for help can get through difficult times with a strong support network. Unfortunately, suicidal people end their lives because they feel that there is no one around them who can help them.

Whoever puts up security for a stranger [for another] will surely suffer, but whoever refuses to shake [strike] hands in pledge is safe (11:15). See 6:1-5.

Giving a guarantee for a neighbor in need can be an act of love, comparable to laying down one's life for a friend. In reality, however, it is not uncommon for the recipient of a guarantee to run into trouble, leaving the guarantor and his or her family homeless and in foreclosure. This proverb emphasizes that careful consideration of this reality is wisdom.

Solomon takes a firm stance against guarantees. He warns that if you guarantee, you will suffer predictably. He also teaches that you can live safely by refusing to guarantee. He means that even if you feel bad about your initial refusal, it's wise to make your intentions clear to avoid long-term ruin.

We need to be clear here that it is not a sin to refuse a guarantee. Christians are free, which means it is not a sin itself to give a guarantee in spite of the possibility of loss or deception. Discernment is required.

It's not easy to be the one asking someone for a guarantee. But it's also not easy for him or her who has to say no. Particularly, people with dependent or avoidant personality disorder who are not good at saying no are more likely to be caught in a "double bind" situation and make the wrong choice. They're torn between the fear of damaging their relationship with the asking person if they say no, and the fear of damaging their relationship with their spouse or family members if they say yes. They also fear that giving the guarantee may cost them their house. Generally speaking, it's wise to say no. It's wise to choose the long-term benefits over the short-term ones. It takes courage to say, "I'm sorry, I can't do this."

A kindhearted woman gains honor [respect], but ruthless men gain only wealth. Those who are kind benefit themselves, but the cruel bring ruin [trouble] on themselves (11:16-17).

There are parallels between "a kindhearted woman" and "those who are kind," and between "ruthless men" and "the cruel." It doesn't matter whether one is a woman or a man. Rather, what matters is whether one is kind and kindhearted. If you have these qualities, you will be respected by people and benefit yourself (16a, 17a). On the other hand, those who are ruthless and cruel in relationships with others "may" gain wealth, but in the end, they will bring harm to themselves (16b, 17b).[102]

A wicked person earns deceptive wages, but the one who sows righteousness reaps a sure reward. Truly the righteous [The

---

[102] Bridges gave the example of Ahab and Jezebel on the proverb, "The cruel bring ruin on themselves." Bridges, *Proverbs*, 120.

truly righteous] attain life, but whoever pursues evil finds [goes to] death (11:18-19).

These two verses form a chiastic structure of A-B-B'-A'. "A wicked person" and "whoever pursues evil" are contrasted to "the one who sows righteousness" and "the righteous." Their results are also contrasted: "earns deceptive wages" and "finds death" vs. "reaps a sure reward" and "attain life."

Wages are a natural reward for one's efforts. Wages are not bad in themselves. The problem is that the reward given to the wicked is deceptive. The life of the wicked appears to be a profitable life in the short term. But in the long run, it is a life of destruction. The wages of sin is death (Rom. 6:23).

But "a sure reward" is not a deserved wage for hard work, it's a gift and grace. This favor is not earned. It is a recognition and praise given to those who sow seeds of righteousness through obedience (18b). Sowing seeds of righteousness rarely produces fruits quickly. Nevertheless, when we sow in obedience to the Word, the God who makes it grow will eventually cause it to bear fruit (1 Cor. 3:7). God promises his laborers who sow or water that "they will each be reward according to their own labor" (1 Cor. 3:8). They reap "a sure reward" (18b).

Those who sow righteousness and hold fast to justice may not be welcome in this world. They may be persecuted. But they will surely reap their reward with joy. The martyrs who laid down their lives for the truth were the wise and righteous who attained eternal life (19a). Some Korean Christians who chose martyrdom, whether under Japanese rule or North Korea Communist rule, in obedience to the invisible God and his Word, have certainly received eternal life as a gift.

The LORD detests those whose hearts are perverse, but he delights in those whose ways are blameless. Be sure of this: The wicked will not go unpunished, but those who are righteous will go free (11:20-21).

127

This proverb can be understood as a chiastic form of A-B-A'-B'. "Those whose hearts are perverse" and "the wicked" are connected to each other. "Those whose ways are blameless" is connected with "those who are righteous. "The LORD detests" is contrasted to "he delight" and "not go unpunished" is contrasted to "go free."

Unhappy are those whom God hates and abhors, because God will punish them even in this world (21a). The NIV Bible translated this as a double negative: "The wicked will not go unpunished." They seem fine in the moment, but God will punish them in an instant, when they least expect it. Furthermore, on the day of the universal end, God will bring them eternal judgment.

On the other hand, blessed are the objects of God's delight, for they go free and saved (21b). Those who depend on God's righteousness through Jesus Christ on the cross have nothing to fear. They are free.

Like a gold ring in a pig's snout is a beautiful woman who shows no discretion (11:22).[103]

The word "discretion" has the same meaning as "prudence," which is one of the goals of Proverbs at the beginning of chapter 1. Solomon describes a beautiful woman with little discretion with an analogy of a pig with a golden ring in its nose. From the sow's point of view, she would be grateful to have a beautiful woman compared to her. However, she would not feel good about being described as a foolish animal, because pigs have also some intelligence. But a pig is a pig! Putting a gold ring on a pig's nose doesn't make it a fancy pig.

Counseling Application: The image associated with "a beautiful

---

[103] Koptak uses Abigail as an example of a woman who contrasts with the woman in this proverb: "She was an intelligent and beautiful woman, but her husband was surly and mean in his dealings" (1 Sam. 25:3). Koptak, *Proverbs*, 322. Abigail's husband, Nabal, was like a pig with a golden ring in his nose. Abigail and Nabal were a mismatched couple.

woman with no discretion" is that of a person with histrionic personality disorder or borderline personality disorder. Those who are outwardly attractive and good-looking, but inwardly insecure and empty and so who seek validation of their self-image in getting attention and interest from others, are likely to have histrionic personality disorder. They are characterized by constantly caring about their their appearance to get attention or acting in a sexually suggestive manner.

The image of a beautiful woman without discretion is also linked to some symptoms of borderline personality disorder. Persons with this disorder are characterized by emotional attraction to, idealization of, and sexual impulsivity toward the other sex who have a certain degree of physical attractiveness but are unstable on the inside. These people are not prudent: they go out easily and break up easily. Examples include some men who travel to foreign countries and have sex with prostitutes. They do reckless things to satisfy their sexual urges. They don't take the risk of contracting a sexually transmitted disease seriously. They get close to the opposite sex in a short period of time. They are characterized by impulsive sexual intercourse (this is also true of homosexuals). Their symptoms include repeated impulsive purchases, such as using a credit card to buy whatever they want at a department store or watching a television commercial and impulsively buying items that look good. It is not an exaggeration to say that these people are like a pig with a golden ring on his or her nose, in that their appearance does not match their inner state. This dynamic is not limited to women. Men with borderline personality disorder also exhibit the same behavioral patterns.

The desire of the righteous ends only in good, but the hope of the wicked only in wrath (11:23).

It would be more convincing to translate the phrase, "the desire of the righteous" into "the hope of the righteous" and "the hope of the wicked" into "the wish (desire) of the wicked." This is because the word "hope" is often used in the Bible with a positive nuance and "desire" with a negative nuance. For example, Paul makes the point that negative desires are the characteristic of old self without Christ when he exhorts us to "put off your old self, which is being corrupted by its deceitful desires" (Eph. 4:22).

However, the "desires" of the righteous are "righteous" desires. When the heart is righteous, the desires that arise from it are righteous. The desires of the righteous are purely functional desires that produce good fruit. For example, eating and drinking for the Lord is a good desire. So "the desire of the righteous ends only in good" (23a). But the desire of the wicked only "ends in wrath" (23b). What the wicked hope for and desire ultimately leads to God's wrath and judgment.

One person gives freely, yet gains even more; another withholds unduly, but comes to poverty. A generous person will prosper; whoever refreshes others will be refreshed. People curse the one who hoards grain, but they pray God's blessing on [blessing crowns] the one who is willing to sell (11:24-26).

The proverb is paradoxical. Generally speaking, a key to getting rich is to be frugal. The more you save, the richer you become. However, it is wise to realize that controlling, saving, and being frugal may not always make you rich. On the contrary, Solomon warns that it can make you poor.

Those who focus on becoming rich in their lives are foolish, for they do not consider that riches, even if they are excessively hoarded, have wings to fly away unexpectedly (24b). Solomon promises that those who are able to share their wealth and use their money generously for the benefit of others, especially for people in need, will paradoxically have more wealth (24a). It's like a spring: the more you draw it, the more water will spring up. But if you don't use it well, the spring will run dry. God fills those who are generous in giving.

God's will for us is to live in this world without being distracted by riches. With what we have, we are challenged to help the poor and those in need. When we are obedient to his command, he provides us with more resources.

If there are presidents, bankers, leaders, or CEOs who want to take advantage of the people by not opening their storehouses in a bad year so that the price of grain will skyrocket, they will hear the people's resentment and curse (26a). To control and manipulate people with the grain that God has graciously given them in order to benefit themselves when survival is at stake is to incur the wrath of God. A nation that monopolizes resources and tyrannizes over them, or causes its neighboring nations to suffer by shutting down oil or gas pipelines in the cold of winter, will incur God's wrath.

But to sell grain at the right price in a bad year is a good deed that saves and enriches people (26b). Such people or nations will also be enriched themselves (25b), because God will bless them. When you do business or trade in a biblical spirit, you save yourself and save others. God will be glorified by you.

Counseling Application: A person's character is revealed in the way he or she manage his or her household finances. Managing one's income and expenses well is a sign of a well-developed ego. Conversely, repeatedly spending more than one's earnings and getting into debt or having bad credit is a sign of an immature ego. On the other hand, excessive frugality is also a sign of psychological immaturity. It is often found among those with obsessive-compulsive personality disorder. Being able to spend appropriately, saving a little for the future, and cheerfully giving financial support to those in need are virtuous attitudes and behaviors of a mature person of faith.

Whoever seeks good finds favor [goodwill], but evil comes to one who searches for it. Those who trust in their riches will fall, but the righteous will thrive like a green leaf. Whoever brings ruin on their family will inherit only wind, and the fool will be servant to the wise (11:27-29).

If we analyze this text as a literary structure, we can understand it as A-B-B'-A'-B"-B"'. "Whoever seeks good" is connected to "the righteous," and "finds favor" to "thrive like a green leaf." On the other hand, "one who searches for it [evil]" is linked to "those who trust in their riches" and "whoever brings ruin on their family" and "the fool."

"Whoever seeks good" seeks God who is good and lives according to God's will. They are those who "hunger and thirst for righteousness" (Matt. 5:6a). They are thirsty for God as a deer is for a stream. They endure the drought. They are like a tree planted by the stream, whose leaves are green, not withered (28b). God will give favor from above to those who seek the things above (27a).

On the other hand, those who search for evil will find it (27b). They who live in trust for their wealth will surely perish forever on the expiration date of their temporary objects that they have been so attached. They will perish like the foolish rich man who stored up grain for many years and died that same night, or like the rich man who lived a life in contrast to Lazarus (28a). Those who walk broad ways, easy ways, and worldly ways, pursuing worldly values, will bring evil upon their family (29a). When they become parents, they teach their children to pursue worldly things. They lead their children to spiritual destruction. The legacy such people leave to their children is "only wind" (29a).

The fruit of the righteous is a tree of life, and the one who is wise saves lives [wins souls]. If the righteous receive their due on earth, how much more the ungodly and the sinner! (11:30-31).

The righteous are the wise. The wise lead people to the way of life. The fruit of the righteous is likened to a tree of life (30a). Not only are its leaves green, but it also yields fruit in season (see Ps. 1:3). It benefits people, gives them rest, and sustains weary souls. In New Testament parlance, the wise are those who are filled with the Holy Spirit. They abounds in the fruit of the Spirit. They keep walking the path of life not only for themselves but serve as a tree of life to those with whom they come across. They lead them to Jesus Christ, the tree of life, so that they win souls (30b).

The righteous already enjoy eternal life in this world (31a). The ungodly and the sinner, on the other hand, already experience eternal judgment in this world (31b). These are those whom God "gave them to a depraved mind, so that they do what ought not to be done" (Rom. 1:28). And they already "received in themselves the due penalty for their error" (Rom. 1:27).

Chapter 12 The Roots of the Righteous Are Unshakable

Whoever loves discipline loves knowledge, but whoever hates correction is stupid (12:1).

One of the goals of Proverbs is for the listener to acquire wisdom and discipline (see 1:2-3). Wise persons like and accept discipline gratefully because they know it is good for them. They know that through correction and discipline they will be refined and will grow and change. Those who desire knowledge and wisdom are willing to take tests and assignments that are required in the process of acquiring knowledge.

In contrast, those who hate admonition stick to their status quo. They feel good about themselves and are not receptive to any advice or feedback. Such people, Solomon says, is "stupid" (1b). In the case of kings, they don't accept feedback from their loyal subjects. They are stubborn in their ruling.

People who listen only to flattery and pleasant words to hear are foolish. Psychologically, such a person is a child: outwardly an adult, but inwardly a child. The Revised Korean Bible translates this kind of person as "like an animal."

Foolish persons are easily deceived and manipulated by others. They are at the level of a child mentally and psychologically. Even if they are Christians, they are still spiritually at the level of a baby (see 1 Cor. 2:2). Their ability to chew and digest solid food is very weak.

Good people obtain favor from the LORD, but he condemns those who devise wicked schemes [condemns a crafty man] (12:2).

"Good people" are contrasted with "those who devise wicked

schemes." God hates and condemns the crafty (2b). But he delights in those who are good in heart and are after God's goodness (2a).[104]

Crafty people are deceitful and cunning. They are opportunists. People see them for what they really are, and that's why they're not recognized and liked by anyone. No one trusts them. In the short term, they may seize an opportunity and succeed. But in the long run, they are not recognized even in this world.

Doeg the Edomite, one of Saul's officials and his chief shepherd, was a cunning man. He accused David of visiting the priest Ahimelech in order to gain favor with Saul (see 1 Sam. 22:9). While the king's officials were reluctant to kill the priests despite the king's order, he volunteered to kill eighty-five of the priests, with the sword, with their men, women, children, infants, cattle, donkeys and sheep (see 1 Sam. 22:17-19). When David heard of his evil behavior, he cursed him with the following poem:

> Why do you boast of evil, you mighty hero? Why do you boast all day long, you who are a disgrace in the eyes of God? You who practice deceit, your tongue plots destruction; it is like a sharpened razor. You love evil rather than good, falsehood rather than speaking the truth. You love every harmful word, you deceitful tongue! *Surely God will bring you down to everlasting ruin*: He will snatch you up and pluck you from your tent; *he will uproot you* from the land of the living (Ps. 52:1-5).

Jonadab son of Shimeah, a friend of David's son Amnon, was "a very shrewd man" (2 Sam. 13:3). He offered Amnon who was so obsessed with his half-sister Tamar, a specific plan to sexually abuse her. His cunning and deceitfulness set the stage for the recurring tragedies that would eventually lead to bloodshed in the David's royal family. When David heard the rumor that Absalom had killed all the princes, he pretended to comfort David by saying,

---

104 Noting that "goodness" is one of the nine fruits of the Holy Spirit, Bridges commented that the good people of the text is one who is filled with the Holy Spirit. Bridges, *Proverbs*, 132. He connected this text with 1 Pet. 3:12, which quotes Ps. 34:15-16, which says "The eyes of the LORD are on the righteous, and his ears are attentive to their cry; the face of the LORD is against those who do evil, to blot out their name from the earth."

"My lord should not think that they killed all the princes; only Amnon is dead. This has been Absalom's express intention ever since the day Ammon raped his sister Tamar. My lord the king should not be concerned about the report that all the king's sons are dead. Only Amnon is dead" (2 Sam. 13:32-33). The writer of 2 Samuel gave him a one-phrase historical assessment: "a very shrewd man." The Bible is silent on what his end was. But God certainly would not have favored his life.

No one can be established through wickedness, but the righteous cannot be uprooted (12:3).

The life of the wicked has a weak foundation (3a). The roots of the wicked will one day be uprooted (3b). Evil and lies do not last long. For example, suppose that some officials take a bribe and get away with it for years without being found out. But then an unforeseen accident happens, and the day comes when a notebook containing the names of those who were involved in the shoddy work and were bribed is made public and they are summoned by the prosecutor. In this way, the wicked are suddenly uprooted. Therefore, Christians should not even think of benefiting from evil behaviors.

The righteous are like a tree that cannot be uprooted no matter what wind blows (3b). A tree by the water endures even in drought. The righteous are also like a house built on the solid foundation. The winds blow and the waters rise, but their house does not fall, because they are rooted deeply on the Word of God and endure. The righteous need not fear being uprooted and disgraced.

Psychologically speaking, the wicked have a "fragile self." They have a weak self-structure. It is likely that they did not experience good enough care and empathy from their parents growing up. They are self-centered and cannot empathize with others, especially with the weak. This type of person's true character comes out in times of crisis. They break down easily. They are unstable and suicidal. Finally, they may commit suicide or kill their family.

A wife of noble character is her husband's crown, but a disgraceful wife is like decay in his bones (12:4).

"A wife of noble character" is contrasted with "a disgraceful wife." A well-developed wife, both spiritually and psychologically, is a crown of honor to her husband. She is one her husband is proud to present in front of others. Living with such a wife, the husband will take after her noble character. This is because he is influenced for good. On the other hand, a husband who behaves shamefully shames his wife. He causes her to worry and suffer. Living with a shameful spouse is painful, like decay in the other's bones (4b). The psychological stress is as bad as the pain caused by arthritis or cervical spinal disc.

The plans of the righteous are just, but the advice of the wicked is deceitful. The words of the wicked lie in wait for blood,[105] but the speech of the upright rescues them.[106] The wicked are overthrown and are no more, but the house of the righteous stands firm (12:5-7).

The literary structure of this passage is A-B-B'-A'-B"-A". The

[105] Bridges found examples of biblical characters who were watching for an opportunity to shed blood in Joseph's brothers, Daniel's enemies, Sanballat and Tobiah, Haman, and King Herod. Bridges, *Proverbs*, 134. Phillips provides a detailed commentary on the wickedness of King Herod, who falsely told the Magi, "As soon as you find him, report to me, so that I too may go and worship him" (Matt. 2:8). Phillips, *Exploring Proverbs*, Vol. 1, 295-96.

[106] Phillips notes that in contrast to King Saul, who sought to shed David's blood, David spared Saul's life by reminding himself that he was God's anointed, even when he had the opportunity to kill him. Phillips, *Exploring Proverbs*, Vol. 1, 296.

proverbs associated with A say that the thoughts of the righteous are upright, the mouth of the upright delivers, and the house of the righteous is strong. The proverbs linked with B say that the counsel of the wicked is deceptive, the mouth of the wicked looks for opportunities to shed blood, and the house of the wicked will be overturned and destroyed.

The righteous are just in their thoughts and plans (5a). It is like pure water flowing from a good spring. The counsel of the righteous is not deceitful (see 5b). The mouth of the righteous saves those in trouble (6b). They speak up and advocate for them. The house of the righteous is stable and secure (7b).

The men who brought the woman caught in adultery to Jesus were wicked, intent on ensnaring him, killing her, and embarrassing him. Outwardly, they spoke as if they were upholding the seventh commandment, "You shall not commit adultery." But inwardly they hated him and wanted to kill him, even breaking the sixth commandment, "you shall not murder."

The plans of these wicked men were exposed by the wisdom of Jesus. Later, these wicked men joined in the charge to crucify Jesus and shed his righteous blood. As a result, the city of Jerusalem, the home city of those who led the charge to kill Jesus, was not long before it was completely destroyed by the Roman soldiers (7a). For nearly two thousand years, the Jews were scattered throughout the world, living without a country. But the house of the righteous Jesus stood firm, and to this day, the church of Jesus Christ stands firm throughout the world (7b).

The same is true in the realm of our personal lives. The families of those who aspire to and practice righteousness and honesty grow stronger over time and overcome difficulties. But the families of those who live wicked, deceitful, and fraudulent lives will be shaken to their foundations and be destroyed over time.

A person is praised according to their prudence, and one with a warped mind is despised (12:8).[107]

---

[107] Bridges gave the example of Nabal, a man with a crooked heart, who was despised even by his own servant and his wife: "He is such a wicked man that no on can talk to

Even in this world, it's a good thing to be praised and recognized. And it would be unfortunate to be despised and looked down upon.

Generally speaking, most people recognize and praise the wise even in this world (8a). And those whose hearts are perverse are despised (8b). This is even more true in our relationship with God. God approves of the wise and despises the perverse in heart.

Better to be a nobody and yet have a servant than pretend to be somebody and have no food (12:9).

A life of substance is better than a life of hollow rhetoric. A man who is full of splendor on the outside but empty on the inside is worthless.[108] Even if you're a nobody, it's much more worthwhile to live a life of substance. If a person lives as a somebody who is known to people, but is actually a poor person who doesn't even have food to eat, he or she is pitiful.

The fig tree, which had lush leaves but no fruit, was cursed by Jesus. God does not recognize those who have a form of godliness but don't have the power of godliness (see 2 Tim. 3:5). He recognizes people who have the power of godliness inside regardless of their appearance.

The righteous care for the needs of their animals, but the kindest acts of the wicked are cruel (12:10).

him" (1 Sam. 25:17); "Please pay no attention, my lord, to that wicked man Nabal. He is just like his name—his name means Fool, and folly goes with him" (1 Sam. 25:25). Bridges, *Proverbs*, 136.

[108] Persons with histrionic personality disorder think they are more attractive than they really are, and think they have more intimate relationships with others than they really do. They mistake the outside for the inside. They may pretend to be rich even when they are actually poor. They rent a nice car and drive around, even if they have to borrow other people's money. Such a person is weak on the inside.

Pastoral care includes individuals, systems, and the ecological environment. Biblical care for the ecological environment begins with the awareness that God is the Creator. It begins with the belief that God created the animals and that they were good in his sight: "God made the wild animals according to their kinds, the livestock according to their kinds, and all the creatures that move along the ground according to their kinds. And God saw that it was good" (Gen. 1:25). God commanded humans, created in the image of God, to rule over all the creatures. The "rule over" doe not mean an oppressive, exploitative rule. Rather, it is a caring, nurturing, and holding rule. It is a "rule over" in the sense of supervision and overseeing.

Peter exhorted elders to "be shepherds over God's flock that is under your care, watching over them" (1 Pet. 5:2). He exhorted them to be examples to the flock, "not lording it over those entrusted to you" (1 Pet. 5:3). Peter's exhortation to be shepherds should be applied to human care and rule over ecosystems. When the creatures that co-exist in ecosystems are seen as "entrusted" to humans by God, their value can be appreciated rightly.[109] Only then will we be able to take good care of them instead of trying to "dominate" exploit them. This is an attitude of obedience to God's cultural mandate for creation.

It is biblical to have this creation theology perspective when raising and caring for livestock and animals. Humans must have the heart of God, who values the life of even a sparrow, in order to be restored to the image of God. The commandment not to muzzle a working ox emphasizes a minimum level of concern and care for animals (see Deut. 25:4). Christians need to remember that in the commandment about the Sabbath, "livestock" was included among the objects of rest (see Ex. 20:10).

---

[109] Fox cites several texts that refer to expressing humanitarian concern for animals: "Do not muzzle an ox while it is treading out the grain" (Deut. 25:4); "Do the same with your cattle and your sheep. Let them stay with their mothers for seven days, but give them to me on the eighth day" (Ex. 22:30); "Do not slaughter a cow or a sheep and its young on the same day" (Lev. 22:28). Fox, *Proverbs 10-31*, 551. The same spirit is found in Proverbs 27:23: "Be sure you know the condition of your flocks, give careful attention to your herds."

When people's hearts are ravaged, individualized, or dysfunctionalized, they are more likely to abuse and exploit animals, including livestock, instead of caring for them. Even when pigs and cows are raised, it is a sin of greed to ignore their nature and force them to be fed in small spaces to gain weight in a short period of time. It is God's will for pigs to live with other pigs until they are slaughtered, in a good environment that suits their nature. Keeping chickens under 24-hour lights to artificially produce eggs and in conditions that prevent them from sleeping well is a violation of God's design.

Raising awareness about animal cruelty through television programs and the internet is a good thing. It is heartless and evil to keep a dog as a pet when it is needed, only to have it become a stray for various reasons. It is a reality in South Korea that thousands of pet dogs are abandoned by their owners every year. The fact that most of them are euthanized before they can be adopted is a clear symptom of the pathology of many Koreans into selfishness.

At the very least, Christians need to renew their awareness of animals as God's creations to avoid practicing this evil. Pastors should use their sermons to call for a change in the hearts of their congregations, urging them to be alert to selfishness and greed. When we have eyes and hearts to see livestock, animals, and plants as valuable parts of creation, we will be able to treat others and our neighbors with compassion and mercy. In an increasingly dehumanized and depersonalized social environment, we need to examine our own state of mind and expand our horizons of awareness to include ecological concerns.

Those who work their land will have abundant food, but those who chase fantasies have no sense [lack judgment] (12:11).[110]

Persons who work and strive to do the best they can with the life

---

[110] Fox points out that this proverb is almost identical to 28:19: "Those who work their land will have abundant food, but those who chase fantasies will have their fill of poverty." Fox, *Proverbs 10-31*, 552.

they have is psychologically healthy and mature. Psychoanalysis views psychological health as linked to the capacity to "be happy" and the capacity to "do good". Solomon was already well aware of this: "I know that there is nothing better for people than to be happy and to do good while they live" (Eccl. 3:12).

Pursuing fantasies without facing reality shows one's lack of judgment (11b). The behavior of pursuing delusions as if they were real is a symptom of impaired mental health.

This proverb can be applied from a different angle. In the eyes of non-Christians, Christians may appear to be chasing fantasies. This is because the only reality they see is this world. In their eyes, Christians may be seen as those who lack a "reality testing" ability. All the people of Noah's days might have thought that Noah and his family were totally out of touch with reality as they were building an ark for many years in preparation for the flood. But in reality, it is the people who are looking at the visible reality and this world only and living hard that lack in judgment and are unable to see reality. On the Day of Judgment of Jesus Christ, it will be clear who had no sense.

Counseling Application: One of the important indicators of good mental health is the ability to test reality. Distorted or partial interpretation of reality is a sign of poor mental health. Furthermore, if a person is unable to distinguish between reality and unreality, he or she may be in a state of psychosis.

Christian counselors need to be able to distinguish between religious experiences and psychosis. Religious experiences and psychosis are dissociated from reality. The symptoms are similar, but the outcomes are different. Religious experiences bring about positive change and maturation in the inner world and spiritual life of the person experiencing them. Psychosis, on the other hand, brings regression and destruction to the life of those who experience. Psychosis destroys a person's life. So it is very important to discern the difference. As Christians, we need to be careful to assess and diagnose people with mental illness because they may often express their symptoms in religious terms.

The wicked desire the stronghold [plunder] of evildoers,[111] but the root of the righteous endures [flourishes] (12:12). See 12:3.

This proverbs is not symmetrical. It only contrasts the wicked and the righteous. The roots of the righteous will flourish and endure even in drought. When drought comes, a tree with deep roots draws water from deep. And it will eventually become fruitful and flourish. The children of the righteous will flourish and be fruitful like deep-rooted trees.

The wicked want to get some portions of what evildoers has taken. There are those who buy stolen goods. Those who buy stolen goods at a bargain price, knowing that they are stolen, are punished by law. They are part of the food chain of crime. The righteous do not do such things.

If we understand the wicked in connection with verse 11, the wicked are those who do not cultivate their land. They seeks to reap the fruit without effort. They chases after illusions. They dream of a quick fortune. And they steal or defraud others of their hard work.

Evildoers are trapped by their sinful talk, and so [but] the innocent escape trouble. From the fruit of their lips people are filled with good things, and [as surely as] the work of their hands bring them reward (12:13-14).

Words bear fruit (14a). They bear good fruit or evil fruit. Words have power. They have consequences in one form or another.

Blessed are the lips that bring good results. Blessed are the lips of a counselor. They speak therapeutic words into the hearts of hurting people, helping them to change. Blessed are the lips of an evangelist, because they bring people to faith and salvation when they hear the gospel.

The righteous don't just talk but work with their hands (14b). The

---

[111] Bridges connected this proverb with 1 Tim. 6:10, which says "For the love of money is a root of all kinds of evil. Some people, eager for money, have wandered from the faith and pierced themselves with many griefs." Bridges, *Proverbs*, 138.

labor of their hands brings good results by God's grace. The result is always more than their labor.

The righteous make fewer mistakes in their words. Because they are prudent, they are less likely to be troubled by their words.

But the wicked get into trouble because of lies and false testimony, just as a deer is trapped (13a).[112] Untruthful words catch up with them. Lies are exposed.

No one is without the slightest slip of the tongue. Most people make unintentional slips of the tongue from time to time. But most of the words of the wicked are impulsive and aggressive. Not only do they hurt the people around them, but their words become a boomerang, and they end up hurting themselves.

In the modern world of recordings and videotapings, sometimes words spoken long ago can get people in trouble. They lose credibility because of inconsistencies between what they said before and what they say now. We live in challenging times indeed. It is wise to be careful what we say.

The way of fools sees right to them,[113] but the wise man listen to advice (12:15).[114]

The characteristic of the foolish is that they rarely see anything wrong with the way they are and the way they live. Therefore, they don't accept or consider advice or feedback. This is because they are so identified with the problem that they have and so they are not able to objectively evaluate themselves. They are called "ego-

---

[112] Bridges cited the case of an Amalekite young man who falsely reported that he had killed King Saul and was killed by David (see 2 Sam. 1:13-16), and the case of Adoniah, who petitioned Solomon to take Abishag, who had attended David in his old age, as his wife and was killed by Solomon(see 1 Kings 2:22-25), as examples of the application of this proverb. It's a very relevant example found in the Bible. Bridges, *Proverbs*, 139.

[113] Fox notes that similar proverbs are repeated several times after chapter 12: 14:12, 16:2, 21:2, 28:11, 30:12. Fox, *Proverbs 10-31*, 555.

[114] Bridges cited the examples of Moses, who took the advice of his father-in-law Jethro, and David, who accepted Abigail's plea. Bridges, *Proverbs*, 140.

syntonic" in psychology.[115]

However, a mature person has the ability to be "ego-dystonic." They have the ability of self-awareness to see themselves objectively and detachedly. They have an insight on themselves. They admit that they may have a problem. And they accept advice and feedback.

Counseling Application: It is difficult for a counselor to work with narcissistic clients because they will not consider or accept the counselor's feedback and will continue to be defensive to the feedback. They feel that the counselor is wrong about them and even become angry. Clients with personality disorders are more likely to be ego-syntonic. This is because they have lived their lives without fully recognizing their personality disorders and they understand their own problems as something wrong with others or their environment. They won't be able to stop being ego-syntonic overnight. They need to increase their self-awareness by gradually using less and less of their old defense mechanisms. The counselor must continue to provide an accepting and empathetic environment, while exercising the wisdom to provide feedback that gradually increases the level of confrontation within the client's tolerance.

Fools show their annoyance at once, but the prudent overlook an insult (12:16). See also 14:17, 29; 29:11.

Solomon calls a person who immediately expresses anger at being insulted a fool (16a). He describes a person who is able to withstand or overlook an insult, even in the face of an actual insult, as "wise" or "prudent" (16b).

It's hard to say in one sentence whether an expression of anger is healthy or unhealthy, because the tolerance of the prudent and the

---

[115] Often, people with personality disorders are ego-syntonic and don't admit that they have a problem in their personality. Those who identify their self with their pathological symptoms have little or no ability to recognize their issues objectively: they have little insight on themselves and therefore no capacity to accept feedback or advice.

anger of the foolish can be pathological when taken to extremes. For example, it may not be a healthy response to overlook whenever insulted. It can be an invitation for the other person to repeat the insulting behavior. Furthermore, if you continue to suppress the anger you feel when you're insulted, you run the risk of transferring that suppressed anger to others and taking it out on them. So when you're insulted or angry, it's sometimes necessary and beneficial to express your anger to the offending party on the spot, within reason. If you are extremely cautious, you may miss the right timing in expressing your emotions.

mature persons have the strength to stand up to insults if necessary. They see the big picture and know how to handle their anger in a way that minimizes the other person's insult. They are able to make rational and reasonable thinking and decisions.

Psychologically immature people, on the other hand, have less control over their anger, so they lash out impulsively. Impulsive people are unable to control their anger and are at risk of over-expressing it and regretting it. People who don't feel remorse are more likely to have narcissistic personality disorder. People with paranoid personality disorder feel insulted by the slightest remark or action and lash out in anger.

Counseling Application: Christian counselors should help clients develop a biblical and balanced understanding, attitude, and approach to anger during the counseling process. Most clients are wrestling with issues related to anger. It's foolish and wrong to condemn anger unconditionally. On the other hand, people who are easily angered are vulnerable to sin.

An honest [truthful] witness tells the truth [gives honest testimony], but a false witness tells lies.[116] The words of the reckless pierce like swords, but the tongue of the wise brings healing (12:17-18).

---

[116] Fox notes that in addition to this proverb, there are several others that exhort us to be true witnesses and warn against false witnesses (14:5, 25; 19:5, 28; 21:28; 24:28; 25:18). Fox, *Proverbs 10-31*, 555.

This proverb has an A-B-B'-A' structure. It connects "an honest witness" with the "wise" and connects "a false witness" with "the reckless."

Truthful witnesses testify honestly and courageously on the witness stand. They speak the truth alone (17a). Truthful witnesses are like a cool spring of water to those in trouble. They are light and hope to the victim, to those in darkness and distress. The testimony of these   truthful witnesses restores and heals those in desperate need (18b). The testimony can be a remedy that restores trust in the world and trust in people to the wounded victim's heart.

False witnesses, on the other hand, testify falsely because they have been paid or threatened to do so (17b). They have no empathy for the devastating impact their false testimony will have on the people involved and their families. There are also some people who volunteer to testify wickedly. Their words pierce like swords to the victimized (18a). They experience like being stabbed. The experience is a kind of "trauma." Reckless, untruthful words can deeply wound the hearer's psyche, like an indelible stigma. Especially if the listener is vulnerable or a child, this traumatic experience can have a long-standing impact on the victim's psyche. In severe cases, the victim may suffer from "post-traumatic stress disorder" for a long time.

Truthful lips endure forever, but a lying tongue lasts only a moment (12:19).[117]

A true testimony remains a true testimony forever (19a), because it is true. Relative truths do not last long, but absolute truths and promises last and are fulfilled, even if heaven and earth were to

---

[117] Bridges cited the example of Gehazi, who lied to General Naaman and lied to Elisha, and was stricken with leprosy as an illustration of the temporary effects of lying. Bridges, *Proverbs*, 143. Koptak notes that this proverb is connected to verses 17 and 22 in the context of chapter 12: "An honest witness tells the truth, but a false witness tells lies" (v. 17); "The LORD detests lying lips, but he delights in people who are trustworthy" (v. 22). Koptak, *Proverbs*, 342.

pass away, without a single detail being changed.

The words of the Bible, inspired by the Holy Spirit, are absolutely true. They are without error. The truth of the Bible will remain. The prophecies of the Old Testament prophets were true and were fulfilled. Every word of Jesus is being fulfilled and will be fulfilled completely.

A false testimony doesn't last long. To cover up the news of Jesus' resurrection, the priests and elders paid the soldiers guarding the tomb a large sum of money to falsely testify that the disciples had stolen Jesus' body. But the lie didn't last long (Matt. 28:11-15), for Jesus himself appeared to his disciples, and in forty days before his ascension he appeared to more than five hundred of them and spoke to them personally. If the disciples had faked the resurrection, Christianity would have already been proven to be a false religion.

A dead body leaves behind scientific evidence that exposes the lies of the perpetrator. Lies don't last long. In this world, lies may be covered up. But in front of the judgment seat of God, they will be exposed as nakedness.

Deceit is in the hearts of those who plot evil, but those who promote peace have joy.[118] No harm overtakes [befalls] the righteous, but the wicked have their fill of trouble (12:20-21).

Like the sentence structure in verses 17 and 18, this proverb is also structured in a chiastic form of A-B-B'-A'. "Those who plot evil" and "the wicked" are linked, and "those who promote peace" and "the righteous" are connected. "Deceit" is paired with "their fill of trouble," and "joy" with "no harm."

---

[118] Bridges saw this proverb and 14:22 as a symmetrical passage: "Do not those who plot evil go astray? But those who plan what is good find love and faithfulness." Bridges, *Proverbs*, 143. Koptak connects the proverb, "those who promote peace have joy," with the preceding second half of verse 15, "the wise listen to advice," noting that the wise who hear counsel find added joy in sharing the digested counsel with others. Koptak, *Proverbs*, 343.

The heart of the evil-doer is deceitful (20a). The consequences are inevitably disastrous (21b). The wicked will fall into a trap of their own making. The ends of the deceiver are miserable. Of course, disaster does not only come to the wicked. Not all calamities are connected to personal sin, but disasters do come to the lives of the wicked. They come suddenly, like a thief breaking in when they least expect it.

The righteous are peacemakers (20b). Blessed are those who promote peace and they will be called children of God (Matt. 5:9). Solomon promises that no disaster will come upon those who seek peace (21a). This is because God will protect them. God uses the righteous to make peace in their homes, churches, and societies. There is joy and peace in the heart of such persons (20b).

The LORD detests lying lips, but he delights in people who are trustworthy [truthful] (12:22).

False lips are a bad object to God. He detests and abhors false lips (22a). But God delights in truthful lips (22b). Trustworthy lips are a good object to him. He delights in and approves of those who testify truthfully.

Even people in the secular world hates those who lie habitually. They have no credibility. But truthful persons and courageous witnesses are trusted and applauded.

The prudent keep their knowledge to themselves, but a fool's heart blurts out folly (12:23).

The thoughtful have the power to keep what they know (23a). They can keep things to themselves if they shouldn't reveal them. They have empathy and concern to keep confidentiality. They are psychologically mature enough not to impulsively reveal secrets.

God hid the mystery of the gospel, which is salvation for all nations including the Gentiles through Jesus Christ, until the fullness of time, when he determined to reveal it (see Eph. 1:9). Wise Jesus did not shout with a loud voice in the streets to be recognized. He spoke in parables about the kingdom of heaven, hiding its meaning so that only those with open ears would understand. He did not reveal that he was the Messiah until the time was right.[119]

In contrast, the mind of the foolish are impulsive, so they blurt out their foolishness (23b). They are unable to distinguish and control what should be concealed and what should be revealed. They foolishly and inadvertently reveal their true feelings when they should not. They make the error of revealing information that should not be revealed.

Those who are aware of what they are saying and can control their tongue is wise and mature. But those who are unaware of what they are saying and disclose secrets in a boastful manner are fools.[120]

Diligent hands will rule, but laziness ends in forced labor [slave labor](12:24). See also 6:6-11; 10:4-5, 26.

The hands of a diligent and hardworking person and the hands of a lazy person don't seem to make much difference at first. But as time passes, the gap widens, and the difference in results is remarkable. One is in a position of leadership, while the other finds himself or herself in a position of being led. The adage "the early bird gets the worm" is a valid one.

God is pleased that humans are zealous and diligent while on this

---

[119] Bridges made a good point that knowledge or truth does not always have to be revealed to everyone. He cited Apostle Paul's supernatural heavenly experience that he had kept hidden for 14 years before he felt obliged to speak out (see 2 Cor. 12:1-6). Additional examples include Abraham hiding his plan to sacrifice Isaac from his wife Sarah, Joseph hiding his identity from his brothers, Esther hiding her true thoughts and feelings from the king and Haman, and Jeremiah hiding the content of his conversation with King Zedekiah at his request. Bridges, *Proverbs*, 145.

[120] Samson was a foolish man to divulge the secret of his power to a Philistine woman.

earth. On the other hand, he is displeased with laziness. It is God's will that we rest and recharge. But God is not pleased with a life of idleness.

Anxiety weighs down the heart [a man down], but a kind word cheers it [him] up (12:25).

Worry, concern, and anxiety weigh down a person's mind. The crushing factor, the process, and the result of the weighing down is called stress. When we are stressed, our energy naturally decreases. We may feel tired and exhausted, and in severe cases, depressed.

The sorrowful and those who are troubled by worry and anxiety can be strengthened by warm words, kind words of comfort (25b). In this way, New Testament believers are called to comfort and encourage for one another in the church community.

Counseling Application: People who struggle with anxiety disorders, where the intensity and frequency of anxiety and fear are severe, will not recover from a warm word. It may make them feel better and reduce your anxiety temporarily, but it cannot be a cure.

It's even possible that people may consciously or unconsciously perpetuate the symptoms of anxiety disorders because it feels good to have friends and family around them when they have those symptoms. This is called "secondary gain." For clients who have reached the level of an anxiety disorder, exploring the causes of anxiety, in addition to a systematic desensitization approach to the symptoms, can be effective. Medication can be some help to relieve the symptoms too.

The righteous choose their friends carefully [are cautious in friendship], but the way of the wicked leads them astray (12:26).

The righteous are prudent and wise in relationships. If a person in a friendship or business relationship naively trust without some information about the other person and experience in the relationship, he or she is likely immature psychologically. Children are weak in their abilities to distinguish between trustworthy and untrustworthy people. Therefore, the righteous in this proverb are the psychologically mature. So they are able to choose their friends carefully.

In the sense of the Revised Korean Bible Version, "The righteous are the guide of their neighbors," counselors can be seen as the righteous. They are guides to their neighbors, their clients. On the other hand, counselors who are not only ineffective but also mislead their clients are the wicked. Counselors who don't examine themselves before God may become deluded and go down the wrong path. And they can delude their clients and lead them astray (26b).

Counseling Application: It is wise for counselors to be "cautious" in their relationships with clients and approach them with caution. It is necessary to be respectful and sensitive to the client. If you're impatient and pushy, the client will shut down.

The lazy do not roast any game, but the diligent feed on the riches of the hunt [the diligent man prizes his possessions] (12:27).

The second half of this proverbs can be understood as "the diligent take what they hunted and cook it and eat it." Then the lazy can be understood people who never hunt for themselves. They may eat what others hunt, cook, and bring to them, but they don't bother to hunt themselves. But the diligent not only hunt themselves, but also take the trouble to cook the game. In a modern sense, a husband who comes home from work and helps his wife with the household chores, rather than thinking that his work is done when he goes to work and collects his paycheck, is a man of integrity and diligence. Such a person reaps the fruits of his labor (27b). He is recognized and respected by his wife and children and enjoys a good life.

In the way of righteousness there is life; along that path is immortality (12:28).[121]

The way of the righteous, the way of walking with God, the way of obeying the Word, is the way of life.[122] It is the way of eternal life. Death cannot overtake them who walk in the path of righteousness. Neither death nor anything present nor anything to come will be able to separate them from the love of God (see Rom. 8:38-39).

[121] Fox notes that the original meaning of the second half of this proverb is unclear, suggesting that it may mean, "The way of [wickedness] leads to death." In this way, the proverb concludes chapter 12 and well summarizes Solomon's core theme that the way of righteousness leads to life, but the way of wickedness leads to death.

[122] Koptak notes that life in this proverb does not refer to eternal life, but to a long, healthy, and safe life on earth. Koptak, *Proverbs*, 345. I take it as the New Testament meaning.

Chapter 13 Walk with the Wise

A wise son heeds his father's instruction, but a mocker does not respond [listen] to rebukes (13:1).[123]

Children who accept and digest the teachings of their her parents are wise (1a). They respect the experience, authority, love, and concern of their parents who have lived longer than they have. They accept their instruction sweetly and are grateful for it.

But foolish children think they are smart. They judge the teachings of their parents through the lens of their own immature thinking. If the teachings don't make sense to them, they talk back to their parents and even refuse to listen to them (1b). They may mock their parents. They think their parents' ideas are outdated and ignore them. So they listen in one ear and let it go out the other. They don't empathize their parents' sincerity. They are arrogant and insist on their own ideas. They do not have the humility to reconsider their own ideas.

It's important to distinguish one's "father's instruction" from nagging. It's a problem when parents scold their children frequently because they're not wise enough or too anxious. Furthermore, nagging is not effective at all. It only creates anger and resentment in their children.

There are fathers who get drunk and scold their children. These fathers are foolish. This kind of scolding is a foolish thing to do. It only builds up anxiety and anger in a child's heart.

---

[123] Bridges connected the example of Hophni and Phinehas, who refused to listen to the counsel of their father, the priest Eli: "His sons, however, did not listen to their father's rebuke, for it was the LORD's will to put them to death" (1 Sam. 2:25b). Bridges, *Proverbs*, 150. There was a parallel between their disregard of Eli's parental counsel and their disregard of God: "This sin of the young men was very great in the LORD's sight, for they were treating the LORD's offering with contempt" (1 Sam. 2:17).

From the fruit of their lips people enjoy good thing,[124] but the unfaithful have an appetite for violence [a craving for violence]. Those who guard their lips preserve their lives,[125] but those who speak rashly will come to ruin (13:2-3).

This proverb has a chiastic structure of A-B-A'-B'. "The fruit of their lips" is connected with "those who guard their lips." "Enjoy good things" is linked with "preserve their lives." "The unfaithful" are "those who speak rashly." "Have an appetite for violence" is connected with "will come to ruin."

The unfaithful are those who opens their mouths wide and speaking impulsively(3b). They hurts others with their words. They don't realize that they have hurt others. They don't remember what they have done, which causes problems in interpersonal relationships, especially with their family. They are alienated and ignored in their relationship with their spouse. They become estranged from their children. They destroy themselves and their families. In the end, they invite violence for themselves and come to ruin (2b, 3b).

Those who "guard their lips" speak the right words and enjoy the fruit of their words (2a). They speak therapeutic words and are loved and respected by others. They make fewer mistakes by thinking and speaking well. They guard their own lives (3a), and even the lives of others. They keep others out of trouble by not saying things that should be kept for their own good.

A sluggard's[126] appetite is never filled [The sluggard craves and

---

[124] Bridges rightly pointed out that the first half of verse 2 is connected with the first half of chapter 12:14, which precedes it: "From the fruit of their lips are filled with good things," Bridges, *Proverbs*, 150.

[125] Bridges associated the proverb in the first half of verse 3 with James 3:2: "We all stumble in many ways. Anyone who is never at fault in which they say is perfect, able to keep their whole body in check." Bridges, *Proverbs*, 151.

[126] Koptak identifies the following relevant proverbs about the sluggard: 6:6-9, 10:26,

gets nothing], but the desires of the diligent are fully satisfied (13:4).

The lazy want and desire something and the diligent also want and desire something. But the lazy want but don't make any effort to get it, so there is no result and no accomplishment (4a). But the diligent will get fully satisfied and filled (4b). The same principle applies to out spiritual lives. It's laziness to want God's grace only without our spiritual discipline and effort.

The righteous hate what is false, but the wicked make themselves a stench and bring shame on themselves [the wicked bring shame and disgrace]. Righteousness guards the person of integrity, but wickedness overthrows the sinner (13:5-6).

The righteous hate falsehood to the point of loathing it (5a). Believers who have the mind of Christ hate lies and deception. They seek truth and honesty. Apostle Paul exhorts us, "Reject every kind of evil" (1 Thess. 5:22). Lies are a classic symptom of evil.

Those who are truthful are free and not disgraced at all (5b). They can defend themselves in any situation (6a). They are not afraid or anxious. They have peace of mind.

The wicked have little conflict in their hearts, even when they lie. They are not distressed, ashamed, or anxious. Their defense mechanism of repression works automatically and naturally. They lie creatively.

Those who make a habit of lying are sure to be disgraced (5b). This is because people don't believe them eventually. In a children's story, the shepherd boy who playfully lied about a wolf coming was eventually bitten to death by a wolf. Similarly, those

21:25, 26:13-16). Koptak, *Proverbs*, 356.

who lie are sure to be destroyed.

A righteous, just society or institution hates falsehood. It treats forgery and fraud as felonies. A common characteristic of people in developed countries is that they seek honesty and make it a virtue. In less developed countries with widespread corruption, falsehood is the norm.

In Korea, we had some ministerial candidates who were defeated because they reported that they had written their research papers as first authors although actually they were not. Some people are disgraced for plagiarizing dissertations or posing as PhDs with fake degree. Some preachers are disgraced for plagiarizing others' sermons. Others misrepresent their education or experience and are ashamed. These are all characterized by lies and deceit. When we sow lies, we will reap the fruit of shame and destruction.

One person pretends to be rich, yet has nothing; another pretends to be poor, yet has great wealth (13:7).[127]

There are people who bluff. There are those who pretend to be rich. There are some people who pretend to be rich or to be graduates of Ivy schools and marry, almost to the point of fraud. There are some professors who talk like they're smart, but actually they're not. There are also some people who live in basement but drive foreign cars with lease. All of them are a kind of hypocrites. They are the ones who exaggerate their appearances without being much good.[128]

---

[127] Bridges interpreted the person described in the second half of this proverb in a negative way too. He thought that it is deceitful to have great wealth and yet live as if he or she is poor. Bridges, *Proverbs*, 154. I interpret this proverb in a positive sense. I see it as a proverb that encourages the virtue of living humbly, without bragging or showing off, even though one is full of wealth.

[128] This histrionic aspect doesn't just apply to the area of wealth. Those who speak pedantically as if they have competence and knowledge although they don't actually are histrionic persons. Spiritual leaders who pretend to be spiritual when they are not are also histrionic. They are no different from the Pharisees and scribes. As Paul

These people are pitiful in that they live their lives hiding their true selves because they are very conscious of what others think of them. They live their lives theatrically, constantly seeking attention and approval of others. Their lives can be deceptive in that they have a high risk of deceiving others.

The Pharisees and scribes had the problem of hypocrisy. They were rebuked by Jesus that they were like the plastered tomb. They seemed outwardly zealous in their observance of the law. They probably thought so themselves. But their hearts were filled with the desire for honor, the desire for riches, and the desire for recognition. That's why they were hypocrites. They deceived others and deceived themselves.

Jesus was different from the Pharisees and scribes. There was a difference in the authority of his words. He was not at all theatrical in his interpersonal relationships and behavior. He was the Lord of all things, yet he was with the weak and the sick. He possessed nothing that he could claim as his own, so much so that he said he had no place to lay down his head. He was full of wisdom, but he did not boast of his wisdom in a pedantic way or do anything to draw attention to himself. He did not raise his voice, nor did he make disciples of the sages or scholars. Rather, he made disciples of Galilean fishermen and tax collectors, and he was active in the fringes of Galilee. He did not have histrionic personality disorder at all.

There are some humble people who live their lives unnoticed. They don't draw attention to themselves. From the outside, they seem so ordinary. They are grateful for their lives even though they are not the center of attention. On the contrary, they find it a burden.

Counseling Application: People with histrionic personality disorder focus their energy into their appearance. They do this to get attention and recognition from others. They exaggerate when they express their emotions. They are psychologically vulnerable

points out, a life "having a form of godliness but denying its power" (2 Tim. 3:5) is histrionic. Bridges connected the Laodicean church to the theatricality and deceitfulness described in this proverb: "You say, 'I am rich; I have acquired wealth and do not need a thing.' But you do not realize that you are wretched, pitiful, poor, blind and naked" (Rev. 3:17). Bridges, *Proverbs*, 154.

and have low self-esteem. Their self-structure are fragile, so they are prone to break down in times of crisis. They seem to have something to say, but there's not much there. Their words and relationships are superficial. They disappoint people who approach them with interest. They end up feeling empty because they can't receive attention continuously from others. Moods rise and fall like a thermometer depending on the favorable or unfavorable environment.

A person's riches may ransom their life, but the poor cannot respond to threatening rebukes [a poor man hears no threat] (13:8).[129]

If the second half of this proverb means that the poor are not threatened, then the first half means, "The rich may be threatened with their lives because of their wealth." There are evil people who kidnap people who appear to be wealthy and blackmail them into depositing money. Or they kidnap their children and demand large sums of money. This may have happened in Old Testament times. So while rich people's wealth protects them like a fortified city (10:15; 18:11), it can also be a source of threats. It's up to the rich man to pay up and avoid death.[130]

Poor neighborhoods may have thieves, but they are petty thieves. So poor people don't worry about leaving their doors open. There is nothing to steal. And the poor need not fear for their lives (8b). For there is nothing to be gained by kidnapping and threatening the

---

[129] In his comment on the second half of this proverb, Bridges insightfully pointed out that if Isaac had not been wealthy, there would have been no enemies to fill the wells he had dug, and if Jacob had not been wealthy, he would not have been envied and threatened by his father-in-law Laban and his sons. Bridges, *Proverbs*, 155.

[130] Riches can be beneficial to save one's life in this world. But they have no effect on the way to eternal life. Bridges connected to 1 Pet. 1:18, which says "For you know that it was not with perishable things such as silver or gold that you were redeemed from the empty way of life handed down to you from your ancestors." Bridges, *Proverbs*, 155.

poor. It only may harm their life. The poor and their children do not have to worry about being kidnapped, so they can enjoy the peace that the rich do not. This is the paradoxical grace of the poor.

In the worldly sense, being wealthy can help you overcome anxiety. This is because money greatly reduces anxiety. So money can be a barrier to salvation because it anesthetizes the fear that leads to salvation.

For some, money is a source of anxiety. They fear of losing it. Those who are rich with stocks, they fear of losing it. If you don't own stocks or don't know about stocks, you don't have to be anxious about them.

The light of the righteous shines brightly, but the lamp of the wicked is snuffed out (13:9).[131]

The light of the righteous is the commandments and Word of God. Their paths are well-lit because they walk in the light of the Word (9a). The righteous do not live the shameful life of walking in darkness. So they do not stumble.

But what the wicked uses as light is their own experiences, the experience of others, and the wisdom of evil. The paths they walk are paths of darkness. They seem wise and reasonable worldly for a time. They seem like "eye-opening" paths. But they are ways of destruction and eternal death (9b).

The righteous live lives that at first go unnoticed. But gradually their light shines brightly, affecting the people and environment around them for good. They live their lives that glorify God. Although their body are passing away with age, they are being renewed inwardly (2 Cor. 4:16). And they become a light and example to those around them. Even after death, their names don't

---

[131] The metaphors used in this proverb, light and lamps, symbolize not only life itself, but also the quality of life, Fox said, adding that the same meaning is found in Job 18:5-6: "The lamp of a wicked man is snuffed out; the flame of his fire stops burning. The light in his tent becomes dark; the lamp beside him goes out." Fox, *Proverbs 10-31*, 564.

decay. Like the stars in the sky, their deeds touch the hearts of others. For example, David Brainerd, a missionary to the Delaware Indians, was called early to his death from pulmonary tuberculosis at the age of 29, but his journals and life have challenged the lives of other missionaries and influenced many for good in later generations.

Where there is strife, there is pride [Pride only breeds quarrels], but wisdom is found in those who take advice (13:10).[132]

The prideful cannot recognize their own faults or mistakes. When interpersonal difficulties arise, they blame others or circumstances. People with narcissistic personality disorder, who are characterized by their self-grandiosity, refuse to admit their faults. They don't believe they can be wrong, so they don't admit when they're wrong. When narcissistic persons get into a quarrel, their argument will never end (10a). They will only blame the other persons.

Dishonest money dwindles away, but whoever gathers money little by little makes it grow (13:11).

Money earned easily without sweating or taken by unrighteous means not only "dwindles away" but also brings ruin to the earner. On the other hand, money earned honestly and with integrity not only increases little by little but also brings reward and joy to the earner.

In the short term, people who make a lot of money unrighteously may seem worldly blessed. But God is not pleased with their lives. In the end, they fail and is

---

132 Koptak connects this proverb with the preceding 13:1: "A wise son heeds his father's instruction, but a mocker does not respond to rebukes." Koptak, *Proverbs*, 358.

disgraced even in this world.

Hope deferred makes the heart sick, but a longing fulfilled is a tree of life (13:12).

Christians also become frustrated when their hopes and wishes are not fulfilled over time. They stop hoping. They become depressed. They become discouraged. Their future narrative becomes negative or meager. They feel like they can't see the light at the end of the tunnel. Their heart is broken and even the desire to pray is lost. They are not discouraged or despaired totally but they feel powerless and helpless. This can be a reality for some Christians in their journey of life.

On the other hand, when what you have long wished for is finally fulfilled, you will experience wonderful joy as if you were eating the fruit of the tree of life, joy that you feel like flying in the sky (12b). It will be like a huge burden has been lifted off your shoulder, and you will feel a rush of gratitude and excitement.

Whoever scorns instruction will pay for it, but whoever respects a command is rewarded[133] (13:13).

God rewards those who value and obey his commandments and words, even on earth (13b). He will also reward them with an inheritance in the everlasting kingdom of God and eternal life. But those who despise and ignore his words and commandments will be punished, even on earth.[134] It is a grave sin for them to despise God, the giver of his words and commandments. They will be destroyed even on this earth, and they will suffer eternal judgment

---

[133] Bridges rightly commented that to fear God and his Word means reverence, not terror. Bridges, *Proverbs*, 159.

[134] Bridges connected this proverb with Noah's flood. Bridges, *Proverbs*, 159.

(13a).

The teaching of the wise is a fountain of life, turning a person from the snares of death.[135] Good judgment [Good understanding] wins favor, but the way of the unfaithful leads to their destruction [is hard] (13:14-15).

The teachings and guidance of the wise are like a spring of life (14a). Those who drink from it have their thirst satisfied and do not thirst for temporary objects. They have wisdom to desire eternal things. They experience the kingdom of God, where there are springs of life and trees of life. Even when they are caught in the net of destruction, they will have a desire to seek the fountain of life again (14b). Like the prodigal son, they courageously return to their Father's home. Then the snares of death that have bound him are broken, and condemnation and judgment are removed. The devil has no more power over them.

The Word of God is like a living, active, double-edged sword. It has the marvelous power to cut through the net of death and rescue those who are bound by sin (14b). The sword of the Word that comes from the mouth of Jesus Christ has the power to liberate those who struggle with addictions and sin of all kinds.

Those who have good wisdom and insight, or who hear, do favor to and receive favor from others (15a).[136] Evil wisdom and foolishness are disbelief in God. The way of unbelievers finally leads to failure and destruction in this world and eternal torment in hell (15b).

---

[135] Fox points out that verse 14 is the same proverb as chapter 14:27 with a slight variation in wording: "The fear of the LORD is a fountain of life, turning a person from the snares of death." Fox, *Proverbs 10-31*, 566.

[136] Noting that the "good judgment" of v. 15 is connected to the preceding "the teaching of the wise" of v. 14, Fox comments that those who have wisdom are those who draw water from the fountain of life, while those who hear and obey it are those who find favor to drink from the fountain of life. Fox, *Proverbs 10-31*, 567.

All who are prudent act with [act out of] knowledge, but fools expose their folly (13:16).

A person is revealed by what is in him or her. The words and actions of those who are thoughtful and discerning come from their knowledge (16a). Even one's face often shows wisdom or foolishness. A minister's face reflects the image of a pastor. An educated person's face reflects his or her sophistication. On the other hand, a swindler's face shows his or her craftiness and deceitfulness. In this sense, it is hard to say that physiognomy has no validity at all. The appearance of the face, especially when it is acquired, often reveals a person's character.

The foolish reveal their folly and immaturity in the words they speak (16b). Speaking in some words is a form of behavior. Words and speech of the foolish reveal their mistakes, pettiness, exaggeration, and contradictions. The immature and unwise Christians also reveal their inner lives through their behaviors. Immature churches and immature communities also exhibit dysfunctional symptoms. They may try hard not to show them, but they will.

A wicked messenger falls into trouble,[137] but a trustworthy envoy brings healing (13:17).

The faithfulness of an envoy or ambassador sent by a king or president on an important mission cannot be overemphasized. The main task of an envoy or ambassador is to deliver the king's or

---

[137] Bridges connects this proverb with Gehazi, Elisha's servant. Gehazi went to General Naaman on his own, even though he had not been sent, and falsely asked for as if Elisha had sent him and received a gift, and was finally chastened with an outbreak of leprosy.

president's message well, or to convey his or her intentions without alteration. When this role is fulfilled faithfully, the envoy brings healing between two nations. Blocked diplomatic channels are restored, trade is established, and mutual cooperation results.

A unfaithful emissary or ambassador, on the other hand, is inconsistent and lacks courage and wisdom, so he or she is swayed by the king or president of the other country and returns home without saving the day. Instead, he or she creates new problems or makes existing ones worse.

We can apply this proverb to our personal lives in a modern sense. The connectivity of the Internet acts as a messenger for many people. In a functional way, the Internet provides good information and fast news that can influence many people for good at once. Many people can be moved and encouraged at the same time by what is posted on the Internet. Watching sermons or testimonies on YouTube anytime and anywhere can be a great source of strength in our faith. In this way, the Internet is like a medicine that can bring healing to an anonymous person who is struggling alone in a distant country.

On the flip side, the Internet can and is used for evil. It's where wrongful meetings take place, where all sorts of evil, obscene information, rumors, and pornographic materials are spread. They are modern-day prostitutes. We must recognize that the Internet can be a dangerous and deep trap for believers, especially children and young adults.

Whoever disregards [ignores] discipline comes to poverty and shame,[138] but whoever heeds correction is honored (13:18).

The fruit of those who heed and obey disciplines and exhortations and the fruit of those who ignore them are in contrast. The one is

---

[138] Bridges connected the first half of this proverb to the metaphor of the ignorant horse and mule in Ps. 32:9, which says "Do not be like the horse or the mule, which have no understanding but must be controlled by bit and bridle or they will not come to you." Bridges, *Proverbs*, 163.

honored, but the other is brought to poverty and shame. Those who are admonished and do not listen predictably end up in poverty and dishonor (18a). You can lead a horse to a stream, but you cannot force it to drink water. Those who reject and ignore corrections intentionally will have correspondingly deadly consequences.

The problem lies in the foolishness of those who don't obey corrections. They deny the consequences of poverty and shame, and then suddenly the consequences are catastrophic.

But those who are disciplined will be honored and glorified (18b). They listen to the Word, obey it, and faithfully live by it. And they will be glorified on the day of their death and on the day of the Second Coming of Jesus. They will be praised and recognized and enjoy eternal life.

A longing fulfilled is sweet to the soul, but fools detest turning from evil (13:19). See 13:12.

At first glance, the first half of this proverb and it's second half don't seem to go together. The conjunction "but" makes it clear that they are contrasted. We can interpret this to mean that even the foolish have longings or desires. The foolish are also temporarily pleased and delighted when their desires are fulfilled, for there is a temporary pleasure and enjoyment that comes from doing evil. All addictive phenomena have this temporary function of giving pleasure or happiness.

The problem is that when the experience of pleasure wears off, pain, anxiety, shame, and guilt follow. These accompanying negative emotions are hard to bear, so the foolish repeat the addictive behavior again. This is why it is so difficult to for them to turn away from foolishness or evil. Paradoxically, they feel ambivalent about their addiction and so they don't want to turn away from evil (19b). So the foolish are unable to repent. They remain attached to their addictive behaviors. Their brain cells are destroyed and their faces age rapidly due to repeated use of drugs. Even their bodily organs are damaged, but they are unable to break the vicious cycle of addiction.

166

Walk with the wise and become wise, for a companion of fools suffers harm (13:20).[139]

There is a Korean saying, "If you are close to red, you will turn red and if you are close to black, you will turn black" (近朱者赤近墨者黑). There is also an old Korean poem, "White herons! Do not associate with a flock of crows." The idea is that white cranes turn black as they hang out with crows. It's a metaphoric warning not to associate with bad company.

Christians live in the world, relating to all kinds of people. But they are not to live "alongside" them. Although we live in the world, we, believers, are not of the world. If we associate with unbelievers to the point of sharing a yoke with them, we will unwittingly be influenced by them. In extreme cases, we may be "harmed" and perish from the way of life (20b).

But when we walk with other believers and commune with them in the "fellowship of the saints," we can grow holistically and live wisely (20a). Furthermore, we can become "good objects" to influence other believers.

Counseling Application: From the perspective of Object Relations Theory, one of psychodynamic theories, if you grow up with "good enough" parents for a certain period of time, especially in the early years, you are likely to be a person with a "good enough" level of self-esteem. However, if you grow up with immature, foolish and aggressive parents, that is, bad objects, you are likely to be immature, foolish and aggressive adult. For "self" is structured and developed through the accumulated experiences of object relations.

No one goes through life alone. You are meant to be "accompanied" by someones on your life journey, such as your

---

[139] Bridges connected the first half of this proverb with Zech. 8:23: "This is what the LORD Almighty says: In those days ten people from all languages and nations will take firm hold of one Jew by the hem of his robe and say, 'Let us go with you, because we have heard that God is with you.'" Bridges, *Proverbs*, 164.

parents, spouse, children, pastors, teachers, friends, coworkers, counselors, supervisors, and other meaningful objects. The importance of companionship experiences, especially during formative years, cannot be overemphasized. It is important to keep in mind that pastors are also meaningful objects who directly or indirectly influence their members in their life journey. Counselors must recognize that in the life of a client, his or her experiences of walking with them in counseling are a relational experience that can be as influential as that of his or her parents.

The experience of working with a counselor, especially one with wisdom and a solid Christian faith, is a providential encounter for Christian clients. This is because it is through this process of "accompaniment" that they can experience a therapeutic environment in which they can grow in wisdom about God and the world and grow stronger in faith. However, Christian clients must be careful in choosing their counselor because the counselor who is blind to his or her own blindness, lacks of insight and wisdom, and lacks of a clear Christian faith may devastate them as much as accompanying experiences with dysfunctional parents.

Trouble [Misfortune] pursues the sinner, but the righteous are rewarded with good things [prosperity is the reward of the righteous] (13:21).

The Book of Proverbs can be well understood even by young children because of its overall dichotomous approach. For example, it's hard for children to understand that disaster can happen to good people. It's also hard for them to understand that even good people can be foolish or evil. It's best to understand this proverb above with this in mind.

The world since the fall into sin has been one of disaster and misery. Wars and catastrophes occur. Natural disasters take place. The problem is that these calamities don't just happen to sinners and the wicked, as stated in this proverb (21a). The case of Job is a classic example. Job's friends understood him only within the paradigm of this proverb, which limited their approach. There are some sinners who die in peace without encountering disaster! It is a reality that those who deserve to die do not die, and those who should not die do. Therefore, we should always be aware that unexplainable calamities can come into the lives of some faithful Christians saints, so that our faith may not be shaken.

But, broadly speaking, there are avenges and punishments of in the life of the sinner (21a). This is true. It is also true that the righteous who love God have prosperous rewards (21b).

A good person leaves an inheritance for their children's children, but a sinner's wealth is stored up for the righteous. An unplowed field produces food for the poor [A poor man's field may produce abundant food], but injustice sweeps it away (13:22-23).

When the goods of a good person are passed on to his or her children and grandchildren, it means that they have been influenced for good by their parents' generation.[140] The families of the righteous are blessed with a good inheritance, not only material, but also mental and spiritual, as it is said, "Apple doesn't fall far from the tree" (22a).[141]

---

[140] Bridges said it is appropriate to apply this proverb as a specific proverb rather than as a universal proverb. The reason for this, he said, is that many of the good have no legacy to leave, have no children, or will never see their children's children. Rather, the wicked leave a legacy and enjoy well-being in this world, he said, citing Ps. 17:14: "By your hand save me from such people, LORD, from those of this world whose reward is in this life. May what you have stored up for the wicked fill their bellies; may their children gorge themselves on it and may there be leftovers for their little ones." Bridges, *Proverbs*, 166.

[141] The tribe of Rechab in the Book of Jeremiah was a great family of faith who had obeyed the command of their forefather Jonadab for nearly 200 years: "Neither you nor your descendants must ever drink wine. Also you must never build houses, sow seed or plant vineyards; you must never have any of these things, but must always live in tents. Then you will live a long time in the land where you are nomads" (Jer.

God-fearing children do not waste their wealth. They have good character and wisdom to manage their wealth well. They do not engage in the impulsive spending that is characteristic of borderline personality disorder. They have a sense of stewardship so that they are well aware of the value of their sweat equity and use it appropriately and wisely.

But the wealth of sinners is not passed on to their children and grand-children well. Even if they do inherit it, they cannot keep it. For the children will imitate the life of their parents, who lived a life of wickedness. Instead, the wealth will be accumulated for the righteous and will benefit them (22b).[142] The children quarrel over the inheritance and fight one another in legal battles. Those who accumulate their wealth wickedly will likely spend it in a short period of time because they did not save it diligently (23b).

In contrast, even though the righteous may have begun their life in poverty, their fields will be blessed with abundant crops (23a). This is because God takes care of them and gives them rain at the right time.

Whoever spares the rod hates their children, but the one who loves their children is careful to discipline them (13:24).

Parents who love their children spare no rod (24a). They discipline them, but do so with wisdom and sensitivity. They discipline appropriately for the child's stage of development. They discipline at the appropriate level, well recognizing their purpose of discipline.

Parents who try to raise up their children perfectly actually stunt their children's development. Parents who strive for perfection are generally anxious. Parental anxiety can stunt a child's

---

35:6b-7).

[142] In his commentary on the proverb, "a sinner's wealth is stored up for the righteous," Bridges saw the passing of much of Laban's wealth to Jacob's, the passing of the gold and silver treasures of Egyptians and the wealth of the Canaanites to the Israelites as an inheritance, and the passing of Haman's wealth to Esther and Mordecai as events that are connected to this proverb. Bridges, *Proverbs*, 167.

psychological development. So parents need to know that even a moderate amount of negative experience and frustration is beneficial so that they don't have to try to be too good in their parenting. A "good enough" level of parenting is enough! Appropriate frustration integrated with good object experiences is rather beneficial for the development of a "cohesive self" of a child.

So parents need to discipline their children enough to feel some pain and suffering, but with sensitivity and knowledge. The discipline should be age-appropriate, developmentally appropriate, and prescribed for each child's level and condition and characteristics. Using a rod appropriately and wisely promotes the child's psychological development and helps him or her to form a healthy psychological structure. The opposite is ineffective and can cause trauma.[143]

Parents who had been disciplined at an appropriate level themselves are able to discipline their children at an appropriate level and in an appropriate context. However, parents who had internalized the bad experience of being spanked too much as children are likely to take their parenting to extremes. They may become overly permissive or repeat the experience they had.

Counseling Application: Counselors who are able to confront their clients at an appropriate level and in an appropriate manner can facilitate their psychological development. Effective

---

[143] Clifford comments that this proverb cannot be used as a proof text for corporal punishment of children. Clifford, *Proverbs*, 140. Koptak comments in the same tone. He sees that the emphasis of this proverb is put on teaching or instruction, not on the means of teaching, that is, the rod, since the Hebrew word *muscar*, used repeatedly in chapter 13, means "teaching" or "instruction. Koptak, *Proverbs*, 362. It is noteworthy, however, that the proverb's reference to corporal punishment is repeated in several places. Fox identified the following verses as proverbs related to corporal punishment 19:25, 29, 20:30, 22:15, 23:13-14, 26:3, 29:15. Fox, *Proverbs 10-31*, 571. How wisely to apply these verses in a modern society that prohibits corporal punishment depends on the level of psychological and spiritual maturity of the parents and their ability to control their anger. Physical punishment of parents that traumatizes their child without seeing the forest but only some trees is as foolish as burning a thatched house to control bedbugs. We need to be wise enough to avoid both extremes in punishment.

counselors don't just empathize with their clients; sometimes they scold, sometimes they frustrate, sometimes they confront them on their level and make them feel some pain. Sometimes they call them for repentance and awaken their dulled conscience.

Counselors who avoid confrontation will be limited in their therapeutic role. Therefore, they must explore why they are afraid to confront their clients. If necessary, they may need to seek supervision or counseling to make changes.

The righteous eat to their hearts' content, but the stomach of the wicked goes hungry (13:25).[144]

In this proverb, in conjunction with verse 4 of the same chapter, the righteous are diligent persons. It is common sense that the diligent are given an abundance of food. For they reap what they sow.

The diligent yet temperate are satisfied when their good desires are fulfilled. They don't overwork themselves to the point of workaholism. They are self-content even in poverty. They are not compulsive with eating because they have learned the secret of being content in both fullness and hunger (see Phil. 4:12).

The wicked, on the other hand, are lazy. The lazy will eventually go hungry because they have nothing to eat (25b). Even if they have something to eat, they are too lazy even to lift a spoon to their mouths (see 26:15).

Meanwhile, the stomach of sluggards is never satisfied, no matter how full it is.[145] Soon they feel thirst and hunger. The appetites of

---

[144] It is unwise if we see only one aspect of this proverb. For even among the righteous there are some people who are hungry, and among the wicked there are some people who eat their fill. In particular, those who are hungry and thirsty for righteousness are blessed: "Blessed are those who hunger and thirst for righteousness, for they will be filled" (Matt. 5:6). The wicked who almost caused Asaph to stumble were described as full: "From their callous hearts comes iniquity; their evil imaginations have no limit" (Ps. 73:7); "This is what the wicked are like—always free of care, they go on amassing wealth" (Ps. 73:12).

[145] In his comment on this proverb, Bridges used the example of King Ahab, who

the wicked are addictive. Even when they become overweight, they eat more and more. Their self-esteem is weak and they constantly feel a sense of inner deficiency. Their need for recognition and admiration is not satisfied, so they try to fill the psychological emptiness by eating. Later on, they will have a hard time controlling their body.

coveted Naboth's vineyard and became restless because he could not find a solution, even though he already owned much as king of Israel: "So Ahab went home, sullen and angry because Naboth the Jezreelite had said, 'I will not give you the inheritance of my ancestors.' He lay on his bed sulking and refused to eat" (1 Kings 21:4). Bridges, *Proverbs*, 169.

Chapter 14 Faithful Witness vs. False Witness

The wise woman builds her house, but with her own hands the foolish one tears hers down (14:1).

Chapter 13 began with a verse about a wise son and a foolish son, but chapter 14 begins with a verse about a wise woman and a foolish woman. This proverb is based on Solomon's own experiences with many women, and his concern for his son is evident. In the context of the entire book of Proverbs, a wise woman is a woman who fears God. A foolish woman, on the other hand, is one who not only doesn't know God, but shakes the very foundations of one's faith in God. She is a spiritually corrupting woman.

The woman in the text can be equally applied to the man. A wise husband knows how to build a stronger marriage with each passing year. This is because he becomes more mature on the inside. He understands his wife better than before and is able to resolve conflicts without much difficulty that may arise in his marriage. A stable marriage allows him to be a functional father to his growing children. And he fears God.

However, an unwise husband jeopardizes the marriage by treating his wife immaturely. They argue violently, even in front of their children, causing them to feel insecure. Finally, they are separated or divorced. Such a husband is a foolish man who destroys his house with his own hands (1b).

Whoever fears the LORD walks uprightly,[146] but those who

---

[146] Koptak notes that the phrase "fear of the Lord" occurs twice as much in the second half of Proverbs as in the first half. This fact suggests that the central concern of Solomon is not so much for us to live a life of wisdom in this world as it is for us to live a God fearing life.

despise him are devious in their ways. A fool's mouth lashes out with pride [A fool's talk brings a rod to his back], but the lips of the wise protect them (14:2-3).[147]

This proverb has a chiastic structure of A-B-B'-A'. The key difference between those who walk uprightly and those who walk in devious ways is their fear of God. Those who despise the LORD go their own way (2b). But those who fear the invisible God and live their lives before his sight walk consistently in the upright way (2a).

Failure to fear God is itself disrespect and contempt for God (2b). Such people are not only foolish but also arrogant. They are the master of their own lives. They are called fools in Proverbs. They are fools who invite "a rod" not only in this world but also in the next (3a). This is because they voluntarily engage in self-defeating behaviors.

But those who fear God are wise, so they confess and praise God with their mouth. Jesus will bring them whose mouths confess Jesus Christ before men into the kingdom of righteousness on the day of judgment. So their lips protect them (3b).

Where there are no oxen, the manger is empty, but from the strength of an ox come abundant harvests (14:4).

This proverb teaches us that in order to have a bountiful harvest, it is necessary to labor to care for and feed the ox that helps to plow the land. In other words, hoping for good results without putting in any effort is nothing more than a foolish illusion.

Oxen are very beneficial in farming. To take good care of them, you need to clean their mangers, provide hay or cut fresh grass, and feed them. Then they will help you with your farming.

---

[147] Bridges noted that the second half of verse 3 connects to the second half of the preceding verse of chapter 12:6: "The speech of the upright rescues them." Bridges, *Proverbs*, 171.

Expecting an output without an input of labor is not only foolish but also deceiving oneself. Similarly, an entrepreneur who expects to make a lot of profit without investing is unscrupulous.

An honest [truthful] witness does not deceive, but a false witness pours out lies (14:5).[148]

Witnesses are required to raise their right hand and swear to tell the truth in court. Unfortunately, there are witnesses who lie under oath. They bravely testify false testimony, denying in their hearts that the truth might be discovered later and humiliate them. How foolish they are! If they could see in a hallucination that the invisible God is watching their lips, their mouths would freeze in panic. It is a sad reality that there are psychopathic so-called Christian leaders who lie without fear because they actually deny the omnipresence and omniscience of God.

Like a cesspool spewing out filth, a false witness feels no remorse and pours out creative lies. It is a fearful behavior that will kill the other person and ultimately lead to their own destruction.

The mocker seeks wisdom and finds none, but knowledge comes easily to the discerning (14:6).

It is very unlikely that the arrogant will seek wisdom. The phrase "seeks and finds not" is more of irony, meaning that they actually don't seek it.[149] They don't seek wisdom because they think they

---

[148] Fox notes that there are several proverbs that address false witness: 6:19, 14:25, 19:5, 9, 21:28. Fox, *Proverbs 10-31*, 574.

[149] Bridges connected the promise to Jesus' words, "Ask and it will be given to you" (Matt. 7:7), to show that it is not a false promise. He noted that when arrogant persons ask for wisdom, their requests are not answered because they are insincere, dishonest in their purpose, joyless, and seek only for their own benefits. Bridges, *Proverbs*, 172. James puts it well: "You do not have because you do not ask God. When you ask, you

176

are already wise.[150] Even if they seek wisdom, they can't find it at all. The reason is that theirs eyes are blinded. The eyes of the proud cannot be open.[151] Only the pure in heart can see God, the source of wisdom (see Matt. 5:8).

In this proverb, wisdom and knowledge are the same thing. True wisdom is based on the knowledge of the LORD. Knowing God is wisdom.

The Holy Spirit is the Spirit of wisdom. Those who are illuminated by the Holy Spirit are the discerning. Not only can they discern right from wrong, but also the will of God from the will of man. For those who have discernment, the horizon of knowledge of the breadth, length, height, and depth of God's love will be enlarged.[152]

---

do not receive, because you ask with wrong motives, that you may spend what you get on your pleasures" (James 4:2b-3). In contrast, he assures those who lack wisdom that God will give it to them if they ask in faith: "But you ask, you must believe and not doubt, because the one who doubts is like a wave of the sea, blown and tossed by the wind" (James 1:6).

[150] Fox comments that the arrogant have wisdom like cunning or craftiness or skill. Fox, *Proverbs 10-31*, 574. People with narcissistic personality disorder are characterized by being smarter and more capable than average people. The problem is that this worldly shrewdness gets in the way of finding true wisdom. For the wisdom-seeking Greeks, the gospel of the cross, or true wisdom, was a difficult obstacle to overcome: "Jews demand signs and Greeks look for wisdom, but we preach Christ crucified: a stumbling block to Jews and foolishness to Gentiles" (1 Cor. 1:22-23).

[151] Pilate was a prime example of the arrogant. He asked Jesus, "What is truth?" (John 18:38), but he was no longer interested in truth. He was face-to-face with Jesus Christ, the source of truth and wisdom, but he didn't know who Jesus was and didn't believe.

[152] Paul prayed that the Ephesians would be enlarged in the knowledge of God through the power of the Holy Spirit: "I keep asking that the God of our Lord Jesus Christ, the glorious Father, may give you the Spirit of wisdom and revelation, so that you may know him better. I pray that the eyes of your heart may be enlightened in order that you may know the hope to which he has called you, the riches of his glorious inheritance in his holy people, and his incomparably great power for us who believe" (Eph. 1:17-19).

Stay away from a fool,[153] for you will not find knowledge on their lips. The wisdom of the prudent is to give thought to their ways, but the folly of fools is deception (14:7-8).

A characteristic of the prudent and thoughtful is that they think over and reflect on their ways, that is, on their life (8a). But the foolish don't reflect about their life. They are not concerned with self-awareness and self-knowledge. When problems arise, they first blame others or circumstances, and then pass them by. They don't think that the problems are related to themselves. They deceive themselves consciously or unconsciously (8b).

It is very difficult to perceive ourselves objectively. It is relatively easy to recognize other people's lives, but it is difficult to recognize and know ourselves. This is because it is very easy to deceive ourselves.[154] It is very difficult to have self-insight or to do self-supervision, especially about unconscious dynamics.

Counseling Application 1: Even with some self-awareness, those who live their lives disconnected from God is being deceived by the devil. No matter how long they may undergo psychoanalysis, no matter how much they become more aware of their unconscious dynamics, they are still in darkness spiritually if they are not illuminated under the light of the Bible. If they are so unconscious of the spiritual realm that they cannot see and hear, they are fools. For they don't recognize themselves as sinners in desperate need of salvation. They may be worldly wise, but if they don't believe in Jesus Christ, they are foolish. Psychoanalysis alone cannot bring the salvation the Bible speaks of. Counseling alone cannot bring

---

[153] Bridges saw the first half of verse 7 as also connecting with 26:4: "Do not answer a fool according to his folly, or you yourself will be just like him." Bridges, *Proverbs*, 173.

[154] For example, persons with an inferiority complex has a weak ability to perceive themselves objectively. Conversely, those who are arrogant and have narcissistic personality disorder also have a weak ability to perceive themselves objectively, which is why they exhibit symptoms of "grandiosity of self." Until we stand in front of the mirror of the Word, we cannot have an accurate self-perception. Even self-awareness through counseling is an experience of standing in front of a somewhat distorted mirror. Even the mirror that the counselor reflects has some flaws.

true salvation and healing. Those who realize this and accept the gospel of Jesus are the wise.

Counseling Application 2: Through the process of counseling, clients can receive objective feedback from their counselor about themselves. They may hear things about themselves that other people in their lives don't give them honest feedback on.

Initially, it is not easy to accept the counselor's feedback because defense mechanisms are activated. However, if you are motivated and courageous enough to be self-aware, you will have the ability to become increasingly aware of your issues, psychodynamics, and symptoms of personality disorders. You will also be able to recognize your strengths that you may not have recognized before.

Christian counselors, like their clients, must be committed to the process of change toward self-awareness. In order to grow, they need to continually seek opportunities to see themselves objectively through their own psychotherapy, supervision, or consultation. Furthermore, they should examine and illuminate themselves through the Scriptures. If counselors lack self-awareness, it is like the blind leading the blind. There is a high risk of getting caught up in the dynamic of countertransference and losing objectivity in their counseling process. If they remain spiritually immature, they become obstacles to their clients' spiritual growth.

Fools mock at making amends for sin, but good will is found among the upright (14:9).

The foolish do not take their sins seriously (9a) and therefore do not feel their need to repent. They do not realize how dreadful sin is and how deadly it is. They do not learn from their mistakes and faults, so they commit the same faults and sins over and over again.

Of course, the upright and honest commit sins too, but they repent. They are well aware of the seriousness of their sin and are willing to change. When they fall, they get back up and try not to repeat the same faults and sins. Grace comes to them (9b).

179

Counseling Application: In the case of foolish, immature clients, Christian counselors help to enlighten them so that they may become more aware of their psychopathology and sins. They facilitate the balanced working of their conscience and superego. They help the clients move toward a life of repentance and change.

Each heart knows its own bitterness,[155] and no one else can share its joy (14:10).

This proverb uses parallelism, meaning that neither the pleasure nor the pain of the heart can be empathized wholeheartedly by others. It can be understood as a proverb that points out that it is difficult to empathize with other people's joy as well as suffering.

Paul exhorts us to "rejoice with those who rejoice; mourn with those who mourn" (Rom. 12:15). Christians are members of an organic church community that share in both joy and pain. Paul points this out: "If one part suffers, every part suffers with it; if one part is honored, every part rejoices with it" (1 Cor. 12:26). However, believers who still have a fallen sinful nature experience in their lives that it is not as easy as it sounds to rejoice together and grieve together. They find within themselves the contradiction of feeling jealous when others rejoice and comforted when others suffer, knowing that they don't suffer the same suffering.

It is characteristic of the image of God to feel the pain and pleasure of others as one's own. God is 100 percent empathetic. So when he created Adam and Eve, he gave them the ability to empathize. The problem is that this ability has been compromised since the fall of Adam. Because fallen humans are born with a narcissistic nature, we don't have the ability to empathize 100 percent like God does. They may empathize 100 percent very shortly, but it's impossible for us to have a 100 percent empathetic heart consistently on this earth.

---

[155] Bridges connected the proverb, "Each heart knows its own bitterness" with 1 Cor. 2:11, which says, "For who knows a person's thoughts except their own spirit within them? In the same way no one knows the thoughts of God except the Spirit of God." Bridges, *Proverbs*, 175-76.

So, sadly, we must humbly accept the reality that true empathy is not something we can experience on this earth. Even in the more idealized setting of counseling, both counselor and client must accept this limitation of reality.

This proverb points out this heartbreaking reality. No parents can empathize with their child 100 percent. They don't know 100 percent what their children are thinking or feeling. Even if they do open up to their parents, it's very difficult to empathize with the depth of their feelings. Even in happy couples who say they can read each other's minds by looking into each other's eyes, it's impossible to be 100 percent empathetic consistently. This is because even while empathizing, human beings are naturally inclined to rejoice and grieve for themselves. This is the same way that pride can creep in, consciously or unconsciously, even in moments of humility.

Counseling Application: Clients feel renewed and encouraged by talking with a counselor who empathizes with them, although it is temporary and limited. This is the same way a "good enough" parental experience is experienced as a "good object" relation experience by a child. When we know and accept our reality that our ability of empathy is limited, we can be less frustrated and less angry when others don't fully empathize with us.

The house of the wicked will be destroyed, but the tent of the upright will flourish (14:11).

The house of those who are not recognized by God is destroyed (11a). Like building the Tower of Babel, those who seek to make a name for themselves and develop a human-centered secular city or secular nation will eventually collapse. No matter how hard they try, if God is not pleased with their plans, they will fail. The houses of the wicked and the castles of wicked people may be built strong, but God will use an earthquake to destroy them.

But the tent of the upright, though shabby and frail, will gradually increase in size (11b).[156] For God blesses those who belong to it.

---

[156] Noting that "house" and "tent" are paired expressions in Hebrew poetry, Clifford

There is a way that appears to be right, but in the end it leads to death (14:12).[157]

Even if most people see a path as wrong, some people may perceive it as right. This statement has both positive and negative connotations. In a positive sense, it means that a path that some people see as right is abnormal. This is when some people insist that something is normal even though most people with common sense would say it's not. For example, a schizophrenic's perception of reality is delusional and hallucinatory to most people. But because the sufferer experiences it as real, he or she thinks everyone else is looking at it wrong. This is a path to destruction. This is a path to ruin, because staying in a schizophrenic state disrupts the functioning of the mind and severely impairs the ability to test reality.

However, the negative implication is that the path that seems right to most people is not necessarily the right path. The path of the unbelieving world is wide, and the number of people walking it is much greater. But the way of the followers of Jesus Christ is narrow, and they are relatively in small number. Therefore, the way of the believers appears to be abnormal to many. But the Bible declares that this narrow way is the way to life.

Thus, those who choose and follow a religion because it looks good in their eyes, or makes sense in their minds, will be led to death absolutely. For Christians who live in this modern world influenced by post-modernism, this proverb, "There is a way that appears to be right, but in the end it leads to death," blows a trumpet of warning.

comments that the wicked's sturdily built "house" will crumble, but the righteous' "tent" will be strong and flourish. Clifford, *Proverbs*, 144.

[157] Clifford points out that the same proverb is also found in 16:25. Clifford, *Proverbs*, 145. Koptak also points this out, identifying 12:15 as a proverb with a similar meaning: "The way of fools seems right to them, but the wise listen to advice." Koptak, *Proverbs*, 376.

Even in laughter the heart may ache, and rejoicing may end in grief (14:13).

Solomon well understands and describes the contradictory and paradoxical nature of human heart and mind. Life is a process filled with ups and downs. Even in moments of laughter, there is unconscious sadness deep inside. This is because humans can experience ambivalent feelings. We can be happy and sad at the same time. We can hate someone and miss them contradictorily. And just as this proverb says, at the end of the joy we experience, there is also sadness. There is a time to laugh and a time to weep (see Eccl. 3:4). Those who understands and accepts this reality are mature persons.

Counseling Application: Some people with depression are so deeply depressed that they can't imagine there will ever be a day in their lives when they feel joy and happiness. Some people are so deeply saddened by the loss of a loved one that they can't imagine ever smiling again. Counselors need to understand and empathize with these clients. They also need to encourage them that "there is a time for everything" and joy and happiness will "surely" come, like the tide rising after low tide.

The faithless will be fully repaid for their ways, and the good rewarded for theirs (14:14).

The word "faithless" has multiple meanings. First, it means "untrustworthy" and "unfaithful." Second, it means "undependable" (of a person or tool). Third, it can mean "without conviction," "skeptical," or "unbelieving." These multiple meanings can all be applied to this proverb. The good have the opposite characteristics against the faithless.

In the first sense, "untrustworthy" people cannot gain others' trust in their interpersonal relationships. So it's hard for them to get help when they're in trouble. They are more likely to be fired from their jobs. They are more likely to lose trust from their spouse or get divorced. These people with a crooked heart bring bad consequences to their own issues (14a). In the second sense, no one would entrust a job to someone they can't depend on. In the third sense, no one follows or respects a leader who has little conviction. Skeptical and negative people don't get anything done. They will demotivate others. And those who have "no faith" in God will receive the retribution of their lives (14a): the dreadful judgment of God.

But the good who are faithful and sincere and keeps his marriage vows, will experience a good reward and recognition worthy of their faithful life. Those who are trustworthy, firm in their convictions, positive, and devout in their Christian faith will be rewarded by God (14b).

The simple believe anything, but the prudent give thought to their steps. The wise fear the LORD and shun evil, but a fool is hotheaded and yet feels secure [hotheaded and reckless] (14:15-16).

This proverb has a chiastic form of A-B-B'-A'. The simple are fools. The word "simple" is sometimes used in a positive sense, such as "pure." However, in the Book of Proverbs "simple" is most often meant in the sense of being foolish and therefore susceptible to deception. The simple are foolish enough to believe anything. They don't have the ability to think in multiple ways. They are like a child. They just believe lies and deceptive words without any questioning.

The simple are susceptible to heresy. They do not have the ability to discern the false teachings of their teachers. The enthusiasm and family-like atmosphere of the cult community make them easily indoctrinated into its teachings. They say "amen" and follow whatever their leader teaches. They are very vulnerable to gaslighting. It is not surprising that many followers of cults are adult children from dysfunctional families. Adult children has an issue of codependency and have a low level of self-differentiation and low self-esteem. So they easily conform to authority figures and their teachings and are unable to think independently.

A quick-tempered person does foolish things, and the one who devises evil schemes [a crafty man] is hated (14:17).[158]

The second half of this proverb expands on the characteristics of the fool mentioned in the first half. In the context of chapter 14 as a whole, one of the symptoms of the foolish is "being easily angered" (17a). This is similar to the characteristic of being "hotheaded and reckless" of fools mentioned in verse 16.

People who have anger management problem and are easily angered by minor provocations are very likely to act foolishly (17a). Hurting others by getting angry easily is a self-defeating behavior. The people around them don't want to be around them. So they lose their family and friends.

The second part of this proverbs doesn't match smoothly with the first. However, if we understand craftiness as another aspect of foolishness and evil, the proverb makes sense: a crafty person is actually a fool. Deceitful people think they are intelligent, but in the end they will be found to be fools. People despise the deceitful and their lying lips. God also abhors "the one who devises evil schemes" (17b) and hates the devil, the father of lies.

The simple inherit folly, but the prudent are crowned with knowledge (14:18).[159]

---

[158] Clifford insightfully comments on the text that it is just as bad to act without reflection as it is to act with evil thoughts. Clifford, *Proverbs*, 145.

[159] Clifford notes that in Proverbs, crowns are symbols of God's blessing, noting that a good wife is a crown to her husband (12:4), gray hair is a crown to the righteous (16:31), and grandchildren are a crown to their grandparents (17:6). Clifford, *Proverbs*, 146. The proverb in 14:24 says, "The wealth of the wise is their crown."

The word "crowned" brings up the image of a royal crown that a king passes on to his successor, a prince. To pass on a crown means to pass on the political, mental, and spiritual legacy of the previous king. A thoughtful prince as the new king will govern his people well by following his predecessor's legacy of knowledge, character, and accomplishments. He will also pass this legacy on to the next generation of princes.

But the simple and foolish do not receive knowledge as an inheritance. Especially they cannot inherit the knowledge of the LORD. Even if it is given to them as an inheritance, they will throw it away. Because they are proud, they do as they think. They inherit only foolishness. Such a prince is, in a word, foolish and stupid. King Rehoboam is a good example. He must have been taught and admonished by Solomon as the first recipient of Proverbs. However, he did not internalize his father's wisdom and understanding. He rejected the wise counsel of the elders who had worked for his father Solomon. He did not inherit the good things that should be inherited from his father, but only the bad things. Because of his foolish judgment, Israel was divided into two kingdom, the northern Israel and Judah.

As one sows, so shall he or she reap. Children raised by dysfunctional parents are at great risk of becoming psychologically immature adults. However, it is possible to have mature, faithful children even in dysfunctional environments exceptionally. Conversely, some functional, pious families may produce an unbelieving, immature child. Therefore, naturalistic causation need to be applied to understanding our family life and personal life with some exceptions. It is not wise and even dangerous to make a blanket statement. Life is a mystery that cannot be understood.

Evildoers will bow down in the presence of the good, and the wicked at the gates of the righteous (14:19).

This proverb says that evildoers and the unrighteous will fall before the good and the righteous. For a time, the wicked may prevail, sitting in high places and exercising power for evil. But evil will never overcome good, so the believer must overcome evil with good (see Rom. 12:21). It is not God's way to use the same evil methods that the evil one uses. When we fight evil with good, good is unwavering because it is true. Evil must eventually be defeated.

Joseph's brothers plotted to kill him, sold him into slavery, and deceived his father Jacob. Evil seemed to triumph and prevail. The truth seemed to be covered up. But their evil was finally exposed in the face of good after many years. The brothers literally "bowed down" before their brother Joseph as those who came to buy food (19a). Not only that, but when the truth was finally revealed, they had to kneel before him and beg for forgiveness.

The poor are shunned even by their neighbors, but the rich have many friends. It is a sin to despise one's neighbor, but blessed is the one who is kind to the needy (14:20-21).

"Neighbor" in verses 20 and 21 have different meanings. In the context of verse 21, one's neighbor means "the needy" or "the one who asks for help." However, in the context of verse 20, neighbors of the poor mean neighbors in the general sense. The poor and the needy in verses 20 and 21 also have different meanings. The poor in verse 20 have a negative connotation, while the needy in verse 21 have a positive connotation.

In verse 20, Solomon encourages the audience to work diligently to become financially independent because when people become poor, even their neighbors avoid them. The reality is that the wealthy have many visitors and friends (20b). But Solomon goes on to warn that it is a sin to hate or look down on the poor, one's neighbor (21a).

It is the way of the world that the poor are seen as a burden and sometimes ignored, even by their neighbors and friends. Even their neighbors dislike and avoid the poor. But believers should not ignore or despise the poor. Rather, they should actively empathize with them and show them mercy. Blessed are those who are kind and generous to them (21b).

The needy are the weak or the minor. They may be economically poor or facing other forms of hardship in their lives. In the parable of the Good Samaritan, the person in need was the man who was robbed; his neighbor was the "one who showed mercy," the Samaritan. To the Samaritan, Jews were not his neighbors. To Jews, Samaritans were not their neighbors. But Jesus expanded the Jewish concept of neighbors. He said that the one who showed mercy, or the one in need, was the true neighbor.

The Samaritan in the parable was blessed (21b). He was recognized by Jesus. On the other hand, the priest and the Levite who "saw" the situation of robbery but "did not have pity" on him (the Samaritan "took pity on" him), but ignored him, were guilty of "no mercy" (21a).

Christians are those who are commanded by the law to "love your neighbor as yourself." Compassion for those in need and concrete acts of mercy should be the hallmark of our lives.

Counseling Application: Christian counseling is an expression of neighborly love. Christian counseling is a process of compassion and mercy for those in need. Therefore, Christian counselors must have both empathy and compassion for those in need. Individuals with severe narcissistic personality disorder or schizotypal personality disorder are very poor candidates to become counselors.[160]

Do not those who plot evil go astray?[161] But those who plan

---

[160] One of the symptoms of narcissistic personality disorder is a lack of empathy and disregard for those who are weaker than the person with the disorder. One of the symptoms of schizoid personality disorder is a lack of even basic concern for others. It's very difficult for someone with that disorder to feel compassion for people in need. They live a self-sufficient, emotionally detached life from others, like an island, with little interaction with the outside world.

[161] Bridges observed that those who "plot evil" are likely to be intellectually superior in areas other than good. Bridges, *Proverbs*, 184. People with antisocial personality disorder and psychopath are often intellectually gifted. It is difficult for a person of average intellectual ability to engage in antisocial behavior, such as fraud.

what is good find love and faithfulness (14:22).

The first half of this proverb is characterized by an interrogative phrase. This change in wording can be understood as a way to get the attention of the listeners of Proverbs.

Those who plan and promote evil things are already out of the straight, righteous way (22a). Their ends are destruction. God's love and faithfulness do not work in them. And there is no mercy or faithfulness to be found in them. But the good who plan and promote good works are people of love and faithfulness (22b).

All hard work brings a profit, but mere talk leads only to poverty (14:23).[162]

This proverb emphasizes the importance of practice and praxis. Theory is important. The words of our lips are important. But if all you have is theory and words, you have no power. Words alone don't change lives. In a sense, they don't benefit anyone. It's just empty talk. It is only when there is concrete action, effort, and labor that life changes and benefits.

The same is true of Christian faith and theology. Mere talk has no power (23b). In fact, those who only talk the talk are rather disgusting. The LORD praises those who are diligent with their hands and feet and who are sincere, even if they are slow of speech and tongue. There is a mocking statement in Korean societies that if Christians are drowning, their mouth is the only part that floats. It means that Christians are very good in talking but not good in their real lives. It's a bitter saying that contains a grain of truth.

Simply saying something but not doing it is a form of lying. If you say you're going to do something and then don't do it, it's deception. Jesus rebuked these people. For example, they would withhold something from their parents by saying "*Corban*" that

---

[162] Bridges understood that this proverb cannot be applied in a universal sense, since the fruit of labor as a servant of sin is death (Rom. 6:21), and the fruit of well-taught lips is clearly positive (cf. Prov. 10:21, 15:7). Bridges, *Proverbs*, 185.

means "devoted to God" without actually giving it to God and to parents either (see Mark 7:11-13). They were only greedy but poor and blind spiritually (23b).

The wealth of the wise is their crown, but the folly of fools yields folly (14:24).

Both wise and foolish people can live in wealth. There are also nouveaux riches. People who suddenly became wealthy and live in a nice house, driving around in an expensive foreign car, are nouveaux riches, even if they try to hide their inner being. Because they became rich overnight, it is difficult to find the character or cultivation to match their wealth.

For wise Solomon, riches were the icing on the cake. Instead of riches or honor, he prayed God for wisdom. As a crowned king, he ruled with wisdom. His incredible wisdom even brought the Queen of Sheba to him with great gifts.

The wise and rich don't think of their wealth as their own. They want to be used as good stewards before God, so they give generously and relieve the poor with compassion. Such people are like trees planted by the waters and they are ever green and fruitful. They benefit those in need and provide them with shade.

A truthful witness saves lives, but a false witness is deceitful (14:25).

It only takes one true witness to help a person in trouble. However, false witnesses drive a stake through the heart of a person in trouble, causing him or her and his or her family to suffer. If a judge sentences him or her to death based on perjury, false witnesses are guilty of murder. It is more natural to read the second part of this proverb as "a false witness kills lives" rather than "a false witness is deceitful" according to the chiastic form.

Jesus Christ is a true witness. He said that he speaks as he has seen and heard: "For I did not speak on my own, but the Father who sent me commanded me to say all that I have spoken" (John 12:49). The testimony of Jesus is the word of life. Whoever hears his word and accepts it has eternal life (25a).

Whoever fears the LORD has a secure fortress, and for their children it will be a refuge. The fear of the LORD is a fountain of life, turning a person from the snares of death (14:26-27).

Solomon reemphasizes the importance of "fearing the LORD" in this proverb. "A secure fortress" is linked with "a fountain of life." "A refuge" is contrasted with "the snares of death." A secure fortress is a place of security and safety. The secure fortress and the fountain of life are promised and guaranteed to those who fear the LORD. The fortress serves as a refuge, not only for them, but also for their children (26b). God protects those who fear him and helps them not to fall into the snares of death or the traps of destruction (27b).

David, Solomon's father, was a living witness to this proverb. He was pursued by King Saul and threatened with death on numerous occasions. Later, he faced life-threatening hardships, such as the danger of abdication because of his son Absalom's treason. But God bound him "securely the bundle of the living" (1 Sam. 25:29), protecting and preserving him and his son Solomon, from Adonijah's rebellion and eventually making him king to succeed his father.

Fear of God is the core issue for Christians. If believers do not fear God, they do not yet know God well. Loving God and yet fearing him must be your basic attitude in your life.

A large population is a king's glory, but without subjects a prince is ruined (14:28).[163]

---

[163] Bridges insightfully commented that it is to God's glory that so many people are saved by the King of the kingdom of God: "After this I looked, and there before me

In most cases, the number of people and the power of a country are proportional. The more people it has, the stronger its military, the more taxes, and the stronger its finances. Countries like the United States, China, and India, with populations in the hundreds of millions, cannot be taken lightly by other countries. Weaker or less populous countries, however, are often ignored or even attacked by strong countries and even their presidents may not be recognized by leaders of other strong countries.

A family with many children or many relatives is strong and powerful. But families with few offspring or few relatives are often shunned by others, especially in times of trouble. In his psalm, Solomon compare those with many children to those whose quivers are full of arrows. He well points out this reality when he wrote, "They will not be put to shame when they contend with their opponents in court" (Ps. 127:5).

Whoever is patient has great understanding, but one who is quick-tempered displays folly (14:29). See also 14:17, 15:18.

The patient are not quick-tempered. They are able to control and manage anger. They can see the whole picture with their great understanding (29a), so they are not easily angered.

God is slow to anger because he sees the big picture and has the enormous strength to be patient. This is exemplified in the attribute of love expressed in 1 Cor. 13:4-7. God is patient, kind, not easily angered and always perseveres.

Those who are easily angered expose their foolishness (29b). They are psychologically immature. Their ego strength to control anger is undeveloped.

After aggression is expressed, some angry people may be able to calm down for themselves. However, because they are so self-centered, they are unable to empathize with the other persons who

was *a great multitude that no one could count*, from every nation, tribe, people and language, standing before the throne and before the Lamb" (Rev. 7:9). Bridges, *Proverbs*, 189.

are wounded by their aggressive words or behaviors. And they may rationalize that they don't hold a grudge. Therefore, they are very likely to repeat the same pattern of being angry. They don't feel their need to be changed. They are called fools in Proverbs (29b).

A heart at peace gives life to the body, but envy rots the bones (14:30).[164]

Connecting with verse 29, those who are easily angered is not peaceful in their heart. Anger is most often a response to a threat. So if the object of their envy threaten their self-esteem, their envy is likely to lead to their anger. Those who are vulnerable to envy and anger cannot maintain a calm mind (30a).

When envy and anger rule one's heart and mind, his or her bones are rotten (30b). In this proverb, "bones" means "whole body." This proverb teaches us that if we are not at peace in our heart and mind, we are prone to illness. Those who harbor envy or anger despite the fact that their body and bones are damaged are foolish: they are actually self-defeating and committing suicide very slowly.

There's a lot of research on the mind-body connection. For example, stress has been shown to contribute to heart disease and cancer. Conversely, studies have shown that laughter can be effective in treating cancer. "Psychosomatic" diseases are strongly associated with psychological causes.

In this way, the mind and body are closely interacted. When you are joyful and peaceful, your body recovers or heals quickly (30a). Conversely, when you are sick, the peace of mind is disturbed. A balanced understanding of the relationship between mind and body is necessary for us to live out our Christian life well. Furthermore, we also need to understand that our body and mind affect our spiritual life as well, and vice versa.

Counseling Application: Anger and envy eventually take their

---

[164] Clifford notes that "flesh" and "bone" are often paired in the Bible (e.g., Gen. 2:23, Judg. 9:2, Job 2:5), but only occur in this text in Proverbs. Clifford, *Proverbs*, 147.

193

toll. They can damage our body and bones and lead to life-threatening illnesses. Rheumatoid arthritis is correlated with prolonged periods of stress for some people who struggle with that disease. Unforgiving, repressing or holding on to anger and retaliation, damages the body and mind. Recent research in the psychology of forgiveness has demonstrated that the primary beneficiary of forgiveness is the forgiver.

Whoever oppresses the poor shows contempt for their Maker, but whoever is kind to the needy honors God (14:31).

In verse 21 of the same chapter, Solomon condemns the passive behavior of not having compassion for those in need, or ignoring them. In this passage, he condemns the wicked who actively oppress, abuse, and exploit those in need rather than show mercy.

Surprisingly, this proverb declares that God identifies with the poor. Those who abuse and oppress those in need or the poor actually despise their Maker the LORD (31a). On the other hand, those who show kindness and mercy to the poor honor him (31b). Those who empathize with the poor please him.

When calamity comes, the wicked are brought down, but even in death the righteous seek refuge [have refuge] in God (14:32).

When disasters like earthquakes and floods occur, the wicked and the righteous die together. This is because disasters don't single out the wicked. It's the same way that radiation therapy or chemotherapy doesn't just kill malignant cells, but often kills healthy cells as well.

This world is a world broken by sin, and the wicked and the good live together. The wicked are benefited with God's common grace too all. However, when natural disasters occur, the good suffer along with the wicked, and so they may die together with the wicked.

The righteous may live or die, but they belong to Jesus Christ.

Blessed are those who die in the Lord. Those who die naturally at their old age are not necessarily blessed. The manner of death is not really important. Those who are really blessed are Christians who have a refuge after death, a home to return to, and citizenship in the eternal kingdom of God. But the wicked have no hope after death. Only the eternal damnation of hell awaits them. When the wicked are afflicted, they fall down and are destroyed (32a).

Again, even believers in Jesus may die in disasters! Their bodies may never be found. But this is not so important, for those who are in Christ, there is a resurrection and eternal life. There is an eternal refuge for us.

Therefore, Christians are ultimately fearless. We know that if we live, we live for the Lord, and if we die, we die for the Lord. We believe that death is a rite of passage into eternal life.

Wisdom reposes in the heart of the discerning and even among fools she lets herself be known (14:33).

This proverb suggests that even the most foolish person may have a bit of wisdom in them. Even in the totally depraved human beings, there are some reserved parts of God's image that are still functioning as common grace. God's wisdom is revealed even in sinful humans and creation. The process of helping people to put this universal wisdom to good use so that they can gradually overcome the foolishness of their daily lives is the process of secular counseling.

The phrase "wisdom reposes in the heart" means that wisdom becomes part of "self" of the discerning. Conversely, foolishness abides in the heart of the foolish. This also means that foolishness becomes part of "self" of the foolish. So their foolishness is known and revealed (33b).

Righteousness exalts a nation, but sin condemns [sin is a disgrace to] any people (14:34).

When the leader is unjust, the people are humiliated. On the other hand, when the leader is upright, the people are honored. When the denominational leaders are just and noble, its stature is elevated. Its local pastors and members are respected. But when a denomination is stigmatized, its pastors and members experience shame.

The same is true for families. Family members in a functional family are proud of their family. But those who are members of a dysfunctional family are not proud of their family and themselves. One of the core issues for adult children of alcoholics (ACOA) is shame.

A king delights in a wise servant, but a shameful servant arouses [incurs] his fury [wrath] (14:35).

In verse 28, a glorious king and a disgraced king are compared through the king's relationship with his people. In this proverb, a wise subject of a king is compared to a shameful servant of the king.

A king must have subjects. Throughout the history of kingdoms, kings have loyalists and disloyalists. No king or president likes to have distrustful henchmen. They can betray him or her at any time. They may act like loyalists at first, so the king needs to be wise and discerning enough to have trustful subjects around him or her.

Chapter 15 Be Slow to Anger

A gentle answer turns away wrath, but a harsh word stirs up anger (15:1). See 15:18.

There is a common saying, "What goes around, comes around." This phrase means that if you say something harsh, the other person will react harshly. Anyway, if someone respond to the other person's anger with anger, he or she can fuel the flames of the other person's anger.[165] But even when the other person says something harsh, one can defuse the other's anger by responding gently (1a).

In chapter 14, Solomon reiterates the foolishness of the "easily angered" twice. At the beginning of chapter 15, Solomon again brings the issue of anger to the forefront.

An incident early in Solomon's reign gives us a glimpse of Solomon's coping with his anger. His brother Adonijah, who had been a political opponent, petitioned Solomon's mother, Bathsheba, to allow him to take Abishag the Shunammite who had been David's caretaker in his old age, as his wife. Bathsheba then took his request directly to Solomon. At this point, the following text does not say that Solomon was angry, but his words and actions well describe his anxiety, displeasure, and anger at the threat of Adonijah to his throne:

> King Solomon answered his mother, "Why do you request Abishag the Shunammite for Adonijah? You might as well request the kingdom for him—after all, he is my older brother—

---

[165] Bridges commented that smooth words are like water that quenches a fire, while provoking words are like oil that makes the flames burn more intensely. Bridges, *Proverbs*, 196. James makes a similar point about the negative power of the tongue: "Likewise, the tongue is a small part of the body, but it makes great boasts. Consider what a great forest is set on fire by a small spark. The tongue also is a fire, a world of evil among the parts of the body. It corrupts the whole body, sets the whole course of one's life on fire, and is itself set on fire by hell" (James 3:5-6).

yes, for him and for Abiathar the priest and Joab son of Zeruiah!" Then King Solomon swore by the LORD: "May God deal with me, be it ever so severely, if Adonijah does not pay with his life for this request! And now, as surely as the LORD lives—he who has established me securely on the throne of my father David and has founded a dynasty for me as he promised—Adonijah shall be put to death today!" So King Solomon gave orders to Benaiah son of Johoiada, and he struck down Adoniah and he died (1 Kings 2:22-25).

Adonijah's unwise, boundary-crossing words provoked Solomon with anger (1b), and he was eventually killed for his words. Solomon used the energy of this anger to get rid of his brother Adonijah, who could have been an obstacle to his dynasty. The writer of 1 Kings described his actions without any judgment.

An excellent example of defusing anger with a gracious response can be found in Abigail's response to David's anger. He was enraged by the disrespectful behavior of her husband Nabal. When she heard about what had happened, she prepared some food quickly and sent her servants ahead of her with that food. And she rode her donkey and met David and his men who were going to kill her husband and all men who belonged to him. She fell at David's feet and pleaded, "Pardon your servant, my lord, and let me speak to you; hear what your servant has to say. Please pay no attention, my lord, to that wicked man Nabal. He is just like his name—his name means Fool, and folly goes with him. And as for me, your servant, I did not see the men my lord sent" (1 Sam. 25:24-25). She was a woman who had the calmness and wisdom to empathize with David who was angered with his murderous rage. She spoke empathically and reasonably. And she spoke with sincerity. And she spoke with "wisdom and authority," as if God was speaking to him through her mouth. In particular, she told him that when he became king, she didn't want him to be stumbled in his conscience by the memory that he had avenged by killing Nabal, a stubborn, foolish man, or that he had shed blood needlessly. Those soothing words helped him to see the meta-narratives and the big picture of God at work beyond the event. Finally, David admired and thanked her for her wisdom, saying, "May you be blessed for your good judgment and for keeping me from bloodshed this day and from avenging myself with my own hands" (1 Sam. 25:33).

Anger causes anxiety, and vice versa. In any case, it's hard to speak wisely and gently when you're anxious or angry. Rather, it's easy to speak defensively or aggressively. It's also easy to make excuses. But those who manage their anxiety and anger well are able to speak wisely and empathetically to defuse the other person's anger (1a).

The tongue of the wise adorns [commends] knowledge, but the mouth of the fool gushes folly (15:2). See 14:34.

A new meaning of this proverb is possible when this verse is connected to verse 1. The tongue and mouth of the wise have knowledge that can calm the anger of others. The tongue and mouth of the foolish, on the other hand, are filled with foolishness, which stirs up the anger of the other person by gushing harsh words.

The mouth of the wise honors knowledge, praising and encouraging knowledge (2a). It especially honors and praises those who seek knowledge of God. But the mouth of the foolish honors what the world says is wisdom. They are not ashamed of their ignorance of God, and they speak with contempt (2b).

The eyes of the LORD are everywhere, keeping watch on the wicked and the good (15:3).

This proverb expresses God's omniscience and omnipresence.[166] God cares about both the wicked and the good. His intentions are different, of course.

---

[166] Fox connects this proverb with verse 11 of the same chapter: "Death and Destruction lie open before the LORD—how much more do human hearts!" Fox, *Proverbs 10-31*, 589.

It is a great comfort to the righteous to know that God is watching them in secret. God knows and sees Christians who suffer. He hears their cryings of prayer. God sees and hears, even if all other people do not. God is not a liar. When he says he sees, he sees.

God is a righteous judge. He watches the wicked in secret and eventually establishes justice by judging them. This fact is a great comfort to the righteous. Although God's justice often does not seem to be realized in the real world, God surely brings judgment on the wicked.

The knowledge that God's eyes are everywhere is a great comfort to the good, but it causes fear and anxiety to the wicked. The knowledge of God's omnipresence and omniscience is like a double-edged sword. It is both comforting and frightening. If the wicked could see directly in hallucination that God is watching them, they would be too afraid to sin. They would be overwhelmed with fear and terror and would develop anxiety disorders, panic attacks, or schizophrenia. They will be mentally broken. Actually we can manage our mental health by using defense mechanisms such as denial and repression of God's omnipresence.

The development of modern technology has made it possible to speak more eloquently about the ubiquity of God's eyes and how accurately he sees. We live in a world where CCTV cameras are installed on streets and buildings to monitor the every move of passersby. The technology for capturing and transmitting real-time images from satellites has improved dramatically to the point where we can see objects on the ground clearly down to 30 centimeters across. To exaggerate, we can even see an ant moving on the ground. Satellites circling the Earth are constantly capturing the surface of the planet with cameras from far away. It has become a world in which the state can spy on the private lives of individuals if it wants to. Considering that man-made technology is developing to such an astonishing degree that humans themselves are amazed, God's power and technology are incomparably "amazing and wonderful."[167]

Counseling Application: Recognizing God's omnipresence and omniscience is powerful for the client. Becoming "conscious" of

---

[167] "Does he who fashioned the ear not hear? Does he who formed the eye not see?" (Ps. 94:9).

the fact that God's eyes and ears are "present" in the counseling room, watching and listening, is a great strength and challenge for both the Christian counselor and the client. Especially in the case of a client who is suffering from a relationship with the wicked, the realization that God's eyes are watching over the life of the wicked gives the client comfort and hope. It gives him or her ability to persevere to the end.

The soothing tongue is a tree of life, but a perverse [deceitful] tongue crushes the spirit (15:4).

This proverb is connected with verse 2. The tongue of the wise not only imparts knowledge to the listener for good, but it also brings healing. A corrupt tongue pours out foolishness and even lies. The result is anti-therapeutic. It crushes and breaks the other person's heart.

This proverb points out the importance of therapeutic words. Healing words restore broken hearts and broken minds. Therapeutic speech is like the tree of life in the Garden of Eden. Ezekiel saw in a vision that the water flowing out of the temple formed a river. The tree of life was like the fruit trees on the right and left sides of the river in the vision: "Their fruit will serve for food and their leaves for healing" (Ezek. 47:12).

There are some people who are like a tree of life. They provide shade for the weary. They provide delicious fruit for the hungry and thirsty. They are "good objects," "therapeutic objects" to them.

On the other hand, there are also many people who, like the thorns, are lonely themselves, unable to give anyone rest and joy. The lyrics of a Korean song "Thorns" describe these people well:

> There's so much of me in me, there's no place for you to rest
> There's no place for you in my heart, with all my vain wishes.
> There's a darkness inside me that I can't control, that takes away your place to rest
> Inside me is a forest of thorns, a grief I can't win.
>
> And when the wind blows, the parched branches cry out to each other.

201

> Young birds flying exhausted in search of a place to rest were pierced by thorns and flew away.
> Whenever the wind blew, I felt lonely and painful and sang sad songs many days.

The poet, Deok-kyu Ha, well-known Korean Christian singer and pastor, like the thorn, is aware that his inner world is divided into many parts and that there is little space in his inner world for others to rest comfortably, including his family. He confesses to his past of pursuing vain hopes and delusions while remaining ungrounded in reality, causing the hearts of those around him to feel sad. The poet sings that there is an unconscious dynamic within him that he cannot control, and that there is a pain and suffering of loss that he cannot overcome by himself. He acknowledges that there is not just one thorny tree, but a lush forest of thorns, making it difficult to change anything by touching one or two. He is also well aware that when the storms of life come, the lifeless, withered branches, striking to one another and screaming that they are painful, are his own reflection and the reflection of his family. He grieves that even the tired young children who have flown back to get empathy and love in their father or mother's arms are hurt by the aggressive words that come from the parents' unrestrained hearts. So they become strangers who do not open their hearts even when they stay at home. Or he has to watch helplessly as they run away from home. The poet's self-portrait of himself, unable to cope with the winds that blow, only feeling sadness, pain, and self-pity for himself and singing a sad song because he is consumed by pain and sorrow, is also a self-portrait of many modern people living today. The families of believers are no exception.

A thorn tree can be turned into a tree of life with the gospel. A cross of shame can be turned into a cross of glory. Only the gospel can transform lives like the thorns.

A fool spurns a parent's discipline, but whoever heeds correction shows prudence (15:5).[168]

Foolish children or students dismiss and ignore parental admonitions or their teacher's guidance (5a). They think they are smart, and therefore their ideas are better than those of their parents or teachers. "True" fools cannot obey their parent's instruction because they don't have cognitive ability to understand it. However, the fools referred to in this proverb is "smart" fools. They have the same dynamic as adolescent children rebelling against their parents, ignoring their teachings and acting out of their own will.

Parents of teenagers need psychological maturity when it comes to discipline. Immature parents fight with their children or blindly ignore their ideas. Or they become helpless in the face of their child's aggression. They may tell their child to leave the house because they can't cope with their conflicts well. These parents are not equipped to handle aggression from their teenagers. This is because they are immature and foolish.

It is through this period of rebellion that the child develops integrated psychological functioning. Therefore, parents need to have faith and trust that their child, though rebellious at the moment, will grow into a child with a balanced development of independence and dependence. Christian parents need the psychological and spiritual capacity to trust, hope, persevere, and endure. They need the wisdom to see the big picture.

Too much nagging will only lead to rebellion. Realize that nagging is rarely digested by your child, so you can cut back.

Those who willingly digest admonitions and teachings and incorporate them into their lives are thoughtful and prudent (5b). Children who see through the crudeness of their parents' expressions and understand their heart are ones who have matured considerably. They don't take what parents say out of love and concern for them as nagging or annoying. They respect their parents despite their own shortcomings.

This dynamic is paralleled in our relationship with God. Those who obey God's Word by faith are wise. Those who violate or disobey God's Word are foolish and unwise. Those who are

---

[168] Bridges rightly pointed out that Solomon's wisdom was a gift from God, but it also resulted from his heeding the precepts of his father David. Bridges, *Proverbs*, 199.

narcissistic are spiritually foolish. They presume their own thoughts to be better than God's Word. In short, they are arrogant. They even judge God's Word, adding to it and subtracting from it.

The house of the righteous contains great treasure, but the income of the wicked brings ruin [them trouble] (15:6).

This proverb can be interpreted in two ways. First, it means that in the house of the righteous there are many treasures, but in the house of the wicked there are no true treasures. Second, it means that the income of the wicked causes suffering, but the income of the righteous brings joy and happiness.

In the first sense, in the house of the righteous, wealth accumulates. It doesn't leak out. Their money doesn't rust. Thieves can't break through the walls and steal their riches (see Matt. 6:19-20). They don't run out of money after helping others. They afford to save.

We can apply this meaning to our faith. In the house of the righteous is the most precious treasure. As Jesus taught in the parable of the pearl merchants and the parable of the man who found the treasure in the ground, Christian home holds the treasure of faith, which is irreplaceable, like no other treasure in the world. A family that confesses and worships Jesus Christ as Lord is a family that possesses true treasure, though it may not have much wealth or honor.[169] The world does not realize that this treasure is of the greatest value.

Conversely, the house of the wicked may be full of visible gold and silver treasures, but the most important treasure is missing. An individual or family without faith in Jesus is missing the most valuable treasure in life. The rich man in the parable of Lazarus the beggar was not morally evil, but he was a wicked man because he

---

[169] Bridges pointed to 2 Cor. 6:10 as evidence, noting that in the house of the righteous there may be no money, but there is true treasure: "Sorrowful, yet always rejoicing; poor, yet making many rich; having nothing, and yet possessing everything." Bridges, *Proverbs*, 200.

did not have God-fearing faith.

This treasure is the seal of the Holy Spirit, which confirms that you have been redeemed by the blood of Christ and possess eternal life. It is the treasure that only confessing Christians possess. In the words of Revelation, the white stone with the new names written on it is the greatest treasure (Rev. 2:17). A family without this treasure is like a family where there is strife, as Solomon puts it, even though they may be full of feasting (Prov. 17:1).

But a family with this treasure can live in peace, giving thanks and loving one another, even over a humble table.[170] A family of believers can live proudly on earth as a family with true treasure. They have joy and peace that others do not know.

There is also a second meaning. The wicked's salary is used to cause suffering and hardship. The wicked only think that the salary they earn is the price of their labor and effort, so they are ungrateful. They think they have earned it, so they boast their work and their strength to their spouse. They even are stingy with their living expenses. And they spend the rest of the money as they please. Some people don't even tell their spouse how much they earn. These egocentric people are the ones who walk the path of the wicked. They spend their money on the wrong things, invest in fraudulent businesses, and get deeply in debt. They end up burdening and hurting their family. They neglect their spouse in managing their income, and later they are abandoned by their spouse when they fail.

But the righteous, who are grateful to God for giving them the opportunity and ability to earn money, have good stewardship. They manage their paychecks well, so they rarely suffer financially. They willingly offer tithes and other offerings and use their money for good works. They know how to use material things frugally but usefully for themselves and their families. The family of the righteous are happy and functional.

---

[170] Bridges noted the connection between this proverb and the proverbs that follow in verses 16 and 17: "Better a little with the fear of the LORD than great wealth with turmoil. Better a small serving of vegetables with love than a fattened calf with hatred." Bridges, *Proverbs*, 199.

The lips of the wise spread knowledge, but the hearts of fools are not upright [not so] (15:7).

This proverb is connected to verse 2. The words of the wise are preached and introduced to many people (7a). So is a good book. A good book is talked about, read, and loved by many. The Bible is the best book of all. It is a book that spreads the knowledge of God.

Foolish parents have nothing to teach their children. They don't have the ability to teach. Some parents are not educated enough to help their children study in middle or high school. They don't know, so they can't teach. Similarly, a person who is psychologically or spiritually unwise cannot teach, exhort, or preach to others about God, the source of all knowledge (see Col. 1:28).

To apply this proverb from another angle, the lips of the foolish also spread something. But their lips spread malice, rumors, and gossip, and so confuse others, the church, society, or the state. We now live in a world filled many fake news that spread easily.

The LORD detests the sacrifice of the wicked,[171] but the prayer of the upright pleases him. The LORD detests the way of the wicked, but he loves those who pursue righteousness. (15:8-9).

This proverb uses a chiastic form of A-B-A'-B' to emphasize the same message. God hates the sacrifice of the wicked. He considers the prayer of the wicked an abomination. He detest the way of the wicked. But God delights in the sacrifice of the upright. He

---

[171] Bridges connected this proverb to Eccl. 5:1, which says "Guard your steps when you go to the house of God. Go near to listen rather than to offer the sacrifice of fools, who do not know that they do wrong." Prov. 21:27 is also relevant: "The sacrifice of the wicked is detestable—how much more so when brought with evil intent!" Bridges, *Proverbs*, 201. The Old Testament speaks of sacrifices that God hates in many places. God spoke clearly through the prophets Isaiah and Malachi (see Isa. 1:13-15; Mal. 1:6-14).

responds to the prayers of the upright. He loves those who pursue righteous ways.

Cain's offering was the offering of the wicked. God was not pleased with his offering (8a). The Bible doesn't say exactly why, but what is clear is that he was wicked. He didn't have the honesty to find fault with himself when his offering was not accepted. Rather he was angry with God, and he transferred that anger to his brother Abel whose sacrifice was accepted and killed him.

Abel's sacrifice, on the other hand, was the sacrifice of the righteous. He became the first martyr who was killed unjustly for his worship. In the early church, Stephen's preaching was a sacrifice pleasing to God, but the wicked did not want to hear him preach and finally stoned him to death. But as he was dying, he was filled with the Holy Spirit and "saw the glory of God, and Jesus standing at the right hand of God. 'Look,' he said, 'I see heaven open and the Son of Man standing at the right hand of God'" (Acts 7:55-56). And he died praying, "Lord, do not hold this sin against them" (Acts 7:60). God was pleased with his sacrifice of the word, prayer, and martyrdom.

"The sacrifice of the wicked" and "the way of the wicked" are connected (8a, 9a). God not only hates the sacrifices of the wicked, but also the ways of the wicked. So the sacrifice of those who walk in the ways of the wicked cannot please him. He is disgusted with people who live in the world without regard to God and then come to church on the Lord's Day to attend services.

"The prayer of the upright" and "those who pursue righteousness" are connected (8b, 9b). God is pleased with those who seek first his righteousness and his kingdom in their lives, not just in prayer.[172] God recognizes such people and delights in their worship.

David was a man after God's own heart. He prayed to God in poetry and praise. And he lived a life sensitive to God's will. He was pursued, persecuted, and threatened with death by King Saul, but when the opportunity to kill him came, he sought God's righteousness. He didn't do it in a humanistic way. He loved his enemy according to God's will. When his enemy Saul died, he mourned his death. God loved him and was willing to make a covenant with him. He promised that his descendants would not be

---

[172] "To do what is right and just is more acceptable to the LORD than sacrifice" (21:3).

cut off from the throne, so that even when his descendants did not serve God faithfully, God remembered David and did not completely destroy Judah.

Even today, God is looking for his people who struggle to align their prayers with their lives. It is not difficult to pray for God's righteousness and kingdom. But it is difficult to live a life in which every decision is made with God's righteousness in mind. However, God is looking for believers who do.

Daniel and his three friends did not live like chameleon, following their own interests in the foreign country Babylon, although their homeland Judah had been destroyed and dismembered. Although their bodies were in Babylon, their hearts and souls were always in Jerusalem. Daniel actually prayed to God three times a day with his window open toward Jerusalem. He and his friends lived in the presence of the God they believed, confessed, and prayed to. His three friends were undaunted in the face of the extreme threat of being thrown into the fiery furnace for refusing to bow down to King Nebuchadnezzar's image. They kept their faith to the end. God was pleased with them and miraculously protected them from the scorching fiery furnace without a hair of their heads singed. And because of his faith in the LORD, Daniel was accused by the other princes and officials and thrown into the lion's den. But God protected him from the hungry lions' mouths. To this day, the faith and lives of Daniel and his three friends shine like bright stars in the night sky.

The Korean church is proud to have great believers like Daniel and his three friends. Many Christians including Rev. Yang-won Son, the protagonist of *The Atomic Bomb of Love*, who adopted and forgave a Communist young man who killed his sons in the Yo-Soon trouble of 1948; Rev. Ki-chul Joo who refused shrine worship in Japan's dominion and died in prison; and Elder Kwan-joon Park, whose name is inscribed on the stone monument in front of the Yangji Martyrs' Memorial. But the Korean church also has a shameful history, with many believers and pastors compromising in the face of persecution and death. So the Korean church has a history of honor and glory but shame as well.

Where do Korean churches stand today? Where do American churches stand today? This is the question we need to ask ourselves repeatedly. We must repent, awaken, and restore our martyr spirit. It must not be swept away by the tide of secularism. We must live a life that is as vital as a salmon swimming upstream.

Stern discipline awaits anyone who leaves the path; the one who hates correction will die. Death and Destruction lie open before the LORD—how much more do human hearts! Mockers resent correction, so they avoid the wise (15:10-12).

"Anyone who leaves the path," "the one who hates correction, " and "mocker" are the same person with with different names. The outcome of this person's life is "stern discipline" and "Death and Destruction" (10a, 11a). No one who sneaks off the path will escape God's severe discipline.[173] For God's eyes are on him (11b),[174] because "the eyes of the LORD are everywhere" (15:2a). And those who are chastened but do not turn will be put to death (10b). They will be cursed with eternal death.

Solomon well describes the characteristics of the arrogant in verse 12. Arrogant people and mockers dislikes any feedback that points out their faults or asks for correction. Furthermore, they

---

[173] God showed Ezekiel in a vision that the elders of Israel were worshiping idols in a secret place in the temple in Jerusalem. God was watching the elders worship idols in secret from the people: "So I went in and looked, and I saw portrayed all over the walls all kinds of crawling things and unclean animals and all the idols of Israel. In front of them stood seventy elders of Israel, and Jaazaniah son of Shaphan was standing among them. Each had a censer in his hand, and a fragrant cloud of incense was rising. He said to me, 'Son of man, have you seen what the elders of Israel are *doing in the darkness*, each at the shrine of his own idol? They say, '*The LORD does not see us*; the LORD has forsaken the land'." (Ezek. 8:10-12).

[174] Before God, the places of Death and Destruction are not closed off and unseen, but clearly exposed. The living human heart is also fully exposed before God. There is no distinction between light and darkness before God. Even in the darkness God sees as he sees in the light. That God knows the secrets and thoughts of each person's heart is a wisdom that cannot be comprehended by human understanding. This is in the same way that people of old could not fathom the fact that thousands of volumes of information can be saved on a USB storage device less than the size of a thumb.

become angry with the feedback giver. They never voluntarily seek advice or counsel from the wise or God.

Counseling Application: The closest clinical description of arrogant people is narcissistic personality disorder. People who identify with an exaggerated image of self as their real selves are unable to recognize their own shortcomings and limitations. And when confronted about their deficiencies or faults that they do not acknowledge, they become narcissistically wounded and very upset, and then counterattack. They defend themselves by denying, projecting or rationalizing.

Another group of people who are sensitive to negative feedback are those with paranoid personality disorder. They have a general distrust of people. As a result, they are more guarded than necessary. If they feel that someone says the slightest negative or offensive thing to them, they will immediately try to protect themselves by striking back. They tend to doubt the credibility of their friends and coworkers unfoundedly. As a result, they misunderstand the intentions of the person giving them feedback and don't take it at face value. They have an groundless fear that others will use what they say against them. So they don't open up, even to a counselor.

When counseling clients with prominent symptoms of narcissistic personality disorder or paranoid personality disorder, it is very important to keep in mind that they have little capacity to accept feedback from the counselor. Their primary need is for a listening, empathetic, and supportive counselor. If confrontation is necessary, it should be done with sensitivity and with a gradual escalation of the level of confrontation after a strong sense of therapeutic alliance is observed.

A happy heart makes the face cheerful, but heartache crushes the spirit (15:13).

The second half of this verse can be associated to the second half of verse 4, "a perverse tongue crushes the spirit." Then a deceitful tongue and heartache break the heart. A lying tongue or a hurtful tongue refers to words heard externally, but heartache comes from within. Of course, anxiety is often a response and consequence of external stimuli. But anxiety also come from internal conflicts, such as conflict between superego and id. The pain and anxiety of the heart can frustrate the mind and spirit. When your heart is hurting, your body can get sick.

The mind is adversely affected by negative feedback or words. Especially if your mind is vulnerable or already in a wounded state, you will be easily frustrated, easily angry, and easily depressed by negative words.[175]

But when you are happy and joyful with good words, your body becomes healthy. You become encouraged and have a positive outlook on the future.[176] You see yourself positively. You feel confident. This confidence is expressed in your words and behaviors. Your voice is strong and full of energy. Your face is naturally cheerful (13a). You smile often, with a radiant expression. You brighten not only your own face, but also the faces of those around them.

If the faces of Christians are darkened or frowning most time, they need to examine themselves.[177] It is truthful, of course, that you show hard faces when times are hard, but even in the midst of suffering, believers' face can shine brightly when it is filled with heavenly joy that sublimates suffering. This glow is not disguised.

Apostle Paul exhorts us to "rejoice always" (1 Thess. 5:16). This, he confirms, is the will of God for us.[178] A life of obedience to this

---

[175] Cognitive therapy understands that some people are vulnerable to depression because they already have a negative schema. The same negative environment will be perceived differently by a person with an already sick mind than by a person with a healthy mind.

[176] Cognitive therapy sees that perspectives and interpretations drive emotions, but it can also be seen as an interactive process in that perspectives and interpretations are sometimes shaped by emotional states.

[177] Bridges said that a person's face is the index of his or her soul in his note on this proverb. Bridges, *Proverbs*, 205.

[178] Paul's exhortation does not teach that Christians should not experience negative emotions or that they should suppress them. In this world we may experience sadness, anger, anxiety, or depression. God says that he will wipe away the flowing tears of believers in heaven (see Rev. 7:17). This means that tears may flow in the lives of

exhortation is holistically beneficial for us.

The discerning heart seeks knowledge, but the mouth of a fool feeds on folly (15:14).

This proverb can be connected to verse 7. While verse 7 characterizes the "lips" of the wise and the "heart" of the foolish, this proverb characterizes the "heart" of the wise and the "mouth" of the foolish. In verse 7, the lips of the wise spread knowledge. In verse 14, a discerning heart seeks knowledge.

To seek knowledge is to thirst after knowing God, the source and beginning of all knowledge. The wise seek the truth, Jesus Christ.[179] The discerning know the meaning of Jesus' words when he said, "Seek first the kingdom of God and his righteousness" (14a). They are able to impart to others the things that are in their heart, the knowledge they have accumulated (7a).

In verse 7, the heart of the foolish is characterized by its inability to spread knowledge and its foolishness. However, the second half of this verse 14 characterizes the lips of the foolish as "feeding on folly." That is, what enters the mouth of the foolish is foolishness alone. If what is eaten is foolishness, then what comes out of the heart is naturally foolishness. Those who have learned from a foolish friend or a foolish teacher are foolish in what they see, hear, and learn; therefore, they become foolish persons and speak foolishly.

All the days of the oppressed are wretched, but the cheerful

believers for many reasons in this world. Solomon also acknowledged that life has its ups and downs, but he said that God made all of them beautiful: "A time to weep, and a time to laugh, a time to mourn, and a time to dance" (Eccl. 3:4); "God has made everything beautiful in its time" (Eccl. 3:11a).

[179] Bridges cited the queen of Sheba, Nicodemus, Mary who listened at the feet of Jesus, the Ethiopian eunuch, Cornelius a centurion, and the Berean Jews as examples of biblical characters who sought truth. Bridges, *Proverbs*, 206.

heart has a continual feast (15:15).

The second half of the verse, "A cheerful heart always feasts," can be connected to the first half of verse 13, "A happy heart makes the face cheerful." This connection allows for the following interpretation: All the days of living under oppression are in reality unhappy (15a), but those who have joy in their hearts despite the adversity always feast (15b). No one can take away their joy. The world can't control or overwhelm them.

Better a little with the fear of the LORD than great wealth with turmoil. Better a small serving [a meal] of vegetables with love [where there is love] than a fattened calf with hatred (15:16-17).

This proverb takes the phrasing structure that teaches wisdom through comparison, "A is better than B." The person who has both A and B would be living a life of the icing on the cake. But that's rarely the case. This proverb teaches us that while the best life may be not possible, wisdom is found in choosing the next best life. It is far better to have "little possessions but fear of the LORD" and "love one another, even though they have a few bites" than to have "many possessions but be troubled and anxious" and "eat all the delicious foods but hate one another." The wise choose the former, but the foolish choose the latter.

When looking for a marriage companion, there are many young people who are foolish enough to choose between a person who believes in God but has not a secure job and an unbeliever or a person of another religion but has a good job or owns a profitable building. Those who choose based on the stability and comfort of the present rather than the vision of the future are foolish. Such a foolish decision can lead to a loss of faith and a broken marriage that ends in divorce. On the other hand, it is much wiser to choose a person of faith and character, even if he or she seems small or not secure financially at the moment, as his or her spouse. In reality, it is not an exaggeration to say that few people have everything going for them. So we need to have the wisdom to choose the next best thing.

Lot was an unfortunate man who made a foolish life choice. It would have been far wiser for him to stay by Abraham's side and keep his faith in the LORD, even if it meant losing a little money in herding. But he chose the east side of the Jordan, which looked like the Garden of Eden and had plenty of water and good pasture. Realistically, he made a wise choice. But he did not consider Sodom and Gomorrah, which lay behind the good pastures. Eventually he entered Sodom and lived in the city as a resident. He ended up living in an environment that made it very difficult for him to keep his faith in the LORD. He failed to choose a life that was, as this proverb says, "better a little with the fear of the LORD" (16a). He was addictively attached to the life of Sodom, and the only way to be delivered from that addiction was to come out of the city alive, even if it meant giving up all his possessions. It was far better to come out empty-handed than to die in the sulfur fire with many possessions. His wife disobeyed the angel's instructions, looked back, and was turned into a pillar of salt. The lives of Lot and his wife provide a great lesson for modern believers in choosing the better life.

From the Christian worldview, the life of believers who live in fearing God on earth, even if they have little possessions, are incomparably better than the life of unbelievers who live a wealthy life on earth but do not fear God, and struggle with worldly cares and worries, and finally are cast into the eternal fires of hell. All Christians are wise people who have chosen the best way.

Christians should place the highest value on fearing and loving God vertically and loving their families and neighbors horizontally. It is wise to be willing to give up anything that can be an obstacle to serving God. It is much better for you to be a part of your family that is happy even though you may not make much money and live in rented housing, than to be a part of an unhappy family although you make a lot of money but rarely talk to your children and are estranged from your spouse, living in a luxurious home.

A hot-tempered person stirs up conflict [dissension], but the one who is patient calms a quarrel (15:18).

This proverb can be associated to verse 1. Verse 1 and verse 18 form an inverse symmetry. "A hot-tempered person" of verse 18 is connected to "a harsh word" of verse 1, and "the one who is patient" of verse 18 is connected to "a gentle answer."[180]

There are some people who calm quarrels and disagreements, and there are also some people who stir them up and fan the flames of a burning house. Solomon calls the former the wise and the righteous, and the latter the foolish and the wicked. The former are those who embody the attributes of God. In their lives, they are restoring the image of God, who is patient and slow to anger. They are peacemakers who resolve misunderstandings, conflicts, and quarrels in their relationships with their neighbors (18b).

However, hot-tempered people have a fiery temper and so easily angered, either by nature or nurture. They easily hurt their family. In the workplace, they are avoided by their subordinates because they get angry badly and unexpectedly. They rarely show remorse or apologize after they lose their temper. They don"t empathize with others, even when they are hurt by their anger. The most relevant personality disorder for hot-tempered people are borderline personality disorder, which is characterized by idealization and devaluation and unstable mood, and narcissistic personality disorder, which is characterized by anger out of narcissistic wound. Paranoid personality disorder and antisocial personality disorder are also related to some degree.

The problem is that people with hot tempers cause strife and argument in relationships (18a). It may be okay if the other person

---

[180] In 1 Cor. 13:4-7, the attributes of love that are most relevant to anger are "love is patient," "love is not easily angered," and "love keeps no record of wrongs. This love is the character of God. God is patient, slow to anger, and forgiving. An important way to cope with and overcome anger is to be slow to anger. To be slow to anger, you must be patient. James has this to say about anger "My dear brothers and sisters, take note of this: Everyone should be quick to listen, slow to speak and slow to become angry, because human anger does not produce the righteousness that God desires" (James 1:19-20).

puts up with their hot temper, but if the other person has the same issue with anger, it becomes a battleground. I happened to see some people a few times who were so angry at the driver who cut them off that they stopped in front of the other driver's car and were fighting with each other. These people are stupid. They have anger management issues. Their anger issue are so internalized in their personality that it is unlikely for them to be changed.

The way of the sluggard is blocked with thorns, but the path of the upright is a highway (15:19).

Interestingly, this proverb contrasts the sluggard with the upright. The lazy and the diligent are a natural pairing of contrast. However, Solomon might have hoped that by changing it up a bit, it would have the effect of awakening the thoughts of the reader or listener. In any case, the connection doesn't seem too far-fetched, since the upright is also diligent. They are diligent and hard-working because they live a life of obedience to God's truth, which is that we reap what we sow (see Gal. 6:7-8).

But the lazy deceive themselves. For they expect fruit without the labor of sowing, tending, and weeding. They are delusional people who chase after fantasies.

The result for the upright and diligent is like traveling on a highway (19b). There are no obstructions. God's guidance is on the way, bringing a joyful harvest to those who sow in tears (see Ps. 126:5-6).

The problem is that not many people seek the path of the upright or the path of the diligent, because although the outcome is a highway, but the process is a narrow way. The path of the upright may be a "thorny path" in this world. People who walk broad ways make moderate compromises, sometimes cheating under the radar. They lie in moderation.

But the upright who walk the way of truth are free. They don't have to fear punishment. They don't take bribes, don't build off the plans, or don't cut corners on the number of rebar. They don't have to go to jail or suffer the financial disgrace of having an accident one day that exposes all of their misdeeds.

If all Christians would walk an upright path, South Korea would be a remarkably just nation. United States of America will be a nation of justice if all Christians walk righteously. For example, if only Christian colleges and universities would pursue honesty and justice, Korea would be different. What makes a Christian university "Christian" is not the presence of a chapel or a large number of Christian students and faculty members. It lies in the rejection of tricks and moderate practices in favor of principles and honesty in academic, administrative, and financial operations. Students who attend such universities will be influenced for good and can serve as salt and light in the world after graduation.

The way of the sluggard is not the way of the wise. It is not the way of the righteous. It is not the way of Christians. It is not the way God wants us to walk. It is the way that non-believers want to go. But it is surrounded with a hedge of thorns, piercing and blocking them eventually (19a). It is a path that leads to destruction.

A wise son brings joy to his father, but a foolish man despises his mother (15:20).

This proverb is connected to the proverb in 13:1, "A wise son heeds his father's instruction, but a mocker does not respond to rebuke." Children who listen to and obey their parents are objects of joy to their parents.

Conversely, children who don't listen to and obey their parents' admonitions are foolish. They disrespect and despise them (20b). They disobey the fifth commandment that they shall honor and respect their parents. Then they are guilty of dishonoring and disobeying God who has given honor and authority to their parents. They think they are wise, but in reality they are foolish. They cause their parents to worry.

The same is true of our faith. Children who listen to and obey God's Word are pleasing to their Heavenly Father. God's children who please and honor God are wise children of God (20a).

Whoever does not believe in Jesus Christ, the Truth, is foolish. Whoever does not accept the truth that there is God the Father who created the heavens and the earth, and that he rewards those who seek him and judge those who do not believe in him through Jesus Christ, is foolish. Furthermore, those who say they believe in God but do not listen to him and live according to their own will are foolish and stupid.

Folly brings joy to one who has no sense [lacks judgment], but whoever has understanding keeps a straight course (15:21).

The second half of this proverb,   "whoever has understanding keeps a straight course," can be connected to the second half of verse 19, "the path of the upright is a highway." Those who consistently walk the right path without shortcuts and detours, not swerving to the left or the right, are people who have understanding (21b). They follow the path of their parents of faith, the path of their faithful ancestors, and the path of the Scriptures. They don't fall or wander by temptations but walk the right path in such a way that it seems foolish. And they walk this path with joy (see 21a).

But those who lack judgment delight in going down crooked paths (21a, 21b), because it seems right to them. Subjectively, they think it's the right way. So they go that way willingly and voluntarily (21a). The problem is that the foolish have a weak or absent capacity in reflection and insight that they lack judgment. Because their ability in cognition and perception function immaturely, they can't see the whole but only a part. Then they are confident that they saw the whole. They deny that they are childish and immature.

Postmodern thought honors subjective viewpoints to an inordinate degree, which is why so many foolish people go down those paths, treating many foolish, subjective ideas as truths. It is difficult for them to turn back to the path of wisdom because they love this foolish life (21a). Believers should keep in mind that the subjective experience of feeling pleasure and accomplishment is not in itself a true measure of truth.

Plans fail for lack of counsel, but with many advisers they succeed (15:22).

This proverb can be understood in conjunction with the preceding verse 21. In verse 21, the ignorant are those who lack judgment. They need to consult the views of others. However, the ignorant do not feel the need to consult others. So they do not seek counsel or advice from experts. It goes without saying that they do not seek God's will.

There are some believers who "plan" their affairs without praying. They are foolish. They are impulsive and have narcissistic fantasies. They think they are always right and don't need to listen to other people's opinions.[181] They plan and push through things at an almost manic level. The problem is that when they fall into a depressive state or things don't go as planned, they fail spectacularly. Eventually, their "plans fail" (22a).

On the other hand, those who listen to advice, judge, and decide are wise. They plan comprehensively and prudently. They voluntarily seek the advice of others. They modify their plans according to their advice. Wise Christians seek God's will above all else. They pray to God to see how their plans connect with seeking God's righteousness and kingdom. So their plans are likely to succeed (22b).

The wise are able to avoid extremes and maintain balance. They seek advice and counsel from others, but not too much. And they have the ability to revise their own thoughts and judgments. They don't procrastinate on decisions for fear of failure. Above all, they know how to humbly ask and depend on God.

Although the following are not the original meaning of this proverb, we can apply it to the opposite situation. There are indecisive people who listen to so much advice that they are unable

---

[181] Bridges made a good point that it is wise for us to distrust ourselves that we may be wrong in our thought. Bridges, *Proverbs*, 213.

to synthesize the conflicting advice and implement their plans. As the saying goes, "too many cooks spoil the broth" and those who are overly cautious procrastinate until an opportunity is lost.

People with dependent personality disorder are unable to make a decision based on the information gathered. They defer or rely on others to make decisions for them. A similar pattern of behavior is seen in people with obsessive-compulsive personality disorder. They have an issue of perfectionism that makes it difficult for them to make decisions while meeting deadlines. They spend most of their energy looking for new information to verify, because fear and anxiety of making mistakes and failing pervade all areas of their life.

A person finds joy in giving an apt reply—and how good is a timely word! (15:23).[182]

This proverb can be understood in connection with the word "joy" in verses 20 and 21. Of the two, the positive "joy of a father" and the negative "joy to one who has no sense," the joy in this proverb is the positive one. It refers to the joy of being able to say the "right" thing in the right situation.

When communicating, the importance of attentive listening to what the other person is saying and responding sensitively and appropriately cannot be overemphasized. It is also gratifying to the speaker to see the other person pleased with his or her appropriate response. "A timely word" is an art (23b). Speaking with exquisite timing and moving the listener is an art.

Counseling Application: When Christian counselors respond to their client thoughtfully, appropriately, and timely in their counseling session, they will feel a sense of accomplishment in their ministry of counseling. When "magic words" come out of their mouth in counseling, they will feel a shiver of joy and gratitude because they sense that those words are not from their

---

[182] Bridges associated this proverb with Proverbs 25:11: "Like apples of gold in settings of silver is a ruling rightly given." Bridges, *Proverbs*, 213.

own ideas but from the Holy Spirit. In that moment, both the counselor and the client experience joy, sometimes even tears of joy together.

The path of life leads upward for the prudent [the wise] to keep them from going down to the realm of the dead [to the grave] (15:24).

The metaphor of "path" is also used in this proverb. The path of the upright (19b), a straight course of one who has understanding (21b), and the path of life (24a) are the same path. Another image used in this proverb is an arrow. The image is of two arrows, one pointing up and one pointing down. The path of life for the prudent is upward direction of an arrow. The path of the foolish, on the other hand, is downward direction of an arrow. It is the path that leads down to Sheol (Hades). It is a slippery downhill slope. It is a path of death from which there is no return.

The way of life is the way of turning the eyes of faith toward heaven (24a). It is a life whose eyes are fixed on God. It is a life of hope in the LORD. Those who desire the LORD ascend.[183] They left the place of Sheol and walk in the "upward path of life" (24a). They came out of darkness and walk in the light (see Col. 1:13).[184]

But the way of destruction, the way of death, is to turn the eyes to the ground. It is the way of living with the eyes fixed on the visible. Those who live this way will fall into the place of eternal death when the visible disappears.

---

[183] "Those who hope in the LORD will renew their strength. They will soar on wings like eagles; they will run and not grow weary, they will walk and not be faint" (Isa. 40:31).

[184] "To fulfill what was said through the prophet Isaiah: 'Land of Zebulun and land of Naphtali, the Way of the Sea, beyond the Jordan, Galilee of the Gentiles—the people living in darkness have seen a great light; on those living in the land of the shadow of death a light has dawned'" (Matt. 4:14-16). Bridges interpreted verse 24 in a Christological way. He identified the upward path of life as Jesus Christ. Bridges, *Proverbs*, 214.

Although Lazarus lived a poor, sick, and painful life, he was taken up and placed in Abraham's bosom. This was the result of his journey of faith. The rich man, on the other hand, lived in affluence and feasting, but after his death he fell into a life of torment in the flames of hell, the result of a faithless, self-centered life. The rich man was a foolish man. For he did not know the true way of life, but followed the way of destruction.

The LORD tears down the house of the proud, but he sets the widow's boundary stones in place [he keeps the widow's boundaries intact] (15:25).[185]

This proverb expresses God's attributes and works in different areas. First, God destroys the house of the proud. Second, God protects the widow's land from the powerful and rich.

God abhors the proud. He hates their proud eyes. And he hates the house to which the proud belong, so he destroys it (25a). Conversely, God loves the humble, and he exalts and builds up the house of the humble.[186]

God has commanded the Israelites to protect orphans and widows through the law.[187] God protects the boundaries of a widow's life

---

[185] Bridges mentioned that God had protected the widowed Naomi and Ruth's inheritance and boundary through their kinsman-redeemer Boaz. He provided a "boundary" for Ruth, a woman from Moab, from the very beginning of his encounter with her: "So he said to Ruth, 'My daughter, listen to me. Don't go and glean in another field and don't go away from here. Stay here with the women who work for me. Watch the field where the men are harvesting, and follow along after the women. I have told the men not to lay a hand on you'" (Ruth 2:8-9). The proverb relating to the boundary stone is repeated in chapter 22:28 and 23:10: "Do not move an ancient boundary stone set up by your ancestors"; "Do not move an ancient boundary stone or encroach on the fields of the fatherless."

[186] After presenting Samuel to the temple, Hannah praised the LORD with the following words: "Do not keep talking so proudly or let your mouth speak such arrogance, for the LORD is a God who knows, and by him deeds are weighed" (1 Sam. 2:3); "The LORD brings death and makes alive; he brings down to the grave and raises up. The LORD sends poverty and wealth; he humbles and he exalts" (1 Sam. 2:6-7).

and her house and land. God is pleased that Christians show care and concern for minorities, the weak, and people in need, such as orphans and widows.

The LORD detests the thoughts of the wicked, but gracious words are pure in his sight [those of the pure are pleasing to him] (15:26).

All human beings have the ability to think, although there are some differences in their ability. Generally speaking, the wicked think evil thoughts, but the good, the pure, think good thoughts.

God hates the thoughts of the wicked (26a). On the other hand, the thoughts of the righteous are pleasing to God (26b). They are "able to test and approve what God's will is—his good, pleasing and perfect will" (Rom. 12:2).

The greedy bring ruin to their households, but the one who hates bribes will live (15:27).[188]

This proverb can be connected to verse 6, "The house of the righteous contains great treasure, but the income of the wicked

---

[187] "Do not take advantage of the widow or the fatherless. If you do and they cry out to me, I will certainly hear their cry. My anger will be aroused, and I will kill you with the sword; your wives will become widows and your children fatherless" (Ex. 22:22-24); "He defends the cause of the fatherless and the widow" (Deuteronomy 10:18a).

[188] Bridges connected 1 Timothy 6:9-10 as a relevant passage: "Those who want to get rich fall into temptation and a trap and into many foolish and harmful desires that plunge people into ruin and destruction. For the love of money is a root of all kinds of evil. Some people, eager for money, have wandered from the faith and pierced themselves with many griefs." Bridges, *Proverbs*, 217. Paul well recognized the self-destructive dynamic of greed. James also pointed out the consequences of greed: "Then, after desire has conceived, it gives birth to sin; and sin, when it is full-grown, gives birth to death" (James 1:15).

brings ruin." While verse 6 emphasizes that the income of the wicked causes hardship for themselves, this proverb emphasizes that it causes hardship not only for themselves but also for their families.

The income of the wicked is a bribe in the context of the text. The riches they accumulate out of bribes end up harming themselves and dishonoring their family. Because bribes are not honest wealth, they become snares.[189] It is not difficult to predict that the greedy will fall into snares and bring shame to themselves and their family (27a).

But those who actively abhor bribery will never be accused of it, no matter what happens. Such people are confident, secure and free. They have nothing to fear. As salt and light they contribute to the purification of their society and nation. A country with a lot of corruption, a country where things don't get done without bribes, is a underdeveloped country. Bribery should not be found both in church politics and in the kingdom of God.

The heart of the righteous weighs its answers, but the mouth of the wicked gushes evil (15:28).[190]

This proverb is connected with verse 2, "The tongue of the wise adorns knowledge, but the mouth of the fool gushes folly." The righteous are wise, so their minds consider and adorn what they are going to say (28a, 4a).[191] They think things through before they speak, so they make fewer mistakes.

The wicked, however, are foolish. Their foolish mouth gushes evil and folly(28b, 4b). Their lips pour out all kinds of filthy language and evil speech impulsively.

---

[189] The motivation for taking a bribe is greed. Greed is a personality trait that is insatiable, so bribe takers don't just take one and be done with it. They take bribes as soon as they get the chance. Eventually, they are caught in a trap and humiliated.

[190] When you think things through, you don't blurt them out or gush out anger. Wise are people who have a properly functioning "brake" on their mouth.

[191] Bridges made a good point about the necessity of prayer in the deliberative process. Bridges, *Proverbs*, 218.

Counseling Application: People with borderline personality disorder have symptoms of "gushing evil." This is because they have a fragile self-structure that is poorly developed in terms of impulse control. So, when they get angry, they may use all sorts of abusive language or even become physically violent. They may also exhibit episodic "dissociation" and "splitting" to the point of temporary insanity.

The symptom of "gushing evil" is also seen in people with antisocial personality disorder. They exhibit argumentative behaviors and a reckless disregard for their own safety or others' safety. When angry, they become violent enough to assault impulsively. In severe cases, they may commit homicide.

The LORD is far from the wicked, but he hears the prayer of the righteous (15:29).

This proverb can be understood in connection with verse 26, "The LORD detests the thoughts of the wicked, but gracious words are pure in his sight." The prayers of the righteous are pure and gracious (26b). They don't pray out of impure motives or greed. God hears and answers the prayers of the righteous (29b). The prayers of the wicked, on the other hand, are rejected (29a).[192] This is because the wicked have an evil heart and their prayers are evil and greedy. James makes this point well when he says, "When you ask, you do not receive, because you ask with wrong motives, that you may spend what you get on your pleasures" (James 4:3).

---

[192] Bridges related the following passages to this proverb "Although they fast, I will not listen to their cry; though they offer burnt offerings and grain offerings, I will not accept them. Instead, I will destroy them with the sword, famine and plague" (Jer 14:12); "Therefore I will deal with them in anger; I will not look on them with pity or spare them. Although they shout in my ears, I will not listen to them" (Ezek. 8:18). He also related Isaiah 1:11, but I think 1:15 is more relevant: "When you spread out your hands in prayer, I hide my eyes from you; even when you offer many prayers, I am not listening." Bridges, *Proverbs*, 219.

Light in a messenger's eyes [A cheerful look] brings joy to the heart, and good news gives health to the bones (15:30).

This proverbs is connected to verse 13, "A happy heart makes the face cheerful, but heartache crushes the spirit." The joy of the heart makes the face shine (13a), but here a cheerful face makes the heart glad (30a). So we see that the face and the heart are interconnected and interacted. "Light in a messenger's eyes" is perceived as a sign of "good news" (30a, 30b). Good news makes the heart happy and the body healthy (30b). Even people who have lost their health become encouraged and strengthened. It can be a trigger for recovery.[193]

Whoever heeds [listens] life-giving correction will be at home among the wise. Those who disregard discipline despise themselves,[194] but the one who heeds correction gains understanding (15:31-32).

Whoever hears rebuke and obeys it that leads to life is wise (31). Whoever hears rebuke and heed it gains understanding (32b).
David had the wisdom and maturity to listen to the prophet Nathan's confrontation.[195] He soon recognized his sin and

---

[193] Bridges associated this proverb to Jacob's reaction when he heard the good news that his beloved son Joseph, whom he thought was dead, was alive and had become prime minister of Egypt: "Jacob was stunned; he did not believe them. But when they told him everything Joseph had said to them, and when he saw the carts Joseph had sent to carry him back, the spirit of their father Jacob revived." (Gen. 45:26-27). Bridges, *Proverbs*, 221.

[194] The meaning becomes clearer when this verse is associated with 6:23: "For this command is a lamp, this teaching is a light, and correction and instruction are the way to life." Failure to receive instruction is suicidal, forsaking the path to eternal life.

[195] The poet Asaph summarized David's life well when he sang: "And David shepherded them with integrity of heart; with skillful hands he led them" (Psalm 78:72). Although David sinned, he had the spirituality and character to repent and turn around.

repented. Although he fell fatally, God forgave him for his repentance.

Those who ignore admonition are foolish. The foolish do not recognize their true worth. They do not understand the heart of the person rebuking them because he or she cares about their souls (32a). They don't accept advice because they take it as criticizing them. They only like words that scratch their itchy ears. So they like keeping such people around. Those who ignore admonishment have strong narcissistic needs. So they understand feedback or discipline as hurtful.[196] They consciously or subconsciously feel threatened that admonishment may destroy their vulnerable narcissistic self, so they reject it as much as possible.

The same is true in our relationship with God. Wise are those whose ears are circumcised. Wise are those whose ears are open to hear what the Holy Spirit is saying. Wise are the Christians who can hear the Holy Spirit saying, "Those whom I love I rebuke and discipline. So be earnest and repent" (Rev. 3:19) and repent.

Wisdom's instruction is to fear the LORD, and humility comes before honor (15:33).

As Solomon concludes Proverbs 15, he restates his core intention. It's to inspire his listeners to live in the fear of the LORD.

God gives wisdom to those who fear him (33a). Specifically, God the Holy Spirit enlightens and illuminates through the written Word.

Those who fear the LORD are bound to be humble. Those who know and love the great and mighty God cannot be arrogant.

God brings the humble to a place of honor. Humility comes before honor (33b).[197] Jesus says it is wise to sit at the backseat

---

[196] The gospel of Jesus Christ hurts people with narcissistic personality disorder. They cannot admit that they are totally incapable of salvation and fallen. It's hard for them to accept that salvation is unconditional grace.

[197] Bridges cited Abigail as an example of humility. When she met David, she dismounted from her mule, bowed her face to the ground, and identified herself as "your servant" (1 Sam. 25:23-24). When David later sent messengers to take her as

when invited to a feast (see Luke 14:10). He says that if you sit at the head table and someone more honorable comes along, you will eventually suffer the humiliation of having to move down to the backseat.

his wife, she humbled herself to the messengers as well: "She bowed down with her face to the ground and said, 'I am your servant and am ready to serve you and wash the feet of my lord's servants'" (1 Sam. 25:41). She went from being the wife of Nabal, a foolish man, to being the wife of King David, a wise man.

Chapter 16 God Directs Each Person's Steps

To humans belong the plans of the heart, but from the LORD comes the proper answer of the tongue (16:1).[198] See also 16:9, 33.

Proverbs 16 is characterized by beginning with verse 1, which refers to God's sovereignty and providence, and ending with verse 33, "The lot is cast into the lap, but its every decision is from the LORD." And each proverb, from verse 1 through 11, is characterized by a connection to the LORD.

The planning of the heart (1a, 9) and the casting of lots (33a) belong to man. But the fulfillment of the work and the response to the words (1b) depend on God. The outcome of the casting of lots also depends on God (33b).

The amazing result of casting lots is epitomized in the story of Jonah (see Jonah 1:7).[199] It is a mystery that human free will and God's sovereignty and providence do not contradict or conflict.

There are times when it seems as though the wicked are taking the lead in the world, making plans and accomplishing things. But their plans can never overcome the great providence of God. The realization of this fact is a great comfort to the believers.

Pharaoh, the king of Egypt, was afraid that Israel was becoming powerful, so he said, "Come, let us be wise against them." The

---

[198] Bridges captured the relationship between divine providence and human free will when he said, "God does not work without us, but with us, through us, in us, and by us." Bridges, *Proverbs*, 224. His words are not an endorsement of synergism. God made all things without human cooperation. He is not dependent on humans.

[199] The word "lot" occurs about 70 times in the Old Testament and seven times in the New Testament. The twelve tribes used the method of lottery to divide their inheritance, and it was practiced in the appointment of offices and functions in the temple (see 1 Chron. 24:5, 31; 25:8-9; 26:13-14). In the New Testament, it occurs once in the case of the casting of lots to replace Judas Iscariot and the making of Matthias as an apostle. Herbert Lockyer (ed.), *Nelson's Illustrated Bible Dictionary* (Nashville: Thomas Nelson Publishers, 1986), 655.

"wise" way he devised was an evil way: he forced the Israelites to do hard labor. He even ordered midwives to kill any male babies that were to be born. Furthermore, he ordered to throw any male babies of Israel into the Nile River to die (see Ex. 1:10-22). But in the meantime, God intervened in Moses' birth and upbringing. Eventually, 80 years later, he called Moses to deliver Israel from slavery to Pharaoh.

Trusting that God is ultimately in control of the outcome of the believers' plans and actions enables them to overcome anxiety and fear and move forward. Those who fail to plan or execute because they are afraid of making mistakes or failing are immature and foolish. When we trust that in all things including failures God works for the good according to his purpose, we can venture out courageously (see Rom. 8:28). Mrs. Ee-sook Ahn's hymnal poem, saying "I don't know what tomorrow will bring, I live one day at a time, I can't control misfortune or good fortune, I'm on a rough road and there's no end to it, Lord Jesus, give me your hand and take me by the hand," expresses this truth well. The wise are those who humbly recognize that failure, frustration, rejection, hurt, loss, pain, and even death are part of God's greater providence. They hold to the fundamental theological truth that "God is good," even when they cannot find the ultimate answers. This is the kind of person the world cannot stand against. Satan cannot tear them down. Job, who confessed, "Naked I cam from my mother's womb, and naked I will depart. The LORD gave and the LORD has taken away; may the name of the LORD be praised." (Job 1:21), is a model for Christians. Those who maintain this attitude are psychologically and spiritually "resilient."

All a person's ways seem pure to them, but motives are weighed by the LORD (16:2).

There are two cases where someone might say that his or her life is blameless. One is someone who, on a conscious level, has a very noble character and lives a life without regrets.[200] The other is

---

[200] The self-evaluation of Paul may be applicable in this case: "I care very little if I am

someone who is unable to make an objective evaluation of himself or herself. These people think they have no problems because they don't have insight and self-awareness.

God weighs one's motives as if on a scale (2b). In both cases mentioned in the previous paragraph, God knows their conscious and unconscious motives. Even those who think they have a virtuous character would not be able to say, "I am clean and pure," if they are to be analyzed their hidden motives or their unconscious motives.[201] Only by looking at our dreams every night we all know that we are not pure and innocent.

Counseling Application: Psychoanalytic psychotherapy is an approach to counseling that helps clients become more conscious of the life stories they tell and the unconscious dynamics that are at work in their attitudes, relationships, and behaviors. The goal is to help clients expand their awareness of what motivations they are already aware but does not want to reveal to others and what unconscious motivations they are unaware of. Through this process, they can experience growth and transformation in their relationship with God and in their relationships with others.

Commit to the LORD whatever you do, and he will establish your plans [your plans will succeed].[202] The LORD works out everything to its proper end [for his own ends]—even the wicked for a day of disaster (16:3-4).

---

judged by you or by any human court; indeed, I do not even judge myself. My conscience is clear, but that does not make me innocent. It is the Lord who judges me" (1 Cor. 4:3-4).

[201] When Isaiah encountered the holy God in the temple, he confessed, "Woe to me! I cried. I am ruined! For I am a man of unclean lips, and I live among a people of unclean lips, and my eyes have seen the King, the LORD Almighty" (Isa. 6:5). His encounter with God led him to his self-examination that expanded his perception of himself.

[202] Verse 3 has connection with 3:6: "In all your ways submit to him, and he will make your paths straight." Bridges also pointed out this connection. He used the example of Abraham's senior servant Eliezer's journey to the land of Aram to find a spouse for Isaac. Bridges, *Proverbs*, 226.

God is the maker of all things to fulfill his purposes and goals. Even evil people are created and used by God to accomplish his will (4b).

Accepting God's sovereignty and providence by faith allows us to endure in the midst of adverse circumstances. Even in the midst of an environment where evil people are triumphant, we are less likely to get angry when we see with eyes of faith that God is working in the big picture. It even frees us up to have pity on evil people. The wicked have only one life, one day on God's timetable to run amok until their expiration date. They will eventually contribute to God's greater will and receive eternal judgment.

The narrative of Joseph is one of the best examples of "reframing" in the Bible. His brothers tried to kill him, and later sold him into slavery to the Ismaelite traders. And they lied to their father Jacob, saying that Joseph had been bitten by a wild animal and died. But they were instruments in God's hands. God brought them to repentance and used them to become the patriarchs of the twelve tribes of Israel. Falsely accused by Potiphar's wife, Joseph seemed to waste time in prison indefinitely, but God used that prison to lead him directly to Pharaoh's throne. Finally, he orchestrated a beautiful event that saved Jacob's entire family from the famine. Joseph rephrased his story to his frightened brothers: "And now, do not be distressed and do not be angry with yourselves for selling me here, because it was *to save lives that God sent me ahead of you...But God sent me ahead of your to preserve for you a remnant* on earth and *to save your lives by a great deliverance*" (see Gen. 45:5-8). The story of Joseph's life, as well as the lives of all Christians, is a story of "re-framing."

The LORD detests all the proud of heart. Be sure of this: They will not go unpunished (16:5).

God looks at the heart, and even if we don't express our pride outwardly (see 1 Sam. 16:7). God hates the thoughts and attitudes of the proud (5a). Overt pride is even worse.[203]

This proverb is a warning to the proud to keep in mind that they will not escape punishment. God humbles the proud, so it would be wise for all the proud to have a humble heart, realizing that they don't know when or how they will be "humbled".[204]

Although Ahab was wicked and proud, he was able to avoid God's judgment by temporarily humbling himself when he heard God's warning. When Elijah delivered God's curses against Jezebel and Ahab for killing Naboth, Ahab "tore his clothes, put on sackcloth and fasted. He lay in sackcloth and went around meekly" (1 Kings 21:27). God postponed judgment, telling Elijah, "Have you noticed how Ahab has humbled himself before me? Because he has humbled himself, I will not bring this disaster in his day, but I will bring it on his house in the days of his sons" (1 Kings 21:29).

Through love and faithfulness sin is atoned for; through the fear of the LORD evil is avoided (16:6).

This proverb is characterized by the fact that it is a proverb about atonement. The doctrine of the atonement is illustrated in this proverb as water that flows beneath the earth occasionally rises to the surface. Solomon's meaning of the redeeming event of Jesus Christ on the cross is well illustrated in this proverb.

In Proverbs, "love and faithfulness" are paired expressions. And love and faithfulness are attributes of the Triune God. It is only in the love of God the Father and through the faithful obedience of Jesus Christ on the cross that our sins can be paid for (6a). And by the power of God the Holy Spirit, who accomplishes the salvation of God-fearing children, we can overcome sin and evil (6b).

---

[203] In particular, so-called scholars who claim that there is no God are arrogant. Those who think they have the ability to evaluate and judge the invisible God with their limited reason are the ones God hates. The act of judging the temporal world and the transcendent world by human limited reason is a sign of pride and ignorance.

[204] Fox notes that the same proverbial phrase is found in chapter 11:21 and comments that "Be sure of this" means "immediately." Fox, *Proverbs 10-31*, 612. If that is the meaning, then the proverb could be interpreted as a warning of the imminent nature of God's punishment to the proud.

However, saved Christians are not free from evil. They still have a sinful nature within them and are exposed to evil in their environment. That is why Jesus taught the prayer, "Lead us not into temptation, but deliver us from evil." We are to pray this prayer continually.

The best way to avoid and stay away from evil is to fear God (6b). Those who are always awake and have a consciousness of *"coram Deo"* are afraid to commit sins. It was Joseph's fear of God that kept him from falling into evil despite the temptation of his master Potiphar's wife in a foreign land: "How then could I do such a wicked thing and sin against God?" (Gen. 39:9).

When the LORD takes pleasure in anyone's way, he causes [makes] their enemies to make peace [even his enemies live at peace] with them (16:7).

Solomon emphasizes to his son, the next in line to be king, that he must rule in a way that pleases God if the nation is to have peace (7a). He promises that God will protect the kingdom of Israel so that even its enemies will not dare to invade (7b). As Korean national anthem says, "God be with us, long live our country."

Israel's defense was in the hands of God alone. As long as they obeyed God and followed the law, Israel was safe. No great power dared to cross them. But the history of southern Judah and northern Israel, beginning with Rehoboam and Jeroboam, was a history of war and suffering. The key cause was the failure of the king and people to live a life pleasing to God. God used Assyria, Egypt, Babylon, Ammon, and Moab to discipline Israel and Judah over and over again.

Solomon taught his sons this proverb, but he himself did not live faithfully to his own precepts. He made agreements with foreign nations and took their princesses as wives. He introduced foreign rituals and idols, and he lived a secular, humanistic life, stockpiling chariots and horses that God had forbidden. He survived his own reign, but his son Rehoboam's reign divided the nation and set the stage for fighting among his own people. Solomon's case well illustrates how difficult it is to know the truth and live by it.

Applying this proverb to the lives of individual Christians, God is pleased with those who live God-centered lives. God intervenes in their lives so that even their enemies come to them for reconciliation. He makes them enjoy shalom in their lives.

Better a little with righteousness than much gain with injustice (16:8).

This proverb is connected to the two proverbs in chapter 15 that precede it: "Better a little with the fear the LORD than a great wealth with turmoil" (15:16); "Better a small serving of vegetables with love than a fattened calf with hatred" (15:17). All these proverbs teach wisdom through comparison, "A is better than B."

An income, even a small one, that is earned through honest and sincere work is uplifting, rewarding, and joyful. On the other hand, if some people earn a lot of money, but it is unjustly earned, they will live an unpresentable, anxious life. They suffer great shame when the injustice is finally revealed.

In their hearts humans plan their course, but the LORD establishes [determines] their steps (16:9).[205]

This proverb connects with verses 1 and 33, "To humans belong the plans of the heart, but from the Lord comes the proper answer of the tongue"; "The lot is cast into the lap, but its every decision is from the LORD." The image used in verse 1 is the mouth whereas the image of the feet is used in verse 9.

We Christians also must make plans while we live in this world. We must also put those plans into action. It is not God's will for us

[205] This proverb is also connected with Jeremiah's confession: "LORD, I know that people's lives are not their own; it is not for them to direct their steps" (Jer. 10:23).

not to plan nor act. It is a life of faith to plan and act, but to recognize that God is the one who guides us through it all. When we trust God to guide our steps, our anxiety and fear of the outcome will be lessened.

The lips of a king speak as an oracle, and his mouth does [should] not betray justice. Honest scales and balances belong to [are from] the LORD; all the weights in the bag are of his making. Kings detest wrongdoing, for a throne is established through righteousness (16:10-12).

Verses 10-15 consist of a proverb that teaches principles for how a king can rule wisely before God. The king's mouth, as an oracle, has the authority and responsibility of taking the place of God's mouth (10a). Therefore, his mouth must be such that it does not betray judicial justice (10b).

All those called to authority should avoid misusing or abusing the authority given to them. For example, parents have the authority to act as kings in the home. They are responsible for raising and disciplining their children well. However, God is not pleased when those in authority abuse or misuse their power by going against the biblical spirit of "justice. It is not justice for a president to act arbitrarily against social justice or to put pressure on relevant institutions. It is not pleasing to God for senior pastors to abuse theirs pastoral authority, to act against justice, or to treat associate pastors and staff with disrespect.

God is pleased that humanly agreed-upon methods of measurement work well. He even goes so far as to say that those methods of measurement are of God's making. He says that the spirit of fair scales and equitable balances comes from the heart of God (11). Therefore, those who try to gain an unfair advantage by deceiving about weight or volume has the mind of the devil, the father of lies. They belong to the devil. Such people have no fear of God's eternal judgment.

The king should hate evil deeds and those who do them (12a). The judiciary, entrusted with the king's authority, must abhor evil behavior. Only then will a nation or society be just. Leaders who aid and abet evil behavior are not worthy of leadership.

The energy required to hate evil behavior is anger. The ability to be aware of and express anger is necessary for leaders. This is because when we feel anger, we can take concrete action with energy of anger for a just life and society.[206]

One of the symbols of the judiciary is the dish scale. It is a symbol of fairness and justice. This also applies to economic activity. It is God's will that his will be done on earth that honest and faithful commerce be established. God watches with care and concern and rewards all economic activities, even those that are conducted in secret.

Kings take pleasure in honest lips; they value the one who speaks what is right [the truth]. A king's wrath is a messenger of death, but the wise will appease it.[207] When a king's face brightens, it means life; his favor is like a rain cloud in spring (16:13-15).

This proverb describes the virtues required of wise kings. The object of wise kings' delight is "honest lips" (13a). They take pleasure in those who speak the truth and keep them around. They are able to recognize and appoint their subjects who speak the truth, even when it is uncomfortable and difficult to speak.

But foolish kings exalt and keep by their side counselors who deceive them by saying only what is good to hear. In the end, these kings destroy themselves and their country.

In verses 14 and 15, "a king's wrath" is contrasted with "a king's

---

206 In the Enneagram, a way of understanding human beings, the core emotion of Type ONE, the Reformer, is anger. Reformer-typed people, including prophets, use their anger to challenge for a better system or nation. For example, King Josiah's disgust and anger at the sin of idolatry drove him to destroy the idols and restore the temple.

207 Clifford gives the examples of Abigail, who calmed David's anger (1 Sam. 25), and Daniel, who appeased the wrath of King Nebuchadnezzar (Dan. 2). Clifford, *Proverbs*, 159.

face brightens." Kings must have a face that is not only merciful and bright, but also stern and fearful. This is because they are to be practitioners of love and justice. Kings who always have a kind face and a bright face are likely to be ones who cannot be angry, who cannot assert their authority, or who cannot say "no." They may even be incompetent. Conversely, if a king always has an angry face, his or her subjects will be reluctant to give him or her advice. As a result, kings with an angry face always will bring ruin to themselves and their country.

"A king's wrath is a messenger of death"(14a). A king's wrath will soon be followed by an order to kill. For example, Solomon's wrath led to the death of Adonijah: "So King Solomon gave orders to Benaiah son of Jehoiada, and he struck down Adonijah and he died" (1 Kings 2:25).

The time for kings to be wrathful is when God is wrathful. If they are angry when God is angry, they are doing a good job as God's stewards. They are used by God when they can feel God's wrath. In case of Phinehas, Aaron's grandson and Eleazar's son, he empathized with God's wrath. So with the energy of that anger, he went into an Israelite man's tent (he was a leader of the tribe of Simeon) and pierced him with a spear because he brought a Midianite woman (she was the daughter of a leader of the Midianites) into the midst of Israel and killed both of them. The wrath of God was relieved by his courageous, just action out of his anger. He was indeed a wise, courageous priest and leader who appeased the wrath of God, the king of Israel.

The wise can appease the king's wrath (14b). In light of the example of Phinehas, he could empathize with God's wrath. The wise can empathize with a king's wrath, which is as fear-inspiring as a messenger of death. By empathizing with the king's anger, they can relieve it.

Jesus Christ, the wise person, became a mediator between God and sinners, taking upon himself the curse of God's wrath on a tree so that God's wrath against sinners might be turned to compassion and mercy. Jesus took all of God's wrath and died so that those who believe in him might be made righteous before God. He himself became a sacrifice of reconciliation.

The brightened face of a king signifies permission to stand before the king (15a). It means not dying despite coming before the king.

The scepter extended by the king on the throne signifies life and acceptance.[208]

The radiance of God's face as King of kings is a "good object image" for his people, signifying grace and favor (15b). God instructed Aaron to use God's face to bless Israel when he blessed them: "The LORD bless you and keep you; the LORD make his face shine on you and be gracious to you; the LORD turn his face toward you and give you peace" (Num. 6:24-26).

How much better to get wisdom than gold, to get insight [understanding] rather than silver! (16:16).[209]

This is a proverb that emphasizes a message by repetition. It says that acquiring wisdom and understanding is much better than acquiring gold and silver. It is a proverb with a clear meaning.

Whoever pursues gold and silver but does not pursue wisdom and understanding is foolish. Those who seek worldly honor and riches but do not seek God are foolish. They are foolish in that they cling to superficial and temporary things, ignorant of the core relationship with God. In that sense, all those who do not know God, the source of wisdom, are fools, no matter how intelligent and wise they may be.

Esau valued a bowl of red bean porridge more than his birthright (Gen. 25:34). Modern people like Esau value gold and silver the most. Esau's descendants will regret it at the end of their life. But it will be no good regretting then.

---

[208] Esther had not been called to appear before King Xerxes for some time and was afraid to go before the king to make her request. However, when she went before the king after fasting for three days, saying, "If I perish, I perish," God caused the king to be pleased with her so that he held out to her the gold scepter. (see Esth. 5:1-2). To her, the king's favor meant "life" for the Jewish people and provided a golden opportunity, like "a rain cloud in spring" (15b).

[209] A similar expression to this proverb appears in the poetry of the descendants of Korah: "Better is one day in your courts than a thousand elsewhere; I would rather be a doorkeeper in the house of my God than dwell in the tents of the wicked" (Ps. 84:10).

The highway of the upright avoids evil; those who guard their ways preserve their lives. Pride goes before destruction, a haughty spirit before a fall. Better to be lowly in spirit along [among] with the oppressed than to share plunder with the proud (16:17-19).

Verses 17 and 18 emphasizes the same message using repetition and verse 19 uses the form of "A is better than B." Verse 18 ties in nicely with 18:12, "Before a downfall the heart is haughty, but humility comes before honor."

Honest persons do not join the ways of the wicked in their journey of life, but keep walking the right path (17a). They do not waver. They do not fall prey to the temptations of the road. They have wisdom and discernment. Therefore, they preserve their lives (17b). They follow the path that leads to eternal life. He does not engage in foolish behavior that mortgages their life for the sake of enjoying the temporary pleasure of sins.

Throughout Chapter 16, the warning against pride appears three times, including in verse 18: "The LORD detests all the proud of heart. Be sure of this: They will not go unpunished" (5); "Better to be lowly in spirit along with the oppressed than to share plunder with the proud" (19). Pride is a key cause of destructive consequences for ourselves and others. After pride has conceived, it gives birth to sin; ans sin, when it is full-grown, gives birth to death (see James 1:15). It is because of this dynamic that greed and pride are included among the seven deadly sins.

"Destruction" and "a fall" mean the same thing (18). There comes a time when persons with an arrogant heart will fall.[210] If they fall, they may not get back up. Paul's warning, "So, if you think you are standing firm, be careful that you don't fall!" (1 Cor. 10:12) is true.

---

[210] Bridges rightly pointed out that haughty persons are characterized by looking up instead of watching their own steps. As a result, they don't see what's in front of them and are bound to fall. And the higher they climb, the more terrible the fall. Bridges, *Proverbs*, 238.

In fact, the higher one rises, the more devastating the fall. The proud are bound to fall.

A good preventative and remedy for overcoming pride is humility (19). Those who use the Bible as a daily mirror are bound to be humble.

A life of humility, even if it means being poor and suffering, is far better than a life of associating with the proud and enjoying temporary benefits (19), because God approves of the former. The latter is a life destined for destruction.

Whoever gives heed to instruction prospers, and blessed is the one who trusts in the LORD (16:20).

The second half of the verse, "Blessed is the one who trusts in the LORD," emphasizes the first half, "Whoever gives heed to instruction prospers." This is because trusting in God means being interested in, listening to, and doing what God says. Trusting and obeying God's Word more than your own thoughts and experiences is the secret to a blessed life. Those who obey God's Word prosper and flourish, especially spiritually.

The wise in heart are called discerning, and gracious [pleasant] words promote instruction (16:21).

The heart and the mouth are closely connected. The mouth is nothing more than a spokesperson for the heart. A good mouth means that the heart is good and wise.

Therefore, the wise in heart know how to speak good words. They have the ability to teach others with what they have already learned, studied, and internalized (21b). Those who learn from them will recognize that they ares indeed wise persons of discernment (21a).

Counseling Application: Counseling supervisors add knowledge and experience to their counselor-in-training in the supervision process. Supervisors with "pleasant words" have the ability to assess their supervisees' learning ability and learning style and supervise appropriately and sensitively. They are well aware that giving positive feedback, praise, and encouragement increases a supervisee's motivation and ability to learn, and that frequent reprimands and unpleasant words increase anxiety and anger, which decreases a supervisee's ability to learn. Effective supervisors have the ability to balance empathy and confrontation.

The same is true for counselors in their relationships with clients. Mirroring words, empowering words, positive words, compliments, and acknowledgments are stepping stones for a client to new change. These positive words facilitate the client to learn new behaviors. Effective counselors also stimulate change by providing an appropriate level of confrontation when necessary.

Prudence [Understanding] is a fountain of life to the prudent [to those who have], but folly brings punishment to fools (16:22).

Even in the world, the wise lead others to a life of vitality. This is what counselors do. When they help their clients become self-aware, the clients become able to make new changes, shake off lethargy, and get up and live a vibrant life.

In the more important spiritual realm, the prudent act as a fountain of life to lead others to the path of eternal life. Those who have theological wisdom and clarity about who and what God is and does, who and what Jesus Christ is and did and does, and who and what the Holy Spirit is and does, can serve as a fountain of life to quench the thirst of those who are spiritually thirsty.

But the foolish will be punished for their foolishness and will be judged (22b). They live by human wisdom and perish because they lack the wisdom and knowledge of God.[211]

---

[211] The wisdom of God, the wisdom of the gospel, seems foolish to the wisdom of the world, and therefore the world ignores it and does not understand it. Their eyes are closed and their ears are deaf, so they do not realize it. Those who are not regenerated by the work of God the Holy Spirit will not believe the gospel and will eventually

The hearts of the wise make their mouths prudent [guides his mouth], and their lips promote instruction (16:23). See 16:21.

Gracious [Pleasant] words are a honeycomb, sweet to the soul and healing to the bones (16:24).[212]

There are words that are pleasant and empowering to hear. There are words that give you courage. When you hear a sincere blessing, you feel a shiver run down your spine. It is like honey that brightens your eyes and energizes you.[213] When you're tired and struggling in your life's journey, words that revitalize you are more effective than restorative medicines.

The Word of God is the word of life that refreshes and revitalizes your soul. It is sweeter than honey. It gives strength and hope to your weary soul.[214]

Counseling Application: Therapeutic words ripple through the client's entire personality. A counselor's heartfelt words are more effective than any psychiatric medication. The right words, spoken in the right tone, with the right words of blessing, with sincerity in the eyes, with the right words that the client have wanted to hear, can bring tears of joy to the client's eyes.

---

perish.

[212] Bridges commented that the expression "bones" refers to the spiritual system. Bridges, *Proverbs*, 244. He saw that this proverb has connection wit proverbs in 3:8 and 4:22: "This will bring health to your body and nourishment to your bones"; "For they are life to those who find them and health to one's whole body."

[213] Exhausted from battle, Jonathan found wild honey and dipped his staff in it. And when he ate it, his eyes brightened and his strength returned (see 1 Sam. 14:27-29).

[214] The Psalmist sings of God's word as sweeter than honey: "How sweet are your words to my taste, sweeter than honey to my mouth!" (Ps, 119:103). He's not exaggerating. Not just anyone can experience the flavor of the Word. For those who meditate on it, who believe and love God, the words of Scripture are the voice and answer of the invisible God.

There is a way that appears to be right [seems right to a man], but in the end it leads to death (16:25).

All paths look right to people except the one that leads to the Way of Life, which is not "a way" but the Way of Life. Even the religions of the world seem right to the human eye. But in the end, they are nothing but the way to death.

The appetite of laborers works for them; their hunger drives them on (16:26).

This proverb connects the words "appetite" and "hunger." It takes a positive stance on the motivations of those who work. Many heads of households say, "I work to feed my family." If you are motivated to work in this way, you will work hard. Without motivation, you become lazy. Work becomes meaningless.

Christians who live a "purpose-driven life" don't work just to eat. They work with a sense of mission that God has sent them to this world. They work out of a sense of vocation, a sense of what God has called them to do. Their sense of calling and mission must be clearer and stronger than any earthly motivation.

A scoundrel plots evil, and on their lips it [and his speech] is like a scorching fire. A perverse person stirs up conflict [dissension], and a gossip separates close friends. A violent person entices their neighbor and leads them down a path that is not good. Whoever winks with their eye is plotting perversity; whoever purses their lips is bent on evil (16:27-30).[215]

This text describes the five sets of evil people. The characteristics and symptoms of antisocial and psychopathic people are well described. First, the wicked are rogues, villains, and scoundrels.[216] They plan and devise evil (27a). Their words are like raging fire, destructive and offensive (27b). They are verbally abusive. They are also very impulsive. There is little good in associating with such people.

Second, the wicked are perverse (28a). They stir up strife and division (28a). They have evil wisdom in creating gossip and driving even close friends apart (28b). They cause the church or society to be dysfunctional by adding or subtracting words, or worse, by writing fiction. They post unverified or false information on social media to make people confused, anxious or angry. Their heart is so perverse that they are subject to legal punishments.

Third, the wicked are violent (29a). They overreact to the slightest conflict with their neighbors and harm them with verbal or physical violence. They also harms their neighbors by deceiving and defrauding them (29b).

Fourth, the wicked wink with their eye with plot (30a). There are good winks and bad winks. A good wink is a means of communication that expresses wholehearted agreement without the need for words. But in this proverb (30a), winkers are ones who plot and scheme to do treacherous things. They signal with their eye without others noticing. They also signal with their hands, feet, and gestures to do evil. They use their God-given bodily parts for evil.

Fifth, an evil person is one who closes his mouth like a purse and does not speak (30b). Some people are soft-spoken by nature. However, the silent person this proverb refers to is one who deliberately does not speak. Shutting your mouth is a very aggressive behavior. Some people express their anger by closing their mouths to the point where the other person feels anxious. These people are building up enough anger to psychologically kill

---

[215] Bridges also commented on the four verses as a group. Bridges, *Proverbs*, 247-48.

[216] Bridges noted that all of these people are servants of their master, Satan, and that the wage they deserve is eternal death. Bridges, *Proverbs*, 248.

the other person. However, these people are foolish enough not to realize that their accumulated anger is killing them first.

Gray hair is a crown of splendor; it is attained in the way of righteousness (16:31).

Gray hair symbolizes old age. Not everyone can live to a ripe old age. Those who live righteous lives are favored by God enough to live that old age (31b).[217] The appearance of the elderly who have gone through many hardships and have been refined and integrated in the process is compared to the wearing of a glorious crown, that is , gray hair.[218] In that respect, the elderly are worthy of respect.

In this modern world that values youthfulness, the lives of the elderly tend to be undervalued. There are strong prejudices against the elderly. Nevertheless, our ears should be open to hear the life story of each old person behind his or her gray hairs. Our eyes should be open to see the "human being" behind the gray hairs and wrinkles. We need to remind ourselves of the sobering fact that he or she, too, had passed through a period of youth to become an old person.

Better a patient person than a warrior, one with self-control [a man who controls his temper] than one who takes a city (16:32). See also 15:1, 15:18.

---

[217] God's curse on the house of priest Eli was that there would be no old man in his house: "The time is coming when I will cut short your strength and the strength of your priestly house, so that no one in it will reach old age, and you will see distress in my dwelling. Although good will be done to Israel, no one in your family line will ever reach old age" (1 Sam. 2:31-32).

[218] "Stand up in the presence of the aged, show respect for the elderly and revere your God. I am the LORD" (Lev. 19:32).

This proverb uses the form, "A is better than B." Solomon says that those who are slow to anger and who control their temper are better than a victorious warrior. He emphasizes that it is more difficult and important to control oneself well and to attack or defend the invisible castle of the heart than to attack and capture a visible castle and win a victory.[219] Even if a warrior wins a battle and captures a castle, if he cannot continue to defend and govern the castle and the people who live in it, his hard work will be in vain.

The lot is cast into the lap, but its every decision is from the LORD (v. 33). See also 16:1.

---

[219] Bridges well recognized that the heart is an invisible battlefield. Bridges, *Proverbs*, 250. David was a warrior who won many battles with enemies, but he was a defeated general in the one battle of the heart. While this proverb refers to the battle of controlling anger, David's battle was the battle of controlling lust. The time David lost the battle of the heart was, paradoxically, when he was taking a leisurely stroll in his castle, not going to war with Ammon.

Chapter 17 Use Words with Restraint

Better a dry crust with peace and quiet than a house full of feasting, with strife (17:1). See 15:16, 17.

This proverb is structured in a form of "A is better than B." People who make a lot of money, occupy a high position, or receive social attention and recognition but whose home is not peaceful is unhappy. They may be less unhappy than someone who doesn't make money, isn't successful or isn't recognized. Those who are unhappy in the most important relationship in the world are really unhappy people. The Korean phrase "family goes well, then everything goes well" (家和萬事成) is a precious phrase that contains a truth.

We can apply this proverb to our relationship with God. Living in poverty but having a reconciled relationship with God is far better than living in wealth but having a "bad object relation" with God. Lazarus the beggar is a prime example of such a life.

A prudent [wise] servant will rule over a disgraceful son and will share the inheritance as one of the family [the brothers] (17:2).

With wisdom, a servant can rise to the position of ruling over his master's shameful son. If a son has no wisdom, he is ruled by a wise servant. In the context of verse 1, it is better to leave an inheritance to a wise servant than to a son who is disgraceful.

To understand the text from the son's point of view, if he fails his sonship, he will suffer the humiliation of being ruled by his father's servant. Solomon even says that the wise servant will have the legal rights of a master's son and will receive a share of the inheritance (2b). This is a warning to the son to get his act together.

It is normal for a servant to be a servant and a son to be a son. It is abnormal for a servant to pretend to be a son or for a son to be a servant. Nevertheless, the meaning of this proverb is that it is better for a wise servant to be an heir than a foolish son.

The crucible for silver and the furnace for gold, but the LORD tests the heart (17:3).[220]

The purpose of the crucibles and the furnace is to smelt ores to obtain treasures such as gold or silver. In order for an earthenware to become a household item or a work of art, it must be fired in the kiln over a hot fire. From the point of view of the ore or the clay, it would be too painful to endure the intense heat. But it must go through the process to become a beautifully colored and patterned vessel. It's only then that valuable and highly pure gold or silver can be extracted from the ore.

Similarly, God refines his children through the furnace or wilderness experiences of life. Wilderness experiences are a necessary part of the sanctification process because they purify the heart and mold it into God's children who look to God alone.

No one voluntarily desires trials and tribulations such as going through the furnace. But for those who endure them, trusting in God's good will to transform and mature them through suffering, they can turn into a refined life like pure gold. Paul expresses this truth beautifully when he writes, "Not only so, but we also glory in our sufferings, because we know that suffering produces perseverance; perseverance, character; and character, hope" (Rom. 5:3-4). Through the furnace experience, a believer's character is refined and spiritually purified.

Counseling Application: Many clients are in the melting pot of life. They are in a situation where they are unable to find a solution on their own, where their pain is mounting, their hope is fading, their courage is dwindling, they are suffocating, and they feel like they are going to die. The Christian counselor will need to help these clients realize that the furnace experience is not meaningless

---

[220] Fox points out that this proverb connects to 27:21: "The crucible for silver and the furnace for gold, but people are tested by their praise." Fox, *Proverbs 10-31*, 625.

and is connected to God's greater providence of transforming and maturing their character, and to help them persevere with living hope.

A wicked person listens to deceitful lips; a liar pays attention to a destructive [malicious] tongue (17:4).

This proverb uses a chiastic structure of A-B-C-A'-B'-C. "A wicked person" connects to "a liar" and "listens to" connects to "pay attention to" and "deceitful lips" connects to "a destructive tongue."

There's a Korean four character phrase that means, "Birds of a feather flock together" (類類相從). Deceitful lips are well heard by the wicked.[221] The term "twin transference" is used in self psychology to describe the idea that when we meet someone with similar traits to ourselves, we experience a sense of identification and use the twin object in our "self" development. The wicked experience twin transference from other evil people who are similar to them, which is why they listen to and follow other evil people with little resistance. They act in agreement, saying, "That's right!" when someone else expresses what they're thinking, even if they haven't expressed it themselves.

Paul pointed out this dynamic well when he said that in the time of distress in the last days, people will "not put up with sound doctrine. Instead, to suit their own desires, they will gather around them a great number of teachers to say what their itching ears want to hear. They will turn their ears away from the truth and turn aside to myths" (2 Tim. 4:3-4). The wicked do not follow good instruction. Rather, they have "many" wicked "teachers" or teachings or ideas that validate and confirm their selfish desires. They love and seek out "deceitful" lips and "destructive" tongues

---

[221] Bridges cited Amnon as the figure he associated with this proverb. Bridges, *Proverbs*, 256. He was led by lust and listened to the counsel of his friend Jonadab, who saw through his heart. Bridges also connected this proverb to the wicked king Ahab, who listened to his even more wicked wife Jezebel and killed the righteous Naboth. Bridges, *Proverbs*, 256-57.

that fulfill their selfish motives.

Liars don't take their problems seriously when they socialize with similar people. They accept themselves and those people as natural (4b). Lying is their routine and normal. They live by deceiving others and being deceived themselves (see 2 Tim. 3:13). They don't mind deceiving others and being deceived themselves, because they are deceptive and deceives others. There are also people who have been deceived many times and are still easily deceived and scammed. These people usually look for easy money. In fact, they deceive themselves by wanting to make easy money.

Heretical churches work well with other heretical churches. The more heretical churches that speak falsehoods because they are false anyway, the less they are attacked and the more they are defended by other heretics.[222]

Whoever mocks the poor shows contempt for their Maker;[223] whoever gloats over disaster will not go unpunished (17:5).[224]

Solomon's overall stance on poverty is negative. He often associates laziness with poverty, and diligence with wealth. In this proverb, however, he emphasizes the need to distinguish between poverty and the poor.

In this proverb, "the poor" and ones in "disaster" are those who are in unfortunate circumstances. Mocking or despising them is a behavior that provokes God to anger. It is an act of contempt for their Maker God (5a). To ignore the poor, even in one's heart, is

---

[222] Those who give heed to "deceitful lips" and "a destructive tongue" do not stand in the truth, but they are liars, who "abandon the faith and follow deceiving spirits and things taught by demons" (1 Tim. 4:1). Paul characterized them as "hypocritical liars, whose consciences have been seared as with a hot iron" (1 Tim. 4:2).

[223] Bridges noted that the first half of this proverb connects with 14:31: "Whoever oppresses the poor shows contempt for their Maker, but whoever is kind to the needy honors God." Bridges, *Proverbs*, 257.

[224] Bridges cited Shimei as a biblical example of one who delights in disaster (see 2 Sam 16:5-8). Bridges, *Proverbs*, 257.

fearful before God, for God created the poor and the afflicted in his image (5a) and he cares for those whom he has made.

Catastrophe strikes for many reasons. Catastrophes and natural disasters cause people to lose their lives or property in a hurry. God punishes those who rejoice when they see people suffer in disaster, even when they might suffer because of their wicked lives (5b).[225] Rather, being fearful and alert is the attitude of those who do not suffer calamity.

Children's children are a crown to the aged, and parents are the pride of their children (17:6).

This proverb is connected with 16:31, "Gray hair is a crown of Splendor" (16:31). It is a blessing for a person to be called grandfather or grandmother.. If his or her children do not marry, or if they marry and have no children, he or she cannot not be called grandfather or grandmother by direct descendants.

Being a grandfather or grandmother means having graying hair and declining strength. But through a grandchild or grandchildren, grandparents' inner self can be strengthened. A grandchild is his or her grandparent's crown of glory and decoration. For parents who have experienced both the bitter and sweet tastes of life through their marriage, to see grandchildren in their old age is an honor and a joy, like wearing a crown. Most grandparents say that they love their grandchildren more than their children. Grandchildren are the joy that God has prepared for us in our old age.

Counseling Application: Children are highly influenced by their parents, so it's not an exaggeration to say that the way parents are shapes the way their children are. Parents are very influential in shaping their children's self-esteem. With appropriate mirroring and idealizing experiences, children can develop a sense of self-worth and form a "cohesive self."[226]

---

[225] God's heart expressed in this proverb was revealed in Judah's destruction. Although Judah was destroyed for its idolatry and other sins, God pronounced judgment on Edom, which rejoiced in its destruction (see Obad. 1:12).

The second half of the verse would not be awkward to change as follows: "Children are the glory of their parents." Children are objects of pride to their parents. When children are growing up and practicing their faith well, parents feel grateful and proud of their children. They feel comfortable talking about and praising their children in public. Parents are especially happy when their children grow up and live independent lives or have successful marriages. Even if they are not much filial, their lives themselves will be a source of pride and joy to their parents.

Parents should be aware of whether they are objects of pride to their their children. Some parents mistakenly believe that they are doing a good job with their children and that their children like them, because of their lack of insight. They may even go so far as to lavish pathological love on their children, thinking that they will appreciate it. They don't empathize with their children's feeling of suffocation and inability to say no to them. They don't understand their children's unexpressed anger and frustration at not being able to say no to them.

Conversely, there are some children who don't care much about the fact that they are the ones who wound their parents' heart. They think they can ignore their parents because they were hurt by them, and so they go on with their lives without understanding, forgiveness, or reconciliation. But in spite of parents' neglect and shortcomings, the path of change and healing is for either children or parents who are enlightened to reach out and reconcile first. Forgiving benefits the forgiver first in many ways. Forgiveness is God's will for us. Otherwise, it won't be long before unforgiving children find themselves wounding the same to their own children. People who have an unresolved relationship with their parents cannot properly love their children. They are at risk of raising their own children with anger.

---

[226] Heinz Kohut, the founder of Self Psychology, argued that children need to experience a "mirroring" from their mother and an "idealizing" from their father in order for their self structure to be cohesive and promote the development of a true self rather than a false self.

Eloquent [Arrogant]lips are unsuited to a godless fool [a fool]—
how much worse lying lips to a ruler! (17:7).

Foolishness and arrogant lips don't always go together: fools
don't necessarily have arrogant lips. To have arrogant lips one
must be smart and intelligent to some degree. This is because many
foolish people often lack confidence and don't know what to say.

But in this proverb, people with haughty lips are considered
foolish. This is because they don't realize that there are many
people in the world who are smarter than they are. Furthermore,
they don't realize that they are not in a position to speak arrogantly
before God.

Even more misbecoming than it is misbecoming for a fool to
speak arrogantly is for a ruler to have lying lips (7b). It is
catastrophic for a ruler to lie. The virtue called for in those in
positions of leadership, both socially and nationally, is honesty and
integrity. If a national leader lies or perjures, it can be a major
reason for removal from office. But the irony of the situation is
that leaders are likely to lie. It is easy for them to say one thing and
do another and end up lying intentionally or unintentionally.
However, habitual liars or psychopaths are not fitting for the
leadership positions, such as head of household, principal, and
political leaders.

Christians are a royal priesthood, a holy nation in this wold.
Christians and lying lips are an unlikely pair. Churches will be able
to fulfill their role of salt and light when the words of Christians
are recognized by the world like certified checks. Pastors who
engage in denominational politics must have honest lips if they are
to be recognized as denominational leaders. We need to repent and
realize that God abhors lying lips, especially from leaders.

A bribe is seen as a charm by the one who gives it; they think
success will come at every turn [wherever he turns, he
succeeds] (17:8).

Even with the second half in mind, it makes more sense to say "a bribe is seductive to the one who receives it." But the text says that a bribe is charming to the giver. What does this mean? It would be appropriate to interpret the second half of the verse as a description of the real-world power of bribery.[227] A misreading of the text could lead to the conclusion that it is teaching us that bribery will get things done in some way. So it is not unreasonable to interpret it as describing the reality that bribery often gets things done.

Bribery works as well in the modern world as it did in Solomon's time. Because they work, bribery methods are attractive to bribe givers. It is also charming because it is not punishable unless the bribe is discovered, and it is rarely discovered. If the giver and receiver do not have a strong ethical value system, they are more likely to use bribery because it is like a defense mechanism that is easily used to cope with anxiety and fear, and it works quickly.

Sometimes bribes are delivered directly, sometimes indirectly. And then there are some brokers who make it their business to deliver bribes. There are also some people who are like a parasitic plant, asking some commission money from both sides, or delivering only a part of the bribe, or not delivering it at all but taking all money for themselves. These people don't feel shame or guilt. It would not be unreasonable to diagnose them as having antisocial personality disorder and/or psychopath. It is shameful that there are such persons even in denominational politics. They have no fear of God.

Whoever would foster [promote] love covers over an offense, but whoever repeats the matter separates close friends (17:9).

One of the biblical options when we became to learn of others'

---

227 Haman offered a large bribe of ten thousand talents of silver to obtain approval from King Xerxes for a decree to exterminate the Jews. The king graciously refused to take it, saying, "Keep the money, and do with the people as you please," and removed his signet ring and handed it over to Haman for approval (see Esth. 3:9-11).

sin is to "cover it up" or "overlook." Of course, there are some cases in which we have to "dis-cover" it or "confront" them. No human being is without sin. If we are exposed to others as we are, we all would feel ashamed as if we are walking around naked.

Thankfully, God designed our eyes in a way that we cannot see the inside of the other person. There may be rare times when our spiritual eyes are opened to see through to the other person's faults (whether this is the work of the Holy Spirit or the devil is to be discerned). However, God took care that Adam and Eve would not feel shame for each other after they sinned by making them permanent skirts of leather instead of the skirts of leaves they had made. This shows us that God covers the inner transgressions of sinful humans for our own benefit of mental health.

Mentioning repeatedly a sin of a person over and over again is a way to continue to humiliate the person. It can be a harassing of the person. Furthermore, to make the sin known and publicized to many people is to cause division among those involved (9b). If it is a sin that can be covered up, it is a neighborly love to cover it up until death. Covering a transgression, even if the other person is unaware of it, is an act of love toward that person.

Those who cover someone's trespasses have the ability to empathize with that person. They cover because they take into account the pain the person will suffer if their transgression is exposed. And they do so by remembering that others also have covered their own transgressions and doing the same for the person.

However, there are times when sins need to be pointed out and confronted. This is when the sin is fatal and contageous to the community. If the offense is serious enough that covering it up risks destroying the individual and the community, we must be angry and have courage and wisdom to confront it. In these cases, direct, personal confrontation is the first step to exhort in a biblical way. If the person does not listen, the next step is to counsel them with two or three witnesses. If the person still do not listen, the next step is to take them through the church community or social justice system (see Matt. 18:15-17).

The virtues of covering up and secrecy do not apply to socially and legally criminal behavior, i.e., when the police or prosecutor needs to be involved. For example, it is not an act of love to cover up for someone who has killed a person.

Counseling Application: Counselors will encounter stories of sin from their clients. Christian counselors with a balanced biblical mindset should be able to cover their clients' transgressions to the end when they need to be covered. The ethics and virtue of confidentiality should be kept in mind at all times.

A rebuke impresses a discerning person more than a hundred lashes a fool (17:10).[228]

For counsel or reproof to be effective, the recipient must be "a discerning person." People of discernment are willing to receive advice, even if it may hurt, and are receptive to applying it to their life. Foolish people, on the other hand, are unlikely to change their minds and behaviors, even if they are struck with a hundred lashes (10b). Solomon confirms this in another proverb: "Though you grind a fool in a mortar, grinding them like grain with a pestle, you will not remove their folly from them" (27:22). Moreover, advice is ineffective to them.

Therefore, it is wise to know who to target when giving advice or rebuking. Not just anyone will listen to a rebuke. There are times when we read sad news stories. For example, a man was beaten up by a group of teenagers when he rebuked their delinquent behavior. Some people are assaulted and in some cases killed because they confronted teenagers not to smoke in public place. So we need to be discerning and wise when giving advice. If you throw pearls before a herd of swine, there is a chance that they will step on them and turn on you (see Matt. 7:6).

Evildoers foster rebellion against God [An evil man is bent only

---

[228] Bridges saw the second half of this proverb is related to 27:22: "Though you grind a fool in a mortar, grinding them like grain with a pestle, you will not remove their folly from them." Bridges, *Proverbs*, 262.

rebellion]; the messenger of death [a merciless official] will be sent against them (17:11).

All fallen humans have a sinful nature and are oriented to sin. Just as a sunflower is oriented to the direction of sunlight, so the wicked will rebel when the circumstances are right. Like the foolish, the evil of the wicked is very difficult to remove. This proverb helps us to understand that the wicked in their adulthood stage of life are already hardwired for aggression and antisociality and cannot be easily changed. People with a so-called "unyielding" temperament is likely to engage in defiant behaviors given the right circumstances.

In this proverb, Solomon suggests sending "a merciless official" to kill those who are at high risk of rebellion (11b). It is understandable that he would have more concerned in this regard, given his traumatic experience with his older brother Adonijah's rebellion before he was installed as king.

Better to meet a bear robbed of her cubs than a fool bent on folly (17:12).

This proverb well expresses how wary Solomon was of fools. For a king to have foolish and stupid subordinates is a sure way to ruin a country. From the perspective of the subordinates, having a foolish and stupid king is a very unfortunate thing. Until the king dies, there is no hope for the future of the country.

King Xerxes was bent on folly. He loved to boast and to be recognized. He was a vulnerable king to manipulation of others who didn't have much of a mind of his own. He was a foolish king who fell prey to the suggestion of his official Memucan and the machination of the evil Haman. He was a "thoughtless" king who entrusted the royal seal to Haman, who was plotting to murder the entire Jewish people, without fully understanding the full extent of the situation. He had dynamics of borderline personality disorder where he impulsively commanded the seven eunuchs to bring before him his beautiful wife Queen Vasti in his high spirits from wine. He wanted to display her beauty to the people and nobles. But when she refused to come, he "became furious and burned with anger" (Est. 1:12). He was a foolish king who dethroned his beloved wife because he had created a double bind for himself in front of his officials and his people the he could neither do this nor that. Moreover, if not for God's amazing providence and protection, he would have been manipulated to wipe out the race of Judah, God's people. It is sad and frustrating for the people to have such a king. It is better for them "to meet a bear robbed of her cubs" (12a). The same is true today. When a foolish person becomes a pastor or a political leader, the church members or the people suffer until he or she leaves office. When a foolish person becomes a university president, the professors and students will be sure to suffer.

Evil will never leave the house of one who pays back evil for good (17:13).

This proverb carries the same meaning of Korean four character idioms, such as "The good triumphs over the evil" (勸善懲惡) or "What goes around comes around" (因果應報). However, it would be unreasonable to apply this proverb to every situation. We need to understand that this proverb contains truth in a general sense.

Solomon counsels against repaying good with evil. Paul goes further and recommends not repaying evil for evil: "Do not repay anyone evil for evil. Be careful to do what is right in the eyes of everyone" (Rom. 12:17); "Do not be overcome by evil, but overcome evil with good" (Rom. 12:21). Paul elaborates on this meaning by giving a specific example: "If your enemy hungers, feed him; if he is thirsty, give him something to drink. In doing this, you will heap burning coals on his head" (Rom. 12:20).

Responding to good with evil is evil and pathological. It not only disregards the other person's goodwill, but also it destroys him or her.[229] Responding to good with good is common sense and unrewarding, but responding to evil with good is acceptable and pleasing to God. This is a difficult attitude of life that all believers are to strive for.

Starting a quarrel is like breaching a dam; so drop the matter before a dispute breaks out (17:14).

When conflicts in the church escalate into litigation, it's often like breaching a dam. Marital conflicts that lead to divorce are also not uncommon, with small arguments escalating into larger conflicts that lead to catastrophic situations. It's like a small crack in a dike that eventually leads to the bursting of the dike (14a).

It's wise to recognize this and back off before it escalates into a big fight. A catastrophic outcome can be avoided if one side backs down and avoids it. When to avoid, it's better to avoid. You don't have to avoid always. There is "a time for war and a time for peace" (Eccl. 3:8b). Paradoxically, losing or withdrawing can be winning. If you react irrationally or emotionally without seeing the big picture up to the catastrophic point, you'll regret it later. It is wise to stop a dispute early on, keeping in mind that small conflicts can escalate into unwinnable battles later on (14b).

Acquitting the guilty and condemning the innocent— the LORD

---

229 Joab, David's military commander, killed Abner, Ishbosheth's military commander, on his own initiative, without being ordered to do so by David, as Abner was returning home after he revealed his will to return Saul's son Ishbosheth's kingdom to David. This was a personal revenge for his brother Asahel being killed by Abner in battle. The problem was that he didn't kill him in the course of battle, but rather "took him aside into an inner chamber, as if to speak with him privately" and "stabbed him in the stomach" (2 Sam. 3:27). Abner's good intentions were repaid with evil. When David heard of this, he prophesied the curse that would come upon Joab and his descendants: "May his blood fall on the head of Joab and on his whole family! May Joab's family never be without someone who has a running sore or leprosy or who leans on a crutch or who falls by the sword or who lacks food" (2 Sam. 3:29). This was an event where the words of this proverb were practically applied.

detests them both (17:15).[230]

God is the source and standard of justice. By nature, God does not take pleasure in unrighteousness. He abhors injustice.

Disliking and hating are not sinful in themselves. We must dislike and hate what we ought to dislike and hate in order for justice to be served. The ability to distinguish between liking and disliking is closely related to the development of the superego (conscience). The healthy functioning of a judge's conscience enables him or her to hate injustice and to rule justly.

Corrupt judges, prosecutors, or police make a country corrupt and dysfunctional. When judicial systems are swayed according to the interest of political leaders or people with power or money, people will be disappointed and angry. It may shake the country's discipline and bring it down. A nation whose police officers are corrupt and accept money from organized crime syndicates to condone or abet crime will be labeled a corrupt nation. God's judgment will come upon such a nation (15b).

Counseling Application: Christian counselors should not take an ethically neutral position in the counseling process. Furthermore, they should not take a distorted view on important issues biblically and ethically. They should not say that sinful behavior is not sinful or unrighteously assign blame to someone who is not responsible in their counseling with clients. It takes discernment and courage to keep a biblical boundary intact and say sin is sin. We are also vulnerable beings ourselves to sin, but if we are unable to call sin sin because of the dynamics of countertransference, we cannot be counselors that God is not pleased with.

---

[230] The same spirit is seen in the book of Isaiah: "Woe to those who call evil good and good evil, who put darkness for light and light for darkness, who put bitter for sweet and sweet for bitter.... who acquit the guilty for a bribe, but deny justice to the innocent" (Isa. 5:20-23). Pilate knew that Jesus was innocent, but he was afraid of a civil uprising, so he released the wicked Barabbas to crucify Jesus. Although he said he was innocent, washing his hands, he was guilty in that he abdicated his responsibility as a judge. His name is mentioned shamefully whenever we recite the Apostles' Creed.

Why should fools have money in hand to buy wisdom, when they are not able to understand it? [since he has no desire to get wisdom?] (17:16).

One meaning of this proverb is that it is foolish for fools to try to buy wisdom with money. We see this in the case of Simon, who practiced magic in the city of Samaria (see Acts 8:18-23). He was a foolish, wicked man who tried to buy the power of the Holy Spirit with money.

Another meaning of this proverb is that the money in the hands of a fools is of no use because they have no desire to gain wisdom. If you have a desire for wisdom, you will go to great lengths to find the wise, even if it means spending money. Like a pearl merchant seeking a costly pearl in a parable of Jesus, you will invest in finding wisdom and knowledge. But the foolish have little desire for wisdom, even if they have enough money, so they do not seek it or invest in it. In the modern sense, fools do not spend money on studying or buying books to improve their intellect or skills. They spend money on entertainment or luxurious things, but not on things that will bring them wisdom in life. The same is true to spiritual wisdom. Fools are not interested in God at all.

A friend is not cut off from love, and a brother comes to the rescue in a time of need [A friend loves at all times, and a brother is born for adversity] (17:17).

□Not all friends are friends. Those who are loving and supportive in times of trouble are true friends. Similarly, not all brothers are brothers. Brothers who are empathetic and concerned in times of crisis are true brothers.

One who has no sense [lacks judgment] shakes hands in pledge and puts up security for a neighbor (17:18).

Solomon sees putting up security for a neighbor as an act of poor judgment. There are times when it's necessary to help someone in a way of giving a guarantee. But in this proverb, Solomon calls it unwise to give a guarantee hastily, impulsively, or without discernment. It's never too late to ask God, seek the advice of your spouse or others with more wisdom before you sign to give a guarantee. It's foolish and dangerous to make a quick decision to pledge without going through this process.

If you can reverse your promise, you can get away with apologizing. However, making an irrevocable contract can be catastrophic. At times, some people vouch for their house in order to keep their friend's loyalty intact. However, a surprising number of people experience the trauma of having their entire family thrown out on the street because of their guarantee for their close friend or relative. It's foolish to risk the future of their children and shorten the life span of their spouse due to the stress that follows the traumatic catastrophe. Therefore, it's important to think twice before taking out a mortgage for others.

Whoever loves a quarrel loves sin; whoever builds a high gate invites destruction (17:19).

There are some people who like to fight and argue. There are some ethnic groups that have a "warlike" temperament. However, Koreans have been called the "white-robed people" which means that they are generally peace-loving. This is because they have often been in the position of being attacked and having to defend themselves rather than invading first.

Are there people who like to argue? Yes, there are actually many who are argumentative and easily angered. The popularity of ultimate fighting game in TV is an evidence that many people like to release their aggression indirectly. The popularity of computer games also supports this reality, as many people like to play aggressive and murderous games. There are a lot of people who have aggression in their hearts even though they don't fight openly.

People who have a lot of anger inside them unconsciously look for someone to take it out on. They lash out, yell, and punch at the slightest mistake. In particular, those who use the defense mechanism of "displacement" take out their anger on people who are weaker than them. It is an immature behavior to suppress the anger that should be expressed to stronger people and then yell and scream at people who are weaker than they are.

As for the second part of the proverb, if you build a high wall and a high gate, you will be safe. This method is wise because a low gate is an easy target for enemies. Then why does Solomon say that those who build a high gate invite destruction? It's not an easy phrase to understand.

Psychologically, the second part of this proverb is easy to understand. A high gate can be interpreted as a strong defense mechanism. It's very difficult to be intimate in interpersonal relationships if the gate is high enough to make it difficult for others to approach. A high and solid gate is safe and helpful in the short term in relationship. However, in the long run, you run the risk of becoming isolated because no one will approach you.

A high gate on your home can be intimidating and keep burglars out, but it can also make you a target for professional thieves. This is because a high gate means that persons living in that house may a lot of valuables. In other words, a high gate invites professional burglars (19b). Furthermore, homes with high gates and walls are harder for neighbors to access and are more likely to be isolated from neighbors.

Counseling Application: With clients who have a high and solid gate to their inner world, it is necessary for the counselor to be empathetic and receptive to help them lower the gate a little bit. Then they begin to open up things slowly that have not been shared with anyone. And they experience some positive changes in their interpersonal relationships with their family and others.

One whose heart is corrupt does not prosper; one whose tongue is perverse [deceitful] falls into trouble (17:20).

Those whose tongue is perverse are the ones whose heart is corrupt because tongue is controlled by heart. Because their heart is corrupt, deceitful words come out of their mouth. The tongue is merely a servant of the mind. The tongue and mouth themselves don't have control.

It may seem like the liar has temporarily won. But lies do not last long. Those who speak lies will soon fall into disaster (20b). Christians should not be frustrated or discouraged, trusting that God is alive and at work to bring the deceitful to their swift defeat (see Ps. 37).

To have a fool for a child brings grief; there is no joy for the parent of a godless fool (17:21). See also 15:20.

The second part of this proverb emphasizes the message of the first part by repeating it. It is natural for parents of foolish children to be anxious and sad. No wonder they have no joy when they are godless. On the other hand, parents whose children are godly, intelligent, wise, and discerning are grateful. They are proud of their children.

A cheerful heart is good medicine, but a crushed spirit dries up the bones (17:22).

This proverb is connected to verse 21. Given the context, the joy of the heart comes from a wise child. And that joy has the same effect as taking good medicine (22a). On the contrary, the anguish of heart comes from an ungodly child, and that worry is so stressful enough to dry up the bones of the parent (22b).

The wicked accept bribes in secret to pervert the course of justice (17:23).

Solomon admonished about bribery in verse 8, and in this verse he confirms again that bribery is evil. No one gives or receives bribes openly. They are given and received in secret (23a).

The wicked take bribes (23a). Conversely, the giver of bribes is also wicked. Both the giver and the receiver are wicked.

It is wicked for a judge, a representation of justice, to take a bribe and judge unjustly (23b). Judges or prosecutors who secretly accept bribes and pervert the course of a trial in exchange for them are evil and psychopaths.

No one will become a politician or lawyer with the goal of taking bribes from the start. No one will enter seminary with the intention of becoming a backroom dealer in denominational politics. But if a person takes a bribe once, and then a second time, he or she becomes a person who lives by a philosophy, "what's good for the goose is good for the gander." Repeated evil deeds dull the function of the conscience. Later on, he or she feels no sense of guilt or shame like those whose consciences have been seared.

The fact that the phrase "One law for the rich and another for the poor" is still in use indicates that those who work in justice are not immune from bribery. If a victim is wrongfully convicted because of a bribe given to the judge, this is an act that provokes God to wrath. God does not look past the injustice done to the weak. Neither the giver nor the receiver of a bribe is immune from God's dreadful judgment.[231] God is well aware of all the ways in which bribes are secretly passed, and he watches over. His eyes are everywhere!

A discerning person keeps wisdom in view, but a fool's eyes wander to the ends of the earth (17:24).

---

[231] Bridges noted two other biblical passages are related to this proverb: "Your rulers are revels, partners with thieves; they all love bribes and chase after gifts. They do not defend the cause of the fatherless; the widow's case does not come before them" (Isa. 1:23); "A gift given in secret soothes anger, and a bribe concealed in the cloak pacifies great wrath" (Prov. 21:14). Bridges, *Proverbs*, 275.

Wisdom is closest. God is close at hand. The Bible is also at our fingertips if we want it.

But the foolish do not know that wisdom is at hand. They do not recognize that precious things are at hand. They see things that are far away as better (24b) and that have little to do with them as relevant. They are more interested in and listen to people who have nothing to do with them. While they fail to empathize with their own family members, they are attentive to others who are not related to them personally. They are what the Bible calls fools. Those who try to love those who are far away while failing to love those who are near is foolish. Paul exhorts us to make our priorities clear: "As we have opportunity, let us do good to all people, especially to those who belong to the family of believers" (Gal. 6:10); "Anyone who does not provide for their relatives, and especially for their own household, has denied the faith and is worse than an unbeliever" (1 Tim. 5:8). It is foolish to provide relief to people in distant lands while neglecting to provide relief to one's own family or people.

This proverb paints a picture of a fool looking to and fro. It is because of psychological immaturity that this seems to be good and that seems to be better. It is a psychological characteristic of children. Therefore, people whose gaze reach to the ends of the earth and whose eyes wander to and fro is immature and foolish.[232]

A foolish son brings grief to his father and bitterness to the mother who bore him (17:25). See 17:21.

---

[232] James makes a good point that people without stability are unstable and doubtful in prayer: "But when you ask, you must believe and not doubt, because the one who doubts is like a wave of the sea, blown and tossed by the wind.... Such a person is double-minded and unstable in all they do" (James 1:6-8). People whose eyes wander are double-minded or triple-minded. It is very difficult for such people to worship God wholeheartedly.

If imposing a fine on the innocent is not good [It is not good to punish an innocent man], surely to flog honest officials is not right [or to flog officials for their integrity] (17:26).

This proverb is connected to the preceding verse 15: "Acquitting the guilty and condemning the innocent—the LORD detests them both." A king or official is responsible for rewarding the righteous and punishing the wicked. However, a king or official who punishes the righteous is an evildoer who misuses and abuses the authority God has given him or her.

It is wicked to convict and punish the innocent. It is also evil before God to discipline a public official who has acted with integrity. To punish the innocent as guilty, the judge must judge the guilty innocent. It is wicked to impute the guilt of the guilty to the innocent.

Jesus was convicted as an innocent man. He was sued and judged unjustly, but he overcame evil with good. By being crucified and executed, he shed his righteous blood to atone for the sins of the guilty. Because our sins have been imputed to him, we are judged innocent and free by God. It is an amazing grace!

The one who has knowledge uses words with restraint, and whoever has understanding is even-tempered (17:27).

People with a temper have little control over their words. When they are upset, they pour out abusive words. But people with understanding and knowledge restrain their speech because their reason controls their emotion.

Counseling Application: Christian counselors should be persons of understanding and knowledge. They know how to speak sparingly. They are able to differentiate what to say from what not to say. They are able to contain what to say next time. They speak with clarity and to the point. They don't say unnecessary things or say things that are tangential.

On the other hand, inexperienced counselors who lack knowledge and understanding, talk a lot. They think that talking more will help the client, but it has the opposite effect. If a verbatim transcript shows more words spoken by the counselor than by the client, it is almost certainly an ineffective session. An effective counselor acts as a catalyst for the client to talk more.

Even fools are thought wise if they keep silent, and discerning if they hold their tongues (17:28).

This proverb is connected with verse 27. The wise have the ability to control their speech. Furthermore, even the foolish will be considered wise when they hold their tongues.

This proverb warns against making mistakes by talking too much. It's not uncommon to say too much and end up borrowing trouble. It's not uncommon to say the wrong thing and end up with a much worse outcome than saying nothing at all.

When people open their mouth to speak, it reveals their level of character, education, and common sense. The accent of speech even reveals where they are from. This is why Solomon advises that it is much better to remain silent than to speak foolishly.

Chapter 18 To Answer before Listening Is Folly and Shame

An unfriendly person pursues selfish ends and against [he defies] all sound judgment starts quarrels (18:1).

Counseling Application: In this proverb, Solomon well describes the core symptoms of narcissistic personality disorder and schizoid personality disorder. Those who separate themselves from others are, first, persons with narcissistic personality disorder.[233] These persons lack empathy for others, especially those in need. They also have an exaggerated sense of self. As a result, they seek to associate with people who are superior and exceptional to them. They don't care about people they consider inferior to them. Even with those who are superior to them, their relationships are selfish and temporary. They seek relationships only with those who satisfy their narcissistic needs. They are psychologically infantile and have not grown out of their childish state. As the proverb says, they pursue their own selfish ends (1a).

People with narcissistic personality disorder dismiss "true wisdom," or "all sound judgment" (1b) because they think their ideas are the best. They don't listen to advice. Generally speaking, they are not good listeners in relationship with others. They listen to people they see as admirable and idealized because they identify with them.

Second, "unfriendly" people may be diagnosed as persons with schizoid personality disorder. These people are selfish on a different level than ones with narcissistic personality disorder. The desire to relate to others is very much absent among them. They're only interested in their own lives. They don't care about or

---

[233] Clifford insightfully points out that being overly preoccupied with one's own thoughts is the hallmark of an antisocial person. He notes that a person who lives in isolation from others cannot become wise. The antisociality he means is more a symptom of schizoid personality disorder than antisocial personality disorder. Clifford, *Proverbs*, 170.

interfere in other people's lives. They don't want others to enter their territory of life. They are isolated, like an island, and don't feel the loneliness or pain that comes from the lack of relationships. Some of them even have little interest in the opposite sex. As long as they're okay with themselves, there's no problem in life. They don't care about other people's praise or criticism. They don't listen to other people's objective advice or wisdom because they are not affected by other people's feedback.[234] They keep their attitude of "my way" to life.

Fools find no pleasure in understanding but delight in airing their own opinions (18:2).

Counseling Application: This proverb can be interpreted in the context of verse 1. Solomon saw people with the aforementioned narcissistic personality disorder or schizoid personality disorder as foolish, or fools. People with narcissistic personality disorder lack a sense of real self and has very little insight into the disorder of their inner world, and therefore do not seek to know themselves in their pursuit of understanding, knowledge, and wisdom. When confronted with their own vulnerability, they withdraw from or resist their reality. They resist because they cannot bear to have their self-image shattered.

Individuals with narcissistic personality disorder like to express their views to others (2b)[235] because they think their ideas are

---

[234] Such people are incapable of loving their neighbor. In some cases, they may be pursuing a solitary life with God. However, a lack of concern for one's neighbors is not a characteristic of a balanced life of faith. Those who do not love neighbors who are visible cannot love God who is invisible. People with schizoid personality disorder are also ones who live a life of pathological self-love, thinking only of their own good.

[235] The problem is that the way they voice their opinions reveals their foolishness and immaturity (see Prov. 17:28). Speaking is a form of behavior. Therefore, people who prefer to speak only their mind are engaging in a behavior that allows others to identify their narcissistic personality disorder. It is important for preachers to recognize the possibility of narcissistic personality disorder tendencies in themselves.

superior and expect people to respond to their ideas with admiration and praise. If people don't praise them, it doesn't hurt them much. This is where they differ from people with histrionic personality disorder. People with histrionic personality disorder are hurt in these situations because their needs for attention and praise are not satisfied. People with narcissistic personality disorder, however, has a self-soothing capacity that allows them to believe that there is something wrong with those around them who don't recognize or praise them. They feel sorry for others who cannot understand their brilliant thoughts and words. Therefore, they are not easily hurt. However, when they receive feedback that confronts them with their weaknesses, it can sometimes wound their self-images that their self structure may collapse. This is called a narcissistic wound.

People who are too opinionated and unable to listen to others are fools. These are prone to social bullying. They may be tolerated a few times, but if their narcissistic behaviors are repeated, most people will dismiss or stay away from them.

It's hard to relate with someone who insists on defending or arguing his or her point no matter what you say. When one makes a mistake, being honest and saying, "I am sorry," or apologizing can restore relationships. However, narcissistic people don't admit their faults or mistakes. If they do, they do it superficially and without sincerity. As a result, people don't want to be in a relationship with them.

When wickedness comes, so does contempt, and with shame comes reproach [disgrace] (18:3).

Shame and disgrace can be seen as synonyms. This proverb is a reminder to anticipate the consequences that follow: if you do evil, insult and dishonor will follow (3a); if you do shameful things, humiliation and dishonor will follow (3b).

Preachers who are unable to understand and empathize with their audience and who are one-sided in their presentation of what they think are most likely to have this disorder.

If we interpret this proverb in connection with the preceding verses 1 and 2, the "wickedness" is a narcissistic or schizoid personality disorder. Then this proverb can be interpreted as a warning of the treatment and consequences those with that disorder will receive from others in social relationships.

The reality is that most people look down on people with narcissistic personality disorder. They especially dislike "explicit" narcissists because their selfishness stands out. People don't get close to them. People don't like to help them when they're in trouble.

The words of the mouth are deep waters, but the fountain of wisdom is a rushing stream [a bubbling brook] (18:4).

In the first part of this proverb a word, "a well," is omitted before "deep waters". The words that come out of the mouth of the wise are wise words and therapeutic words. They are life-saving words. Drinking the words from a well of deep waters refreshes and empowers.

The fountain of wisdom never stops flowing as one draws from it. The mouth of the wise is not a mouth that has nothing to say after a few words. It is a mouth from which inexhaustible wisdom continues to flow (4b).[236]

David, Solomon, and Paul were God's men of wisdom whose mouths were the spring of wisdom and knowledge. David wrote many of the Psalms. Solomon, who was greatly influenced by David, wrote the gems of Proverbs, Ecclesiastes, and Song of Songs. The book of Proverbs, in particular, is a treasure trove of wisdom, each verse alone. Paul brilliantly expounded the core truths of Christian beliefs in his epistles.

However, the wisest and most life-giving of lips is Jesus Christ. His every word contains core wisdom and penetrates the hearts of

---

[236] This is contrasted with the mouth of the foolish, which gushes out evil and foolish words. The mouth of the wise also has an empathetic ear, listening to the counsel and wisdom of others, unlike the mouth of the foolish, which speaks only of their own will and thought.

people. His one word, "Let any one of you who is without sin be the first to throw a stone at her," cut to the hearts of the entire crowd that brought the woman caught in the act of adultery to her death (John 8:7). It was a word that caused every single one of them, without exception, to lay down the stone in their hands and turn around.[237] His word was "alive and active. Sharper than any double-edged sword, it penetrates even to dividing soul and spirit, joints and marrow; it judges the thoughts and attitudes of the heart" (Heb. 4:12). He was such an inexhaustible fountain of wisdom that to record all the words of wisdom he spoke and the works he did would require "even the whole world would not have room for the books that would be written" (John 21:25). He was the river of living water that Ezekiel saw in his vision.[238]

It is not good to be partial to the wicked and so deprive the innocent of justice (18:5).

This proverb directly connects to 17:26, "If imposing a fine on the innocent is not good, surely to flog honest officials is not right." God likes to be fair and impartial. God is not "partial." God explicitly prescribed a few times in Leviticus and Deuteronomy not to make partial judgments.[239] God is a righteous judge. He will

---

[237] The amazing thing is that they retained a minimum of self-awareness. If even one of them had thrown a stone, thinking he or she was innocent, the woman would have died.

[238] Jesus himself said, "Let anyone who is thirsty come to me and drink. Whoever believes in me, as Scripture has said, rivers of living water will flow from within them" (John 7:37-38).

[239] "Do not pervert justice; do not show partiality to the poor or favoritism to the great, but judge your neighbor fairly" (Lev. 19:15); "And I charged your judges at that time, 'Hear the disputes between your people and judge fairly, whether the case is between two Israelites or between an Israeltie and a foreigner residing among you. Do not show partiality in judging; hear both small and great alike. Do not be afraid of anyone, for judgment belongs to God'" (Deut. 1:16-17); "For the LORD your God is God of gods and Lord of lords, the great God, mighty and awesome, who shows no

274

never judge unjustly on the Last Judgment Day. He will not judge unrighteously those who have been justified by faith in Jesus Christ.

The scales, which symbolize the judiciary, symbolize that judgments should be unbiased. It is evil for a judge to take sides with the wicked or the rich (5b).

The lips of fools bring them strife, and their mouths invite a beating. The mouths of fools are their undoing, and their lips are a snare to their very lives (18:6-7).[240]

The text can be understood as a "lips-mouth-mouth-lips" structure. The consequences of the lips and mouth of the foolish are described in four ways. First, they bring contention and strife (6a). The foolish cannot speak "therapeutic words," like cool water drawn from a deep well mentioned in verse 4. Instead, they speak impulsively and recklessly and thus cause unnecessary strife. A word may pay off a debt of a thousand dollars, but they owe a thousand dollars with a word! This is especially common in family relationships. A single impulsive word of a fool can deeply hurt a spouse, child, or parent.

Second, the lips and mouth of the foolish invite a beating (6b). By speaking foolishly, they are counter-attacked and humiliated by the other person.

partiality and accepts no bribes. He defends the cause of the fatherless and the widow, and loves the foreigner residing among you, giving them food and clothing. And you are to love those who are foreigners, for you yourselves were foreigners in Egypt" (Deut. 10:17-19); "Do not pervert justice or show partiality. Do not accept a bribe, for a bribe blinds the eyes of the wise and twists the words of the innocent. Follow justice and justice alone, so that you may live and possess the land the LORD your God is giving you" (Deut. 16:19-20).

[240] Bridges refers to the foolishness of the young men of Bethel who mocked Elisha, saying, "Get out of here, baldy! Get out of here, baldy!" (2 Kings 2:23). As a result of Elisha's curse, forty-two of them were mauled by two bears that came out of the woods. Bridges, *Proverbs*, 284.

Third, the lips and mouth of the foolish bring ruin to themselves (7a). A foolishly uttered word has deadly consequences. It brings ruin to themselves or ruin to others. In a sensitive situation, under heightened anxiety, a foolish word can bring irreversible ruin. It can cause great losses in marriage, family, career, honor, or material possessions. A person may commit suicide because it has wounded his or her traumatically. Furthermore, foolish words spoken unconsciously can psychologically kill the other person. This is truly frightening.

Finally, the lips and mouth of the foolish become a snare for their soul and inner world (7b). Foolish words get them into situations where they can do neither this nor that. They shoot themselves in the foot.

A wisdom in relationship is not to say anything that should never come out of the mouth. No matter how angry you are, you need a sense of control and wisdom to know what to say and what not to say.

Counseling Application: If you don't want to be a person of foolish lips and mouth, you need to restore your inner world. You need to work with your repressed anxiety, anger, aggression, sadness, unresolved issues, and so on. When you are subject to the dynamics of the unconscious world, you may say something unintentionally and unconsciously without realizing what you are saying. It's only when you come to your senses that you realize you've already said something that has a huge impact destructively.

The words of a gossip are like choice morsels; they go down to the inmost parts (18:8).[241] See 26:22.

Verse 8 can be interpreted in the context of verses 6 and 7, which

---

[241] Koptak rightly points out that the same proverb as this one is found in 26:22: "The words of a gossip are like choice morsels; they go down to the inmost parts." Koptak, *Proverbs*, 450. He also notes that the Hebrew word, *"mitlahmim"* for "choice morsels" is used only in this verse in Proverbs and the word was used to mean "complaining" or "grumbling" in the Old Testament (see Deut. 1:27, Ps. 106:25, Isa. 29:24). Koptak, *Proverbs*, 450.

warn that the mouth and words of the foolish stir up strife and contention, invite a beating, are their own destruction, and are a snare to their own souls. Solomon compares a gossip to a delicious dish. Gossiping is a vulnerable area for women, who, generally speaking, need to speak about fifteen to twenty thousand words a day to feel good.[242] It's fun to gossip. It's fun to listen to gossip. Gossip can go deep into the mind and heart, into the depths of one's psyche. It can change the personality of the gossiper and the listener. As a result, they become more of gossipers or people who like to hear more gossip. One's habits becomes one's character.

Gossip is remembered even when you don't try to remember it. As the saying goes, "Bad news travels fast," gossip travels fast. This is especially true on the Internet. Gossip can eventually lead to the strife and destruction mentioned in verses 6 and 7.

There were gossips in the early church. The apostles were wary of them. Paul exhorted Timothy to be on guard against young widows, saying as follows:

> As for younger widows, do not put them on such a list. For when their sensual desires overcome their dedication to Christ, they want to marry. Thus they bring judgment on themselves, because they have broken their first pledge. Besides, they get into the habit of being idle and going about from house to house. And not only do they become idlers, but also busybodies who talk nonsense, saying things they ought not to. So I counsel younger widows to marry, to have children, to manage their homes and to give the enemy no opportunity for slander (1 Tim. 5:11-14).

One who is slack in his work is brother to one who destroys (18:9).

Solomon warned against laziness in a negative light on several occasions. "Go to the ant, you sluggard; consider its ways and be wise!" (6:6) is a classic proverb. He also warned of the

---

[242] I'm not saying this to demean women. I'm just stating a general characterization of women.

consequences of sloth: "Poverty will come on you like a thief and scarcity like an armed man" (6:11). Now in this proverb, he warns of the consequences of laziness again. He sternly warns that lazy people will suffer the same fate as those who destroy themselves and their house (9b).

There is a difference between rest/relaxation and idleness. Rest/relaxation is a grace given to those who labor hard, but idleness is a way of life for those who are slack in their work (9a). Like the servant who received one talent, they will be condemned by their master as "wicked and lazy servants!" because they have little sense of mission and purpose (see Matt. 25:26). Believers should be alert lest they live an idle life on earth and be judged as "wicked and lazy servants" before the Lord in their final day.

Paul exhorts us to live a responsible life in our spheres of responsibility, saying, "Each one should carry their own load" (Gal. 6:5). He also warns that those who do not sow will not reap: "Do not be deceived: God cannot be mocked. A man reaps what he sows" (Gal. 6:7). And He also encourages us not to lose heart: "Let us not become weary in doing good, for at the proper time we will reap a harvest if we do not give up" (Gal. 6:9).

The name of the LORD is a fortified tower; the righteous run to it and are safe. The wealth of the rich is their fortified city; they imagine it a wall too high to scale [an unscalable wall] (18:10-11).

"The name of the LORD" is contrasted with "the riches of the rich" and "a fortified tower" with "their fortified city." The connection is made between being "safe" and "an unscalable wall."

According to the values of this world, the wealth of the rich serves as a "fortified city" (11a). A castle with "an unscalable wall" guarantees safety and security from outside attack (11b). So, in reality, it is true that people who have a lot of money enjoy a sense of security and stability in this world. However, wealth cannot provide true security and stability. What it gives is a sense of pseudo-security. Although someone lives in a castle with a high wall and is very wealthy, if a virus spreads in the castle, he or she will not be safe.

There is only one solid castle, shield, or fortress for believers, and that is the Eternal, Living LORD (10b). Whenever we are troubled, whenever we are anxious and afraid, we must run to the strong tower and climb on it. It is the one that cannot be set on fire from below. For God protects it with a flaming sword.

Jerusalem in the Old Testament was a stronghold that no power could overcome as long as the people of Judah remained faithful to the LORD (10a). It was the place where the name of the LORD dwelt. It was home to the temple, the place of God's presence, the place he had guarded like the pupil of his eye. In the New Testament, each believer is a temple (see 1 Cor. 6:19). The eyes of God watch over and protect the saints. In the time of tribulation, God is the refuge of his children.

God's name represents his power, honor and glory.[243] The name of Jesus Christ also has power, honor and glory. Christians are entitled to pray "in the name of Jesus Christ" when they end their every prayer. The devil is powerless before the name of Jesus. He has no choice but to flee. We are weak, but the name of Jesus is strong. Therefore, those who rely on the name of Jesus are the righteous (10b).

Before a downfall the heart is haughty, but humility comes before honor (18:12).

The first half of this proverb is similar to 16:18 and the second half of this proverbs is the same as 15:33. Through repetition, Solomon emphasizes the danger of pride and the importance of humility in the path of the wise.[244]

The haughty are people who unconsciously desire to be

---

[243] Bridges connected this proverb to Ps. 9:10: "Those who know your name trust in you, for you, LORD, have never forsaken those who seek you." Bridges, *Proverbs*, 287.

[244] Bridges saw this repetition as having the same intent as Jesus' repetition of parables with similar meanings, that is, to emphasize its importance. Bridges, *Proverbs*, 289.

destroyed. t God humbles the proud and even tears down. Hannah beautifully warns the haughty in heart: "Do not keep talking so proudly or let your mouth speak such arrogance, for the LORD is a God who knows, and by him deeds are weighed" (1 Sam. 2:3). Honor, on the other hand, is a crown that God gives to the humble (12b).

To answer before listening—that is folly and shame (18:13).

   Those who respond without listening are foolish. If we connect this proverb to verse 12, they are arrogant. Arrogant people don't listen well. They don't empathize well. The arrogant don't think they need to listen out for the other person, so they interrupt and respond. This shows little consideration or empathy for the other person's point of view. It's a behavior that will make the other person angry, and they'll end up humiliated.

   We sometimes see some persons on quiz battle programs who think they know the answer to a question before they hear it well, and then lose the opportunity to answer it. This is because they don't listen to the question completely, and they answer by guessing. Solomon makes a good point that guessing in conversation is foolish and shameful.

   Counseling Application: Counselors must be careful not to respond or diagnose before listening to the client fully and carefully. If they do, they are not effective counselors. Furthermore, this attitude is likely to anger their client. It's reckless and foolish to prejudge where the story of the client will be going or what the punchline will be.

The human spirit can endure in sickness, but a crushed spirit who can bear? (18:14).

   The word "spirit" here means the mind and heart. Positive thinking and attitudes can overcome illness (14a). On the other hand, a broken heart and a discouraged mind cannot overcome illness that can be cured (14b).

The mind and body interact closely. This is why people who suffer from physical illnesses often need psychological support and healing. For example, a study found that cancer patients who had participated in group counseling lived longer than those who had not, which shows that the mind and body are organically connected. The invisible world of the mind plays a vital role in supporting a person's life and health.

A helpless and hopeless person cannot overcome illness. Without motivation to live, even healthy people are vulnerable to illness. Victor Frankl, the founder of "logotherapy," witnessed this firsthand in a Jewish concentration camp, where he saw that people without meaning and hope whose wings of mind had been broken, died more easily than those in poor physical condition. He also observed that people who were in a state of illness and near death could still maintain a sense of humor and hope and survive camp life longer than expected. He later advocated an existential psychology called logotherapy.

There's a saying, "Mind over matter." People who live with a strong faith are resilient. The world cannot defeat such believers. Even illness is hard to knock them down.

The heart of the discerning acquires knowledge, for the ears of the wise seek it out (18:15).

The second part is logically more convincing when it comes first. Both the wise and the discerning seek knowledge. Knowledge can only be obtained by seeking. Knowledge is given to those who have ears to hear.

God answers those who seek. Jesus said, "Ask and it will be given to you; seek and you will find; knock and the door will be opened to you" (Matt. 7:7). Knowledge and wisdom are God's grace to those who ask (see James 1:5). Wild ginseng stands out to those who seek it, although some find it by accident, some by good fortune.

The wise digest what they hear in their minds and eventually gain knowledge (15a). They make it their own. Then they become even wiser.

Those who do not have ears to hear, do not understand and digest what they hear. The same is true of spiritual knowledge. The uncircumcised ears cannot gain spiritual knowledge, the knowledge of God, by reading the Bible or listening to a sermon. Nor do they seek it.

A gift opens the way and ushers the giver into the presence of the great (18:16).

This proverb describes the positive function of gifts. Solomon says that a gift paves the way for givers to reach the greater than themselves.[245]

There is a distinction between gifts and bribes. A gift is a sign of good intentions, while a bribe is a sign of selfish intent. However, there is a risk that a gift one feel pressured can become a bribe.

We need to be able to give and receive love. People who only give one way have problems, and people who only receive one way have problems. Gifts have a good function of enriching relationships. We experience joy when we give and receive gifts. A gift from the heart is worth a hundred words.

When people with narcissistic personality disorder receive a gift, they don't empathize with the giver and don't appreciate it. This is because they have a sense of entitlement, believing that they are smart, capable, and deserving of gifts.

Common graces that God gives to all people are unconditional gifts from God. Air, water, nature, and health are the most precious gifts. Many take these gifts of God for granted. In that sense, they are "disordered people" with narcissistic personality before God. They are ungrateful and foolish.

---

[245] Bridges gave several examples of biblical events that are related to this proverb. These include Abraham's servant Eliezer's gifts to Rebekah's house, Jacob's gifts to Esau to sooth Esau's anger, and Abigail's food to appease David's anger. Bridges, *Proverbs*, 295.

In a lawsuit the first to speak [The first to present his case] seems right, until someone comes forward and cross-examines [till another comes forward and questions him] (18:17).[246]

The importance of maintaining objectivity in a perpetrator-victim or plaintiff-defendant scenario cannot be overemphasized. Everyone is egocentric, and it is common to understand and interpret reality from their own perspective first. Therefore, people have different opinions about the same event. That's why it's important for judges to hear both sides of the story so they can make fewer mistakes.

People who hear only one side of the story and make a judgment are impulsive and immature. And people who hear both sides of the story but are unable to make a wise judgment by comparing and analyzing them are persons with poor ego function, that is, persons who lack wisdom and discernment.

Counseling Application: Counselors must listen to both perpetrator and victim, both husband and wife, or both parent and child without bias and assumptions. Empathizing too much with one side of the story can prevent them from hearing the other side of the story and cause them to lose their sense of objectivity in counseling. Counselors need to listen attentively and empathetically, but have the wisdom to hear both sides of the story with reservations and "skeptical ears," asking themselves, "How much of this story is true and how much is distorted? Are there any inconsistencies or contradictions in the narrative?"

In marital counseling, it is very important to remain objective. It is easy to take sides with one spouse, especially when caught up in the dynamics of countertransference. When counselors lose their objectivity, they become ineffective or even destructive.

---

[246] As an example from the Bible that connects to this proverb, Bridges mentioned an incident in which Ziba came and spoke about Mephibosheth in a way that misled David, but later when he heard from Mephibosheth about what really had happened, he found out that he was misled by Ziba (see 2 Sam 16:1-4; 2 Sam 19:24-30). Bridges, *Proverbs*, 296.

Casting the lot settles disputes and keeps strong opponents apart (18:18). See also 16:1, 16:33.

It is very difficult to make a final decision when there is contention, conflict, or differences of opinion. A method used in biblical times to discern God's will in these situations was the casting of lots. Casting lots was used to catch Achan in sin, to choose Saul as king, to choose Jonah to be thrown into the sea, and to choose an apostle to replace Judas Iscariot in the early church.[247] In all of these cases, God intervened in the human act of casting lots to accomplish his will.

However, it is not advisable to turn the casting of lots into a game of chance. It is not biblical to use it in a way that encourages purchasing lottery ticket or gambling, even if it is done in the same way. The reason or motivation for the casting of lots is important, that is, discerning God's will or seeking greed.

When conflicting values are both valid and justifiable in their own way, casting lots can be a good way to stop an argument or strife. However, when one option is evil or immoral, there should not be a lottery at all. Joseph and Matthias were both qualified to be apostles who could testify to the resurrection of Jesus among those who had traveled with Jesus. Because they were both qualified, casting lots was a good way to ensure that Joseph, who was not chosen, was not hurt (see Acts 1:21-26).

A brother wronged [An offended brother] is more unyielding than a fortified city; disputes are like the barred gates of a citadel (18:19).[248]

---

[247] Bridges made a good point that when the twelve tribes were allotted land in Canaan, they were allotted by lot. It was a good way to avoid disputes by casting lots rather than deciding by sibling position or by the number of people. Bridges, *Proverbs*, 296.

[248] Bridges mentioned the relationships between brothers that are relevant to this proverb, noting Cain's heart for Abel, his brothers' hearts for Joseph, Absalom's heart

Getting hurt is most often experienced in relationships with persons close to us. It's easy to get over a hurt from someone far away or someone you are not related with. But when you're hurt by a family member, relative, or friend, the wounds are often deep and lasting.

When Jacob and Esau met again, they hugged and kissed each other around the neck and wept (see Gen. 33:4). They seemed to be restored to a peaceful relationship. However, biblical history shows that Israel and Edom remained enemies until the fall of the kingdom of Judah. They never truly forgave and reconciled each other. The history of Israel and Edom shows that it is more difficult to truly reconcile with a brother or sister who has offended you than it is to take a fortified city.

Counseling Application: If you focus on the hurt rather than understanding the offender, you're more likely to use defense mechanisms. It's like "the barred gates of a citadel" (19b), and you won't open up to the other person. That's what Absalom did to his brother Amnon: "Absalom never said a word to Amnon, either good of bad; he hated Amnon because he had disgraced his sister Tamar" (2 Sam. 13:22). He finally retaliated by murdering him.

Therefore, the closer you are with someone, the more careful and sensitive you need to be with him or her. It's wise to be careful not to create situations that can cause hurt because once hurt, it's not easy to reconcile. But the reality is that in interpersonal relationships, people who are close to you speak with less defense mechanisms. So you need to be understanding and forgiving each other because the other person may unintentionally hurt you.

From the fruit of their mouth a person's stomach is filled; with

for Amnon, and the heart of the rest of the tribes for the tribe of Benjamin. He also cited the Reformation history as an example of the difficulty of reconciliation between Luther and Calvin due to their differences in theological views. Bridges, *Proverbs*, 297-98. We see this same dynamic in conflicts between churches and denominations. It is the mission of believers to strive to keep the unity of the Spirit.

the harvest of their lips they are satisfied. The tongue has the power of life and death, and those who love it will eat its fruit (18:20-21).

When you hear good words, blessing words, therapeutic words, and words you wanted to hear, your stomach will be filled even if you don't eat (20a). It is more energizing than taking a pack of restorative herb medicine. It is more grateful than being treated with a lavish dinner. Therapeutic words empower people incredibly.

The same is true in the spiritual realm. The joy we derive from meditating on and digesting the Word of life is more than the pleasure of eating. When Jesus was tempted in his hunger in the wilderness by Satan, he quoted from the Word of life: "Man does not live by bread alone but on every word that comes from the mouth of the LORD" (Deut. 8:3). God's words feed our soul (20a).

The Word of God makes people alive. It also kills. The word of God is like a two-edged sword. On the one hand, it is a knife that saves lives, like a surgical knife.[249] It is the sword of the Spirit that enables the believer to resist the devil. But on the other hand, it is a sword of judgment, condemning unbelievers to death.

A word well spoken can save your life, and a word poorly spoken can lead to social burial. The power of the tongue is great indeed. James likens the tongue to the "very small rudder" that moves a large ship (James 3:4). Those who love to use their tongue will eat the harvest it brings (21b). The harvest can be good or bad, so we need the wisdom to be careful with our words.

He who finds a wife finds what is good and receives favor from the LORD (18:22). See also 19:14.

---

[249] In exegeting this proverb, Bridges connected it to 2 Cor. 2:16, which points out the ambivalence of the gospel: "To the one we are an aroma that brings death; to the other, an aroma that brings life. And who is equal to such a task?" Bridges, *Proverbs*, 299.

This proverb applies to both women and men. If you are given the opportunity to find a spouse by God's grace and providence, you should be very grateful. There are an increasing number of Christian young adults who want to get married but remain single because they do not have a suitable partner. The difficulty of finding a steady job and the high cost of housing make it more difficult for young adults to find a spouse to whom they are psychologically and spiritually attracted. It is no exaggeration to say that finding a faithful spouse in such a situation is a special favor from the LORD.[250]

Meeting and marrying your spouse can be likened to finding a treasure. In the final chapter of Proverbs, the sayings of King Lemuel, his mother emphasizes the value of a wife of noble character when she says, "A wife of noble character who can find? She is worth far more than rubies" (31:10). Blessed indeed are those who found a spouse whose psychological growth and spiritual maturity are commensurate with his or her age. Blessed are people who found a good enough husband or wife who serves as a good object.

If your spouse is psychologically immature and spiritually blind, you may wonder if you are truly blessed by God to have to live with such a person. God's thoughts are different from our thoughts. However, your spouse is also favored by God in that there is a wonderful will and providence of God even in the midst of

---

[250] One might ask, "Are Christian young adults who give up marriage for various reasons out of favor with God?" The answer is no. We need to understand it in terms of the universality of suffering. Christian young adults who are living in a time when it is difficult to fulfill their dreams should not be discouraged by remembering the fact that there are many others who are struggling and suffering like them. Many young adults choose to marry in unbelief. They should recognize that there is definitely pain in being yoked with an unbelieving spouse (see 2 Cor. 6:14-18). If a marriage with unbelieving spouse leads to the destruction of one's soul, it is a foolish and unwise decision to marry. This is because marriage is a "transitional object relation" that is only valid on earth. Furthermore, from a New Testament perspective, marriage is not a requirement for Christians. In 1 Cor. 7, Paul endorsed the positive implications of singleness. If one is so attached on marriage relationship, the relationship can be an idolatry. Christians need to be clear about their priorities.

immaturity, sin and dysfunction. It is meaningful if you are being used to heal and restore your childish or dysfunctional spouse. There is more responsibility and power to you, if you are healthier, to ensure that the influence of your relationship with your childish or dysfunctional spouse is not passed on to your children. A word of caution: marriage is not a rescue!

The poor plead for mercy, but the rich answer harshly (18:23).[251]

This proverb describes the reality of the world. Realizing the harsh reality of life is part of life's wisdom. Knowing the reality that it is not easy to live in this world is a way to avoid romanticizing life like a child.

The reality of the world is that the poor and the rich are mixed. And even if poor persons beg for mercy because they owe rich people money or can't pay their rent, they have no place to plead if the rich people treat them harshly without any excuse. In particular, it is a reality that banks often foreclose or auction off borrowers' homes without any excuse.

However, believers need to act differently from the real world. We need to be considerate and empathetic with the poor and the needy. We need to be willing to give extra time or chance to repay, reduce or even forgive their debts, taking into account the circumstances of the poor. In the case of rent, a grace period of a few months should be granted. If some people force you to go one mile, you need to go with them two miles (Matt. 5:41). You need to be gracious to charge a right amount of rent or even to make it cheaper even when others increase a significant amount for rent. Then you can become salt and light in the world.

---

[251] Bridges connected the rich man Nabal's rejection of David's petition to this proverb: "Nabal answered David's servants, 'Who is this David? Who is this son of Jesse? Many servants are breaking away from their masters these days. Why should I take my bread and water, and the meat I have slaughtered for my shearers, and give it to men coming from who knows where?'" (1 Sam. 25:10-11). Bridges, *Proverbs*, 301.

288

One who has unreliable friends [A man of many companions] soon comes to ruin, but there is a friend who sticks closer than a brother (18:24).[252]

If you have many friends, you may have a relatively strong support system. The same goes for having a wide network of contacts. These are advantages in life. However, Solomon highlights the downside of having many friends. From the Family Systems Theory perspective, having a lot of friends means that you're more likely to be affected by changes in their lives because you are connected with them. For example, you might provide a financial guarantee for a friend and then find yourself bankrupt due to his or her failure.

Another disadvantage of having many friends is that you're more likely to have superficial friendships with them. In this case, you may not find some friends you can confide in in times of crisis. Then you are pitiful, as Solomon says, "But pity anyone who falls and has no one to help them up" (Eccl. 4:10). Although not explicitly mentioned in the parable of the prodigal son, the friends (or women) with whom he associated while squandering his wealth were not there for him when he was in need (see Luke 15:13-16): "He longed to fill his stomach with the pods that the pigs were eating, but no one gave him anything" (Like 15:16).

Jesus is the only faithful friend to believers. Jesus is the friend, closer than our family.[253] He is the only friend with whom we can relate more intimately than with anyone else in the world. This intimacy and attachment is not temporary, but permanent. Jesus is your friend to whom you can confide in and whose confidentiality is guaranteed. He is accessible 24 hours a day and dwells in your heart through the Holy Spirit. He is the one with whom you can have a closer relationship and companionship than anyone else in

---

[252] Bridges connected David and Jonathan's friendship to this proverb: "I grieve for you, Jonathan my brother; you were very dear to me. Your love for me was wonderful, more wonderful than that of women" (2 Sam. 1:26). Bridges, *Proverbs*, 302.

[253] Bridges made this point well in his commentary. He noted that Jesus is a good friend who is a rod and staff even as we walk through the valley of the shadow of death. Bridges, *Proverbs*, 303.

the world. In terms of mysticism, Jesus is in "symbiosis" with us: he is in us and we are in him (see John 15:4).

Counseling Application: Counseling is a unique friendship and relationship. It's not a superficial friendship. A counselor can be closer than a family member. It's a relationship where clients can open up and talk about things they can't even talk about with their own family. This friendship is different from a normal friendship in that it is temporary and one-sided, primarily for the benefit of the client.

Chapter 19 A Prudent Spouse Is from the LORD

Better the poor whose walk is blameless than a fool whose lips are perverse (19:1).

   This is a proverb of the form "A is better than B." Although it is not explicitly mentioned in the text, it can be seen that "the 'rich" counterpart of "the poor" is hidden in the proverb. Then this proverb means that the blameless poor is better than the rich but foolish whose lips are perverse. People with perverse lips are persons with perverse heart. God does not recognize the rich with corrupt heart. He recognizes the poor but righteous.[254] Accordingly, the righteous poor who are pleased by God are far better than the perverse rich.

Desire without knowledge is not good [It is not good to have zeal without knowledge]—how much more will hasty feet miss the way! [nor to be hasty and miss the way] (19:2).

   Being zealous or passionate is a hallmark of a healthy life. It's similar to the case of desires. There are some people who live as "sick souls," without zeal and passion. Like the Laodicean church members, they live in a way that is neither hot nor cold (see Rev. 3:15-16). The Lord warns those who are lukewarm in their faith, "So, because you are lukewarm—neither hot nor cold—I am about to spit you out of my mouth" (Rev. 3:16).
   However, this proverb warns against zeal or desires without knowledge (2a). Here, knowledge is linked to the image of hasty feet. Hasty feet signifies behaviors that are impulsive, rash, and

---

[254] Bridges quoted Jesus' praise for the church in Smyrna: "I know your afflictions and your poverty—yet you are rich!" (Rev. 2:9). Bridges, *Proverbs*, 304.

reckless. Hasty feet means that reason is not functioning properly. Without knowledge, we become impulsive. Action gets ahead of thought. Impulsive people without knowledge miss the way or become astray (2b).

To use an analogy of marathon, life isn't about running hard. You need to know what your goal is and what the path is to get there. If you run hard but end up in the wrong place or on the wrong path, you're running with zeal without true knowledge.

One of the diagnostic measures of a healthy faith life is zeal and passion. A faith that is weak in commitment and conviction is obviously unhealthy, but zeal does not necessarily make a faith healthy. So-called fanatics believe passionately. There are also people of other religions who are passionately committed. They may even give their lives for the cause of their faith.

Passion and the right knowledge must be balanced. Passion without knowledge is blind. Knowledge without passion is cold. It is knowledge without practice. A heart function without a head function is not good. A head function with little heart function is also not healthy. When passion/emotion and knowledge/reason are balanced, we can live a healthy life in our relationships with others as well as with God.

A person's own folly leads to their ruin, yet their heart rages against the LORD (19:3).

There's a saying that goes, "One takes credit for the good, but blames one's ancestors for the bad." It's a phrase that well expresses the narcissism of humans.

There are some people who blame God for their lives that have been ruined by their own foolishness and stupidity.[255] When life

---

[255] Blaming God implies that the foolish person who blames God is at least aware of God's existence. Normal people use defense mechanisms to rationalize, project, blame, or deny when bad things happen because of their own foolishness. They usually blame other people or circumstances. They rarely recognize that the problem is within themselves. Many believers with immature psychological structures blame God when they face crises or difficulties. This was the behavior of the Israelites in the

does not go well, many fools blame others or even blame God instead of recognizing their own problems. Those who do self-defeating things themselves and then blame God for not restraining them are foolish (3a).

Cain was unable to recognize that he himself had not offered a sacrifice that was pleasing to God. Instead, he was angry with God for not accepting his offering. He projected his own problems onto God. The writer of Genesis recorded that he "was very angry, and his face was downcast" (Gen. 4:5b), meaning he did not look up. He averted his gaze from the heavens, where God was. He kept his eyes on the ground.

Cain's anger was actually directed at God. He was angry with God for accepting Abel's sacrifice and rejecting his own. He did self-defeating behavior for himself and then he became with God for rejecting his offering (3b). He was a foolish and wicked man who eventually "displaced" his anger toward God upon Abel.

Wealth attracts many friends, but even the closest friend of the poor person [but a poor man's friend] deserts them (19:4).[256]

This proverb describes the reality of the world. It is a wake-up call to realize that this is the way the world works, regardless of whether it is right or wrong.[257] In the world, if you have money and background, you will have a lot of so-called friends. They want to associate with you, they want to put your number in their phone as an acquaintance, and they want to see their name in your

wilderness, and it is the behavior of many believers today.

[256] Bridges made a good point that the most relevant proverb to this one is 14:20: "The poor are shunned even by their neighbors, but the rich have many friends." Bridges, *Proverbs*, 310. He pointed out that the friends of the rich are often selfishly motivated and are not the true friends of 17:17: "A friend loves at all times, and a brother is born for a time of adversity." Bridges, *Proverbs*, 310.

[257] Solomon refers to this reality again in verse 7, "The poor are shunned by all their relatives—how much more do their friends avoid them! Though the poor pursue them with pleading, they are nowhere to be found."

phone as a contact.

Most friends in the the world pretend to know you because they think you have something for them to gain from you. But suppose that you suddenly go broke or become poor, most of your friends will stop talking to you. If you call them, they don't return your calls. If you realize that this is the reality of the world and deal with it, you can be wise as serpents and innocent as doves in the world. It is wise to realize that friendships made with wealth do not last long. It is also wise not to be offended by what most friends avoid when you are poor. No need to be angry. If you know the world and know yourself, then you are unbeaten.

Differently from worldly friends, Jesus Christ is the most faithful friend of believers. He is the good friend who laid down his life and suffered the judgment and death we deserved. He is the Savior who redeemed us with his own flesh and blood. He is the faithful friend who accompanies us in his faithful love to the end of the world and never forsakes us. He loves us regardless of our appearance, education, or wealth. He is not ashamed of us, even though we are utterly lacking. The hymn, "Though all the world may forsake me, but you never forsake me, Lord Jesus, you look back to the end," expresses this truth well.

A false witness will not go unpunished, and whoever pours out lies will not go free (19:5).[258]

The role of witnesses is very important. They can make the difference between life and death. True witnesses testify truthfully about what they have seen or heard. When Peter and John were questioned before the council of Sanhedrin, they boldly stated, "Which is right in God's eyes: to listen to your or to him? You be the judges! As for us, we cannot help speaking about what we have seen and heard" (Acts 4:19-20). If the apostles' testimony had been false, they would have been punished by God (5a). In Old

---

[258] Bridges made a good point about the connection between this proverb and 14:25: "A truthful witness saves lives, but a false witness is deceitful." Bridges, *Proverbs*, 310.

Testament times, many prophets were false witnesses.[259] Some were judged directly by God for prophesying as if they had seen and heard things they had not seen or heard.

The second half of this verse is a proverb about lying. In the context, lying is linked to false testimony. Lying is punishable in some cases. Specifically, those who give false testimony that harms the well-being of others can be punished for defamation or perjury. Furthermore, God will not tolerate the lips that give false witness (5b).

False testimony leads to more and more lies. In severe cases, it can lead to a pathological state where the false testifiers believe their own lies to be true.

The devil is the father of lies. Those who perjure are in voluntary obedience to the devil. False witnesses are evil and destructive. A surprising number of people lie in court, even after they take an oath to tell the truth. God hears and remembers their false testimony. When their hidden guilt is revealed before the righteous Judge, Jesus Christ, on the Last Day, they will be condemned to eternal judgment with their father, the devil.

Many curry favor with a ruler, and everyone is the friend of one who gives gifts (19:6).

This is another proverb that reminds us of the reality of this world. There is no one who doesn't like the giver of a gift. As the saying goes, "those who are given a gift and dead men tell no tales," gifts are often the catalyst that opens people's hearts.

People in public office often receive many personal requests. If they accept them generously, it won't be long before they are

---

[259] Bridges well pointed out that false witnesses do not become false witnesses overnight, but those who often lie become increasingly wicked. He also pointed out that false witness is directly related to the third commandment, "You shall not misuse the name of the LORD your God," and to the sixth commandment, "You shall not murder," and the ninth commandment, "You shall not give false testimony against your neighbor," which are related to loving neighbors. Bridges, *Proverbs*, 311.

forced to step down from their position. Therefore, it is wise to distinguish between public and private affairs, even if it seems heartless to do that at first. If they are known as persons who do not take personal requests, there will be few people to ask them to do favor for them personally.

This proverb describes the reality of this world that many people flatter people in power in order to please them. In our society, there are people in positions of power and authority, such as president, governor, or mayor, superintendent, police chief, military general, CEO, principal, and university president. It is a reality of the world that people who have interests with these people will inevitably bow down to them and try to please them. This is because they have selfish motives for doing so. Therefore, persons in authority should not mistake their flattery for their true self. If they recognize themselves for who they are, they will not be arrogant and will be respected in their position of authority.

Counseling Application: Adult children who grew up in dysfunctional families are more likely to have low self-esteem. One of the common symptoms they struggle with is difficulty relating to authority figures. This is because the representations of authority they experienced as children from dysfunctional parents were negative. As a result, they feel intimidated or anxious around authority figures. They often feel angry and are likely to react to oppressive authority figures in a dependent way or in a passive-aggressive way. Dependent adult children are likely to behave in a flattering and deferential way to an oppressive authority figure. Passive-aggressive adult children resist or show aggression. They may be passive-aggressive in a way of not following directions well.

These symptoms indicate the need for restoration and healing in the hearts of adult children. Believers should have an attitude of respect and recognition for authority. They recognize them as God-appointed authorities. But there is no need to be unnecessarily flattering or cowed. And being submissive to tyrannical authorities is extreme, because each person has God-given dignity and freedom of conscience. Christian counselors must have the knowledge and wisdom to recognize and balance the dynamics of adult children in their counseling process.

The poor are shunned by all their relatives—how much more do their friends avoid them! Though the poor pursue them with pleading, they are nowhere to be found (19:7). See also 19:4.

This proverb is longer than other proverbs because of the addition of a subordinate clause. This is another proverb that reflects the reality of this world.

If a person is poor and his or her brothers dislike or hate him or her because he or she is poor, God will not be pleased with them. The same goes for neglecting a friend and having estranged relationship with him or her because of poverty. Demonstrating to prevent low-income apartments from being built in neighborhood or ignoring the children of poor families is an offense to God. Solomon says this proverb to remind us that the world actually works that way. We are responsible to see and confront the reality of this world and we are not to just look for the ideal.

In a good, healthy sibling relationship, you'd feel sorry for a poor sibling or support him or her financially. However, unlike parent-child relationships, sibling relationships often become selfish after marriage. Parents are willing to give their children. However, it's not easy for grown-up siblings to help financially. It's even harder to do it, especially if one sibling continues to be dependent on the other siblings. This is likely to cause irritation and anger to them.

Solomon urges us to see that this is true of sibling relationships and even more likely of friends who are not blood relatives. Even if you follow them around and beg them to help you, you are unlikely to get help. Therefore, believers should live their lives to the best of their ability so as not to be a burden to their siblings and friends.

The one who gets wisdom loves life [his own soul]; the one who cherishes understanding will soon prosper [prospers]

(19:8).

Those who value themselves are concerned about what they put into their inner world. They place a core value in life on acquiring and holding wisdom and understanding. In that way, they love and care for themselves in a healthy way (8a).

Blessed are those who have attained wisdom and understanding that lead them to prosperity and eternal life (8b). Trees planted by the waters do not wither and bears fruit even in times of drought. Similarly, blessed are those who are rooted in God, the source of wisdom and understanding, who bear the fruit of eternal life.

Understanding this proverb from a New Testament perspective, those who acquire and cherish wisdom and understanding seek wisdom and understanding not only for the love of their own souls but also for the love of their neighbors' souls. For example, when they study, they study not only for themselves, but for the benefit of others. They use their knowledge and understanding to help others do well, not just themselves.

A false witness will not go unpunished, and whoever pours out lies will perish (19:9). See 19:5.

It is not fitting for a fool to live in luxury— how much worse for a slave to rule over princes! (19:10).

Some things go well together, like "a golden apple and a silver tray," while others do not. Solomon says that the foolish living in luxury and extravagance are not a good match (10a). However, the wise living in luxury and extravagance is also not a good match, because they do not seek out outward splendor and do not overspend.

This proverb emphasizes that if those who are unable to manage wealth properly become rich and use it to fulfill their own desires, it would not be a good match. The unfortunate reality is that there are many rich people in the world who are not fitting with their wealth. People who do not know why wealth and honor have been given to them, and who drive a fancy and expensive foreign car in this world just for their own happiness including their family, are foolish. People who live in a house worth millions or tens of millions of dollars and live only for themselves and their family are pitiful persons from the perspective of the kingdom of God.

Solomon also points out that an even worse case is one in which a slave rule over princes (10b). Such a society is not only disordered, it is not God's will. However, this proverb should not be used as a proof text for the lawfulness of slavery.

A person's wisdom yields [gives him] patience; it is to one's glory to overlook an offense (19:11).

An attribute of God is to be slow to anger. It is also God's character to overlook trespasses. Having received the love that flows from the character of God, Christians have the ability to persevere in life.

In 1 Cor. 13:4-7, the first attribute of love is patience. Those who are able to be patient are mature. The mature can see the big picture. So even if they're angry about the situation at hand, they have the ability to look around, to look at the past, present, and future, and cope with their anxiety and anger. They are able to "overlook" an offense without counterattacking. Having experienced God's patient love, when hurtful situations arise, they remember Jesus' words, "But I tell you, do not resist an evil person. If anyone slaps you on the right cheek, turn to them the other cheer also. And, if anyone wants to sue you and take your shirt, hand over your coat as well. If anyone forces you to go one mile, go with them two miles" (Matt. 5:39-41). And they obey his words.

Solomon says that overlooking an offense ends up being the glory of those who persevere (11b). Those who do not retaliate with "tooth for tooth and eye for eye" but give food when their enemy is hungry glorify God (see Rom. 12:20).

A king's rage is like the roar of a lion, but his favor is like dew on the grass (19:12). See also 20:2.

This proverb can be seen as a proverb that describes the realities of kings as they maintain their power. In context, it can be understood in connection with the anger I mentioned in the previous verse. While verse 11 was about controlling anger and overlooking it whenever possible, this verse is about describing the king's anger.[260]

The king's rage at the traitor can be interpreted psychologically as "narcissistic rage." The king's rage and aggression is experienced when he experiences threats to his kingship.[261] He must experience anger to protect his kingship and his kingdom.

"Good objects" to the king are loyalists who contribute to the kingship and protect the king. So it is natural and proper for the king to grant them favors. As the text puts it, the favors are gentle and benevolent, like the dew on the grass. The problem with pathological kings is that they are often in and out of hot and cold water, exhibiting symptoms of borderline personality disorder. They have an issue of instability in their perception and mood so that they fluctuate between idealization and devaluation in their relationships.

We can also interpret this proverb in a positive way. The king's wrath is a necessary experience in order to punish those who do evil. As Paul explains, kings need to exercise their power to be wrathful if they are to be "God's servants, agents of wrath to bring punishment on the wrongdoer" (Rom. 13:4b).

God is the King of kings. Not only is he the God of love, but he is

---

[260] "Rage" and "his favor" are opposite emotions and images. This is an example of extremes, one of the symptoms of borderline personality disorder.

[261] Generally speaking, kingship is based on an egocentric notion. Even in the context of Bridges' time (1794-1869), he well recognized the dangers of unlimited royal authority. Bridges, *Proverbs*, 315.

also the God of wrath who judges with justice. God is wrathful against sin. This was evident in the events of Noah's flood and the fire judgment of Sodom and Gomorrah. God judges by being wrathful. On the Last Day, God will judge righteously in wrath against all those who have no relationship with Jesus Christ. But for those who have been made righteous in Christ, he will be gracious, like the "dew on the grass," as this proverb says.

A foolish child is father's ruin, and a quarrelsome wife is like the constant dripping of a leaky roof.[262] Houses and wealth are inherited from parents, but a prudent wife is from the LORD (19:13-14).

Foolish children are a worry and a disaster to their parents (13a). Such people do not have the wisdom to keep their property and home properly, even if they inherit from their parents. Foolish children are very unlikely to find a wise and thoughtful person as their spouse.[263] They are more likely to find a spouse with a similar level of foolishness, with a similar level of self-differentiation. In context, foolish sons are likely to find quarrelsome wives. Therefore, they are a worry and a disaster for their parents.

Religiously speaking, foolish children do not fear the LORD. They are likely to reject or be rejected by a God-fearing spouse. Even if they do marry and inherit wealth, their marriage is likely to be filled with conflicts and quarrels. Therefore, those who find a wise spouse through God's providence are much more blessed than those who inherit a house or wealth from their parents (14b).

"A quarrelsome wife" is contrasted with "a prudent wife" (13b, 14b). A quarrelsome wife, a fighting cock, is a disaster for her

---

[262] Bridges pointed out other proverbs that connect with this one: "A quarrelsome wife is like the dripping of a leaky roof in a rainstorm" (27:15); "Better to live on a corner of the roof than share a house with a quarrelsome wife" (21:9, 25:24). Bridges, *Proverbs*, 316.

[263] It is surprising that Nabal, whose very name means "foolish one," married Abigail, a wise and beautiful wife. There are exceptions in life.

husband, and vice versa (see 13a). She is not a gracious, favorable wife, like the image of "the dew on the grass" in verse 12. "Like the constant dripping of a leaky roof," a marriage that is a constant stream of quarrels is a dead marriage, even though it appears to be alive.[264]

A wise and thoughtful spouse doesn't argue unnecessarily. He or she is mature psychologically and spiritually. Such a spouse is "from the LORD" (14b).

Parents can leave their home or possessions to their children. And they can counsel their children to find a wise and thoughtful spouse. But ultimately, it is in God's administration and providence (14b). We need to remember that "in all things God works for the good of those who love him" (Rom. 8:28a). We know that God works for the good even with a quarrelsome wife or husband.

Laziness brings on deep sleep, and the shiftless go hungry (19:15).

Those who live their best can sleep deeply. God gives a deep sleep to those He loves (see Ps. 127:2). A deep sleep is a restful sleep.

But the deep sleep of a lazy person is a sleep of escape from reality. A lazy person is half-asleep even when awake, and when it's time to sleep, they fall into a deep sleep that consumes most of their day.

Solomon warns that the lethargic, the deep-sleeper, and the lazy will starve (15b). A life without effort is unlikely to bear good fruit. Those who are negligent at work will one day be fired. Then the balance in their bank accounts will decrease. Finally, it

---

[264] Those who endure to the end, even their contentious marriages, are ones that God approves of. Perseverance in the midst of suffering can lead to character formation and sanctification. And there is hope, because suffering does not last forever. In his comment on this passage, Bridges asked, "Who knows, even a quarrelsome spouse, if one perseveres in prayer and perseveres in patience, he or she will become an co-inheritor of God's inheritance?" Bridges, *Proverbs*, 316.

becomes difficult for them to provide basic food for their family.

Counseling Application: Some people are lethargic not because they are lazy by nature, but because they are depressed and spend most of their day lethargically or sleeping. When you're depressed, it's hard to get out of bed in the morning. You feel so lethargic that you wish you could die without opening your eyes. So we need to be careful not to condemn depressed persons as lazy. Once the symptoms of depression are gone, they will regain their normal rhythm of life.

Whoever keeps commandments keeps their life, but whoever shows contempt for their ways will die (19:16).

Those who hear and obey God's commandments and commands are wise persons who preserve their life (16a). Those who disobey despite multiple admonitions and warnings bring them ruin and death (16b).

Even though they know that obeying God's Word is the way to life, many people sin because they are driven by greed and lust. It is not uncommon for people to surrender and return to God only when their lives are bitter and miserable. It is God's will that we should be able to live consistently according to his Word without experiencing "*mara*." However, in reality, there are many believers who repent and return only after experiencing *mara*. Those who do return are those who are favored by God, for there are some people who stubbornly refuse to return even after the experience of bitterness.

Whoever is kind to the poor lends to the LORD, and he will reward them for what they have done (19:17). See also 21:13.

Solomon discusses the poor in verses 1, 7, 17, and 22. Verse 1 is positive about the poor living righteously before God. Verse 7, on the other hand, mentions the negative aspects of the poor. Verse 22

303

compares the poor to a liar and says that the poor is better than liars. So we can see that there are different kinds of the poor. However, the poor in verse 17 and 21:13 are characterized by the fact that they are the ones God is interested in.

To have compassion on the poor is to honor God (17a).[265] Therefore, God will surely repay the good deed (17b).

These poor people are different from the poor who are lazy as mentioned in verse 15, "Laziness brings on deep sleep, and the shiftless go hungry." They are poor because of the oppression and usurpation of the rich who are self-centered.

Counseling Application: Who are the poor in counseling and how can we show them we care? How can we distinguish the work of social workers from the work of counselors? How far can counselors go in helping the poor? There's a lot that can be said about poverty and social justice from a Christian counseling perspective. However, I'd like to make a connection to counseling fees even though it may be tangential.

The poor also should be able to benefit from counseling service. However, the reality is that professional counseling is often out of reach for the poor. So Christian counselors should consider ways to make professional counseling accessible to them. A practical suggestion is to set aside some of their counseling time as free time for poor clients, or to charge a minimal fee based on the client's economic level. Or, in the spirit of tithing, they may consider offering counseling for free or with a minimal fee to the poor up to the amount equal to one-tenth of their total fee income. It's much better to charge a minimal fee for counseling than no fee at all, unless it's unavoidable. It can be beneficial for poor clients to maintain basic dignity during the counseling process. Regular

---

[265] James equated care and concern for the poor with godly living: "Religion that God our Father accepts as pure and faultless is this: to look after orphans and widows in their distress and to keep oneself from being polluted by the world" (James 1:27). Christian wealthy people have a responsibility to care for the poor. Paul made this point when he said "Command those who are rich in this present world not to be arrogant nor to put their hope in wealth, which is so uncertain, but to put their hope in God, who richly provides us with everything for our enjoyment. Command them to do good, to be rich in good deeds, and to be generous and willing to share" (1 Tim. 6:17-18).

sponsorship of Christian counseling centers by local churches is also a very beneficial way to contribute to free or low-cost counseling for the poor.

In any case, God sees and approves of counseling the poor for free or for a minimal fee. He will repay the counselor's good deeds done in secret.

Discipline your children, for in that there is hope; do not be a willing party to their death (19:18).

There are parents who take both extremes when it comes to discipline of their children. Some parents are very strict and use physical punishment. On the other hand, some parents raise their children with a level of neglect, rarely reprimanding them when they do something wrong.

Solomon was such a proponent of proper physical punishment saying that children will not die with spanking. So in this proverb he is saying that proper discipline is a way to have hope for children. Parents who spoil their children liberally can be complicit in their children's destruction.

So how can we discipline our children in a good way? I already mentioned about this issue in other texts, so I won't repeat it here. As a brief refresher, it's wise to discipline and scold our children at a level that is appropriate for their stage of physical and psychological development and appropriate to the issue at hand. Unreasonable spanking or scolding is foolish and can lead to assault.[266]

---

[266] Bridges commented that in the context of his time, children's sinful nature should be corrected by disciplining them with a rod from a very young age. Bridges, *Proverbs*, 322-23. Today, there are many considerations that make it difficult to simply apply that rule. Especially in the United States, where parents accused of child abuse may not only lose custody of their children, but also face jail time. It's foolish to literally obey a proverb like 23:13-14 and use physical punishment without considering each child's characteristics, age, and sensitivity: "Do not withhold discipline from a child; if you punish them with the rod, they will not die. Punish them with the rod and save them from death." Bridges was more cautious about corporal punishment,

A hot-tempered person must pay the penalty; rescue them, and you will have to do it again (19:19).

Solomon insists that hot-tempered people must suffer the loss or punishment for their behavior (19a). He warns that if we sweep their bad consequences under the rug, they will repeat the behavior (19b).

Counseling Application: An effective behavioral approach to modifying dysfunctional behaviors is to use a combination of rewards and punishments. For example, we may praise or reward children or adults when they are less angry or mildly angry, but hold them accountable for the consequences or punish them when they are more angry or cannot control their anger. When they are punished or lose money because of their behaviors, they are more likely to come to their senses and to be modified in their behaviors.

Listen to advice and accept discipline, and at the end you will be counted among the wise (19:20).

No one is wise from the start. A wise "self" needs a wise "object" to develop. We become wise when we "internalize" the advice and admonitions of a wise "external object."

This proverb says what Solomon likes to say over and over again. It's about listening to and digesting advice and instruction so that we can think and act wisely.

Many are the plans in a person's heart, but it is the LORD's

commenting on 19:25: "But the word and ordinance of God is our standard. However, great wisdom is called for in the degree [of corporal punishment] and the manner [of its application]." Bridges, *Proverbs*, 330.

purpose that prevails (19:21).[267] See also 16:1, 3, 9, 33.

Humans are thinkers. We plan and prepare for the future. We make schedules, make promises, and prepare for the future, even though we don't know what tomorrow will bring. But despite planning and preparation, it is wise to humbly acknowledge that life's steps are not in the hands of the walker, and it is wise to seek God's help (see Jer. 10:23).

What a person desires is unfailing love; better to be poor than a liar (19:22).

At first glance, the first and second part seem unrelated. And the comparison between the poor and liars seems out of place. Comparing the poor to liars seems like a bias against the poor.

This proverb means that even if one lives a life of poverty, the life of one who receives unchanging love is better.[268] The opposite interpretation is that those who love with variable love or those who receive variable love, are unhappy, even if they live a wealthy life.

This proverb can be understood as two separate proverbs, one that says, "People who are generous are loved and respected by others," and the other that says, "It is better to be poor than a liar." To add to the first half of the proverb, the generous attract people. They attract people because they have a good object image. When people get close to them, they experience love, warmth, acceptance, and healing through them.

When interpreting the second half of the proverb, it is important

---

[267] Bridges connected the second half of this proverb with Job 23:13-14: "But he stands alone, and who can oppose him? He does whatever he pleases. He carries out his decree against me, and many such plans he still has in store." Bridges, *Proverbs*, 326.

[268] Koptak supports this exegesis. He notes that the text is the last of five proverbs that speak of the poor throughout chapter 19, and can be understood especially in connection with verse 1: "Better the poor whose walk is blameless than a fool whose lips are perverse." Koptak, *Proverbs*, 472.

to keep in mind that Solomon takes a generally negative stance toward poverty and the poor. We can interpret this proverb to mean that the poor don't have a very good life, but a liar has an even worse life. Compared to a liar, the poor are better off.

The fear of the LORD leads to life; then one rests content, untouched by trouble (19:23).

In this proverb, Solomon reaffirms the central theme of living in the fear of the LORD. The one who fears the LORD walks in the way of life (23a).

On the contrary, whoever does not fear God walks in the way of death. It is not a path of possible destruction; it is a path of one hundred percent certain destruction.

Those who fear the LORD have peace of mind because they walk in the way of life (23b). They do not suffer the plagues of sin (23b). They are ultimately not afraid of the calamities that befall everyone, because they know that when they die, they will live forever. Those who fear God are self-content in any circumstance and are not overwhelmed by hardship. They have shalom and happiness that are not dependent on circumstances.[269]

A sluggard buries his hand in the dish; he will not even bring it back to his mouth! (19:24).[270]

The lazy don't even bother to scoop their food with their own hands. They act like children who want to be fed.

---

[269] Bridges noted that the triple fruit of the fear of the Lord is life, satisfaction, and security. Bridges, *Proverbs*, 327.

[270] In chapter 19, a proverb that addresses the issue of laziness is found in verse 15. Koptak notes that an identical proverb to this one is found in 26:15. Koptak, *Proverbs*, 473. Chapter 26 continues to address the foolish in verses 1 through 12 and continues to address the lazy in verses 13 through 16.

In that sense, the lazy are dependent. They want others to live for them. It is infantile to want to share in the labor of others without making any effort of their own.

Counseling Application: The reason the lazy can remain lazy is because they have helpers around them. If you help lazy people, they stay lazy. Only by not helping them you can shake off their laziness. This dynamic is seen in the lives of codependents. A husband's alcoholism is difficult to cure if the wife continues to accept her husband coming home drunk almost every day, and is responsible for his share. If she over-connects in her relationship with her husband, it's hard for them to heal. When the wife is able to differentiate herself from her husband, she can function well and he begins to function. Only when the couple makes changes in their level of differentiation, their children become healthy with their growing ability to differentiate themselves with other family members.

Alcoholism is a sin of sloth. It's a deadly sin that wastes precious time until alcoholics are sober and do not damage their families and people around them.

Flog a mocker, and the simple will learn prudence; rebuke the discerning, and they will gain knowledge (19:25).[271]

The first and second part of this proverb have the same structure. It consists of an exhortation to flog a mocker and an exhortation to rebuke a discerning man. Then the fool, or scorner, will gain wisdom and learn prudence (25a). A discerning man will gain knowledge (25b).

In this proverb, mockers are fools. Solomon sees the possibility that the arrogant and foolish might learn prudence through flogging.

The first half of this proverb can be understood as follows "Scourge the arrogant, and the foolish who see it will understand

---

[271] Bridges pointed out that there is a proverb in 21:11 with almost identical wording: "When a mocker is punished, the simple gain wisdom; by paying attention to the wise they get knowledge." Bridges, *Proverbs*, 330.

and gain wisdom." The idea is that seeing the arrogant humiliated will indirectly educate the foolish.

The arrogant, the mockers, the scornful, the foolish, and the simple are psychologically immature, although they may be labeled differently. An effective method of discipline for them is to modify their behavior by inflicting physical pain rather than verbal rebuke (25a). This is the same way that discipline is effective when used appropriately on a child.

But for those who are discerning and psychologically and spiritually mature, verbal rebuke and exhortation are effective enough. It is ineffective to prescribe the opposite approach to the arrogant or the discerning.[272]

Whoever robs their father and drives out their mother is a child who brings shame and disgrace (19:26).[273]

There are six commandments in the Ten Commandments that deal with human relationships. The first commandment that deals with human relationships is "Honor your father and your mother." In the Old Testament law, God commanded that children who disobey, hit, or curse their parents be stoned to death. God's good will in this law is for children to honor their parents and recognize their authority.[274]

Solomon points out that there are those who do not honor their parents, but instead beat their father, rob their father of his money, or kick their mother out of their homes.[275] Neglecting or kicking

---

[272] See 17:10, "A rebuke impresses a discerning person more than a hundred lashes a fool."

[273] Fox cites 20:20 and 28:24 as proverbs about children who treat their parents badly: "If someone curses their father or mother, their lamp will be snuffed out in pitch darkness"; "Whoever robs their father or mother and says, 'it's not wrong,' is partner to one who destroys." Fox, *Proverbs 10-31*, 661.

[274] Paul referred to this commandment as the "first commandment with promise" and expanded its scope, exhorting, "Fathers, do not exasperate your children; instead, bring them up in the training and instruction of the Lord" (Eph. 6:4).

out an elderly parent who is unable to live independently is an act of parental abuse holistically. It is an offense to God. God will put such children to shame (26b).

Even if parents have done something to anger their child, it is shameful to beat and drive them away in retaliation (26b). God is not pleased with those who retaliate. Such children must seriously listen to God's words, "Anyone who does not provide for their relatives, and especially for their own household, has denied the faith and is worse than an unbeliever" (1 Tim. 5:8) and repent. Otherwise, they will suffer shame and disgrace in their own lives (26b). It is very likely that they will receive the same treatment from their own children when they become parents.

Stop listening to instruction, my son, and you will stray from the words of knowledge (19:27).[276]

The discerning are able to distinguish between general knowledge that can be connected to the knowledge of God and general knowledge that conflicts with the knowledge of God. Knowledge that leads away from the knowledge of God is humanistic, secular, and even demonic.

Solomon implies that sweetly accepting instruction and lessons, even if they are painful to hear, is the way to avoid shame and humiliation (see 26b). Those who refuse to listen to their parents or to God's Word because they don't want to hear it have already deviated from the right path.

---

[275] Bridges cited Absalom's rebellion against his father David and his dishonoring of his father's concubines in daylight as an example of this proverb. Bridges, *Proverbs*, 330.

[276] This proverb can also be applied to the realm of doctrinal knowledge. Bridges pointed to 2 Cor. 11:13-15 as an example, noting that there are many servants of Satan who teach doctrines that deviate from the truth: "For such people are false apostles, deceitful workers, masquerading as apostles of Christ. And no wonder, for Satan himself masquerades as an angel of light. It is not surprising, then, if his servants also masquerade as servants of righteousness. Their end will be what their actions deserve." Bridges, *Proverbs,* 331.

A corrupt witness mocks at justice, and the mouth of the wicked gulps down evil (19:28).[277]

The first half part describes the attitudes and values of corrupt witnesses. The second half part describes their specific behaviors.

Corrupt and wicked witnesses dishonor justice and the judiciary (28a). They testify falsely even after taking an oath to tell the truth. They even lay their hands on the Bible and testify falsely. This is wicked behavior that dishonors God.

Corrupt witnesses have no fear of the consequences of false testimony. They are not concerned that their lies will soon be discovered and they will be shamed and severely punished. The defense mechanism of denial works too well. They seek only the temporary benefits that come from acting as false witnesses. They are completely incapable of empathizing with the victim who will suffer unjustly because the truth is distorted by their false testimonies. They have seared conscience. They have little superego functioning. They are likely to have antisocial personality disorder and sociopath. Furthermore, they are children of the devil, the father of lies.[278]

Corrupt and wicked witnesses devours evil chug-a-lug (28b). They gluttonously eat evil. They gobble up evil and eat it all up, and then they act innocent as if they haven't done anything evil. But God says that the evil they have swallowed will cause their stomach, liver, and intestines to rot.

These wicked men are the same today as they were in Solomon's day. As Martin Lloyd-Jones repeatedly emphasized in his sermons, all human beings since Adam are essentially the same. These evil

---

[277] Fox notes that the metaphor of "the mouth of the wicked gulps down evil" is also used in other proverb: "They eat the bread of wickedness and drink the wine of violence" (4:17). Fox, *Proverbs 10-31*, 662.

[278] Bridges pointed out that the "corrupt witness" in this proverb is the "witness of belial." Bridges, *Proverbs*, 333. Fox reveals that the Hebrew for 'corrupt witness' is *'ed beliyyaal'*. Fox, *Proverbs 10-31*, 662. In the New Testament, it is rendered "belial" in the sense of Satan or Satan's minion (2 Cor. 6:15). In the Old Testament, it is used of a "scoundrel" who does nothing but harm in society (Judg. 19:22).

and corrupt witnesses do not disappear as the quality of life improves. There are those who devour evil and manifest evil in both developed countries and underdeveloped countries.

Because of the corrupt and wicked, those who live by basic ethics, morals, and values suffer losses and pain. Until the kingdom of God is fully established, the wicked will become even more wicked. And the righteous will still suffer for the sake of righteousness.

Our consolation lies in that the wicked receive their due judgment here on earth when justice is served through the judiciary. Sometimes it is heartbreaking that this is not the case. But when the kingdom of God fully comes, they will surely receive eternal judgment from God.

Penalties are prepared for mockers, and beatings for the backs of fools (19:29).

Mockers refer to the verb, "mock" in verse 28. "Penalties" are reserved for those who despise and disregard justice and bear false witness at will (29a). There will be punishment and judgment commensurate with the false testimony. Even through the judiciary of the world, such people will have corresponding "beatings" inflicted on their back (29b). When punishments like these are administered justly, the desire of the wicked to sin can be controlled to some extent.

Chapter 20 The LORD Detests Differing Weights and Measures

Wine is a mocker and beer a brawler; whoever is led astray by them is not wise (20:1).

Wine and beer weaken the function of reason. Alcohol affects the brain. The chemicals in alcohol affect the brain. That's why, when we're drunk, we have a distorted perception of reality. We may experience feelings of self-exaltation and self-aggrandizement. Our judgment may be clouded and we may impulsively say or do things we wouldn't normally do. As a result, drunk people "talk too much" and get into arguments easily (1a). People who act unpredictably because of alcohol are foolish (1b). They do things they will regret later. The wisdom of life is not to do things we regret.

Leaders in society should be especially careful about drinking. This is because there are times when they make a mistake in a place of drinking and are criticized by the media. It's not uncommon for some leaders to make a sexually harassing remark or grope in a bar and be removed from their position overnight.

In the Book of Esther, King Xerxes' anger was not unrelated to his drinking: he "was in high spirits from wine" and ordered seven eunuchs to bring his queen Vasti to the feast. In his high spirits, he impulsively wanted to show off the queen's beauty to the dignitaries and people at the feast. When she refused to come to the feast in defiance of his royal command, "his heart was burning with wrath" (Esth. 1:12). In his drunkenness, he listened to his officials and did the foolish thing of deposing his beloved queen by his own hand. Nevertheless, God used his foolish behavior to prepare Esther and to accomplish his providential administration in saving the scattered people of Judah from the coming carnage.

A king's wrath strikes terror like the roar of a lion; those who anger him forfeit their lives (20:2).[279] See 19:12a.

In the monarchical era, the king's wrath was primarily related to treason. Treason was the king's greatest source of anxiety. To be traitors meant that their whole families including their relatives would be exterminated. Nevertheless, rebellion has been a recurring theme throughout history. People have challenged kingship, even at the risk of their own lives and the lives of their families.

Most reviews of rebels are negative, but there are some positive ones in the Bible. Some of those who challenged wicked kings were people who were just, courageous, and with conviction. For example, Jehu's rebellion against the Ahab dynasty in northern Israel was treason in the eyes of Ahab's son, King Joram (see 2 Kings 9:23). But in God's eyes, Jehu was an instrument of God's righteous judgment. Jehu pleased God by killing all of the priests of Baal who had opposed Ahab's dynasty.

It is to one's honor to avoid strife, but every fool is quick to quarrel (20:3).

Solomon says that those who are easily provoked are foolish (3b). Quarrelsome people are often "easily angered." Being easily angered is a symptom of psychologically immature persons, especially people with borderline personality disorder. Another personality disorder that is related to this symptom is paranoid personality disorder. One of the symptoms is that the person feels hurt by the slightest thing that the other person says or does, and he or she lashes out in anger.

When there are many people who are easily angered, the community they belong to is bound to fall apart. It consumes too much unnecessary energy. Today, Korean churches or church-

---

[279] Bridges cited the example of Adonijah, who sought to take Abishag, David's attending servant, as his wife, incurring Solomon's wrath and ultimately being killed. Bridges, *Proverbs*, 335.

related institutions are experiencing a bizarre phenomenon of many litigation. Even minor disputes within the church are being tried to be resolved in the courts. In some cases, it is possible and necessary to resolve issues through the judiciary. However, in many cases, litigation is not in the spirit of the biblical teaching. It's a sad reality. When a church community becomes embroiled in litigation, it unnecessarily expends energy and money and scatters members. A church, presbytery, or denomination can be devastated by protracted litigation, which can take at least two to three years for a single case to be decided by the Supreme Court. It is no exaggeration to say that most of the lawsuits in Korean churches are spiritually foolish and demonic.[280]

In that regard, it is God's will that quarrels be avoided as much as possible and that peace be sought, and it is consequently honorable for those involved (3a). Paul exhorts us to keep the peace with all people as far as it depends on us (Rom. 12:18). If we continue to argue when a dispute arises, we become irrational and emotionally unstable. As a result, we become wicked toward each other by fighting without an end in sight. Therefore, we should obey the Bible's instruction to seek peace so that minor quarrels do not escalate into major fights.

Pursuing peace should be distinguished from the neurotic and immature behavior of avoiding conflicts at all costs. It means having the psychological and spiritual maturity not to return evil for evil, but to "overlook" and tolerate the offense of the other side. In doing so, we can avoid a bitter lawsuit. As a result, there is honor for peacemakers (3a).

"Every fool is quick to quarrel" in verse 3b can be interpreted in conjunction with verse 1. Intoxication by wine or strong drink increases the risk of getting into an argument or fight. Fighting

---

[280] Paul makes it clear that unresolved anger can provide a platform for the devil to intervene: "In your anger do not sin: Do not let the sun go down while you are still angry, and do not give the devil a foothold" (Eph. 4:26-27). Bridges pointed out that strife is not wisdom from above, citing James 3:14-16 as an example: "But if you harbor bitter envy and selfish ambition in your hearts, do not boast about it or deny the truth. Such 'wisdom' does not come down from heaven but is earthly, unspiritual, demonic. For where you have envy and selfish ambition, there you find disorder and every evil practice." *Bridges*, Proverbs, 336.

while drunk is a foolish and unwise behavior. People who drink in bars and get involved in violent incidents are also foolish.

Sluggards do not plow in season; so at harvest time they look but find nothing (20:4).[281]

Interpreting this proverb with Korean farming culture in mind, persons who do not plow their rice paddies or fields in the spring are lazy farmers. If they don't sow seeds and expect to reap grain or vegetables, they are delusional. They may rub their eyes to see if there is anything in the field, but they will not find any harvest (4b).

The purposes of a person's heart are deep waters, but one who has insight draws them out (20:5).

Generally, people don't show their "real self" or "true self" outside of a safe environment or safe relationship. Many people even identify themselves with their superficial "false self" or "*persona.*" Just as it is difficult to draw water from a deep well, many people go through life without being in in-depth touch with their inner selves. They are unconscious to their core issues and core feelings.

Counseling Application: Insightful and understanding counselors have the wisdom and ability to make clients feel comfortable revealing what they are hiding or what is hidden in them. When they relate with their clients with empathy, understanding, and compassion, clients feel comfortable trusting them and the counseling process. This allows them to reveal parts of themselves that they have never shared with anyone else. In the process, they can gain a new awareness of what they really want in

---

[281] Koptak suggests that the proverb can be interpreted in conjunction with the preceding verse 3 as a recommendation to expend energy on something productive rather than on arguing. Koptak, *Proverbs*, 484.

life and who they really are.

From the perspective of depth psychology, the deep water in the text symbolizes the unconscious mind. The unconscious part of the human mind is much larger than the conscious part. And even one's own motives, or the purpose of one's life, are often unconscious. There are a surprising number of people who are unaware of what they really want. In the case of Christians, many are unaware of the presence and work of the Holy Spirit who indwells their hearts.

In the course of long-term counseling, the counselor can help the client explore the realm of the unconscious, expanding and deepening his or her horizons of consciousness. It's not easy to draw deep water, but if the counselor can draw deep water from the client's inner world, both the counselor and the client will enjoy the taste of cool water.

Many claim to have unfailing love, but a faithful person who can find? (20:6).

Most people are not very aware of their true inner beings, so they tend to think of themselves either too positively or too negatively. People who think positively without knowing who they really are think, "I'm such a mature and decent person,"[282] and overestimate their psychological maturity. In contrast, people who think themselves negatively devalue their potentials and talents and think that they are not lovable or they cannot love others enough. Anyway, it is difficult to find people who have both the maturity of faith and psychological maturity enough to love with unfailing love and to keep "object constancy" in relationships (6b).

Human beings are limited in their capacity to love. We may endure and sacrifice up to a certain point, but it is difficult to have a n object constancy that allows us to endure and love to the end.[283]

---

[282] Bridges connected the preceding verse 5 with this proverb, insightfully commenting that most people do not recognize the deceit and pride that lie deep within their own hearts. Bridges, *Proverbs*, 339.

[283] Most people overestimate their ability to maintain "object constancy" because they

Human beings with sinful nature are bound to have limitations in loving. However, by continually experiencing the love of Jesus Christ and being empowered by the Holy Spirit, we can grow in loving and being loved.[284]

One of the classic examples of stable, faithful, and enduring relationships is found in the parent-child relationship or the marriage relationship. But even these relationships often become unstable. Nevertheless, these are the two key human relationships that most visibly express God's love in the world.

The righteous lead blameless lives; blessed are their children after them (20:7).

Blessed are the children of parents or ancestors whose lives are blameless. They are influenced by godly parents or ancestors. They finally inherit a legacy of faith and transmit the legacy to the next generation.

When a king[285] sits on his throne to judge, he winnows out all evil with his eyes (20:8).

Kings or a judges entrusted with judgment must have the wisdom to discern matters. They must have knowledge, discernment and

have a poor ability to perceive themselves objectively. They claim to be able to do so confidently, but it doesn't take long for them to crack under the pressure of reality.

[284] In Paul's case, he was "under great pressure, far beyond our ability to endure" so that he despaired of life itself. But he learned that "this happened that we might not rely one ourselves but on God, who raises the dead" (2 Cor. 1:8, 9).

[285] Bridges pointed to Ps. 5:4-6 as a relevant passage, noting that all sins and deceits are exposed before God, the eternal King: "For you are not a God who is pleased with wickedness; with you, evil people are not welcome. The arrogant cannot stand in your presence. You hate all who do wrong; you destroy those who tell lies. The bloodthirsty and deceitful you, LORD, detest." Bridges, *Proverbs*, 341.

wisdom to distinguish between justice and injustice. Only then will falsehood and iniquity be revealed before their eyes (8b).

Spiritually understood, Christians who experience the indwelling and working of the Holy Spirit can see things through spiritual eyes. They are sensitive to the temptations and interventions of the devil. They are also able to discern evil and have the power to depart from it. The devil has no access to Christians spiritually alert, well armored in the Holy Spirit.

Counseling Application: Understood on a psychological level of an individual, there is a king inside each person called the ego. This king is not powerful enough to wield total power, but it can control impulses and dominate thoughts and emotions to a certain extent. It is sometimes subject to unconscious dynamics and suffers from the intervention of the superego. However, a person with a well-developed ego has a healthy and powerful king ruling the inner world. This king is able to discern between good and evil, distinguish truth from falsehood, and seek justice.

Who can say, "I have kept my heart pure; I am clean and without sin"? (20:9).

This proverb ends with an interrogative sentence. The answer, of course, is "No one!" However, some who do not understand the biblical concept of sin may answer, "I am clean." On a conscious level, they may perceive that way. On an ethical and moral level, they might even say, "I am clean and sinless." But the Bible declares that there is not a single person who is free from the sinful nature since the fall of Adam and Eve. If we understand the dynamics of the unconscious world, the Bible's declaration that there is not a single person who can say that he or she is without sin makes more sense. Jesus' statement that anyone who looks at a woman with lust in their hearts has already committed adultery can be understood in the same way.

Differing weights and differing measures—the LORD detests

them both (20:10).[286]

Scales and rulers for measuring weight and length are symbols of social agreement and justice. They are the promised institutions and devices of human society that enable people to trust one another. So to use different scales and rulers is anti-social behavior and a sin that displeases God (10b).

God sees and knows who uses deceitful scales and who uses honest ones. And he rewards and punishes according to their behavior. If they are aware of God's judgment, they cannot cheat the scales. People with normal psychological development, whether religious or not, would not do such a shameful thing. Unfortunately, there are many people in the world who fearlessly practice this evil behavior that God hates. There are too many human beings who are not developed even in basic morals.

Even small children are known by their action, so is their conduct really pure and upright? [by whether his conduct is pure and right] (20:11).

Action or behavior is an important area of human understanding. In a strict sense, we can say that no behavior is meaningless. From a psychoanalytic perspective, even mistakes are meaningful. Even a tongue slip can be interpreted as meaningful.

This proverb tells us that children's actions have meaning. Even when they say they are not lying, their behavior reveals that they are. For example, averting your eyes, touching your nose, tensing your face, wiggling your eyes, overreacting, and blushing are unconscious behaviors that reveal you are not being truthful with your words.

Counseling Application: Behavior is an important symbol and symptom in understanding and diagnosing people. Identifying and

---

[286] A similar proverb is found in verse in the same chapter: "The LORD detests differing weights, and dishonest scales do not please him."

categorizing symptoms help us to make an accurate assessment or diagnosis. Therefore, effective counselors listen sensitively to the client's every word. They have the ability to pick up on even the most insignificant behaviors.

Ears that hear and eyes that see—the LORD has made them both (20:12).

God didn't just give us ears and eyes. God is the Creator of all things. He created every animal, every plant, every mineral, from microbes to humans, by his words. He created all the stars in the universe. And he is omniscient and omnipresent, remembering and calling them by name.

The eyes and ears are the most important organs for humans to grasp and perceive the external reality. Being blind or deaf makes life very inconvenient and difficult. It is a mystery that God created these wonderful eyes and ears. We should be thankful that we have eyes to see beautiful things and ears to hear birds chirping.

God, who made eyes and ears, watches over the world and all its inhabitants. The psalmist affirmed this fact by saying "Does he who fashioned the ear not hear? Does he who formed the eye not see?" (Ps. 94:9). Our answer is an unhesitating "Yes, he hears and he sees us."

Do not love sleep or you will grow poor; stay awake and you will have food to spare (20:13).

This proverb is a warning against the lazy. Lazy people love to sleep. They doze off whenever they can and sleep whenever they can. To borrow a phrase from 19:15, sluggards sleep a deep sleep.

People who sleep too much are likely to be impoverished in many ways (13a), spiritually, materially, and physically. Excessive sleep is emotionally depressing and can even jeopardize their physical health.

Solomon encourages us to stay awake and be active and do our best. When we do that, we will have food to spare financially and spiritually (13b).

Counseling Application: A symptom of depression is usually insomnia, but it can also manifest as sleeping too much. Some depressed people sleep too much because they don't have to face reality while they sleep.

"It's no good, it's no good!" says the buyer—then goes off and boasts about the purchase (20:14).

This proverb describes the psychology of people in the world. The position of a buyer and the position of a seller are different. Buyers feel good when they get a bargain. But sellers try to sell at a profit. They bargain with each other while considering their own interests.

There are some buyers who talk about things to buy in a disparaging way or say they're not interested in them. In effect, they are lying and bargaining. They hide their true feelings. There are also people who boast about their bargaining skills.[287] In the world, this is called haggling. It's a human psychology to feel good when you buy something for less than the full price while everyone else pays full price for it.

This proverb neither praises nor condemns this tactic. It tells us that this is the way it is. Believers in the position of sellers should sell reasonably and not cheat. Believers who are in the position of buyers should also buy wisely so that they should not take advantage of the seller's predicament to sell or be foolishly deceived by lying sellers. Christians need to be wise as snakes and innocent as doves, knowing full well that there are those who will deceive others by saying that they are sincere deacons or elders of

---

[287] Bridges insightfully commented that while verse 10 of this chapter warns of the immorality of the seller, this verse exposes the selfishness and falsehood of the buyer. He noted that the buyer's boastfulness in mocking the seller's simplicity may be shrewd in the world but is vanity: "As it is, you boast in your arrogant schemes. All such boasting is evil" (James 4:16). Bridges, *Proverbs*, 347.

a certain church, and then commit fraud after they have disarmed them.

Gold there is, and rubies in abundance, but lips that speak knowledge are a rare jewel (20:15).[288]

Gold and pearls are precious. They're scarce. But you can buy gold or pearls if you have the money. But wise lips are a "rare jewel." Wise lips are more valuable than gold. They are more precious than expensive pearls.

Counseling Application: Christian counselors with wise lips are a rare gem in Korea. There are not many counselors who are spiritually and psychologically mature, well versed in counseling theory and practice, and confidently speak theological language. Christian counselors who are as Christ-centered and therapeutically skilled as Peter, who said, "Silver or gold I do not have, but what I do have I give you. In the name of Jesus Christ of Nazareth, walk" (Acts 3:6), are a treasure for Korean churches as well as for Korean-American churches. We need more of them.

The grain is ready for harvest, but there is a shortage of trained laborers. It is encouraging to see church counseling centers and privately run Christian counseling centers popping up all over the place in Korea, and more people studying for degrees and training. There is a desperate need for more Christian counseling services.

Take the garment of one who puts up security for a stranger; hold it in pledge if it is done for an outsider [for a wayward woman] (20:16).

[288] Koptak points out other proverbs that are relevant to this proverb, including "She is more precious than rubies; nothing you desire can compare with her" (3:15); "For wisdom is more precious than rubies and nothing you desire can compare with her" (8:11); "A wife of noble character who can find? She is worth far more than rubies" (31:10). Koptak, *Proverbs*, 487.

The sentence structure, A-B-A'-B', suggests that a stranger and a wayward woman are synonymous. Those who put up security for a stranger, a foreigner, or a wayward woman are fools. Solomon recommends that if such foolish persons ask to borrow money for a stranger or a wayward woman, one is better to ask for their most important asset, that is, their outer garment, as collateral.[289] If one trusts the foolish persons and lend them money, he or she is also a fool. In this case, collateral is required. Then the foolish persons are likely to reconsider their decision when they are asked to pledge their most important asset as collateral.[290]

Food gained by fraud tastes sweet,[291] but one ends up with a mouth full of grave (20:17).[292]

Eating in secret, rather than just eating, activates the senses more due to tension, anxiety, and excitement. Some people who shoplift from department stores or shops do so because although they have

[289] Bridges noted that while this proverb may seem to contradict the Mosaic law, which warns against pledging outer garments of the poor as security and not returning it when they borrow money, it actually does not contradict the Mosaic law. The distinction should be made because the target of this proverb is not the poor person who has to worry about putting food on the table, but the person who borrows money while living a reckless and inconsiderate life. Bridges, *Proverbs*, 349-50.

[290] Judah, one of Jacob's sons, acted foolishly. He was foolish to have sex with a woman he thought was a prostitute. He was also foolish to give her with his seal as a pledge. From Tamar's perspective, his seal was a safeguard against the consequences of having sex with his father-in-law. In that sense, she was wise and Judah was foolish.

[291] This is connected to the words of the foolish woman to deceive the foolish: "Stolen water is sweet; food eaten in secret is delicious!" (9:17).

[292] Bridges connected to a biblical event in which Achan's secretly taken riches at the Battle of Jericho resulted not only in the death of himself and his family, but also in the defeat of the Israelites at the Battle of Ai (Josh. 7:21-24). He also connected Gehazi's deception of General Naaman and taking his gold and coat, to his curse from Elisha, which resulted in his leprosy from Elisha's curse (2 Kings 5:20-27). Bridges, *Proverbs*, 350.

the money, they want to enjoy the high they get when they succeed in shoplifting. The reason why taking drugs gives people such a strong high is because they are legally prohibited. Doing something legally forbidden increases the pleasure even more. The problem is that these behaviors are short-lived and often lead to disgrace, shame, and ruin (17b). There comes a time when they realize that what they ate as delicious food was actually indigestible gravel.[293] It is wise to realize this beforehand and avoid doing anything foolish.

Plans are established by seeking advice; so if you wage war, obtain guidance (20:18).[294]

This proverb emphasizes the importance of consultation and advice. It is much wiser to take the advice of others when making decisions in business or planning.[295]

Good commanders have good staff officers and know how to listen to their advice. Good commanders are humble. Furthermore, leaders of faith pray for God's guidance. They ask for the Holy Spirit's help. Joshua was that kind of commander.

---

[293] The narrative that connects to the metaphor of "food and pebbles" is the story of Jesus' temptation by the devil in the wilderness. The devil came to Jesus, who had fasted for forty days, and tempted him to make bread out of stones and eat them. The taste of food after fasting is incomparable to the taste of normal food, and it brings tears to the eyes. The devil's temptation to turn the pebbles into bread and eat them was an insidious temptation to undermine Jesus' work on the cross: to avoid suffering and seek only glory. It's natural to want to eat when we're hungry, and it's beneficial to do so. The important thing is to have the spiritual wisdom to discern whether it is a worldly teaching or a divine teaching.

[294] Koptak comments that the story of Hushai and Ahithophel illustrates that warfare is not waged with "military power," but with "strategy." Koptak, *Proverbs*, 487.

[295] In Ecclesiastes, Solomon captured this truth when he said, "Two are better than one, because they have a good return for their labor: If either of them falls down, one can help the other up. But pity anyone who falls and has no one to help them up." (Eccl. 4:9-10).

However, commanders with narcissistic personality disorder trust their own thoughts. They don't consult or seek advice from officers around them. If they ask for advice, it's a formality. And managers with obsessive-compulsive personality disorder don't know how to delegate, so they make decisions and handle things on their own. They don't take the views of others seriously.

A gossip betrays a confidence; so avoid anyone who talks too much (20:19). See also 18:8.

Those who love to gossip may serve as an epicenter for unfounded rumors. The phrase "silence is like gold" applies to keeping confidentiality, especially when it comes to things that are said in trust.

Most of us have tongue slips, as James said that no one is perfect in speaking. The more we talk, the more likely we are to slip. Freud believed that even a "tongue slip" is meaningful. He interpreted a tongue slip as an unconscious meaning and motivation behind a word or phrase, even if it was completely unintentional. In the same way, there are times when words slip out of our mouths without our intention, and we happened to fail to keep them secret. Such mistakes are inevitable when we talk a lot. So it's wise to be careful with our words and watch what we say.

Evil people intentionally break promises of confidentiality. There are even those who say, "Don't ever tell anyone about this," and then pass the word on. It is foolish to tell them your secrets.

Counseling Application: The importance of confidentiality in counseling cannot be overemphasized. When counselors fail to keep their clients' secrets, they are seriously hurt. Counselors who don't keep confidentiality strictly to themselves get rumored. Rumors can stop prospective clients from coming to see them. They may even be sued for violating confidentiality ethics. Confidentiality is a core ethical rule that counselors should strive to uphold.[296]

---

[296] In the age of television and the internet, where sermons can be easily watched or listened to via YouTube, radio, or recordings, preachers need to be very careful when

If someone curses their father or mother, their lamp[297] will be snuffed out in pitch darkness[298] (20:20). See also 19:26.

Adult children who curse their parents have violated a boundary that should not be crossed. Anger to the point of cursing is extreme anger. Saying things we shouldn't say or crossing boundaries we shouldn't cross even when we are angry is a deadly sin that disobeys God's commands.

In the Ten Commandments, God gave the commandment, "Honor your father and your mother," and a law that those who who curse their parents were stoned to death. This was because when they curse their parents, they are actually cursing God, who gave every parents an authority over their children.

Solomon warns in this proverb that those who curse their parents will be cursed themselves. Adult children who curse their elderly parents, in particular, are likely to be cursed by their own children. There's a dynamic of "parallel process" at work.

In New Testament times, cursing one's parents doesn't result in stoning to death under the Old Testament law. If physical violence against a parent goes unreported, the police don't get involved. As a result, it's not uncommon for children to cross generational boundaries within a family system, or for their parents to be abused and abandoned. Of course, some of the parents who are treated this way have been abusive in many ways when raising their children.

However, God is not pleased when a adult child abuses an elderly parent in retaliation for the hurt he or she received in growing up.

citing specific cases in their sermons. They lose credibility from their congregation if they casually mention a story even though the story is not from their own churches, and they may even be sued by the person of the story.

[297] Fox sees "lamps" as a metaphor for life, generational permanence, the permanence of a throne, or prosperity. Fox, *Proverbs 10-31*, 672.

[298] Fox notes that 30:11 and 30:17 are related to this proverb: "There are those who curse their fathers and do not bless their mothers"; "The eye that mocks a father, that scorns an aged mother, will be pecked out by the ravens of the valley, will be eaten by the vultures." Fox, *Proverbs 10-31*, 672.

Abused children may not be able to actively show love to their parents. However, actively using physical, verbal, or emotional violence against parents is a criminal offense and must be prohibited. As a Christian, if you happen to have children who repeat this kind of anti-social behavior, you need to understand that they don't fully appreciate that they themselves have been given grace and forgiven through Jesus Christ and their behaviors detest God.[299]

An inheritance claimed too soon [quickly gained at the beginning] will not be blessed at the end (20:21).

This proverb contrasts "at the beginning" with "at the end." There is a Korean four character phrase, "bright beginning but dull finish" (龍頭蛇尾). It refers to a case in which a person starts out like a dragon's head but end up like a snake's tail. This proverb warns against the case of starting like a dragon's head.

People who start from scratch with their inherited money don't know the value of money because they've never had to work hard for it. They may even have the misguided notion that it's okay to lose. They're likely to fail because they haven't learned to manage their money through trial and error.

Most unearned income is not beneficial, and it disappears as quickly as it has wings to fly away. This is often the case with lottery winners. Most people who dream about winning a "jackpot" and then find that it has become a reality for them are unable to manage it properly. They are likely to experience a family breakdown and end up in a miserable situation. In the end, the miraculous lottery win becomes a curse instead of a blessing.

Do not say, "I'll pay you back for this wrong!" Wait for the

---

[299] Such a person is like the foolish man who incurred the king's wrath. He imprisoned a fellow who owed him a hundred denarii, even though he was forgiven ten thousand talents in full what he owned to the king.

LORD, and he will avenge [deliver] you (20:22).

  This proverb advises against our possible saying to the wrongdoer, "I will surely retaliate against you for this evil," when we are in trouble because of the wickedness of a person. Solomon encourages us to be God-centered and to keep our eyes fixed on God in our dealings with the wicked. It is very important to look vertically first, not just horizontally, when dealing with the evil-doers.

  David, Solomon's father, actually lived such a life. Saul tried to kill him many times, but he did not retaliate with evil. He overcame evil with good until the end. He trusted that God would ultimately intervene. He recognized God's sovereignty and providence. When he was fleeing from Absalom's rebellion, Shimei, a member of Saul's extended family, cursed him and threw stones at him, but he did not retaliate. Rather, he interpreted it as God's permission for Shimei to curse him. Solomon must have learned this valuable faith and truth from his father.

  It takes total trust and faith in God to look to him and trust him with our lives when we suffer injustice at the hands of the wicked. Waiting on him and praying to him in the face of evil is faith.[300]

The LORD detests differing weights, and dishonest scales do not please him (20:23). See also 20:10.

A person's steps are directed by the LORD. How then can anyone understand their own way? (20:24).[301]

---

[300] Paul gave the same exhortation: "Do not repay anyone evil for evil....Do not take revenge, my dear friends, but leave room for God's wrath, for it is written: 'It is mine to avenge; I will repay,' says the Lord" (Rom. 12:17-19).

[301] "LORD, I know that people's lives are not their own: it is not for them to direct their steps" (Jer. 10:23).

The journey of life is a journey that each person must take one step at a time. At the same time, there is the intervention of an invisible God who guides and directs each step (24a). This is a paradox. If we hope only for God's guidance and do not take any steps ourselves, we cannot move forward. We must take our own steps, trusting in God's providence and guidance.

Humans cannot know the path they are walking. No one can even accurately predict what path they will take tomorrow (24b). And worrying about tomorrow won't help us much. We can plan for the future, but no one can guarantee that it will turn out the way we want it to. So we must be humble before God. We can overcome the anxiety and fear that accompany the journey of life when we trust God to guide our every step in the way.[302]

It is a trap to dedicate something rashly and only later to consider one's vows (20:25).

This proverb warns us that impulsive vows to God can be a trap. It is foolish to impulsively pledge things or people to God.[303]

---

[302] Bridges commented that this proverb reveals man's utter dependence and helplessness in contrast to God's sovereignty and power as a foundational principle of human life. Bridges, *Proverbs*, 357.

[303] The Old Testament story of Jephthah is a prime example of this proverb. He made an impulsive vow that led to the unfortunate consequence of offering his daughter as a burnt offering. Clifford also points out his impulsive vow in his commentary on this proverb. Clifford, *Proverbs*, 186. Herod was so enamored with the dancing of Herodias' daughter that he impulsively vowed to her to give anything she asked, which ultimately led to the beheading of John the Baptist. In the case of Ananias and Sapphira, it's not clear from the Acts 5 text, but it's likely that they impulsively pledged to sell their land and give all. We can infer this from Peter's rebuke, "Didn't it belong to you before it was sold? And after it was sold, wasn't the money at your disposal?" (Acts 5:4). If they had thought it would be a good idea to sell their possessions and give only a portion, and if they had discussed it as a couple and then promised that they would offer a portion of the money, there would have been no

Impulsive promises in interpersonal relationships can also be a trap.

God does not make impulsive promises in his relationship with humans. The covenant relationship God has with his children is not a promise to be made or broken on a whim. God's covenant is indeed trustworthy. They are faithful. The hymn, "The covenant of my Lord is everlasting, He keeps me till I reach his land," captures the truth.

Counseling Application: In terms of MBTI personality types, Sensing (S), Thinking (T), or Judging (J) is more cautious and deliberate than iNtuitive (N), Feeling (F), or Perceiving (P). Sensing people process all information through their five senses, so they need to see it to believe it. They confirm each stepping-stone before before crossing a stream. Therefore, they are less likely to make mistakes. Thinking people are less impulsive because they think rationally and not emotionally. Judging types are far from impulsive because they plan things out. However, iNtuitive, Feeling, or Perceiving people have weaknesses in terms of impulsivity. Therefore, people with these personality types need to be especially cautious.

A wise king winnows out the wicked; he drives the threshing wheel over them (20:26).

This proverb uses the agricultural metaphors of winnowing and threshing. Winnowing separates the kernels from the chaff. When a farmer puts a sheaf of rice into the threshing wheel, the grain is sifted out and only the chaff and straw remain.[304] The wicked are

reason for Peter to discipline them for giving a portion. But they had either promised to sell and give all of their possessions, or they had concealed some and falsely said it was all they had sold. In the end, their impulsive behavior proved to be a trap, with fatal consequences.

[304] Bridges connected Jesus' ministry of threshing, prophesied by John the Baptist, to this proverb: "His winnowing fork is in his hand, and he will clear his threshing floor, gathering his wheat into the barn and burning up the chaff with unquenchable fire"

"like chaff that the wind blows away" (Ps. 1:4), and when God threshes them, they cannot survive. The following poetry well describes this: "Therefore the wicked will not stand in the judgment, nor sinners in the assembly of the righteous" (Ps. 1:5).

A wise king has the discernment to winnow out the wicked from the good (26a). Solomon was a king who exercised great wisdom in sifting the wickedness of the woman who insisted on the other woman's baby as her own. Her wickedness was exposed as soon as she was put into the threshing wheel (26b).

The human spirit is the lamp of the LORD that sheds light on one's inmost being (20:27).

The soul is God's gift to humans that sets us apart from other animals. The soul is like a lamp, enabling spiritual sight, enlightenment, and insight. Only when the soul is alive we can discern good and evil and have fellowship with God.

After the fall of Adam, the lamp of the soul was extinguished in every human being. They lost the light of knowing God. It is like the blind whose optic nerve is dead, unable to see even when light shines on them. The ability to feel and search for the divine remains faintly, but they are unable to recognize God as the Light, and so they live in idolatry and other religious practices.

No one can know and believe in the God revealed in the Bible unless God the Holy Spirit regenerates this dead soul. But the soul of believers who are regenerated by the Holy Spirit in Jesus Christ is enlightened by the Holy Spirit with the Word of God. So they realize and believe that they are sinners and that Jesus Christ is the Savior for their sins. Their spiritual eyes are opened so that they are able to connect every creation with God the Creator. They become worshippers in reverence and awe for God.

The NIV Bible translates the text as "The human spirit is the lamp of the LORD that sheds light on one's inmost being."[305] As a

(Matt. 3:12). Bridges, *Proverbs*, 360.

[305] *The Anchor Yale Bible* translates, "He examines all the rooms of the belly." See Fox, *Proverbs 10-31*, 676. God knows what is in every room of our hearts. Even the secret

special revelation, the Bible is a lamp and a mirror to each person's heart. It is a healing ray that penetrates to the deepest depths. As the Holy Spirit indwells the believer's heart, he continually illuminates and enlightens our inner world through the written Word. He helps us to accurate self-awareness. He prays with unspeakable groans, even when we are unaware of it. So we walk in the path of righteousness even in the valley of the shadow of death, relying on the lamp of the Word.

In the Old Testament times, the priests were responsible for providing a constant supply of oil to keep the lamp of the LORD burning in the sanctuary. In the New Testament era, each believer is a royal priest. And our body and soul are the temple in which the Holy Spirit dwells (see 1 Cor. 5:19-20).

But sin increases the risk of extinguishing the fire of the Holy Spirit. Even we are vulnerable to the devil when we sin. When we sin, we cannot properly discern God's will and examine our own hearts. All kinds of greed and sin darken our soul. It is instructive to note that Samson, who was set apart as a Nazarite from his birth and filled with the Holy Spirit, was blinded by greed and lust. And he actually had both his eyes plucked out and was reduced to the status of an animal grinding a millstone. With his physical eyes plucked out, but his spiritual eyes opened, he was finally clothed with God's grace again and was used by God to perform amazing feats and die a spectacular death.

Love and faithfulness keep a king safe; through love his throne is made secure (20:28).

Love and faithfulness are the character of God. The throne of a king with God's character is safe and secure. It is recognized by God. The king is loved and honored by his officials and peoples. The second part of this proverb is a paraphrase of the first part, emphasizing the same meaning.

rooms we don't show others, God can enter. Even the rooms of our unconscious mind that we don't know about, God is familiar with.

When kings ignore and oppress their peoples, there is a high risk of riots and rebellion. Their wicked behaviors and attitudes are self-defeating and foolish. Their thrones will not be safe and secure.

Unfortunately, Solomon's son, Rehoboam, ignored the legitimate demands of the people and declared his plan of violent dominion, which resulted in the loss of ten tribes and the division of the nation. As we can see from this outcome, Solomon's proverbs were of little help to his son Rehoboam. Solomon himself lived a life that did not live up to the words of the proverbs he taught. The foolish lives of Solomon and Rehoboam offer challenges and lessons for us as parents and children.

The glory of young men is their strength, gray hair the splendor of the old (20:29).

The old are ones who has been through youth. The young have plenty of strength and energy. But the old do not have the same strength and energy as the young. On the other hand, generally speaking, the old are more mature and integrated than the young, as symbolized by gray hair.[306] Therefore, both the young and the old have their strengths and weaknesses. Thus, life is beautiful and glorious at each stage of development. A young child has the glory and beauty of being a child. Life in old age is not without beauty. It is as if the beauty of the late fall foliage is a beauty that cannot be seen at any other time of the year.

Therefore, those who are depressed or sad because they have reached old age are foolish. Wise persons are ones who embrace their gray hair as a natural part of life.

Blows and wounds scrub [cleanse] away evil, and beatings

---

[306] Not everyone who grows older achieves the wisdom and integration that gray hair symbolizes. Some people grow old ugly. Those who have not attained the maturity appropriate to each stage of life from their youth will spend their old age in depression, regret, and sorrow.

purge the inmost being (20:30).

Solomon endorses the positive effects of beating and punishing with a rod. Spanking and punishment are effective when the purpose and method are appropriate. A proper spanking removes evil that is already in a child and is effective in breaking bad habits (30a).

The experience of suffering has the same effect.[307] Suffering can be life-changing. It can refine one's character, for suffering "purge the inmost being" (30b).

On the other hand, excessive or frequent use of punishment is counterproductive to removing evil. Using excessive punishment or creating a level of fear that is beyond a child's ability to handle is not only ineffective, it is evil. It's a foolish way to discipline a child that sows seeds of anxiety and anger in his or her mind. Parents should be aware of the danger that an unwise discipline can destroy a child's inner world. Parents should recognize that the devil delights in the destruction of a child's psychological world through the foolish choice of a parent.

---

[307] Bridges connected this proverb to the words of 1 Cor. 5:5: "Hand this man over to Satan for the destruction of the flesh, so that his spirit may be saved on the day of the Lord." Bridges, *Proverbs*, 363.

Chapter 21 Living with a Quarrelsome Spouse Is Very Stressful

In the LORD's hand the king's heart is a stream of water that he channels toward all who please him (21:1).

Kings are the sovereign rulers of their country. Their heart is like a stream of water, and they can change its course as they pleases.

But what God-fearing kings must recognize is that there is the LORD God who controls their hearts. When they recognize that they make decisions in every activity, but God controls their hearts (see 16:9), God recognizes and uses them.

When Joseph was thirty years old and in prison in Egypt, God moved like a stream of water in the heart of King Pharaoh. He intervened in Pharaoh's dreams and used them to bring Joseph out of prison. And he made Joseph the ruler of Egypt and redeemed Jacob's entire family out of famine.

God controlled the heart of Pharaoh, king of Egypt, the greatest empire of Moses' day. Pharaoh made arbitrary decisions at every turn. But the Bible says that God hardened his heart. God used Pharaoh's repeated disobedience to reveal God's glory and greatness to all creation.

God doesn't just control the hearts of powerful people like kings or presidents. He intervenes the hearts of all who dwell on this earth. He even controls the thoughts of the ravens (see 1 Kings 17:4-6).

A person may think their own ways are right, but the LORD weighs the heart (21:2).[308]

---

[308] The second half of this proverb connects with the second half of 20:27, which precedes it: "that sheds light on one's inmost being." Bridges noted that this proverb is a repetition of 16:2: "All a person's ways seem pure to them, but motives are weighted by the LORD." Bridges, *Proverbs*, 365.

Most people tend to be egocentric, which means that they often see their points of view and ways of life as the right one (2a). Some people even believe that their ideas are right and that they are fine, even though other people objectively see them as wrong and problematic. This is most often seen in people with personality disorders or schizophrenia.

But God sees and knows the heart's center (2b). Even hidden motives are naked before God's eyes. When believers stand before the Word of God, they realize what they had not recognized before and repent.

Filled with the Holy Spirit, Peter saw through Ananias and Sapphira's hidden sin and deceit as if he could see them with his own eyes. Peter rebuked Ananias, saying, "Ananias, how is it that Satan has so filled your heart that you have lied to the Holy Spirit and have kept for yourself some of the money you received for the land?" and "You have not lied just to human beings but to God" (Acts 5:3, 4). God cannot be deceived.

To do what is right and just is more acceptable to the LORD than sacrifice (21:3).

Solomon argues that God takes more pleasure in our doing righteousness and justice than in our sacrifice. Samuel also rebuked King Saul that his obedience would be better than his sacrifice (1 Sam. 15:22). Isaiah identified what fasting was pleasing to God (see Is. 58:5-7).[309]

Some people think that attending worship services is enough for their faith in God. But God is more pleased when his children live out his will in their lives.

---

[309] The prophet Amos captures the meaning of this proverb: "I hate, I despise your religious festivals; your assemblies are a stench to me. Even though you bring me burnt offerings and grain offerings, I will not accept them. Though you bring choice fellowship offerings, I have no regard for them" (Amos 5:21-22).

Haughty eyes and a proud heart—the unplowed field of the wicked—produce sin [Haughty eyes and a proud heart, the lamp of the wicked, are sin!] (21:4).

The previous NIV Bible (1984) translated "the unplowed field of the wicked" as "the lamp of the wicked." The old NIV understood that "haughty eyes and a proud heart" is "the lamp of the wicked."

One of the physical manifestations of a proud heart is "haughty eyes" (4a). Some people have "haughty eyes" when they are looking for a mate. Persons with haughty eyes are satisfied with few prospective mates. They see the other person through the lens of self-grandiosity. They only notice people who are in a higher position than they are, and they like to associate with them. They envy them and fantasize that they will one day be like them. And they live in the fantasy that those who are lesser than them will envy them. Solomon declares that living this way is a sin in itself. A life of pride is an antithesis of a life according to the gospel, and it is a devilish life. The devil has been a person of pride from the beginning.

There are many Christians who still live with narcissistic personality disorder. It's unfortunate and dangerous that they don't recognize their own issues and think they are doing well in their lives of faith.[310] Living a self-centered life is a sin in itself before God. Like the lamp of the wicked, it will eventually go out and lead to destruction. We must recognize it and repent and renew ourselves.

The plans of the diligent lead to profit as surely as haste leads to poverty (21:5).

---

[310] One of the core problems of the Laodicean church was pride: "You say, 'I am rich; I have acquired wealth and do not need a thing.' But you do not realize that you are wretched, pitiful, poor, blind and naked'" (Rev. 3:17).

The "diligent" and the "hasty" are contrasted.[311] "Profit" and "poverty" are contrasted. The opposite of diligence is laziness, so we can interpret the hasty in the text as ones who have an issue of laziness.

A synonym for "haste" is "impulsivity." The opposite of the impulsive is the cautious, so the diligent can be understood as the cautious persons. Plans and management of the prudent are less likely to fail. Those who discern the left and right, compare the future with the present, and plan and act are very likely to gain profit.

But the hasty people are more likely to get things wrong because of their impulsivity. Not thinking and planning carefully is laziness. As a result of sloth, they will lose even what they have and become poor (5b).

A fortune made by a lying tongue is a fleeting vapor and a deadly snare (21:6).

Making a wealth by deception is fraud. Solomon compares this to a "fleeting vapor" (6b). Life itself is like a mist that is driven by the wind (see Jam. 4:14b). A wealth accumulated by fraud even more like a mist that lasts only a moment and then vanishes.

Those who take riches by unrighteous means are as foolish as ones who try to grasp at sand. They dig their own graves (6a). They commit a suicide financially and spiritually. They will soon be exposed for their deceitfulness, and they will be ashamed by others. Socially, they will not escape the judgment of the law. Even

---

[311] A diligent person is an industrious person. Erikson, a developmental psychologist, saw the developmental task of childhood as industry. The opposite, he understood, was inferiority. He believed that establishing a habit of hard work in childhood influences the next stage of development, adolescence, which is identity development. When students are diligent and hardworking, they get good grades and recognition, which give them a sense of confidence and competence. This experience leads to a positive attitude toward the future, a positive self-image, and a clearer sense of what they want to do with their lives. The plans of a child with a developed industry are not vain dreams or fantasies, but more concrete and realistically achievable.

when they are well fed and well off in this world with their unrighteous wealth, they cannot escape the deadly snare, i.e., the terrible judgment of God.

The violence of the wicked will drag them away,[312] for they refuse to do what is right. The way of the guilty is devious, but the conduct of the innocent is upright (21:7-8).

"The violence of the wicked" is contrasted with "the conduct of the innocent." The behavior of the wicked brings defeat and destruction to themselves (7a). Their violence destroys themselves. Their paths are crooked and pathological (8a). They not only actively do evil, but also passively hate to do what is right (7b).

Better to live on a corner of the roof than share a house with a quarrelsome wife (21:9).

This proverb most likely comes from Solomon's own issues. It can be seen as a counsel to his sons based on his own troubled marriage. Similar proverbs appear four times in Proverbs.[313]
Verse 19 of the same chapter is paraphrased as the proverb, "Better to live in a desert than with a quarrelsome and nagging wife." Living on a corner under the same roof is a representation of closer physical distance than living in the wilderness.
It's normal to have some conflicts in a marriage. When two

---

[312] Bridges understood "the violence of the wicked" to mean "the theft of the wicked." Bridges, *Proverbs*, 370. If so, verse 7 can be interpreted in conjunction with verse 6. Fraudulent behavior and theft of wealth can be seen in the same context. "A deadly snare" and "drag them away" can be understood interchangeably. In conjunction with verse 5, those who are impatient to gather wealth are not gathering it in a diligent manner. Those who gather wealth through fraud and steal to fill their storehouses will only end up in poverty.

[313] Koptak gives each of these texts: 19:13, 21:9, 25:24, 27:15. The texts of 21:9 and 25:24 are identical. Koptak, *Proverbs*, 501.

different persons come together, conflict is inevitable. But the problem lies in their inability to face or resolve the conflict that comes with their marital relationship. This proverb sounds like an exhortation to avoid conflict. However, this proverb needs to be interpreted in light of 17:1, which states that it is better to live in harmony and happiness while eating a piece of dry bread than to live a house full of feasting but in contention and unhappiness.

Before marriage, it is difficult to discern whether a spouse-to-be is a quarrelsome person or not. Nevertheless, it is wise to find out as much as possible about whether he or she is easily angry, irritable, suspicious, vindictive, or unforgiving. It is very difficult to maintain a healthy marriage with a partner who has severe personality disorders. With such a partner, even a relatively healthy spouse is likely to become a person with personality disorders.

The wicked crave evil; their neighbors get no mercy from them (21:10).

In context, evil refers to the calamity, failure, ruin, or death of neighbors. The wicked take pleasure in seeing their neighbors fail or die (10a). It is characteristic of the wicked to want bad things to happen to others, or to rejoice when bad things happen to them. For example, evil persons see their neighbor's house burning down and rejoice in its destruction.[314] Another example is a mother-in-law who is psychologically attached to her married son and secretly rejoices that her daughter-in-law is not very happy in her relationship with her husband because she feels jealous of her daughter-in-law.

It is important to recognize that our sinful heart has a psychology

---

[314] The iniquity of Edom, which God revealed through the prophet Amos, was that they rejoiced in the destruction of their brother nation Judah, and persecuted people of Judah: "For three sins of Edom, even for four, I will not relent. Because he pursued his brother with a sword and slaughtered the women of the land, because his anger raged continually and his fury flamed unchecked" (Amos 1:11).

of evil that delights in the suffering of others. It is the heart of sinful human beings that makes it difficult to share in the joy of our neighbors and difficult to grieve and suffer with them in their sorrow and pain. Recognizing and repenting of this self-centered and antisocial psychology deep within our hearts is the path to transformation and maturity. Those who deny or repress their sinfulness are unaware of their unconscious aggression and therefore unaware of their problems, and therefore unaware of the need for repentance.

When a mocker is punished, the simple gain wisdom; by paying attention to the wise they get knowledge (20:11).[315]

Even the most self-centered person still has a potential to gain wisdom when punished. Suffering and punishment open up the possibility of realizing one's pride and humbling oneself. It is often the case that those who used to live a life of pride, laughing at others, suddenly become bankrupt or suffer a great crisis, which cause them to repent and live a humble life. This was the case with King Nebuchadnezzar.

Fools have an opportunity to become wise. That opportunity may come when they witness someone who lives a life of arrogance being punished by God. They can be warned indirectly and gain wisdom. For example, an alcoholic who is shocked to learn that a close friend has died after hitting a median while driving drunk may become sober and free from alcoholism as a result of the shock.

The Righteous One takes note of the house of the wicked and brings the wicked to ruin (21:12).

---

[315] Bridges noted that a proverb with nearly identical wording to this proverb is found in 19:25. Bridges, *Proverbs*, 373.

Solomon uses two verbs to describe what God does. God "takes note" and "brings down." The act of watching over and the act of bringing to ruin are connected in that God watches over and then brings to ruin.

God observed the wickedness of the world in Noah's day: "The LORD saw how great the wickedness of the human race had become on the earth, and that every inclination of the thoughts of the human heart was only evil all the time. The LORD regretted that he had made human beings on the earth, and his heart was deeply troubled" (Gen. 6:5-6). Allowing many years to pass since his first decision to judge with the flood, God was patient and finally wiped all of his creation off the face of the earth. God also took note of the wickedness of the people of Sodom and Gomorrah, sent angels to see what was really going on, and finally rained down burning sulfur from heaven to destroy all but Lot's family (see Gen. 19:23-25).

In this way, God watches over and judges wicked groups or nations, but also wicked individuals. God observed the religious corruption and moral wickedness of Ahab and Jezebel and judged them for taking Naboth's righteous blood in order to take his vineyard in greed by force.

For a time, it may seem that the wicked prosper and things are going according to their schemes. But it is an immutable biblical truth that the end of the wicked is destruction and judgment. Believing that God is living, watching, and intervening in history, Christians do not participate in the schemes of the wicked. The wicked must perish. God's judgment is only suspended.

Whoever shuts their ears to the cry of the poor will also cry out and not be answered (21:13).

There are always poor people in the world. In the world broken by sin, the rich and the poor live together. There are those who are relatively poor and those who are absolutely poor.

It is a sin not to empathize the poor who live in sorrow, pain, crying, frustration, shame, and helplessness. From the point of view of ecclesiology, churches, society, and the state must be organic to each other. Christians and churches are not immune from their responsibility to care for the poor. It is God's will that we empathize with the suffering of the poor, share in their pain, and provide concrete help.[316]

Those who close their eyes or stop their ears when the poor ask for help are wicked. To ignore the requests of the poor in favor of one's own life is to ignore the request of God, who created the poor. It is also not good to remain ignorant of the presence of the poor.

There are some people who pose as beggars and manipulate others' hearts to do good. There are also antisocial people who have their own homes and pose as beggars, ask homeless children to beg and extort money. Therefore, we need to have a wisdom to discern when we give. If they use the money to buy alcohol or do evil things with it, we will be encouraging them to sin more. However, since we do not have accurate information to discern properly in many cases, it is right to respond to the cry of the poor as soon as we have the opportunity and as much as our means permit. The consequences of deceiving or exploiting will be the portion of those who do so to be reckoned with before the judgment seat of God.

For a variety of reasons, even the wealthiest of people can find themselves in the ranks of the poor. It's not uncommon for them to become bankrupt overnight and be evicted from their homes and for their families to be scattered. It's a fact of life that the misfortune of others will one day become your misfortune. Wisdom is being able to think about the possibility that life's crises, not just economic poverty, can come to you, not just to others. If there are many such wise people, we will have a society where the poor can receive help. In such a society, there will be some people who will help and comfort them when they are in trouble themselves.

---

[316] God commanded that the poor be relieved and cared for by those who have. Orphans and widows, who were vulnerable to poverty, were specified.

A gift given in secret soothes anger, and a bribe concealed in the cloak pacifies great wrath (21:14).

"A gift given in secret" and "a bribe concealed in the cloak" are used synonymously. "A gift given in secret" is not difficult to understand. Jesus himself said to be "in secret" in our giving (see Matt. 6:4).

However, in this proverb, the recipient of a secret gift and a bribe concealed in the cloak is an angry person, one who feels great wrath. This proverb, then, can be interpreted as a statement of life wisdom that a secret gift or bribe can be one way to deal with a very angry person. "A bribe concealed in the cloak" can be understood as describing the possibility that angry feelings can be tempered by an unexpected twist when a gift or bribe is given without others noticing and without the recipient noticing. However, this method cannot be applied to all angry people, because the attitude of using money or gifts to resolve a broken heart may end up fueling the fierce anger.

When justice is done, it brings joy to the righteous but terror to evildoers (21:15).

The place where justice is administered is in a court of law. If the judge's ruling is right, the plaintiff's pain and wounds are relieved or healed. They experience relief and healing. The defendant, on the other hand, is called out for their evil deeds and held accountable for the consequences of their sin. They experience shame and fear.

The day Jesus returns is the day justice is executed. Those who belong to him will rejoice when the Righteous Judge judges. They will rejoice because Jesus will wipe away the tears from their eyes. On the other hand, those who do not belong to Jesus will tremble and be panicky (15b).[317]

---

[317] We see this in the fearful reaction of the people at the opening of the sixth seal in

> Whoever strays from the path of prudence comes to rest in the company of the dead (21:16).

People may wander off temporarily. Adolescents, especially those going through puberty, can be rebellious and disobedient to their parents. However, if the period is prolonged, they will develop antisocial personality disorder, which will cause difficulties in interpersonal relationships. The deviation from the right path can be fatal.

There are some people who temporarily wander from their relationships with God and, like the prodigal son, leave their Father's house and live a life of profligacy. But if they continue to live such a life, they may end up on a path that leads to eternal destruction. Then they will be among the multitudes of the perishing and will suffer eternal torment. It is a fearful thing.

> Whoever loves pleasure will become poor; whoever loves wine and olive oil [wine and oil] will never be rich (21:17).

Pleasure and joy are positive. However, when we pursue pleasure and joy as a goal in life, we live a hedonistic life. As hedonists, humans are no different from animals.

Solomon compares pleasure to "wine and oil."[318] The end of

John's vision: "Then the kings of the earth, the princes, the generals, the rich, the mighty, and everyone else, both slave and free, hid in caves and among the rocks of the mountains. They called to the mountains and rocks, 'Fall on us and hide us from the face of him who sits on the throne and from the wrath of the Lamb! For the great day of their wrath has come, and who can withstand it?'" (Rev. 6:15-17).

[318] Isaiah characterized pleasure-seekers when he said, "Woe to those who rise early in the morning to run after their drinks, who stay up late at night till they are inflamed with wine. They have harps and lyres at their banquets, pipes and timbrels and wine, but they have no regard of the deeds of the LORD, no respect for the work of his hands" (Isa. 5:11-12).

those who seek wine and oil is poverty and destruction.[319] Furthermore, the spiritual end of hedonists is eternal death.[320]

The wicked become a ransom for the righteous, and the unfaithful for the upright (21:18).

Soteriologically speaking, the positions of the wicked and the righteous in the text would have to be reversed. The righteous can provide the ransom for the wicked. The righteous God himself paid the ransom for sinners and redeemed them. The wicked or evil cannot be ransom for the righteous and upright.

So what does this proverb mean? We can interpret it to mean that while the wicked and evil may seem to flourish at first, the righteous and upright will eventually flourish and be saved. In place of the righteous and upright who are now suffering, the wicked and evil will suffer forever (18b).

Better to live in a desert than with a quarrelsome and nagging [ill-tempered] wife (21:19).

This is a parallel proverb to verse 9. The intensity of the suffering is expressed more strongly than in verse 9. Living in a desert would be a painful life of being cut off from all relationships. "Living on a corner of the roof" would be less painful because it involves living among people. In any case, Solomon says that it is

---

[319] This includes becoming financially impoverished. Most addictions have a hedonic component and involve financial loss.

[320] Peter described these hedonists well: "But these people blaspheme in matters they do not understand. They are like unreasoning animals, creatures of instinct, born only to be caught and destroyed, and like animals they too will perish. They will be paid back with harm for the harm they have done. Their idea of pleasure is to carouse in broad daylight. They are blots and blemishes, reveling in their pleasures while they feast with you. With eyes full of adultery, they never stop sinning; they seduce the unstable; they are experts in greed—and accursed brood!" (2 Pet. 2:12-14).

very painful to live with a spouse who is often quarrelsome and nagging.

Solomon's caution for his sons is more focused on the symptom rather than the core problem of having multiple wives. "A quarrelsome and nagging wife" is a symptom, not the core problem.

Counseling Application: There are families with high levels of marital conflicts. Some couples fight to the point of rage, treating each other like enemies. As a result, the home often turns into a battlefield. And the children who grow up in that battlefield are likely to suffer from post-traumatic stress disorder. Parents who fight without considering their influences on their children are foolish. The psychological dynamics of their children are similar to those of "veterans" who have survived the war.

This proverb should not be misused as a text that allows or encourages separation or divorce. Rather, it should be interpreted as a proverb that empathizes with how difficult it can be to live with an arguing, angry spouse.

The wise store up choice food and olive oil [oil], but fools gulp theirs down [a foolish man devours all he has] (21:20).

The wise prepare for the future by stockpiling food and oil. The foolish, on the other hand, use up their resources (20b). They waste without thinking about the future.

The prodigal son was foolish in that he spent his father's inheritance. He failed to keep what he should have kept. He was the one who devoured the "choice food and olive oil" for his own selfish desires.

Adam and Eve were prodigals. God's presence was in the Garden of Eden, and there were choice food and and oil, but they lost them all by sinning. They caused the loss of the precious treasure and oil, not only for themselves, but for all of humanity. As a result, all humans, without exception, became prodigals. Prodigal children cannot regain their lost status and the precious treasure and oil unless they return to their Father's house.

"House" symbolizes the ego or self. The ego of the wise functions well to guard "precious things" well. It knows how to preserve and value what is valuable. But the ego of the foolish is like that of a pig that does not recognize the value of a pearl and tramples it underfoot.

Whoever pursues righteousness and love finds life, prosperity and honor (21:21).

Righteousness and love are the attributes of God. Those who pursue righteousness and love are those who seek to restore the image of God in their lives. The verb "pursue" in the proverb is active. From the gospel perspective, Christians are passively "clothed" with the righteousness and love of Christ. At the same time, they are to be seekers after God's righteousness and his kingdom.

The fruit of those who pursue righteousness and love is life and eternal life, prosperity and honor.[321] They are sowers for the Holy Spirit and they are promised to reap eternal life from the Holy Spirit (Gal. 6:8b).

But those who sow to please their flesh will reap destruction and eternal judgment. They are deceived themselves. God cannot be mocked (Gal. 6:7).

One who is wise can go up against the city of the mighty and pull down the stronghold in which they trust (21:22).[322]

---

[321] Koptak notes that life, prosperity, and honor are the three typical blessings promised by Proverbs (see 3:16; 22:4). Koptak, *Proverbs*, 504.

[322] This proverb applies to spiritual battles as well. The power of the gospel of God is wisdom to pull down strongholds and rescue those who are in bondage to the devil. Bridges pointed to 2 Cor. 10:4-5 as a related passage: "The weapons we fight with are not the weapons of the world. On the contrary, they have divine power to demolish strongholds. We demolish arguments and every pretension that sets itself up against the knowledge of God, and we take captive every thought to make it obedient to

This proverb uses the metaphor of battle. To attack a castle guarded by warriors, a strategy is needed. It is foolish to attack blindly. A tactical wisdom is to recognize the weaknesses of the enemy and of their castle, and to focus military power on those weak spots.

Counseling Application: Although it is not the original meaning of this proverb, the stronghold can be understood as defense mechanisms. Insightful counselors can go up against the strong wall of a client and pull down the defense mechanism on which the client depends. Defense mechanisms are like walls that the client has long relied on and trusted to survive in this world. The problem is that they become stumbling blocks in interpersonal relationships. Those who frequently use defense mechanisms, even in unnecessary situations, have difficulties in intimacy in close relationships. In counseling, this makes it difficult for the client to have a therapeutic alliance with the counselor. When the counselor strategically explores and targets his or her client to get to the in-depth issues, the client with strong and rigid defense mechanisms is very likely to resist and use defense mechanisms consciously or unconsciously. However, wise counselors will identify and understand what the client's unconscious defenses are. They empathize with the client's vulnerability, which is why the client uses the defense mechanism. They make sure the client that they are trying to help, not attack the client. They provide a safe space to make the client feel less anxious. They also help the client facilitate self-awareness by explaining the function and meaning of the defense mechanisms. As this process goes well, the client's defenses are gradually released and used less. The client is then able to tell his or her inner story, one by one, that has been suppressed many years. In this way, wise counselors are able to break down the barriers that the client has relied on.

Those who guard their mouths and their tongues keep themselves from calamity (21:23). See also 13:3.

Christ." Bridges, *Proverbs*, 386.

The power of the tongue is very great. It has both positive and destructive powers. It is difficult to keep the tongue balanced: "We all stumble in many ways. Anyone who is never at fault in what they say is perfect, able to keep their whole body in check (James 3:2). Impulsive speech has the potential to be self-destructive as well as destructive to others. James warns that "those who consider themselves religious and yet do not keep a tight rein on their tongues deceive themselves, and their religion is worthless" (James 1:26). Those who aspire to a godly life should recognize the potential danger of their tongue: "No human being can tame the tongue. It is a restless evil, full of deadly poison" (James 3:8).

The proud and arrogant person—"Mocker" is his name— behaves with insolent fury [overweening pride] (21:24). See 21:4.

The core problem with "Mocker" is pride and arrogance. Arrogance is the behavioral fruit of pride. Pride is an attitude and character of the heart. The proud are disrespectful in interpersonal relationships. They consciously or unconsciously act to exalt themselves and disregard others. If we connect this to the preceding proverb in verse 23, the proud speak hastily and impulsively. They don't consider or empathize with others, so they say hurtful things and feel no remorse. Eventually they lead to their own destruction.

If we were to give a name to the proud, it would be "Mocker." The name represents the person. Mockers are those whose pride is ingrained in their personalities. Such people are not afraid of even the name of God. They mock Christians who believe in God. Their self-grandiosity reaches the heavens.[323]

---

[323] Bridges connected this proverb with Psalms 12:3-4: "May the LORD silence all flattering lips and every boastful tongue—those who say, 'By our tongues we will prevail; our own lips will defend us—who is lord over us?'" Bridges, *Proverbs*, 387. He noted Pharaoh of Egypt as an illustration of the mockers: "Pharaoh said, 'Who is the LORD, that I should obey him and let Israel go? I do not know the LORD and I will not let Israel go'" (Ex. 5:2). Bridges, *Proverbs*, 387.

The proud "behave" (24b). Their pride is expressed in their behaviors. They show their pride in their haughty eyes. They put themselves up. They speak pompously. They walk with their neck stretched out.

The craving of a sluggard will be the death of him, because his hands refuse to work (21:25). See also 6:11; 13:4; 20:4; 24:34.

Laziness is a sin that leads to death. It is a self-destructive and self-defeating behavior and way of life (25a). As James well points out that "After desire has conceived, it gives birth to sin; and sin, when it is full-grown, gives birth to death" (James 1:15), the craving of the lazy leads to death. The cravings of the lazy are not realistic but illusory. Especially spiritual laziness breeds eternal death and judgment.

Sluggards hardly use the two hands God gave them (25b). They are passive and dependent in life. They do not live a responsible life as adults. It is normal for children to be lazy. It is normal for babies, especially, to eat and sleep. But adults should be diligent and industrious. They should labor and strive hard for themselves, for others, and for God.

In developmental psychologist Erik Erikson's theory, childhood is a time of fulfillment of the psychological task of "industry." Students who study hard are psychologically healthy. If some children are not interested in studying or don't even do their homework, laziness becomes their habit and finally a part of their character. There are some adolescents who spend most of their time playing computer games and don't study. They usually stay up late and barely attend school. They are likely to sleep on their stomach for most of the class hours.

Lazy children are vulnerable to depression. Conversely, depression leads them to sloth. They can't even take care of themselves. In severe cases, depression can lead them to suicide.

All day long he craves for more, but the righteous give without sparing (21:26).

The NIV Bible translates verses 25 and 26 by linking them: the sluggard craves for more all day long. But the righteous are not only diligent and industrious but also generous and giving (26b). They are willing to spend money where it should be spent.

But the lazy have nothing to give, for they have not labored with their own hands. Furthermore, they have no concern for others.

Counseling Application: There are some people who are pathologically diligent. A typical example is people with obsessive-compulsive personality disorder. One of the symptoms of OCPD is workaholism. Workaholics are pathologically diligent and cannot rest, because resting makes them anxious. They don't experience intimacy in their relationships. Another symptom of OCPD is being very frugal with money. They're too frugal because they're anxious about the future. This makes it difficult for them to live the life of the righteous that this proverb talks about. Living a life of generosity cures them from OCPD. Tithing with joy to God can cure them from OCPD, because they are not attached to material things and anxiety about the future.

The sacrifice of the wicked is detestable—how much more so when brought with evil intent! (21:27). See also 15:8.

The sacrifice of the wicked is an abomination to God.[324] God said through Isaiah that the sacrifices of the Israelites, who worshiped idols and yet offered sacrifices to God, were detestable (see Isa. 1:13-14). He told them that he would not listen to them when they prayed: "When you spread out your hands in prayer, I hide my eyes from you; even you offer many prayers, I am not listening" (Isa. 1:15).

---

[324] The wicked have no faith in God. Bridges connected this proverb to Heb. 11:6: "And without faith it is impossible to please God, because anyone who comes to him must believe that he exists and that he rewards whose who earnestly seek him." Bridges, *Proverbs*, 390.

A worship that honors man is abhorrent to God. What kinds of worship are abhorrent to God in the modern church today? One of them is humanistic worship. It is not worship that exalts God in reverence, but worship that exalts man and entertains man. Worship that exalts the preacher or entertains the worshipers is an abomination to God. Worship services labeled as "doctoral degree conferral thanks service," "publication thanks service," "thanks service for elected denominational leaders" should be reconsidered because they are likely to be man-centered services.

A false witness will perish but a careful listener will testify successfully [whoever listens to him will be destroyed forever] (21:28). See also 12:19.

False witnesses are doomed. Those who believed and acted on their witnesses are also destroyed (28b). Falsehood must be defeated, because God is alive. Perjury will one day be exposed. There comes a day when justice is restored. False witnesses will be judged on the day justice is established. Truth will always prevail.

The word of those who have heard with their own two ears is powerful. The testimony of those who have seen with their own eyes cannot be challenged by false witnesses.[325] Falsehood cannot overcome truth.

The wicked put up a bold front, but the upright give thought to their ways (21:29).

The faces of the wicked are hardened. You pierce them with a needle and then the needle would break. This is because the wicked have hearts of stone. Their hearts of stone are only revealed

---

[325] Peter and John boldly testified to the gospel before the council because they had been eyewitnesses to Jesus' resurrection and experienced the filling of the Holy Spirit at Pentecost: "As for us, we cannot help speaking about what we have seen and heard" (Acts 4:20).

by their hard faces.

In this proverb, the wicked are those who are not honest. They even don't blink their eyes when they lie.[326] They lie with a bold face and a voice that does not tremble. They lie on a whim, without rethinking about their lives or the consequences of their lies. They give false testimony with a bold face, even though they have taken an oath to tell the truth.[327]

Those who appear courageous are not necessarily good. The devil gives people boldness and courage when they sin. This is why a fearful person can be brave in sinning. This is because his or her anxiety and fear system is not activated.

The wicked can have the same faces as those of angels. The devil masquerades as an angel of light. Similarly, psychopathic evil persons may appear to be good persons, contrary to what you might expect. They may consciously or unconsciously wear a mask of "persona." These people's faces are ever-changing. Depending on their mood and who they're talking to, their faces can be angelic one minute and devilish the next.

There is no wisdom, no insight, no plan that can succeed against the LORD (21:30).

It's a common sense proverb. No man can prevail against God. No amount of human wisdom, cleverness, or cunning can defeat the mind of God.

The Way of the Cross is the wisdom of God. This wisdom was kept secret for a long time. It was foolishness to the Greeks and shame to the Jews, but through the Cross God revealed the marvelous wisdom and understanding of redeeming sinners. "None

---

[326] Bridges connected the face of the wicked with that of a deceitful prostitute: "She took hold of him and kissed him and with a brazen face she said" (Prov. 7:13). Bridges, *Proverbs*, 392.

[327] Fox makes a good point that verse 29 can be interpreted in conjunction with verse 28. The wicked in this verse are false witnesses. They don't change their facial expressions to hide their false testimonies. Fox, *Proverbs 10-31*, 692.

of the rulers of this age understood" this wisdom (1 Cor. 2:8).[328] By comparison, "The foolishness of God is wiser than human wisdom, and the weakness of God is stronger than human strength" (1 Cor. 1:25). God solved the problem of human sin that no human power or method could solve. God the Son destroyed the power of death by the power of his resurrection and triumphed over the power of the devil and his deception.

God is not deceived by man. The Creator cannot be mocked by the creature. God was not defeated by the schemes of the devil, the fallen archangel. The devil hindered the coming of the Savior in redemptive history, but he could not defeat God's plan.

All wisdom that is made against God is foolishness. It is all foolishness in the sight of God. All the philosophies, sciences, and knowledge of the world are "drops in the ocean" compared to God's wisdom and understanding.

The folly of the worldly wise is that they not only do not glorify but do not acknowledge the God who gave them wisdom. It is foolish and evil to deny that there is God or to not even care about his existence.[329] It is disrespectful.

The horse is made ready for the day of battle, but victory rests with the LORD (21:31).

There's a Korean four character phrase (有備無患) which means "An ounce of prevention is worth a pound of cure." If you're prepared, you won't be troubled. This is realistic and biblical. It is laziness to not do our part to prepare and bear our share of the burden only thinking that victory rests with the LORD. God's sovereignty and human freedom and responsibility must be in healthy tension. Overemphasizing either is not a biblical idea.

---

[328] Bridges connected Psalms 33:10-11 with this proverb: "The LORD foils the plans of the nations; he thwarts the purposes of the peoples. But the plans of the LORD stand firm forever, the purposes of his heart through all generations." Bridges, *Proverbs*, 393.

[329] David put this as follows: "The fool says in his heart, 'There is no god.' They are corrupt, their deeds are vile; there is no one who does good" (Ps. 14:1).

When we connect this proverb to Solomon's personal life history, a new interpretation is possible. He was the first king to disobey the law against training horses and horsemen for war.[330] He trained horsemen for war.[331] He disobeyed the law in which God explicitly forbade.

Solomon knew in his heart that victory in war depended on God, but he kept horsemen and cavalry. Solomon's act of disobedience set the stage for the disobedience of the subsequent kingdoms of Israel and Judah. He took the ambivalent position of serving God and serving the world. He acted with two hearts.

---

[330] Bridges also pointed out this problem with Solomon in his commentary: "The king, moreover, must not acquire great numbers of horses for himself or make the people return to Egypt to get more of them, for the LORD has told you, 'Your are not to go back that way again'" (Deut. 17:16). Bridges, *Proverbs*, 394. Koptak cites Isaiah 31:1 as a relevant text: "Woe to those who go down to Egypt for help, who rely on horses, who trust in the multitude of their chariots and in the great strength of their horsemen, but do not look to the Holy One of Israel, or seek help from the LORD." Koptak, *Proverbs*, 694.

[331] Koptak notes that the preceding references to wisdom, insight and plan in verse 30 can be interpreted as having a military connotation when read in conjunction with verse 31. Koptak, *Proverbs*, 507.

Chapter 22 Do Not Walk with One Easily Angered

A good name is more desirable than great riches; to be esteemed is better than silver or gold (22:1).

Gold or silver is one of the most valuable things in the world. The same goes for wealth. Money has a commodity value. The more of it you have, the more valuable it is. But it's not as valuable as honor, which is an invisible, intangible value.

There is value in being well-liked and respected in the world.[332] That's why it's said that "tigers die and leave behind their skins, but people die and leave behind their names." A name reflects a person's life and character. If some persons pursue riches while being dishonored, they will be remembered with a stigma.

Furthermore, if some people are recognized and respected in the world, but do not have eternal life, they are foolish and pitiful. Those who are not saved, no matter how well they are recognized in the world, are very unfortunate. Jesus' words are true: "What good is it for someone to gain the whole world, yet forfeit their soul?" (Mark 8:36).

Choices are important. Especially choosing eternal life cannot be repeated. We only get one chance while we're alive. Those who make the wrong choice will gnash their teeth and regret it forever. Those who follow the values of this world will surely regret it.

Rich and poor have this in common: The LORD is the Maker of them all (22:2).

This proverb can be connected to Jesus' words, "The poor you will always have with you, but you will not always have me"

---

[332] Bridges connected the text to one of Paul's criteria for an overseer, that is "a good reputation" with outsiders (1 Tim. 3:7). Bridges, *Proverbs*, 396.

(Matt. 26:11). Rich and poor, male and female, educated and uneducated, those with status and those without, are equal in that they are all God's creations. They have the same intrinsic worthiness in that they are all made in the image of God. Furthermore, God is the one who makes people poor or rich.[333]

Therefore, in our relationships with the weak, the poor, or the marginalized, we should fear God, because they are connected to God. When we help the poor, God remembers and repays our helping hand. Conversely, if we ignore or show no compassion for them, God remembers and repays our evil deeds.

The prudent see danger and take refuge, but the simple keep going and pay the penalty (22:3).[334]

The prudent have an adequately developed ability to detect danger. The simple, on the other hand, have little ability to detect danger signals. Their alarm systems don't work well. So they don't realize that they are in danger, so they go on and get harmed (3b).

There are the opposite fools with danger. For them, the devices that detect danger work too sensitively. As a result, they unnecessarily feel anxious or fearful and suffer from anxiety disorders.

When psychologically immature people are faced with anxious situations, they often use avoidance as a defense mechanism. Mature people, however, have the ability to recognize anxiety, face it, and work through it. They know how, when, what to avoid situations that they have to avoid. They recognize their limitations and avoid them.

Humility is the fear of the LORD; its wages are riches and honor

---

[333] Bridges cited 1 Sam. 2:7 as a related text to this proverb: "The LORD sends poverty and wealth; he humbles and he exalts." Bridges, *Proverbs*, 398.

[334] Koptak notes that "a prudent man" is singular, but "the simple" are plural, suggesting that this proverb implies that the majority is not always right. Koptak, *Proverbs*, 517.

and life (22:4).

In this proverb, Solomon emphasizes that two key values in the life of believers are humility and the fear of God. The humility in this passage is not humility in the ordinary sense, but the humility that comes from the fear of God. It is a way of life. In that sense, humility and the fear of the Lord are inseparable.

Those who live humble lives in the fear of the LORD reap good fruit in this world and in the eternal world. And the fruit is "riches and honor and life."[335]

We do not fear God to gain riches, honor, or life. These are graces that are given as a result. If one fears God in the hope of reward, he or she would be a rudimentary believer.

In the paths of the wicked are snares and pitfalls [thorns and snares], but those who would preserve their life [he who guards his soul] stay far from them (22:5).

This proverb can be understood as a parallel to verse 3. "Snares and pitfalls" are the "danger" described in verse 3. The prudent can "see" the thorns and snares in front of them. Therefore, they avoid them (5b). But the foolish and wicked, because of their greed, do not see the thorns and snares that are waiting for them. As a result, they are pierced by thorns and ensnared by snares.

Those who keep their souls are vigilant and alert through the Word of God. They do not live a life of laxity or sloth. They live a life of alertness, with an attitude that they never know when or how the devil's schemes will strike. So they are not deceived or ensnared by sin.

Start children off on [Train a child in] the way they should go,

---

[335] The same three blessings are mentioned in 21:21: life, prosperity, and honor. In this proverb, the order is reversed: riches (prosperity) and honor and life.

and even when they are old they will not turn from it (22:6).

The importance of a good nurturing environment during developmental stages cannot be overemphasized. It can't be perfect, and it doesn't need to be. A "good enough" environment is enough for a child to develop and grow as a whole person.

In psychological terms, "the way they should go" means developing the "superego."[336] It's about teaching what to do and what not to do. It is important and effective to teach children from an early age to live a moral and conscientious life.

It's been said that "What is learned in the cradle is carried to the tomb." From the perspective of post-Freudian theories such as object relations theory and ego psychology, this statement makes a lot of sense. These theories understand that the foundations of psychological structures are formed between the ages of three and five, when the superego begins to form. Therefore, children need to be disciplined when the superego begins to form. It is important to use discipline children appropriately and sensitively during this period and teach them to distinguish between right and wrong behavior. As the saying goes, "A thief who steals a needle becomes a thief who steals an ox," if parents do not correct their children when they misbehave, they are likely to grow up to become antisocial.

We reap what we sow. If we neglect our children during their formative years, they will grow up to be persons with severe personality disorders that will cause or contribute to difficulties in relationships.

The rich rule over the poor, and the borrower is slave to the lender (22:7).

Money wields power, so those who are in debt are taken away

---

[336] Bridges insightfully commented that there are two paths a child is given, one that the child "would go" and the other that the child "should go. The would-go path is the path of destruction and the should-go path is the path of eternal life, he added. Bridges, *Proverbs*, 402.

their power and freedom. If you go into debt and can't pay it back, everything you have is taken away.

This proverb is a descriptive proverb of reality in the world. It is real that the rich rule over the poor (7a). When you are in debt, you are psychologically bound to the person who lent you the money (7b). In the old days, people were actually sold as slaves when they were not able to pay their debts.

It's wise to face this harsh reality and stay out of debt whenever possible. Some people have repetitive symptoms of impulsive spending without considering their financial situation. This is one of the symptoms of borderline personality disorder.

Moneylenders who practice usury are wicked. On the other hand, those who borrow money at usury are foolish, single-minded and psychologically immature. They are self-defeating themselves.

Whoever sows injustice reaps calamity [He who sows wickedness reaps trouble], and the rod they wield in fury [the rod of his fury] will be broken (22:8).

It is an immutable truth that we reap what we sow. Therefore, if whoever sows evil will reap trouble and calamity (8a).

A problem with this proverb is that the meaning of the second half of the proverb is not easy to interpret. If the second half of the verse is interpreted in conjunction with the first half, then the "sower of evil" is the "wielder of the rod of wrath," who, with God's permission, wields the rod of wrath against an individual, community, or nation.

The wielder of the rod of wrath is an instrument of God, albeit a wicked one. God uses even the wicked "at the right time" and "for the right purpose." The problem is that the wicked fail to recognize this fact and act arrogantly. Usually, wicked people or wicked nations act arrogantly, thinking that they own the rod, that is, power and military might. And so when they are used, the rod they hold is broken and they find themselves in disaster. And they themselves are destroyed by a more severe blow from one more wicked than themselves.

363

The generous will themselves be blessed, for they share their food with the poor (22:9).

The generous empathize with the poor. They are generous not because they are wealthy but because they have empathy for the poor.[337] On the other hand, those with prideful eyes are incapable of empathizing with the poor. They ignore them. Many wealthy people are self-centered. They don't realize that others are hungry as long as they are full.

Nabal was a wealthy man, but he was a "fool" (see 1 Sam. 25:25), as his name implies. In the assessment of his servants, he was "such a wicked man that no one could speak to him" (1 Sam. 25:17). He responded rudely to the request of David's men to share food on a good day for shearing sheep. His narcissism is evident in his word "my bread," "my water," and "the meat I have slaughtered for my shearers" (see 1 Sam. 25:11). He had no compassion for David and his men in their time of need. In the end, he was cursed, his body turned to stone, and he died.

Boaz, on the other hand, was a generous man. He didn't look down on Ruth, the Moabite woman, even though she was a poor gleaner and a Gentile. Rather he let her drink from the water jar the men have filled whenever she was thirsty (Ruth 2:9). He showed consideration for her by commanding the boys, "Let her gather among the sheaves and don't reprimand her. Even pull out some stalks for her from the bundles and leave them for her to pick up, and don't rebuke her" (Ruth 2:15-16). He was generous and compassionate enough to send her back with a promise of keeping a kinsman-redeemer law, giving her six measures of barley and

---

[337] Believers of the Macedonian churches were "the generous." Paul commended them for "In the midst of a very severe trial, their overflowing joy and their extreme poverty welled up in rich generosity" (2 Cor. 8:2). They gave beyond their means because they sympathized with the members of the Jerusalem church who were suffering from famine and poverty, while they themselves were also in poverty. They were blessed to be remembered in Christian history as an exemplary church for giving.

saying, "Don't go back to your mother-in-law empty-handed" (Ruth 3:17).[338] Finally, he was blessed to have Ruth as his wife, Obed as his son, and to be the great-grandfather of King David (9a).

Drive out the mocker, and out goes strife; quarrels and insults are ended (22:10).

There are some people who are arrogant, proud, and haughty. If you keep them near you, you will have quarrels, fights, and shame.

Solomon taught his son with this proverb. But when his son Rehoboam became king, he made the foolish decision to listen to the young men who had grown up with him and overruled the old, experienced officials. The younger men who advised him were arrogant and proud. Rehoboam was also arrogant. The fact that they were arrogant is evidenced in that they had no ability to empathize with their people's sufferings. The result was a division between southern Judah and northern Israel, and quarrels, fights, and envy continued between the two nations until they are destroyed (see 10b).

The arrogant stir up quarrels and strife wherever they go, just as a loach stirs up mud. It is a sad reality that there are many such arrogant people in churches, denominations, and society. The arrogant must be removed from the community. The arrogant are not fit for the kingdom of God.

One who loves a pure heart and who speaks with grace will have the king for a friend(22:11).

A king needs advisors and loyalists who are consistent on the inside and outside. Vassals who obey blindly to the king but think

---

[338] Boaz modeled generous leadership as a spiritual legacy for David, the most revered of Israel's kings. And he was blessed with a honorable name in biblical history. Furthermore, he became a representation of the redemptive work of Jesus Christ.

differently on the inside are great obstacles to the king. An immature king or one with a narcissistic personality disorder is easily swayed by the cunning words of those vassals.

Kings who befriend vassals who are unpleasant to listen to but who can speak truthfully and profitably are mature kings.[339] Such officials are pure in heart and with integrity. A king who befriends them is also pure in heart and with integrity.

Blessed are the pure in heart, for they will see God, the King (see Matt. 5:8).[340] And God, the King, is the friend of the pure in heart (11b). He opens his heart to them.[341]

As descendants of Adam, we humans are not by nature pure in heart. We have all sorts of contradictory motives and desires, and even when we are humble, we can be proud. No one is one hundred percent pure in heart. Nevertheless, there are those who love and pursue purity of heart. They are born again of the Holy Spirit. Those who have received Jesus Christ desire to have the heart of Jesus. God recognizes believers as righteous in Christ, even though they are still impure, and treats them as his children and friends.

The eyes of the LORD keep watch over knowledge, but he

---

[339] Barzillai was a loyal official and friend of King David. He was a man of pure heart. He was not greedy for power. He served King David when he fled from Absalom, but he did not expect a reward. When the restored David offered him a reward, "Cross over with me and stay with me in Jerusalem, and I will provide for you" (2 Sam. 19:33), he refused, saying, "How many more years will I live, that I should go up to Jerusalem with the king?" (2 Sam. 19:34). His next answer reveals even more of his wisdom and generosity: "I am now eighty years old. Can I tell the difference between what is enjoyable and what is not? Can your servant taste what he eats and drinks? Can I still hear the voices of male and female singers? Why should your servant be an added burden to my lord the king....Let your servant return, that I may die in my own town near the tomb of my father and mother" (2 Sam. 19:35-37). Barzillai was a true friend to David. Blessed are those who have such a friend!

[340] Bridges also connected Matthew 5:8 with this proverb. Bridges, *Proverbs*, 410.

[341] Abraham was a friend of God. God told Abraham in advance of his plan to destroy Sodom and Gomorrah. Moses was also a friend of God. God communed with him for forty days on Mount Sinai during the giving of the law.

frustrates the words of the unfaithful (22:12).

In this proverb, "knowledge" is the knowledge of the fear of God. God always watches over and protects those who have the knowledge of the fear of God (12a). Their every move is always on God's radar, and he hears and answers their words and prayers. In times of crisis, God protects and delivers them. He works to fulfill their prayers.

God is invisible to our physical eyes, but he is alive and his eyes watch over us. God's eyes are everywhere (see 15:3). He knows us well.

If you drive a car with a GPS, you can rely on satellites to give you accurate directions in real time. Likewise, in the lives of believers, even when we deviate from our planned path, God works together for good. He opens up new paths and ultimately leads us to our destination.

The sluggard says, "There's a lion outside! I'll be killed in the public square!" ["There is a lion outside!" or, "I will be murdered in the streets!"] (22:13).

If you think there's a lion or a tiger outside, you won't go outside. If you think you could be killed by someone if you go outside, you won't go outside. In modern terms, if you think you might die in a car accident while driving, you won't get behind the wheel. People who are too afraid of accidents won't take the train, bus, or airplane. They won't leave the house at all. They're afraid of dying in an accident. The problem is that if they continue to live like this, they'll end up with invisible shackles and a self-made prison.

Failure to overcome anxiety and fear makes people lazy. Issues of laziness and anxiety go hand in hand. The lazy use anxiety as an excuse not to work.

Anxiety and fear are worse when you are uneducated, ignorant, or psychologically immature. When anxiety reaches the level of an anxiety disorder, life is painful. Avoiding anxiety and fear drains your energy. It becomes difficult to live with a sense of mission.

You spend a lot of energy trying to keep yourself alive.

The devil delights in stirring up anxiety and fear, to which anyone is susceptible, to sap the motivation and energy from life. He makes us fear physical death more than God, who is able to destroy body and soul in the fires of hell (see Matt. 10:28). He amplifies anxiety and fear so that we focus our attention on the threatening environment rather than on God, who is in control of life and death.

To overcome this intervention of the devil, we must apply to our lives the words of Jesus, "Whoever wants to save their life will lose it,k but whoever loses their life for me will find it" (Matt. 16:25). If you face your anxiety and fear with faith in God, you will live a vital life.

The mouth of an adulterous woman is a deep pit;[342] a man who is under the LORD's wrath falls into it (22:14).

After the proverbial warning against prostitutes in chapter 7, another warning against prostitutes appears briefly here.[343] The lips of an adulterous woman are tempting and flow honey, but it is a mouth that kills and a snare that entraps (14a).

A sexually degrading trap is often difficult to escape. It's hard to escape even when you have some awareness of it, because the process is addictive.

Those who persist in sexual sins may live for a while with momentary pleasure. But their lives are deadly diseased. They are under the wrath of God (14b) and they are already sentenced to death, even though there is a grace period for them. They must hear the Bible's stern warning that they will not receive an inheritance in heaven. And they must do everything in their power to escape from adultery.[344]

---

[342] A similar proverb is found in 23:27: "An adulterous woman is a deep pit, and a wayward wife is a narrow well."

[343] The proverb in 9:16-18 indirectly alludes to the temptation of a prostitute.

[344] "For of this you can be sure: No immoral, impure or greedy person—such a person is an idolater—has any inheritance in the kingdom of Christ and of God. Let no one

Folly is bound up in the heart of a child, but the rod of discipline will drive it far away (22:15).

The Bible takes a position on human understanding that is diametrically opposed to the modern humanistic view of man. The Bible declares that humans are born sinful from the womb. The "foolishness" in this proverb is the sinful nature that is present from birth.[345] Foolishness, ignorance, and narcissism are present in a child's life from the beginning.

Healthy parents can spank their children with love and at the appropriate level at the right time. If parents have personality disorders, they are not able to distinguish between a "spanking" and a "whip." Whipping is a great risk of traumatizing a child rather than helping to discipline him or her. It can be a child abuse and a crime against law. Therefore, physical discipline should be used with care and wisdom.

Education theories and counseling theories based on humanistic psychology presuppose that children have fundamental goodness and potential. However, it's just a premise. Humanistic psychology believes that the nurturing environment has a profound impact on human psychological development. There is some validity to this. However, the Bible teaches us that even babies are naturally self-centered and sinful after the fall of Adam. We need to recognize this fact and combine adequate nurturing with appropriate discipline according to the developmental stage. Children who grow up without adequate punishment and frustration are at risk of becoming adults with narcissistic personality disorder or antisocial personality disorder.

One who oppresses the poor to increase his wealth and one

deceive you with empty words, for because of such things God's wrath comes on those who are disobedient" (Eph. 5:5-6).

[345] Bridges also noted that the foolishness of children is "innate." He traced the cause of children's foolishness to Adam and Eve. Bridges, *Proverbs*, 413-14.

who give gifts to the rich—both come to poverty (22:16).

Two kinds of antisocial human beings are depicted. One class of them abuse and oppress the poor in order to accumulate wealth for themselves. The other class of them give gifts or bribes to the rich. Both will end up poor.

Those who oppress the poor and abuse the weak in pursuit of their own interests have narcissistic personality disorder and antisocial personality disorder. They have psychological traits at the level of psychopaths. They cannot empathize with the suffering, pain, and hunger of the weak. Employers who can't help but cut, delay, or don't pay the wages they owe for one reason or another fall into this category.

There are many instances where selfish and abusive business persons or employers oppress or exploit their employees or workers. Some disrespect and exploit workers, especially those from other underdeveloped countries. God will not overlook any business or enterprise run by such people. They will be held accountable not only on the Last Judgment Day, but also in this world. They will be judged for the sin of not paying wages on time.[346]

Using one's position and authority to mistreat the weak and the foreigner, represented by orphans and widows in the Old Testament, with disrespect is a grave sin that provokes God's wrath. One of the three or four core sins of Israel that Amos identified was taking advantage of the weak: "For three sins of Israel, even for four, I will not relent. They sell the innocent for silver, and the needy for a pair of sandals" (Amos 2:6-7). God said he would not turn away from punishing them.

The second category of people are those who want to be associated with the wealthy or powerful. They are not ashamed to give gifts or bribes to get their help. They use illegal methods to achieve their goals. They are characterized by symptoms of narcissistic personality disorder. God abhors the behavior of these

---

[346] "Look! The wages you failed to pay the workers who mowed your fields are crying out against you. The cries of the harvesters have reached the ears of the Lord Almighty. You have lived on earth in luxury and self-indulgence. You have fattened yourselves in the day of slaughter" (James 5:4-5).

people, and he causes their worldly efforts to fail. It won't be long before their bribery is discovered and they are humiliated.

Pay attention and turn your ear to the saying of the wise; apply your heart to what I teach,[347] for it is pleasing when you keep them in your heart and have all of them ready on your lips (22:17-18).

No matter how good a proverb you hear, if you are not interested in it or hear it halfheartedly, it will have no effect on you. You don't take it to heart, so you don't remember it.

Unfortunately, the foolish are attracted to the words of the wicked. They are easily influenced by evil. They don't need to be taught much about evil to act wickedly. Moreover, it is very easy for them to ruin their lives by listening to the wicked.

But it takes a long time to listen to the wise and educators and to make changes. In order to listen to the wise, you have to read a lot of books or go out of your way to seek education in person. If we understand education as education up to college years, we have to persevere through a process that takes at least 16 years to complete and to be well influenced by your teachers and professors and by your friends.

Internalizing the words of a wise person or a mature parent makes us wise and mature. Therefore, we must "feed" on good teaching, especially the Word of life. One cannot become wise by eating only bread. For our souls live by every word that proceeds from the mouth of God (see Matt. 4:4).

What is in the heart comes out of the mouth at some point (18b). Wise words come out of the mouth of one who has heard and digested words of wisdom. Even the manner of speaking are taken after. What adult children heard from their parents in their

---

[347] Bridges rightly pointed out that from verse 17 to the end of chapter 24, Solomon departs from the style of Proverbs that contrasts the life of wisdom and understanding with the life of foolishness and folly, and presents a style of proverbs that preaches to an audience as well as to the individual. Bridges, *Proverbs*, 416.

childhood often comes out unconsciously when they teach their own children. What we internalize will be externalized.

So that your trust may be in the LORD, I teach you today, even you. Have I not written thirty sayings for you, sayings of counsel and knowledge, teaching you to be honest and to speak the truth [teaching you true and reliable words], so that you bring back truthful reports [give sound answers] to those you serve? (22:19-21).

Solomon restates his reasons for instructing his sons in more proverbs than they may even remember. The first one is to teach us to trust in the LORD (19a), that is, to rely on God in all things without trusting in our own wisdom or understanding. Proverbs are "sayings of counsel and knowledge" (20b) that help us to rely on God. They are "true and reliable words" of truth (21a).

The second one is to equip us to answer with the word of truth. It is to discern the will of God so that we may answer wisely.[348]

Who are "those you serve" in the text? To whom serve Solomon's sons, the primary listeners of Proverbs? Koptak interprets that "those you serve" mean "messengers." If so, then Solomon's son as king is instructed on how to respond wisely to envoys from other countries in a diplomatic context.[349]

Do not exploit the poor because they are poor and do not crush the needy in court, for the LORD will take up their case and will exact life for life [plunder those who plunder them]

---

[348] Bridges connected this proverb to 1 Pet. 3:15-16: "But in your hearts revere Christ as Lord. Always be prepared to give an answer to everyone who asks you to give the reason for the hope that you have. But do this with gentleness and respect, keeping a clear conscience, so that those who speak maliciously against your good behavior in Christ may be ashamed of their slander." Bridges, Proverbs, 419.

[349] Koptak, Proverbs, 534.

(22:22-23).

Solomon cautions against oppressing the weak and needy in the judicial process. The decisions made by a tribunal must be fair. Courts are supposed to be places where justice is done. However, the reality is that this is sometimes not the case. If you're represented by a big law firm, you're more likely to get a favorable ruling from the judge, whether it's just or not. It's an unfortunate reality that the person who pays the most money for a lawyer is more likely to win.

Solomon makes it clear that to ignore the cryings of the weak and poor in judgment is to anger God. God will judge those who judge unjustly (23b). God is angry when the judiciary is corrupt.

There is One greater than kings. There is One greater than judges. All judges, fear God who watches over in secret!

Do not make friends with a hot-tempered person, do not associate with one easily angered, or you may learn their ways and get yourself ensnared (22:24-25).

This is a precious proverb with insights and teachings about anger. Anger is an important emotion and function in human life. Too many people are unable to recognize it, express it well, or cope with it in others. Many Christians suppress their anger at all costs or feel guilty when they lose their temper because they think anger itself is a sin.

Solomon teaches us not to befriend or mate with someone who cannot express anger in a healthy way. "Hot-tempered" persons do not express anger in a healthy way. They are easily angered (24b). They have poor impulse control, and any situation that upsets them will cause them to lash out without restraint. Most of them are self-centered and psychologically immature. They don't have the ability to consider or empathize with the other person. They don't take into account the embarrassment and fear that the other person may experience when they lose their temper over small things. They only focus on what has upset them. They create obstacles for themselves in interpersonal relationships.

Solomon warns against accompanying someone who is easily angered. In general, people don't like to be around short-tempered persons. Eventually, these persons become loners.

Hot-tempered people can be understood in the framework of personality disorders. They may have characteristics of narcissistic personality disorder, borderline personality disorder, and/or antisocial personality disorder. Being diagnosed with personality disorder means that they are very likely to interact in the same patterns unless they become self-aware and work to change and heal. It would be nice if they are changed on the inside. But if not, it is wise to reconsider working with or marrying these people. One sensible approach is not to associate with these persons from the beginning if possible.[350]

There are many reasons to avoid associating with or accompanying the short-tempered. Solomon is primarily concerned about the consequences of companionship with them, because one becomes influenced by them and becomes like them (25a). In other words, there is a great risk that one will internalize the anger of the companion and become a hot-tempered person too.

One person's anger affects those around him or her, and their anger affects other people around them. One person's anger can have an exponentially negative impact on the people around. It's like a contagious disease. This would make the world a very difficult place to live in. If we have more people who get angry and violent over minor issues, we all have to be on edge in this world.

In today's world hard to live, there are more and more people who are easily offended. Some people will honk their horns and turn on their high beams as they follow you because they think that you cut them off. Some drivers will even cut in front of you on the highway and slam on their brakes to intimidate you. A growing number of foolish people get angry too easily and too much, with destructive results, over something that can be overlooked with a little patience and grace.

---

[350] Believers are not expected to have good interpersonal relationships with everyone. It's important to recognize that even when Paul encouraged reconciliation, he said, "*If it is possible, as far as it depends on you,* live at peace with everyone" (Rom. 12:18). We need to admit that there are times when we can't live peacefully with everyone.

Anger can be understood as the dynamic of learning and modeling. In some cases, we learn not because you want to learn, but because learning takes place with unconscious process of introjection and internalization. For example, a son who grows up with a father who gets angry easily grows up with a lot of anxiety and fear. The problem is that when he becomes grown up, his father's behavior is likely to be repeated in his interpersonal relationships, especially in his relationship with his own children. At some point, the victim becomes the perpetrator.

As a result, if you are in the company of someone who is easily angered, you are at high risk of being influenced and caught in the "snare" of destruction and death (25b). Once caught in a snare, it is very difficult to escape. It is wise to be cautious and careful not to get caught in a snare. Once you're in the snare, it's hard to cut ties with someone who is easily angered, even if you want to. He or she will not let you go. This is especially true in a marriage.

Anger, anxiety, depression, and even psychosis can be contagious.[351] Who is your companion to accompany with matters a lot. We live by influencing each other. Being part of a healthy church community is very important in this regard. Being part of a dysfunctional family or a heretical church is soul-sickening. It can lead to destruction. Therefore, it is important to become more aware of who you primarily associate with.

Do not be one who shakes hands in pledge or puts up security for debts; if you lack the means to pay, your very bed will be snatched from under you (22:26-27). See also 11:15, 17:18.

Whereas verses 24 and 25 warned against associating with people with anger and bitterness, this proverb warns against associating with people who ask for guarantees of debt. Two primary functions in life, that is, making association and making differentiation, are

[351] In his comment with this proverb, Bridges began with the statement, "Sin is contagious." Bridges, *Proverbs*, 420. Bad things are contagious and good things are also contagious.

the most important life skill and wisdom that cannot be overemphasized. There are times to associate with others and times not to associate with others. When it comes to differentiation, it is wise in the long run to differentiate. What you need to make differentiation, you need to mobilize the ability to say no.

"To shake hands in pledge" in this proverb means "to guarantee." Holding hands means an expression of assurance. Of course, there are times when you should hold hands and help. But when you shouldn't, you need to have the courage to say no. There are many people who suffer and regret in the long run because of the consequences of not being able to say no.

The Bible teaches that we should love our neighbors as ourselves. This commandment captures the core spirit of the law. But loving our neighbors also requires wisdom and knowledge. Saying no to our neighbor when you need to say no is also a necessary part of healthy neighborly love.[352]

Paying someone's debt for him or her is a commendable act. If you have resources to pay the debt and you do so voluntarily, it's a good act. You are redeeming for the person who owes debt. However, it is not wise to guarantee a debt at the request of a debtor when you are unable to do so, because the consequences can be devastating. As described in this proverb, even your household goods will be mortgaged, and you will remain in debt. It is an irresponsible behavior that can lead not only you but also your family to poverty overnight.

There are quite a few people who have tasted bitterness in life because they made a guarantee that went wrong. It's a sad and unfortunate thing when the person who owes money can't pay it back and his or her debt falls solely on the person who made the guarantee. Some vulnerable people even commit suicide when a guarantee wipes out everything they've worked for. So it's wise to be mindful of this possible outcome.

---

[352] Some psychological reasons for not being able to say no when you need to can be found in the dynamic of codependency. Adult children with low self-esteem are often unable to say no because they fear conflict with others or rejection from others. People who are unable to maintain healthy boundaries for themselves are unable to love their neighbors in a healthy way. Instead, they are at risk of being taken advantage of in relationships.

Being an adult presupposes the ability to consider the well-being of one's own family. Family relationships take priority over friendships. If a friendship is broken because you refuse to guarantee, it's not really a friendship because it is conditional. The person who asks for a guarantee should consider and understand the friend's position. The friend who has to decline must be able to say no while still understanding the asking friend's position. In that case, their friendship can remain healthy.

In your life journey, it's wise to live by the principle of never making guarantees. There is a danger that a "Never" will end up with a "Real" of the catastrophic consequences of making a guarantee. If you can think ahead to the potentially fatal consequences and still feel compelled to make a guarantee, it's only right to do so with a full consent of your family.

The lesson to be learned from this proverb is that neighborly love is healthy within proper bounds. Unconditional neighborly love is not necessarily biblical. It is immature and foolish to strike hands in pledge to a neighbor's request without common sense and wisdom to protect yourself and your family.

Do not move an ancient boundary stone set up by your ancestors (22:28). See 23:10.

There are two reasons to move a boundary stone. The first is voluntary. This is when people are forced to sell their land that was distributed to them by their ancestors.[353] The second is when a boundary stone is moved without the landowner's knowledge. This is when a greedy neighbor secretly moves a boundary stone from a land adjacent to his own and claims it as his own. The law of Moses explicitly forbade this behavior (see Deut. 19:14, 27:17). In this proverb, it has the first meaning. This is because we can

[353] For example, when Jeremiah was trapped inside the courtyard of the guard, his uncle's son Hanamel came to him and offered to buy his field in his hometown of Anathoth. He sold it to Jeremiah, who had the right of a kinsman-redeemer. Through this event, God prophesied that Judah would be restored after its destruction: "Houses, fields and vineyards will again be bought in this land" (Jer. 32:15).

understand this text in the context of the preceding warning in verse 27 that "your very bed will be snatched from under you," and that even the land you inherited from your ancestors may be taken from you.

We can apply this proverb to our faith. The boundary stones are the boundaries of the orthodox Christian faith, inherited from our ancestors of faith. These boundaries must be kept. Biblical truths should not change over time.[354] Changing absolute truths into relative truths is the sin of moving the boundary stone.

Do you see someone skilled in their work? They will serve before kings; they will not serve before officials of low rank [before obscure men] (22:29).

Solomon's father, King David, was a man who was skilled in his works. The poet who wrote Psalms 78 sang of him, "And David shepherded them with integrity of heart; with skillful hands he led them" (Ps. 78:72). His two qualities are worth noting. One is that he shepherded his people "with integrity of heart."[355] The other is that he shepherded them with skillful hands.

Those who possess these two qualities in a balanced way are truly skillful leaders. David was a shepherd who had the skill and ability to shepherd his sheep well. He was called by God from his life of shepherding. He was skilled at throwing a sling in his battle with Goliath. He was scouted by Saul when he was looking for a man who could play a lyre well to cast out evil spirits. David's musical

---

[354] In a postmodern world, Christian believers are expected to pass on to the next generation the truths of historic Christianity, which run through the Old and New Testaments and the history of the church. The core doctrines, the creeds, and the infallibility of the 66 books of the Old and New Testaments are indispensable boundary stones.

[355] David's integrity is exemplified in the testimony of God concerning him, "I have found David son of Jesse, a man after my own heart; he will do everything I want him to do" (Acts 13:22). He was honored and loved by God as well as by his people. His faith and integrity are also seen in the incident where he was given the opportunity to kill his opponent, King Saul, but did not.

skill was such that he was chosen from all of Israel.[356] In addition, he was a skilled poet who beautifully expressed his faith in the LORD in poetry. He was also a man of integrity who sympathized with the weak and could care for the people with sensitivity. Finally, he was called by God and anointed as king.

Joseph, Daniel, and Daniel's three friends were all skilled at what they did. Above all, they were men of great faith and integrity.[357] Despite living in difficult times, they became valued instruments of God.

---

[356] "These are the last words of David: 'The inspired utterance of David son of Jesse, the utterance of the man exalted by the Most High, the man anointed by the God of Jacob, the hero of Israel's songs'" (2 Sam. 23:1).

[357] Bridges also mentioned these names and ministries, including the name of Nehemiah. Bridges, *Proverbs*, 423.

Chapter 23 Drunkards and Gluttons Become Poor

When you sit to dine with a ruler, note well what is before you, and put a knife to your throat if you are given to gluttony. Do not crave his delicacies, for that food is deceptive (23:1-3).

There are two possible interpretations of this passage, depending on who is being addressed. First, if this is a lesson for Solomon to teach his sons, then "a ruler" is not a king, but a person in authority or a high-ranking official. Second, if this is a lesson for the general congregation, then a ruler is a king or someone in authority.

In the first case, the wisdom of Solomon's son to take the throne is to be wary of undeserved catering from those in power. It has been said that "Those who have eaten and the dead are silent." This saying means that if someone is well treated with delicacies, he or she cannot speak against the person who treated. So if someone in power invites you to his or her home and treats you to an expensive meal, he or she possibly has an ulterior motive. The problem is that it's hard to turn down the person's solicitation after you've eaten a delicious meal. "Delicacies" in this proverb don't just mean a delicious dinner but also mean bribes, which are much more valuable than a dinner.

In the second case, "his delicacies" refers to food served by a powerful person.[358] The idea is that when someone in power, including a king, serves delicious or expensive food, you should not take it at face value. Solomon points out that "delicacies" are

---

[358] Koptak comments that the proverbs in 23:1-8 are related to each other. Koptak, *Proverbs*, 544. Verses 4 and 5 seem to have a weaker direct connection. This proverb is a warning against wealth. If the connection is between dinner invited by an official and wealth, then the invitee is looking for an opportunity to take unrighteous money by dining with the official. Conversely, the person in power may be using the invitee to further his or her own interests. Verses 6 through 8 focus on the theme of "Do not crave delicacies," warning us to be wary of invitations to eat from those with evil intentions.

"deceptive" (3). It is wise to see that a sharp knife is hidden in the delicacies.

In the Garden of Eden, the devil packaged the forbidden fruit as "delicious food" or "magical food" that could make Adam and Eve like God. But it was a deception that lured them. It was deadly food that led not only them, but all of humanity into sin. It was "poisoned food." It was food with a hidden edged knife.

Although a context is different from this proverb, Haman was invited to a special feast by the queen, Esther, to which he was the only one to be a guest to the king. But he had no idea that the feast was a feast of deception. Excited by the queen's recognition of him, he went unsuspectingly to the feast and fell into a "snare" that ultimately led to his death by being hanged from the same pole he had prepared to hang Mordecai. The special meal proved to be a death trap for him.

Applying this proverb to modern life, it's wise to be wary when your boss or president of your company calls you in person and offers you delicious food. Sometimes it's a genuine gesture of encouragement. But more often than not, it's to ask for a favor that's hard to refuse or to take advantage of you. Another reason to be wary of dining with your boss or someone in authority is that you may be unwittingly judged by him or her. For example, if you're labeled as someone who doesn't have good table etiquette or as a glutton, you'll end up losing out.

Do not wear yourself out to get rich; do not trust your own cleverness [have the wisdom to show restraint]. Cast but a glance at riches, and they are gone, for they will surely sprout wings and fly off to the sky like an eagle (23:4-5).

Wanting to live a wealthy life in the world is a desire that most people have. It's true that this desire motivates us to achieve and succeed. This desire is not a sin in itself.

Striving to make money to the point of burning yourself out and losing sight of the true value of life is a sign of misplaced priorities. It's foolish if you lose your health or your relationship with your family because you care about making money. It is even more foolish to neglect your soul and neglect a life of the Word and prayer in order to make more money.

Therefore, moderation is necessary. Showing restraint is a wisdom (4b). Even when you're trying to make money, you need to be disciplined, like controlling the reins of a horse.

Money and riches are temporary and transitory.[359] If you lose your health, even the money you earned is quickly wasted on hospital bills. In particular, unearned or unrighteous income flies away as if it has wings (5). The wealth of the wealthy with whom God does not please flows away like water poured into a jar without a bottom, through whatever channels it may take. We see this most starkly in the case of the rich in stocks. Overnight, their stocks can turn into scraps of paper. The fact that money is actually nothing more than a print bill is instructive.

Do not eat the food of a begrudging host [a stingy man], do not crave his delicacies; for he is the kind of person who is always thinking about the cost. "Eat and drink," he says to you, but his heart is not with you. You will vomit up the little you have eaten and will have wasted your compliments (23:6-8).

Chapter 23 contains many warnings about eating and drinking. Verses 1-3 warn against eating with those in power, while verses 6-8 warn against eating from a begrudging host or a stingy person. Verses 20-21 counsel against associating with wine drinkers and meat eaters, and verses 29-35 warn of the disaster that will come to the drunkard.

The same warning in verse 3, "do not crave his delicacies," against food from people in power is repeated in verse 6. "A begrudging host" seems to fit in the context than "a stingy man,"

---

[359] Bridges commented on the second half of verse 5, connecting it to 1 Tim. 6:17, which reads "Command those who are rich in this present world not to be arrogant nor to put their hope in wealth, which is so uncertain, but to put their hope in God, who richly provides us with everything for our enjoyment." Bridges, *Proverbs*, 426.

because stingy people rarely treat others with delicacies.[360]

The food of a begrudging host is related to the food of the one in power warned about in verses 1-3. It is so in that it is food with intent. He invites you to "eat and drink," but his heart is "not with you" (7b). You need to know that he is "the kind of person who is always thinking about the cost" (7a). He cares about the cost of the food he invests in. He also expects more than he gives and has an agenda for his delicacies.[361] Recognizing hidden motives is a wisdom of life.

Do not speak to fools, for they will scorn your prudent words [the wisdom of your words] (23:9). See also 9:7-8; 26:4-5.

This proverb can be viewed as a stand-alone text, distinct from the previous verse 6-8, but it can also be viewed as a connected text. As a connected text, "a fool" are another expression of "a begrudging host." "Your compliments" in verse 8 is connected with "your prudent words" in verse 9.

Even if you eat and drink with a begrudging host and speak words of compliments or wisdom to him, it will be of no use, for the one who treats you with delicacies has other things on his mind and will not listen or empathize with you. The foolish and evil person pretends to listen, but doesn't really listen. He will take your compliments for granted and ignore your words of wisdom because he does not listen attentively (9b).

A dinner with such a person is a waste of time and energy. At the

---

[360] Stinginess can be associated with obsessive-compulsive personality disorder. People with OCPD are characterized by stinginess. They don't treat others even with average meal, not to mention expensive dinner. This is because they don't like to spend money in general.

[361] Peter insightfully characterized them, saying "Their idea of pleasure is to carouse in broad daylight. They are blots and blemishes, reveling in their pleasures while they feast with you. With eyes full of adultery, they never stop sinning; they seduce the unstable; they are experts in greed—an accursed brood!" (2 Pet. 2:13-14); "For they mouth empty, boastful words and, by appealing to the lustful desires of the flesh, they entice people who are just escaping from those who live in error" (2 Pet. 2:18).

end of a meal, you will "vomit up the little you have eaten" (8a). Therefore, it is wise to discern beforehand and avoid such a person and place. Blessed is the one who does not "sit in the company of mockers" (Ps.1:1).

The basic rule for avoiding these temptations is to hate freebies. When someone offers you something for free or money, they usually have an ulterior motive. People who are prone to scams are characterized by their love of freebies. They fall for the promise of easy money without effort. It's human nature to like freebies, which is corrupted by sin. This is something we all need to be careful and vigilant about.

Do not move an ancient boundary stone or encroach on the fields of the fatherless, for their Defender is strong; he will take up their case against you (23:10-11). See also 22:28.

In this proverb, the act of moving an old boundary stone is associated with greed. In a time when cadastral maps were not as clearly drawn and surveyed as they are today, it was easy to move boundary stones. It was easy to be tempted by greed to move them. It would have been easy to sneak around to move them at night and claim the land as one's own, leading to lawsuits.

There was no point in protesting or suing, especially if the boundary stones of the field of orphans and widows were moved. There was a high probability that the case would be decided in favor of the wealthy and powerful. Therefore, God forbade the act of moving a boundary stone in the law. Nevertheless, there were cases where the boundary stones were moved.[362]

The fatherless were weak socially because they had no "father," a hedge to protect them and keep them out. So God became their Defending Father. God is the fence for orphans and widows, so trespassing on their fields is trespassing on God's boundary. God will be the attorney and judge in their legal cases, defending the

---

[362] Isaiah's accusation illustrates this: "Woe to you who add house to house and join field to field till no space is left and you live alone in the land" (Isa. 5:8).

fields of the orphan and widow. He will hear the grievances of the orphan and the widow and advocate them.

In today's society and church, it is imperative to maintain a spirit of protecting a boundary stone. We need to recognize that encroaching intentionally or unintentionally on the boundaries of small businesses or planting churches that are not able to defend their own boundaries is an action that can trigger the wrath of God. We hear stories of megachurches coming into an area and killing off most of planting churches around them. Megachurches should be careful for this reality.

Counseling Application: Individual boundaries and boundaries between subsystems within the family and between the family and the outside world are healthy for the individual and the system when they are maintained at appropriate levels. Violating other people's boundaries, especially the boundaries of the vulnerable, is antisocial behavior. In the name of loving children, it is evil for parents to ignore their children's boundaries and become too controlling or manipulative. Furthermore, rigid or blurred boundaries are a major symptom of a pathological and dysfunctional individual or family. The importance of appropriate boundaries cannot be overemphasized.

Apply your heart to instruction and your ears to words of knowledge (23:12).

Counseling Application: Some parents call their children over to admonish them when they are drunk. What they say when they're drunk is not wise nor effective. The words that they keep inside come out in rambling. It's hard for the children to listen to their parent. It will only make them angry.

Do not withhold discipline from a child; if you punish them with the rod, they will not die. Punish them with the rod and save them from death (23:13-14).[363]

It is a proverb expressed in the double negative. The idea is not to withhold or delay discipline.

Humans, corrupted by sin, tend to swerve left or right. The same is true when it comes to discipline. Some parents rarely discipline their children. They don't restrain their children when they run around in the public restaurant. They don't even like it when other people stop them. On the other hand, some parents are too strict. They are overly controlling and punish their children for the slightest misbehavior. Both of these are foolish ways of disciplining.

In Solomon's time, it was acceptable to beat children with a rod. But now that we live in a society and nation that value human rights, we need sensitivity and wisdom in applying this proverb. If you take this proverb literally and beat your children with a rod, you may go to jail for child abuse. So how do we apply this proverb?

The Korean Revised Standard Version translates "a rod" as "a whip." The word "whip" is a strong word. We use whips when dealing with animals. Slaves were also whipped when disciplining slaves. But children are not animals, nor are they slaves. They are human beings who bear the image of God. They are human beings, even if they are young in age and young in understanding and thinking. Therefore, it is wise and biblical to discipline sensitively, taking into account a child's level and personality trait.[364] Discipline at the right level and at the right time will help a child develop. For example, it is effective to use the rod when a child is old enough to differentiate good from bad, which is at least three years old. Using a rod to children when they don't know what they've done wrong will only confuse and frustrate them. In disciplining, we should also explain to our child what we're doing and control our own anger.

Impulsive spanking or spanking out of anger leaves a child with

---

[363] Fox lists the relevant passages that advocate physical punishment as follows: 13:24, 19:25, 29, 22:15, 26:3, 29:15. Fox, *Proverbs 10-31*, 734.

[364] Bridges also noted the importance of using a rod wisely, firmly, and in love. Bridges, *Proverbs*, 429.

indelible trauma. It's foolish to risk your life for disciplining your child for small things. Spanking should be done in the context of the big picture. You need to consider the intensity and number of spanking that the child can cope with. And it should be proportionate and appropriate to the severity of the offense.

Furthermore, it is biblical for Christian parents to obey the laws of the state. Many states outlaw physical punishment as excessive in child rearing. It is biblical to honor and obey the authority of the state and society, as long as it is not evil. The core spirit of discipline is still to be kept, but the wisdom of applying them does not have to be literal.

Extreme behavior in disciplining children is ineffective and unbiblical. Foolishly taking discipline to the point of physical assault is an act that provokes the wrath of God. Remember that children belong to God, not just to their parents.

Counseling Application: The counseling process also requires appropriate discipline. Making confrontation to the clients without considering their emotional, mental level, or confronting them even when they are not yet ready to accept it, is a foolish approach that will act as a stumbling block in counseling process. It will only undermine trust in the counselor.

My son, if your heart is wise, then my heart will be glad indeed; my inmost being will rejoice when your lips speak what is right (23:15-16).

Beginning in the middle of chapter 23, Solomon calls attention to his son three times with the phrase "my son" (15, 19, and 26), reaffirming his earnestness. This proverb takes the form of a metonymy. It has the structure A-B-B'-A'.

When children are wise and truthful, their parents' hearts are glad and thankful (15, 16). They will be proud of their children and worry-free.

Do not let your heart envy sinners, but always be zealous for the fear of the LORD. There is surely a future hope for you, and your hope will not be cut off (23:17-18).

Solomon reemphasizes that the true purpose of Proverbs is to "fear the LORD. Those who fear God do not envy sinners' well-being (17a).[365] Those who serve God, the most worthy, are not stirred by sinners' worldly wealth. They do not envy them, even when they are temporarily prosperous in the world, because their attention is focused on the invisible God. So they are not envious or angry at the visible prosperity of sinners.[366] Those who are connected to God are bound to live a wise life. Those who always keep their eyes on God have a sure future and hope (18).

Listen, my son, and be wise, and set your heart on the right path: Do not join those who drink too much wine or gorge themselves on meat, for drunkards and gluttons become poor, and drowsiness clothes them in rags (23:19-21).

This proverb begins with the imperative "listen." This doesn't just mean to listen. It means to listen and digest what is said. Those who hear but do not understand and digest what they hear are fools whose ears are uncircumcised.

Those who hear and digest can consistently walk in the right way (19b). Their life is predictable and stable. But the unenlightened

---

[365] Bridges connected this proverb with Asaph's poem: "But as for me, my feet had almost slipped; I had nearly lost my foothold. For I envied the arrogant when I saw the prosperity of the wicked" (Ps. 73:2-3); "How suddenly are they destroyed, completely swept away by terrors!" (Ps. 73:19). Bridges, *Proverbs*, 432.

[366] David expressed this well in poetry: "Be still before the LORD and wait patiently for him; do not fret when people succeed in their ways, when they carry out their wicked schemes. Refrain from anger and turn from wrath; do not fret—it leads only to evil. For those who are evil will be destroyed, but those who hope in the LORD will inherit the land" (Ps. 37:7-9). It is wisdom to stay connected to God and differentiate ourselves from the wicked.

are as unstable as the waves of the sea (see James 1:6).

Alcoholism is a mental illness that harms alcoholics, their family, and society. Solomon points out that a typical result of alcoholism is poverty (21a). Another harm is that alcoholics are vulnerable to physical illnesses and are very likely to die younger than the average life expectancy for a variety of reasons. But the bigger problem is that alcoholism makes their family dysfunctional.

Adult children who grew up in an alcoholic family often struggle with common symptoms of low self-esteem and a weak sense of identity. Spouses of alcoholics suffer as they grapple with issues of co-dependency.

The "wine-lover" and the "meat-lover" and the "sleep-lover" are linked to each other. This is because they are the ones who commit the deadly sins of gluttony and sloth. In human psychological development, beginning with oral stage, eating plays an important role in the formation of major psychological tasks such as trust. Psychoanalysts understand alcoholism and bulimia as conditions that are fixated in the oral stage. They believe that a baby is more likely to become stuck in the oral stage when he or she does not develop a sense of security and trust in the relationship with the mother. The process of trying to solve most of our psychological needs by eating or drinking leads us to gluttony. Of course, there are biochemical processes and environmental and social variables that contribute to binge eating.

Modern people live in a world where there is an abundance of food. Many people seek out so-called "gourmet" restaurants, which are known for their delicious food. The desire to eat delicious food is normal, but there is a danger of overspending God's provisions to please one's own mouth. For those who cannot afford it, gluttony can lead them to poverty (21a).

In the first half of the text, Solomon advises not to associate with drinkers of wine and lovers of meat (20), because in their company you are likely to become like them. Gluttony, or food craving is also a type of addiction. Therefore, it's difficult for you to abstain from it. Your body adapts to food, so if you don't eat a certain amount of food, you'll feel hungry and psychologically anxious. It's a symptom of withdrawal in addiction.

Drunkards or gluttons have little vitality in their lives. They are lethargic, as if they are sleepy. Those who sleep in the streets because they are drunk are foolish, as are those who eat a lot and feel sleepy after eating. We need to eat in order to work!

Those who love to doze or sleep too much are guilty of the deadly sin of sloth. This proverb warns of the consequences of living in rags (21b). Gluttony and sloth are brotherly sins.

Listen to your father, who gave you life, and do not despise your mother when she is old (23:22). See also 1:8; 6:20.

When parents are powerful, children may obey even out of fear. However, it is biblical to honor and obey our parents even when they are old and weak. We are not to disrespect them because they look old and powerless. It is a sign of pride and foolishness for adult children to disrespect their parents because they have financial power and social status.[367]

Buy the truth and do not sell it—wisdom, instruction and insight as well (23:23).

Truth includes wisdom, instruction and insight. All these are more precious than gold or silver. Therefore, we should buy them but not to sell (23a). We should digest them as our own.

And the truth is to be shared. You should make others wise by telling them the truth. But the truth is not to be sold (23a). Nothing should be exchanged for it as more valuable than the truth. Especially we Christians should not exchange Jesus the truth, the way, and the life with anything in the world. We are not to sell the truth to an adulterous woman of verse 27. It is too foolish to give up eternal life for her, a transitory object. It is also too foolish to sell one's life and family to choose her.

---

[367] Bridges connected this proverb to some of the symptoms of people in the last days: "lovers of themselves...proud...disobedient to their parents" (2 Tim. 3:2). Bridges, *Proverbs*, 435.

The father of a righteous child has great joy; a man who fathers a wise son rejoices in him. May your father and mother rejoice; may she who gave you birth be joyful! (23:24-25). See also 10:1; 17:25; 23:15-16.

My son, give me your heart and let your eyes delight in my ways [keep to my ways] (23:26). See 23:15.

There are children who outwardly pretend to obey their parents' precepts and teachings, but inwardly do not give their hearts to their parents. They obey their parents out of obligation. This obedience is not voluntary and therefore does not bring joy to their parents.

The same is true of God's children. God is not pleased when we worship him out of habit without loving him wholeheartedly. God is not pleased with forced offerings. He is pleased with those who worship in spirit and truth. He delights in those who seek him wholeheartedly. He is pleased with heartfelt worship.

For an adulterous woman is a deep pit, and a wayward wife is a narrow well. Like a bandit she lies in wait and multiplies the unfaithful among men (23:27-28).

Both "a deep pit" and "a narrow well" refer to the fact that an adulterous, wayward woman is very dangerous and deadly.[368] The phrase, "like a bandit she lies in wait" is reminiscent of the behavior of the wicked described in 1:10-19. She devours people alive like the grave, shedding innocent blood (1:11, 12). She

---

[368] Bridges connected the symbolism of a deep pit and a narrow well to 2:19: "None who go to her return or attain the paths of life." Bridges, *Proverbs*, 441.

swallows them whole (1:12). She goes after ill-gotten gain (1:19).

Who has woe? Who has sorrow? Who has strife? Who has complaints? Who has needless bruises? Who has bloodshot eyes? Those who linger over wine, who go to sample bowls of mixed wine. Do not gaze at wine when it is red, when it sparkles in the cup, when it goes down smoothly! In the end it bites like a snake and poisons like a viper. Your eyes will see strange sights, and your mind will imagine confusing things. You will be like one sleeping on the high seas, lying on top of the rigging. "They hit me," you will say, "But I'm not hurt! They beat me, but I don't feel it! When will I wake up so I can find another drink?" (23:29-35). See also 23:20-21.

Verse 29 well describes the devastating consequences of alcoholism: woe, sorrow, strife, complaints, needless bruises (physical wounds, psychological wounds, and biochemical changes in the brain), bloodshot eyes, and finally death by a venomous snake bite (32). Verses 33-35 describe the symptoms of a drunkard. First, there are temporary hallucinations, inferred from the phrase "your eyes will see strange sights" (33a). The phrases "sleeping on the high seas" and "lying on top of the rigging" also refer to the hallucinatory symptoms of drunkenness. These are hallucinatory experiences that are also characteristic of withdrawal symptoms.

Second, there is a symptom of temporary thought confusion and paranoid thinking, inferred from the phrase "your mind will imagine confusing things" (33b).

Third, there is a physical symptom that the drunkard doesn't feel hurt when he or she is actually hurt.[369] Alcohol is a chemical that

[369] Solomon's detailed description of the symptoms of drunkenness makes it very likely that he had experienced drunkenness himself.

reduces pain and increases pleasure.

Fourth, there is a symptom of relapse. When the drunkard is sober, he or she engages in relapsing behavior (35b). Life revolves around drinking. Alcoholics spend most of their time drunk or drinking.

After repeated episodes, the alcoholic's brain adapts to alcohol. The brain cells become impaired, causing serious problems with impulse control, thinking, emotions, and interpersonal relationships. Alcohol also adversely affects the body's tissues. It has a high fatality rate, especially in acute alcoholism.

Solomon strongly admonishes, "Do not gaze at wine when it is red" (31a). This exhortation is reminiscent of Paul's admonition to "reject every kind of evil" (1 Thess. 5:22).

If we connect this paragraph of proverbs to verses 27-28, fornication and alcohol are linked. Fornication is also addictive and deadly. Those who fornicate out of control destroy themselves as alcoholics do. They destroy themselves and their families.

Chapter 24 Do Not Envy the Wicked

Do not envy the wicked, do not desire their company; for their hearts plot violence, and their lips talk about making trouble (24:1-2). See also 23:17.

In this proverb, we see the characteristics of the wicked. First, the heart of the wicked is violent. They plot violence (2a). The plot and characteristic of the heart of the wicked is "violence."

Second, the wicked can be prosperous (1a). Envy suggests that the wicked are doing well. The unearned income of the wicked is clearly unjust and anti-social. However, we may envy such unearned income. Asaph, a psalmist, was troubled by the well-being of the wicked (see Ps. 73).

Those who plan and carry out violence are usually in positions of power, and it is wise not to associate with them (1b). It is "dysfunctional," spiritually "pathological," and "demonic" behavior to aid them or agree with them.

By wisdom a house is built, and through understanding it is established; through knowledge its rooms are filled with rare and beautiful treasures (24:3-4).

The word "house" in the text can be interpreted in three ways. The first is the physical house. The second is home, which means family. The third is the psychological home.

First, when you build a physical house, you need a design and specific construction work. Then there's the interior work. All of this building process requires wisdom, understanding, and knowledge.[370] If you don't design for every situation, you'll have to

---

[370] God is the designer and architect of the entire universe. With immeasurable wisdom and understanding, he stretched out the heavens and created the earth and the seas. He

tear it down. You can't put precious and beautiful furniture in each room if you don't make doors that can fit most of the furniture. You can't build a solid house if you don't build a foundation and columns that can withstand the load.

Second, it also takes wisdom, understanding and knowledge to make sure your home is a healthy one.[371] You need both life experience and common sense. You also need a knowledge of psychology to understand differences between males and females and children's psychology. Foolishness, ignorance, and unawareness are the quickest way to create a dysfunctional family. Especially spiritually wise parents can build a God-fearing home. This is a home that is built on the rock. It will not be destroyed by the winds and the floods.

Third, to build a psychological structure with a well-developed psychological self requires wisdom, understanding and knowledge. Those whose psychological structure is stable and secure are less biased to the left or right. They have a well-developed "true self" and a "cohesive self."

On the other hand, people whose psychological structure is fragile generally lack wisdom, understanding and knowledge. They make judgments and decisions based on partial information, leading to foolish results. They have few precious and beautiful treasures inside of them. These persons suffer from low self-esteem. They don't share with others much of their inner world. They feel ashamed to show their inner chambers.

The wise prevail through great power, and those who have knowledge muster their strength [A wise man has great power, and a man of knowledge increases strength]. Surely you need

set boundaries so that the waters would not overflow the land. He created all kinds of precious and beautiful animals, plants, and minerals on the earth. He created the most precious and beautiful of them all, human beings.

[371] Bridges connected "house" in the sense of home to the text of 14:1: "The wise woman builds her house, but with her own hands the foolish one tears hers down." Bridges, *Proverbs*, 445.

guidance to wage war, and victory is won through many advisers (24:5-6). See 11:14, 15:22, 20:18.[372]

We can interpret this proverb in conjunction with verses 3 and 4, which emphasized the need for wisdom, understanding and knowledge in the process of building a house. Now wisdom, understanding and knowledge are needed in waging war, beyond the scope of an individual or family.

Strategy and tactics are essential resources in waging war. There's a saying, "If you know your enemy and yourself, you can win every battle." The knowledge of one's enemy and oneself, wisdom and tactics are essential factors in winning a war.

The power of a wise person is as great as a wise person with a good strategy can win a war. This is especially true if the wise person is a king. If the king is a fool, he will lose every battle.

It's not just a king, but a prophet of God can make a difference in a war. The prophet Elisha was Israel's shield.[373] As long as Elisha was there, Israel was safe.

We can apply this proverb to our faith. The secret to living a victorious life is to live in the presence of God, the supreme wisdom. The help of the Holy Spirit, the best advisor and counselor, is absolutely necessary. We must recognize that God the Holy Spirit, who has deep and wide wisdom, dwells and works within us.

For a nation to stand strong, intellectuals and experts in their fields must serve in each branch of government. In spiritual warfare, a believer needs many advisors and counselors. The writings and books of the seniors of faith, theological knowledge and insights, and even universal wisdom and knowledge from

---

[372] Fox notes that the first half of verse 6 is the same as the second half of 20:18, and the second half of verse 6 is the same as the second half of 11:14. Fox, *Proverbs 10-31*, 744.

[373] The king of Aram wanted to attack Israel, but Elisha knew all about Aram's strategy and had the king of Israel defend himself. The king of Aram even suspected that there was an informer in the royal court. Then his servant said to him "Elisha, the prophet who is in Israel, tells the king of Israel the very words you speak in your bedroom." (2 Kings 6:12).

liberal arts can serve as counselors.

Wisdom is too high for fools; in the assembly at the gate they must not open their mouths [he has nothing to say] (24:7).

The gate was the place where trials were held. In the court of justice, the unwise cannot argue the defense of the wise. They cannot even understand the words of the wise (7a). They will only be publicly humiliated.

We can apply this text to God's relationship with humans. The wisdom of God is too high and too deep for human beings to fathom and measure. Even the wise in the world are but fools compared to the wisdom of God.[374]

Whoever plots evil will be known as a schemer (24:8).

"A schemer" is a person who is contrasted to "advisors" in verse 6. evil schemers are not advisors who use wisdom, understanding and knowledge to fight in a war. They are people with antisocial personality disorder or psychopaths who use their good brain for bad.

The father of the wicked is the devil. The chief of those who misuse their good brains is the devil. The devil is always up to something destructive. It's been that way since the Garden of Eden.[375]

Solomon's brother, Absalom, plotted evil. He hid his plots and remained silent for two years in order to kill Amnon, who had sexually assaulted his sister Tamar.[376] In his relationship with his

---

[374] Job and his friends were all wise men, but their foolishness was revealed before God.

[375] Bridges also pointed out that the representative of the wicked is the devil. Bridges, *Proverbs*, 447.

[376] Solomon's older brother Amnon was a predator who sexually assaulted his half-sister Tamar. His sexual assault was not accidental, but premeditated. His behavior toward her after his sexual assault demonstrates devaluation, a classic symptom of borderline personality disorder. His attitude toward her before the sexual assault was one of

father David, he also hid his plots to rebel, waiting for the right time to win the favor of the people and finally revolted.

Another of Solomon's brothers, Adonijah, carried out his own plans to become king without King David's approval and finally died at Solomon's hands. As such, Solomon had witnessed evil-doers in his own life, so he used this proverb to teach his sons to be wary of the potential for betrayal and treachery.

This proverb does not apply only to sons of kings. Christians need to be aware that in this fallen world there are some people who conspire to do evil. In particular, we must know that the invisible devil is the chief of evil-doers, holding the power of the air and continually recruiting and managing those who do evil.[377] We must live spiritually alert lives, recognizing that evil can be committed even within the church community. A naive view of the world is an infantile mindset.

The schemes of folly are sin, and people detest a mocker (24:9).

This proverb is connected with verse 8. Schemers devise evil thoughts and plans. They plot plans that God hates. Their thoughts and schemes are sinful in the sight of God (9a).[378]

The schemes of the wicked are actually foolish schemes because the schemes eventually lead themselves to fall into their own schemes. Their schemes bring judgment from God.

Those who do evil deny that imprisonment awaits them even in this world. They don't realize that after death, an eternal hell awaits them.

In this proverb, the foolish and mockers are the same people,

idealization.

[377] This includes heretics who sneak into the church community. They are, in Paul's words, "false believers" who "had infiltrated our ranks to spy on" (Gal. 2:4). Those who secretly take the property of a church or Christian institution and privatize it are "evil-doers."

[378] Plotting and thinking are invisible behaviors, but even inner behaviors are sinful before God. God looks at the heart. Jesus also emphasizes the importance of internal motivations when he says that a man who looks at a woman with lustful eyes has already sinned.

Fools who plot evil schemes are arrogant. They think they're smart and their schemes will work. They may succeed temporarily, but soon they will fall into their own schemes.

If you falter in a time of trouble, how small is your strength! (24:10).

Psychological strength and spiritual strength are not usually on display. They are revealed in times of crisis and hardship. For example, those who are psychologically vulnerable are overwhelmed with anxiety and experience great fear when faced with a crisis. As Jesus used in metaphor, these persons have a psychological structure like a house built on sand. When the wind blows and the flood waters rise, the house built on sand collapses.

People with borderline personality disorder or dependent personality disorder are characterized by weakness. People with borderline personality disorder are unstable in their thinking, mood, impulse control and relationships. They are likely to perceive mild stresses as intense and they easily experience rejection, alienation and abandonment. They are at risk of having strong suicidal thoughts or attempting other impulsive behaviors. People with dependent personality disorder seek out others to lean on when faced with difficult situations because they see themselves as weak and vulnerable.

But people with a cohesive self are like the wise who built their houses on a rock. Their psychological structure is strong. They can withstand winds and floods without being shaken. They have resilience to endure.

It is not the tribulation or suffering that is the problem; it is the person's inner response to it. People who have psychological and spiritual strength will not be shaken. Believers with a deep sense of trust and faith in God are able to endure tribulation without much fear.

Rescue those being led away to death; hold back those

staggering toward slaughter. If you say, "But we knew nothing about this," does not he who weighs the heart perceive it? Does not he who guards your life know it? Will he not repay everyone according to what they have done? (24:11-12).

Verse 11 is a firm exhortation.[379] It is God's will to rescue those who are being led to the place of death and those who are about to be killed and murdered. God watches over those who know and do nothing or turn a blind eye. God "weighs the heart" (12a).

God rewards each person according to their deeds (12b). He has compassion on those who have shown compassion. He knows and remembers the deed of those who give a cup of ice water to the thirsty in the name of Jesus Christ. He makes the evil deeds of the wicked return to their own heads. God repaid for the blood of Naboth shed by King Ahab and his wicked wife Jezebel to them and their descendants. He is the God of justice.

In the movie "Schindler's List," the protagonist used his wealth and resources to escape many Jews being sent to concentration camps. There were some devout people in American history who hid escaped black slaves, even breaking state law to do so. These are the people who obeyed the words of this proverb. God will repay their good deeds.

Eat honey, my son, for it is good; honey from the comb is sweet to your taste. Know also that wisdom is like honey for you [is sweet to your soul]: If you find it, there is a future hope for you, and your hope will not be cut off (24:13-14).

---

[379] Bridges gave several examples of biblical characters connected to this proverb. Hebrew midwives in Egypt delivered male babies in defiance of Pharaoh's orders. Esther saved her people from Haman's hand with an attitude, "If I perish, I perish." Jonathan risked his own life to protect David from Saul's hand. Michal also rescued her husband David from the hand of her father Saul. Obadiah, Ahab's palace administrator, risked his life to hide and feed a hundred of the prophets of the LORD in caves. Ahikam and Ebed-melech rescued Jeremiah. Bridges, *Proverbs*, 451.

Solomon compares wisdom to honey. Honey is beneficial to the body and has a sweet taste.[380] Solomon characterizes wisdom with the phrases "it is good" and "honey from the comb is sweet to your taste" (13). Like honey, wisdom is beneficial and sweet to the heart and soul. Through wisdom, the mind and soul can be strengthened and refreshed (see 1 Sam. 14:27).

In this proverb, wisdom refers to God and God's Word. God's Word is sweeter than honey. When Ezekiel ate the scroll with God's words on it, it was sweet as honey (Ezek. 3:3). When John ate the scroll given to him by the angel, it was sweet as honey in his mouth, but after he ate it, it turned sour in his stomach (Rev. 10:10). A psalmist confessed that God's word is sweeter than honey (Ps. 119:103). In this way, God's Word is sweet, profound and wonderful and has the power to revitalize the soul.

But Solomon warns against consuming too much honey in 25:16: "If you find honey, eat just enough—too much of it, and you will vomit." But wisdom and the Word of God, which is likened to honey in the text, can never be consumed in excess.

The future of the wise is clearly bright and hopeful (14b). Believers who are indwelt by God the Holy Spirit will never be discouraged. We may fall, but we will rise again. Our hopes will not disappoint us (see Rom. 5:5a). We rejoice in tribulation because we have eyes to see and wisdom to know that through suffering we learn to be patient, and through patience our character is renewed and refined (see Rom. 5:3-4).

Do not lurk like a thief near [Do not lie in wait like an outlaw against] the house of the righteous, do not plunder [raid] their dwelling place (24:15).

---

[380] Solomon already pointed out that the lips of a prostitute also drip honey: "For the lips of the adulterous woman drip honey, and her speech is smoother than oil" (5:3). The lips of a harlot are easy to seek, but her honey will soon turn to "bitter" flavor. But the words that come from the mouth of God are not easy to obey, but their honey is sweet and beneficial.

The reason for hiding and waiting is to plunder the dwellings of the righteous. The wicked and their father Satan lie in wait to plunder the houses of the righteous. Our enemy Satan lies in wait for an opportunity to stumble even elected believers. He prowls around like a roaring lion, looking for someone to devour (see 1 Pet. 5:8).

Those who are consciously or unconsciously followers of the devil (see Eph. 2:2) are on standby today to attack the homes of the righteous by any means necessary. When they see an opportunity, they swarm like bees and plunder. They attack churches and pastors without revealing their identity. They attack in the name of human rights and propagate heretical ideas in the name of faith, especially those heretical groups that used to operate in secret but are now out in the open and actively attacking. They even indiscriminately send emails offering theological discussions, identifying the recipient and sender. We should all be aware that we are living in challenging times where it is easy to be targeted if we are not vigilant.

For though the righteous fall seven times, they rise again, but the wicked stumble when calamity strikes [are brought down by calamity] (24:16).

We can interpret this proverb in conjunction with verse 15. No matter how much the devil tries to attack the house of the righteous, he cannot completely destroy it. No matter how hard he tries to attack God's churches, he will eventually be defeated. Even if it happens that the house of the righteous falls seven times, God raises up the house of the righteous, holding them with his strong right arm, as the hymn goes, "He raised me up."[381]

---

[381] Fox connects this proverb to Ps. 34:19: "The righteous person may have many troubles, but the LORD delivers him from them all." Fox, *Proverbs 10-31*, 749. Jesus Christ was revealed as walking among the seven golden lampstands, holding the messengers of the seven churches (Rev. 2:1).

Therefore, God's children need not to fear total defeat. Even if we fall down and stumble, we can get back up again with the spirit of perseverance. Even if we commit a sin, we can repent and get back up again. The righteous have hope even in the midst of sin.

The devil and the wicked who attack and plunder the houses of the righteous will be defeated (16b). They will be killed and judged by disasters that will come upon them in an instant. The wicked may appear to be temporarily victorious. But they will perish as suddenly as green vegetables wither.[382]

Do not gloat when your enemy falls; when they stumble, do not let your heart rejoice, or the LORD will see and disapprove and turn his wrath away from them (24:17-18).

Verse 17 can be interpreted in conjunction with verse 16. The wicked will certainly be overthrown and destroyed by a sudden calamity. From the perspective of the righteous, the fall of the wicked is the result of God's justice. Nevertheless, Solomon cautions against rejoicing in the heart when the wicked, who have been enemies, fall. As we look at the fall of the wicked, it is wise for us to be awakened and reflect on ourselves. It is not God's will that we rejoice in their downfall.

God wants even the wicked to repent and turn around. So God does not like the behavior of rejoicing in the downfall of the wicked. God demonstrated this will in biblical history. In the destruction of the southern kingdom of Judah, that was stained with the sin of idolatry, the people of Judah were severely judged for their sins before God. At this time, Edom, an enemy of Judah,

---

[382] King Ahab tried to avoid dying on the battlefield, so he had King Hezekiah of southern Judah put on his royal robes and he himself went to battle in plain clothes. But an arrow randomly shot by an enemy soldier pierced through the seam of his armor in his body. The random, accidental arrow pierced through all of his defenses and severely wounded him, despite his best efforts to avoid disaster. Unable to escape the ranks due to the intensity of the battle, he eventually bled to death on his chariot. God's providential judgment is amazing.

rejoiced in the destruction of Judah. God was not pleased with this behavior and was angry with Edom and brought judgment upon them.[383]

It is our natural response that when an enemy who has been tormenting us finally falls, we are more likely to react by exulting that God has answered. Certainly, God works to bring the enemy down; it is an answer to the prayers of believers and a just judgment of God. However, the enemy's fall is not something to rejoice and celebrate. We should be prudent believers who are alert and use it as an opportunity to examine ourselves.

Do not fret because of evildoers or be envious of the wicked, for the evildoer has no future hope, and the lamp of the wicked will be snuffed out (24:19-20). See also 23:17; 24:1.

This proverb can also be interpreted in the context of verses 17 and 18. While the preceding two verses are about warning against rejoicing in the destruction of the wicked, verse 19 is about warning against being envious or angry at the temporary prosperity of the wicked.

There are many people in this world who are healthy and prosperous despite the fact that they continue to do evil. Even in lawsuits, the wicked continue to win. When we see this reality, we

---

[383] In the destruction of northern Israel and southern Judah, God was watching over the Edomites, who, instead of hiding those who fled or were taken captive, rejoiced and pursued them, actively accused them, captured them, and sold them: "On the day you stood aloof while strangers carried off his wealth and foreigners entered his gates and cast lots for Jerusalem, you were like one of them. You should not gloat over your brother in the day of his misfortune, nor rejoice over the people of Judah in the day of their destruction, nor boast so much in the day of their trouble. You should not march through the gates of my people in the day of their disaster, nor gloat over them in their calamity in the day of their disaster, nor seize their wealth in the day of their disaster. You should not wait at the crossroads to cut down their fugitives, nor hand over their survivors in the day of their trouble" (Obad. 1:11-14). God pronounced judgment on Edom, saying, "As you have done, it will be done to you; your deeds will return upon your own head" (Obad. 1:15).

may be confused and angry.[384] If God is alive and God is just, the wicked should be judged and punished soon, but the reality is not that simple! A psalmist and the prophet Habakkuk wrestled with this problem (see Ps. 73, Hab. 1). This proverb answers that question. The wicked have no future and no hope. The lamp of the wicked will be soon extinguished. God's neglect represents his judgment. Their richness and well-being are a curse of God. Because the wicked are prosperous, they are not anxious and do not fear God. Therefore, they do not sense that judgment and disaster are coming. They miss the opportunity to repent. Finally, when the time of judgment comes, the wicked die of irreversible calamity and are subject to eternal judgment.

Christians, knowing the end of God's work, do not envy the riches of the wicked. Rather, we feel sorry for them.

Our hearts are often contradictory and ambivalent. We are angry at the prosperity of the wicked, but we also envy their prosperity. We are angry because it is motivated by righteousness and justice, but contradictorily, we are also angry because we are jealous of the other's prosperity. Therefore, we must examine our own feelings and motivations with the wicked.

Fear the LORD and the king, my son, and do not join with rebellious officials, for those two will send sudden destruction on them, and who knows what calamities they can bring? (24:21-22).

Solomon calls his son back to attention in verse 13 by calling him "my son" again. He teaches him to revere God, the invisible king, and to fear the king with visible power.

Those who are wicked in their relationships with God or with the king is "rebellious officials." They fearlessly disregard the power and authority of both God and the king. For the rebels, destruction will come "quickly" and "suddenly" (22). And all who are

---

[384] Fox comments that the reason for fretting over the wicked is found in nearsightedness and lack of faith in God's justice. Fox, *Proverbs 10-31*, 751.

associated with these rebels will be destroyed with them. Therefore, Solomon warns, "Do not join with rebellious officials."[385] The chief commander Joab who joined in Adonijah's rebel was killed by Solomon. Adonijah who rebelled against David was also suddenly killed by Solomon.

Both God and the king have strategic weapons to judge the rebellious officials. God is the almighty King who exercised the ten plagues in his relationship with Pharaoh of Egypt. God's weapons for the sudden destruction of the kingdom of Judah were the sword of Babylon, the plagues, and the famine out of being besieged. A king or ruler has authority granted by God and carries a sword to judge those who do evil (see Rom. 12:4).

These also are sayings of the wise: To show partiality in judging is not good: Whoever says to the guilty, "You are innocent," will be cursed by peoples and denounced by nations. But it will go well with those who convict the guilty, and rich blessing will come on them (24:23-25).

In severe cases, as in the text, "to show partiality" means to judge the wicked as right and the righteous as wrong.[386] If there is such a wicked judge or king, peoples will hate and curse him (24b).

God does not judge by appearances. He hates showing partiality in justice. He even does not unconditionally take sides with the poor. He loves justice and righteousness. He delights in seeing the

---

[385] King Hezekiah, who had a friendly relationship with the wicked king Ahab, joined the war and was pursued by the enemies and almost faced death. Without God's help, he would have been mistaken for Ahab and killed. This was the result of his associating with the wicked Ahab.

[386] It is not just for a judge not to be able to keep an objective stance in a trial for a variety of reasons. It is common sense and common practice for judges to recuse themselves from cases where they have a personal connection to the plaintiff or defendant. Furthermore, if a judge's personal experience or psychological issues are involved, it is advisable for him or her to recuse from the case because of possible dynamics of countertransference.

law enforced justly. He recognizes and is pleased in the judgment of a king or judge who rebukes the sinner and judges justly. He will give a king or judge "rich blessing" (25b).

Counseling Application: The principles of justice can be applied to the counseling process. Counselors' primary roles are to empathize with and advocate for their clients, but they should never lose their objectivity. If they identify too much with clients, they won't be able to give objective feedback. In the case of marital counseling, it is important not to get caught in a triangle, because losing objectivity makes counseling ineffective.

An honest answer is like a kiss on the lips (24:26).

In the context of the preceding verses 23-25, an honest answer means an honest judgment. An honest verdict that the guilty party is guilty of sin will give the plaintiff the same joy as a kiss. It will give the plaintiff the joy of comforting and healing the hurt and pain thus far.

Put your outdoor work in order and get your fields ready; after that, build your house (24:27).

This proverb seems to have the opposite meaning of a Korean phrase, "When ones' home is happy, all goes well" (家和萬事成). It sounds like it's telling us to prioritize outside work. A literal meaning of this proverb would be, "Do your farming properly before you build your house." Building a house here can mean building a visible home, or it can refer to an invisible home.[387]

---

[387] To understand this proverb, Fox says, one must consider the context of an agrarian society. He sees it as a proverb that teaches the importance of taking care of one's own fields before they build their own houses or before children move out on their own and start their own families. Fox, *Proverbs 10-31*, 772. Bridges interpreted the proverb as a proverb to prepare the building materials for the house outside before building the house. Bridges, *Proverbs*, 458.

Do not testify against your neighbor without cause—would you use your lips to mislead? [without cause, or use your lips to deceive.] Do not say, "I'll do to them as they have done to me; I'll pay them back for what they did" (24:28-29). See also 20:22.

It is natural to interpret verses 28 and 29 together. If taken separately, verse 28 means not to bear false witness against one's neighbor for no reason and without foundation. Some people slander, accuse, and libel for no reason at all. This is a kind of random murdering. There are even those who bear false witness against their neighbor even though they have received a favor from the neighbor.

When interpreted in conjunction with verse 28, verse 29 reveals the motive for bearing false witness. To bear false witness is to hurt a neighbor in retaliation because they think that they were hurt by the neighbor. If so, it would not be "without cause." But in verse 29, Solomon counsels against retaliation even in such cases.[388]

I went past the field of a sluggard, past the vineyard of someone who has no sense [lacks judgment]; thorns had come up everywhere, the ground was covered with weeds, and the stone wall was in ruins. I applied my heart to what I observed and learned a lesson from what I saw: A little sleep, a little slumber, a little folding of the hands to rest—and poverty will

---

[388] Paul expressed this spirit when he wrote "Do not repay anyone evil for evil. Be careful to do what is right in the eyes of everyone. If it is possible as far as it depends on you, live at peace with everyone. Do not take revenge, my dear friends, but leave room for God's wrath, for it is written: 'It is mine to avenge; I will repay,' says the Lord. On the contrary: 'If your enemy is hungry, feed him; if he is thirsty, give him something to drink. In doing this, you will heap burning coals on his head.' Do not be overcome by evil, but overcome evil with good" (Rom. 12:17-21).

come on you like a thief and scarcity like an armed man (24:30-34).

Solomon was a wise man who reflected about what he "saw," and through his reflections, he compiled wise proverbs. For the people of Israel, fields and vineyards symbolized workplace. It is God's grace that even the lazy and the unwise are given fields and vineyards.

But the sluggard, like a servant in Jesus' parable who was given a talent, leaves his fields and vineyards unattended and makes no effort at all. The slogan of his life is: "Sleep a little longer, doze a little longer, lie down a little longer."

There are some adolescents who don't get up even when their parent wakes them up for school in the morning. The problem is that if this behavior is repeated, it becomes a habit and eventually a personality. These children are likely to grow up without purpose and meaning in life, as the field is covered with weeds (31b).

The issue of sloth is not just related to some teenagers. There are some adults who are lazy too. This is especially true for people with antisocial personality disorder. People who cheat others without actual work are antisocial and lazy. The same goes for robbers. Men who rely on their wives' income and don't want to work are also lazy.

This laziness also applies to the spiritual life. Those who are spiritually drowsy or sleepy do not realize that their inner world is covered with weeds and thorns. They don't care even when thorny bushes are damaging their souls. It is difficult to grow spiritually, but it is all too easy to regress. Laziness is one of the deadly obstacles to psychological and spiritual development.

Chapter 25 Apples of Gold in Settings of Silver

These are more proverbs of Solomon, compiled by the men of Hezekiah king of Judah:[389] It is the glory of God to conceal a matter; to search out a matter is the glory of kings. As the heavens are high and the earth is deep, so the hearts of kings are unsearchable (25:1-3).

The glory of God and the glory of the king are both associated and differentiated. God is connected to the glory of the king in that he is the King of kings. If a connection between God and kings is found in the text, both the hearts of kings and the heart of God are "unsearchable" "as the heavens are high and the earth is deep" (3). But the mind of God is distinct and different from the mind of a human king as far apart as the heights of the heavens and the depths of the earth.[390]

The king's mind and heart is differentiated from the minds and hearts of the people. The people cannot fathom the king's heart and mind. When the king's thoughts are superior and wiser than the people's, the king is honored by the people.

Needless to say, God's thoughts are far superior and wiser than all human thoughts. Paul puts it well: "For the foolishness of God is wiser than human wisdom, and the weakness of God is stronger than human strength" (1 Cor. 1:25).[391] So God is worthy to be

---

[389] Bridges noted that the Holy Spirit not only inspired Solomon, the author of Proverbs, but also intervened with those who wrote the manuscripts of Proverbs. Bridges, *Proverbs*, 462.

[390] Bridges connected Rom. 11:33 with this proverb: "Oh, the depth of the riches of the wisdom and knowledge of God! How unsearchable his judgments, and his paths beyond tracing out!" Bridges, *Proverbs*, 463.

[391] Foolishness and weakness are not at all compatible with God. Nevertheless, Paul emphasizes God's wisdom and power in comparison to humans in order to make it easier for humans to understand.

410

glorified by all humans and all creation: "Amen! Praise and glory and wisdom, and thanks and honor and strength be to our God for ever and ever. Amen!" (Rev. 7:12).

What distinguishes God from kings is that God reveals his glory in concealing a matter. Kings, on the other hand, reveals their glory in searching out a matter (2). In the Book of Job, God did not reveal the ultimate meaning of Job's suffering at the end. He left it in the realm of mystery and secrecy. The salvation providence of Jesus Christ, the Son of God, dying on the cross to redeem us from eternal condemnation and judgment of sin was, in Paul's words, a "mystery" in Old Testament times. When the mystery was finally revealed, the light of the glory of the gospel shone into the hearts of God's elect children.

When kings in Israel were wise enough to meditate on the meaning of God's law, to discern its meaning, and to implement it, God endorsed them and blessed their kingdoms. Hezekiah and Josiah were kings who brought forth the glory of God brilliantly in the kingdom of Judah by practicing the law faithfully.

Counseling Application: Christian counselors need to counsel like wise kings. They must have wisdom and knowledge and skills to sensitively and wisely navigate the deeply hidden life stories and secrets of their clients' minds. Effective counselors have an ability to empathize and probing skills to help their clients reveal areas they may not have been aware of. Such counselors are honored by their clients. They may idealize their counselor saying that they have found an exceptional counselor.[392]

Remove the dross from the silver, and a silversmith can produce a vessel [and out comes material for the silversmith]; remove wicked officials [the wicked] from the king's presence,[393]

---

[392] If the client had few idealized experiences with people in their life, such as a father figure, this experience of idealization can be a good resource for building a cohesive self-structure.

[393] Fox points out that this proverb has connection with 20:26: "A wise king winnows out the wicked; he drives the threshing wheel over them." Fox, *Proverbs 10-31*, 779.

411

and his throne will be established through righteousness (25:4-5).

Verses 4 and 5 begin with the imperative verb "remove." Verse 4 can be understood as a metaphorical expression of what verse 5 is about. Wicked officials are like impurities, dross, or rust on pure silver. They add nothing to the kingship, only damage it. Even one wicked official can make the throne untenable.[394]

In contrast, when a king lacks wisdom and discernment, he may act foolishly in trying to eliminate his loyal officials because he thinks they are wicked officials. King Saul suspected his loyal official and son-in-law David, of being a threat to his throne, so he mobilized his army to get rid of him. Consequently, his throne was destroyed like a house built on sand because of his unrighteousness and lack of fear of God.

Evil people and evil ideas in the church community are like leaven that must be removed. If left unchecked, they can have an evil effect on the entire church. Jesus told his disciples to beware of the leaven of the Pharisees. Paul considered the legalists as leaven and was very wary of them (see Gal. 5:9). Emphasizing love and tolerating heresy or tolerating heretical ideas are destructive for a church or a denomination. Christian churches must strive to maintain purity, especially in doctrine. Only then they can be pure brides of Jesus Christ.

Do not exalt yourself in the king's presence, and do not claim a place among his great men; it is better for him to say to you, "Come up here," than for him to humiliate you before his nobles (25:6-7).

---

[394] King Saul's guards and officials were reasonable, loyal persons who hesitated to obey the king's order to kill the priests and their families. But Doeg the Edomite, Saul's shepherd, was an evil man. He was a psychopathic official who did not hesitate to slaughter entire villages of priests and their families with the sword. He was an evil official who hastened the destruction of Saul's kingdom.

Verse 6 can also be understood in conjunction with verse 5. The phrase "the king's presence" is repeated in verse 6. Those who exalt themselves in the presence of the king are wicked officials. They are arrogant and proud.[395]

It will be an honor if the king asks a person who sits in a lowly place to come up to the top-of-the-table. But it will be also a disgrace if the king orders a person who sits in a high place without permission to move out of the place so that someone else can sit there.

God exalts those who humble themselves. He humbles those who exalt themselves to the ash heap (see 1 Sam. 2:7-8)[396]

Jesus "made himself nothing by taking the very nature of a servant, being made in human likeness. And being found in appearance as a man, he humbled himself by becoming obedient to death—even death on a cross!" (Phil. 2:7-8). "Therefore God exalted him to the highest place and gave him the name that is above every name" (Phil. 2:9).

What you have seen with your eyes do not bring hastily to court, for what will you do in the end if your neighbor puts you

---

[395] Haman was a wicked official who rose to the position of second in command to King Xerxes. But he eventually suffered the humiliation of being placed in the position of entourage in front of Mordecai's chariot. He who wanted to be exalted higher was humbled. Finally, he and his sons were hanged to death from the same high pole from which Mordecai was to be hanged.

[396] Jesus once said something along the lines of this proverb when he was warning against the Pharisees who liked to sit at the places of honor at the table. He told them the following parable: "When someone invites you to a wedding feast, do not take the place of honor, for a person more distinguished than you may have been invited. If so, the host who invited both of you will come and say to you, 'Give this person your seat.' Then, humiliated, you will have to take the least important place. But when you are invited, take the lowest place, so that when your host comes, he will say to you, 'Friend, move up to a better place.' Then you will be honored in the presence of all the other guests. For all those who exalt themselves will be humbled, and those who humble themselves will be exalted" (Luke 14:8-11).

to shame? (25:8).

If you rush to sue or accuse, even if you have seen it with your own eyes, your perception and interpretation of what you saw may turn out to be wrong. Moreover, when the person is your neighbor or someone close to you, it is necessary and wise to think prudently and reconsider.

What is seen phenomenologically may be a part of reality. Just because you see something doesn't mean it's accurate and real. If you exaggerate or distort what you perceive, it can be very hurtful to the other person. You will be also humiliated. So we need to be careful not to be hasty and impulsive in our relationships.

If you take your neighbor to court [argue your case with a neighbor], do not betray another's confidence, or the one who hears it may shame you and the charge against you will stand [you will never lose your bad reputation] (25:9-10).

This proverb can be connected to verse 8. Verse 8 is a proverb about not deciding and proceeding with a lawsuit hastily. Verse 9, on the other hand, tells us that if we do decide to sue, we should not reveal the weaknesses or secrets of others in order to defend ourselves in court.

It is selfish and antisocial to divulge the other's secrets to further your own interests during a defense. If your acquaintances happen to see your unethical behavior, you will be branded as untrustworthy. Even if you win the case by exposing your opponent's weaknesses, it is foolish to lose a lot to gain a little.

Counseling Application: This proverb can be applied to counselors' ethics of keeping confidentiality. It is a violation of counseling ethics to quote counseling contents in a sermon or seminar without the client's permission. Realistically speaking, you can't compulsively ask permission from clients every time you use a counseling story. If you must use them, you must be sensitive and considerate enough to adapt them in an educational setting and in a way that fully protects the client's identity.

Like apples of gold in settings of silver is a ruling rightly given [A word aptly spoken is like apples of gold in settings of silver] (25:11).[397]

Solomon well uses analogies to educate the listener. Verses 11-14, 18-20, 23, 25-26 start with "Like…." When words "like golden apples on a silver platter" is uttered, it's an art. Silver apples on a golden platter don't look good. If you put rotten apples on a silver tray, it would look ridiculous. Conversely, golden apples on a low-quality, chipped plate would also look out of place. Likewise, it's not easy to say the right things at the right time, in the right way, and in the right context.

We need to meditate on the words of Paul's exhortation to the church in Colossae: "Let your conversation be always full of grace, seasoned with salt, so that you may know how to answer everyone" (Col. 4:6). To elaborate his exhortation, first, let your speech always be full of grace. Words full of grace are life-giving and empowering to the other person. Second, when you're having a conversation, speak with words well seasoned with salt. It's not good to be too salty and to be little salty. In order to season your speaking good enough, you need to put yourself in the other person's shoes and be considerate.

Counseling Application: Speaking with a fitting answer and an insightful answer at the right moment is a communication skill every counselor wants to have. If counselors can say something like golden apple on a silver platter once or twice in every session, they will be excellent counselors. Responding at the right time, at the right level, and with the right words is an art. "Magic" words that combine the right choice of words with sincerity, genuine expression, and empathy are fantastic. The client will feel understood, empowered and motivated to change.

---

[397] Bridges mentioned that this proverb is connected to 10:32a: "The lips of the righteous know what finds favor." Bridges, *Proverbs*, 468.

Like an earring of gold or an ornament of fine gold is the rebuke of a wise judge [a wise man's rebuke] to a listening ear (25:12).

Solomon uses an analogy of an earring of gold or an ornament of fine gold in this proverb. We can understand this proverb in four ways. First, the rebuke of a wise person and a listening ear are a golden combination. As the text says, it's a combination that fits together like a gold ring around an obedient ear. Or, as verse 11 puts it, it's like golden apples on a silver platter.

Second, when the rebuke of a wise person is combined with a disobedient ear, the rebuke is ineffective. Rather, the rebuke may cause the other person with a disobedient ear to respond with anger. In fact, Pharisees and the scribes who heard Jesus' rebuke sought to kill him with anger and jealousy.

Third, it is a thankful thing when the rebuke of the unwise is combined with an obedient ear. Those who can bear and digest the reproof that is crude and clumsy, are truly mature.

Fourth, when the reproof of the unwise meets a disobedient ear, both are foolish. The one who gives ineffective reproof is foolish, and so is the other who is unable to digest it.

Like a snow-cooled drink [Like the coolness of snow] at harvest time is a trustworthy messenger to the one who sends him; he refreshed the spirit of his master (25:13).

A king will feel secure and confident if he has an envoy who understands and can speak for him (13b). A president who relies on a trusted ambassador to deliver a message will be secure and confident. Solomon uses the metaphor of "a snow-cooled drink in the harvest."[398] When it's hot, a bowl of ice-cold water or a cup of cold coffee will refresh us. So a trustworthy messenger is like this

[398] Fox notes that the time of harvest in this proverb seems to be the wheat and barley harvest of May through June, as in Ruth 2:23. Fox, *Proverbs 10-31*, 783.

to his or her sender.

Paul had these "loyal messengers" who could deliver his letters and convey his feelings to the church members in Asia Minor.[399] Jesus Christ was a faithful and loyal messenger of God the Father. He was a loyal proclaimer of the gospel who told all that he had heard from the Father. He was one hundred percent discerning and obedient to the will of God the Father. Likewise, Jesus asked his disciples and believers to be loyal messengers, preaching, teaching, and exhorting the gospel. Those who obey his commands are pleasing to the Lord.

Counseling Application: Christian counselors should be messengers of the gospel of Jesus who can refresh the spirit of their master. When they are renewed in their mind, they will be able to discern "what God's will is—his good, pleasing and perfect will" (Rom. 12:2b).

Like clouds and wind without rain is the one who boasts of gifts never given (25:14).

Some clouds and winds bring rain, while others do not. We also need clouds and winds that don't bring rain. Clouds are beautiful to look at and cool us down. However, the "clouds and wind without rain" in the text are clouds and wind as a precursor to rain. Especially in a drought, people get excited when they see clouds that look like they're going to rain, but when they disappear without dropping any rain, it's even more disheartening.

In the same way, when a person promises to give a gift and makes the other's heart buoyed up, but does not follow through with that gift, the other person is left feeling manipulated and deceived.

---

[399] These include Timothy, Barnabas, Priscilla and Aquila ("They risked their lives for me," Rom. 16:4), Stephanas, Fortunatus and Achaicus ("Because they have supplied what was lacking from you. For they refreshed my spirit and yours also. Such men deserve recognition," 1 Cor. 16:17-18), Epaphroditus ("My brother, co-worker and fellow soldier, who is also your messenger, whom you sen to take care of my needs," Phil. 2:25), and Tychicus ("Tychicus will tell you all the news about me. He is a dear brother, a faithful minister and fellow servant in the Lord," Col. 4:7).

When the promises made by candidates during the election season end up as empty promises, peoples feel betrayed and deceived. These politicians are like clouds and wind without rain.

In our relationship with God, we often make promises and fail to keep them. The Israelites repeatedly promised in vain that they would follow God as their only bridegroom and worship him. In that regard, they were like clouds and wind without rain. They repeatedly disappointed God and provoked him to anger.

Through patience a ruler can be persuaded, and a gentle tongue can break a bone (25:15).

This proverb emphasizes a need for patience in dealing with decision-makers or approving authorities. A good official or ruler is considerate of the people who bring complaints to him and expedites matters. But an evil official or ruler is self-centered and unable to empathize with the people who ask justice to be done. They often delay deliberately the process. Those who are powerless have no choice but to be patient. However, if they don't give up and keep in touch again and again, even evil officials will likely be persuaded (15a).

When Jesus taught about prayer, he told the parable of a widow who was persistently appealing to a wicked official. He said that even though he was wicked, he would listen to her, because her persistent behavior was troublesome to him. Jesus argued, "Will not God bring about justice for his chosen ones, who cry out to him day and night? Will he keep putting them off? I tell you, he will see that they get justice and quickly" (Luke 18:7-8).

The proverb in the text expresses a paradoxical truth: a soft tongue, a meek tongue, can break bones. Bones are strong, but the tongue is weak, and yet the weak one breaks and crushes the strong one. There's a similar saying, "The pen is mightier than the sword." Bones can break, but a tongue is flexible and boneless and cannot break. No matter how much you twist it, it will bleed, but it won't break.

The implication of the metaphor of a tongue is that speaking gently and generously can open the door to even the most hardened of hearts. Solomon recommends patience here. Even the proud and stiff-necked have a potential to be persuaded if they are treated with patience.

However, it's very hard to put this into practice. In most interpersonal relationships, when the other person has an overbearing attitude, it's easy for us to get angry, to raise our voice, to stiffen our face, and to give up after a few tries. We need wisdom to remember this proverb and respond with patience in difficult relationships.

If you find honey, eat just enough—too much of it, and you will vomit (25:16). See 24:13.

This proverb means that too much of a good thing is not good for us. Honey is a natural food that is rich in nutrients and has a sweet flavor. Jonathan found natural honey in battle, dipped his staff in it, ate a little bit, and his eyes were brightened and his strength was recovered. John the Baptist's staple food was locusts and wild honey. Anyway, in a world of suffering, honey brings comfort and joy to those who eat it. It provides energy.

However, eating too much honey can cause one to vomit. One vomits because honey is no longer beneficial to the body. Similarly, something good is not beneficial if it is used or eaten in excess, which is why Solomon advises us to "eat just enough."

To eat too much honey means that one is greedy. Greed, whether in eating or in possessions, is not beneficial to our body and soul.

Eating honey in moderation can be applied to our sexual life. Sex is sweet, fun, and pleasurable, but too much of it can throw our lives out of balance and harm our health. It can lead to sex addiction. It's important to keep in mind the truth of moderation. A mature person has the wisdom to be self-sufficient and maintain balance.

Seldom set foot in your neighbor's house—too much of you,

419

and they will hate you (25:17).

This proverb can be connected to verse 16. The issue is an "excess." Eating honey in moderation is good for the body. It is beneficial and good to go to and from your neighbor's house in moderation. But going to your neighbor's house "often" is not beneficial. Solomon says this is because "they will hate you."

It is too extreme to be disconnected with our neighbors. But it's also extreme to be too open. The boundaries between your home and your neighbor's home should be differentiated. Even within a house, boundaries should be respected between husband and wife and between parents and children. Frequent visits with neighbors can have both good and bad effects. If they come over when you want to rest, you'll feel burdensome and even angry. Our human hearts are contradictory. On the one hand, we want to get along well with our neighbors, but on the other hand, we also want to keep our distance from them.

There are some people who are hated and disliked by their neighbors, but they keep visiting them without sense. They are psychologically young. They have a poor ability to empathize with the other person.

Like a club or a sword or a sharp arrow is one who gives false testimony against a neighbor (25:18).

Verses 18, 19, and 20 are characterized by the use of analogies to describe their meanings metaphorically. Solomon warns us to be wary of those who show aggression in their relationships with their neighbors. Unfortunately, there are some people who bear false witness to harm their neighbors. They don't hear the voice of the superego or their superego is not functioning at all. They are like those who use offensive weapons cowardly: hitting on the back of the head with a club, stabbing sneakily with a knife, or shooting a sharp arrow from hidden places.[400]

---

[400] Bridges made a good point that the weapons described in this proverb are all

To crucify Jesus, the priests and Pharisees set up false witnesses. Their tongues were like sharp arrows and sharp swords. The men who came to arrest Jesus were actually armed with swords and clubs.

God takes false witness against one's neighbor seriously. In the ninth commandment of the Ten Commandments, he explicitly warned, "You shall not give false testimony against your neighbor" (Ex. 20:16).

Like a broken tooth or a lame foot is reliance on the unfaithful in a time of trouble (25:19).

The untruthful or unfaithful are not to be trusted. Moreover, to rely on them in times of trouble is like a broken tooth or a lame foot.[401]

Some people trust and rely on unfaithful people and are betrayed. These are usually codependents. They are foolish people who have low self-esteem and are swayed by a few words from an unfaithful person, only to be manipulated or betrayed again.

Like one who takes away a garment on a cold day or like vinegar poured on a wound [soda], is one who sings songs to a heavy heart (25:20).

Verse 18 speaks metaphorically of people who strike their neighbors and bear false witness, and verse 19 speaks metaphorically of trusting in the unfaithful in a day of trouble. Now verse 20 speaks metaphorically of singing to the

murderous weapons. False witness is a sin comparable to murder. Bridges, *Proverbs*, 473.

[401] Bridges commented that a broken tooth and a lame foot are not only incapacitating, but also painful and uncomfortable. Bridges, *Proverbs*, 474. Relying on an unreliable person is a foolish act that invites suffering.

brokenhearted.

Singing to a brokenhearted person or a person with a heavy heart is ambivalent. The text emphasizes the negative side. If you sing joyful songs without empathizing with the brokenhearted, it's like taking off their clothes on a cold day, or like pouring vinegar on a wound (20b).

It's cruel to strip someone of his or her clothes on a cold day. Unempathetic actions or words cause deeper wounds to people whose hearts already have been broken.

Although this is not what the text means, if we interpret the act of singing in a positive light, a well-chosen song can be therapeutic for the brokenhearted. Singing hymns, especially those that are appropriate to the situation, is a great way to heal a broken heart. A folk song from a bygone era can have a therapeutic effect on someone who feels like crying. David used to sing for King Saul, playing his lyre whenever Saul was afflicted by an evil spirit. The music of the lyre surprisingly caused the evil spirit to leave and his symptoms to improve.

If your enemy is hungry, give him food to eat; if he is thirsty, give him water to drink. In doing this, you will heap burning coals on his head, and the LORD will reward you (25:21-22). See also 20:22; 24:29.

Old Testament law prescribes the principle of "an eye for an eye and a tooth for a tooth" as a way to implement justice in relationships. It doesn't necessarily mean retaliation, but rather teaches that compensation should be made in proportion to the harm done. Solomon's advice in this proverbs is aligned with the spirit of New Testament in that it goes beyond the rules of the law. It specifically mentions the ways of loving our enemies.

Feeding our enemies when they are hungry and giving them a drink of water when they are thirsty are concrete acts of loving our enemies. If our enemy's ox or donkey is carrying a load and collapses from exhaustion, we are not to leave it there but help them (see Ex. 23:4-5).

"The Lord will reward you" (22b) not only means that God will repay our enemies, but also that he will compensate us for our losses, wounds, and pain.[402] Furthermore, it means that God will reward us for our expressions of love toward our enemies.

Like a north wind that brings unexpected rain is a sly tongue— which provokes a horrified look [As a north wind brings rain, so a sly tongue brings angry looks] (25:23).

The devil has a sly tongue; his tongue is cunning. The devil tempted Eve with his sly tongue to stir up anger in her heart. By saying, "For God knows that when you eat from it your eyes will be opened, and you will be like God, knowing good and evil" (Gen. 3:5), he made her suspect as if God had deceived Adam and Eve. The deadly sins of greed, gluttony, pride, anger, and jealousy were at work in Eve's heart.

Counseling Application: Sneaky, accusing words can act as a stimulus and result in an emotional response of anger (S-R model). However, the response can vary depending on the maturity of the organism interpreting the stimulus (S-O-R model). If the frontal lobe of the brain interprets the information to dismiss or overlook the stimulus as trivial, the intensity and frequency of anger will decrease.

Better to live on a corner of the roof than share a house with a quarrelsome wife (25:24). See also 19:13; 21:9; 21:19; 27:15.

It would be very painful to live with a spouse who reacts aggressively to every little thing and provokes arguments, not just for a day or two, but for a lifetime. Therefore, this proverb means that it is better to live alone in a cottage than to live in a large

---

[402] Paul quotes Deut. 32:35 in Rom. 12:19: "For it is written: 'It is mine to avenge; I will repay,' says the Lord."

423

house with such a spouse. The idea is that it's better to live alone in an attic or under the eaves where one can get out of the rain.

Marital conflicts are an inevitable reality of marriage. When two people with different upbringings, different personalities, and different sexes live together as a couple, the potential for conflict is inevitable. However, if your spouse has a personality disorder with uncontrolled anger that leads to extreme verbal and physical violence, you may seriously consider living alone.

Violence in marriage can destroy one's self-esteem and damage one's mental health. In severe cases, it can be fatal. Both a perpetrator and a victim of domestic violence often don't realize the severity of the problem. Therefore, a spouse who is constantly subjected to physical violence needs a safe and secure place to go, such as a state-run shelter. He or she may also need to seek legal action to keep the abusive spouse away from him or her. Marital violence is a serious sin that destroys one's image of God. The covenant of a marriage in which violence takes place regularly already has been broken, even if the couple is still legally married.

Like cold water to a weary soul is good news from a distant land (25:25).

This proverb connects to verse 13 in the same chapter. For those who are waiting for good news, good news is like an oasis found by a thirsty and weary person.[403] Moreover, good news that comes "from a distant land" will bring even more joy to those who wait to hear. News from a distant land takes a long time to arrive, which makes them impatient. They become impatient because they doesn't know whether the news will be good or bad and when the news will arrive. But when the good news finally arrives, they will be glad and happy, knowing that all their works of waiting have not been in vain.[404]

[403] Bridges gave examples of biblical events in which thirsty people actually experienced the cold water they needed: Hagar and Ishmael's discovery of a spring of water while wandering in the wilderness, the Israelites finding water at Rephidim, and Samson finding water at Lehi. Bridges, *Proverbs*, 480.

All human beings outside of Jesus are spiritually thirsty and dying. The news that eternal life is available through Jesus Christ, the one who came from heaven with good news, is the gospel itself. Jesus Christ is the good news. The news that the way of salvation has been opened through Jesus is good news, like cold water, to all those who are bound to die because of sin. The word of God to the Israelites, who were dying from the bites of venomous snakes, that whoever looks at the bronze snake that was put up on a pole will live, was a representation of Jesus' salvation on the cross (see Num. 21:8-9, John 3:14-15).

Like a muddied spring or a polluted well are the righteous who give way to the wicked (25:26).

Like verse 25, verse 26 is a proverb expressed in the metaphor of "A is like B." Both verses 25 and 26 are connected by the use of water as a metaphor.[405] If the righteous give in to the wicked, it is as if wells and springs become polluted and muddied. A polluted well cannot be used. A world in which the righteous must yield to the wicked is not worthy of existence because it is too evil to live in.

Christians are to live lives of righteousness in the world.[406] We must live in awareness of our missions as salt and light, despite our shortcomings and limitations. If we give up our faith and values

---

[404] Deborah and Barak described in their hymn how the mother of Sisera, the military minister of Jabin, king of Canaan, anxiously awaited the news of victory that her son would bring her: "Through the window peered Sisera's mother; behind the lattice she cried out, 'Why is his chariot so long in coming? Why is the clatter of his chariots delayed?'" (Judg. 5:28). But the news she had to hear was shocking: Jael, the wife of Hebel the Gennite, had driven the stake holding the tabernacle in place into Sisera's temple, killing him.

[405] Fox makes this point well. Fox, *Proverbs 10-31*, 790.

[406] Bridges contrasted this proverb with 10:11: "The mouth of the righteous is a fountain of life, but the mouth of the wicked conceals violence." Bridges, *Proverbs*, 481. When the righteous yield to the wicked, the fountain of life will become a fountain of bitter water.

because we are overwhelmed by the evil forces of the world, we are like a polluted spring. We become like salt that has lost its functions. It has no useful value and is thrown away and trodden underfoot.

The leading figures of the Reformation did not cower in the face of the wicked. Jan Hus did not cower in the face of the threat of burning at the stake. He lived by his life's motto: "Speak the truth, love the truth, and defend the truth." Martin Luther did the same. Like Ezekiel's vision of the water from the temple forming a great river and reviving all kinds of fruit trees, they were reformers like wells and springs, restoring and purifying the streams of Christian truth.

Why do the righteous bow down before the wicked? There are several reasons. First, they are afraid. The wicked will do whatever it takes to win. They skillfully use appeasement, intimidation, deception, and trickery. Second, the wicked are in the majority. They often have power. They push through with force, numbers, and even laws. Third, the life of the persecuted is painful to endure. It seems better to compromise and live in moderation.

God honors those who are persecuted for the sake of righteousness and the kingdom of God. He actively encourages us to rejoice when we are persecuted.[407] At first, the wicked may prosper and the righteous may suffer and be ignored, but God approves of the ways of the righteous. The wicked will be defeated and face eternal judgment.

Secularization is a symptom of a dirty well. When believers and churches go down the path of secularization, they lose their identity and value and what it means to be a church. Jesus does not recognize this kind of church. He says, "Because you are lukewarm—neither hot nor cold—I am about to spit you out of my mouth" (Rev. 3:16) and urges, "Those whom I love I rebuke and discipline. So be earnest and repent" (Rev. 3:19).

---

[407] When they had no other alternative but to release the apostles who had proclaimed the gospel before the members of the Sanhedrin, they had them flogged and ordered "not to speak in the name of Jesus, and let them go." The apostles rejoiced "because they had been counted worthy of suffering disgrace for the Name" (Acts 5:40, 41).

It is not good to eat too much honey, nor is it honorable to search out matters that are too deep [to seek one's own honor] (25:27). See 25:16.

The proverbial saying goes that too much honey is not good and even good things are bad in excess. This proverb reiterates the proverb in verse 16 of the same chapter.

Verse 16 connects honey with health, whereas this proverb connects honey with honor. Both honey and honor are good things. It is good to seek our honor. Those who dishonor themselves are foolish. However, excessive pursuit of our own honor is not good, just as excessive consumption of honey is not good. Excessive honor-seeking can result in "vomiting."

If you seek your own honor too much, you become narcissistic and histrionic. You become overly influenced by other people's feedback or attention. If your honor is suddenly damaged, your life can fall apart. You may take your own life. You may end up with dishonor.

Like a city whose walls are broken through [down] is a person who lacks self-control (25:28).[408]

This proverb is also metaphorical. Solomon compares people who lack self-control to a city wall that is broken down. A city with broken walls is vulnerable to attack.[409] It can be attacked at any time. It can't protect itself. It can't defend its own boundaries.

Self-control is the last of the nine fruits of the Holy Spirit. Believers who are controlled by the Holy Spirit are able to control

---

[408] Bridges mentioned that this proverb is connected to 16:32: "Better a patient person than a warrior, one with self-control than one who takes a city." Bridges, Proverbs, 483.

[409] Walls have a defensive function. They keep the inhabitants of a city safe from outside invasion. It's a boundary that separates the outside from the inside and that confirms a sense of identity of the city.

themselves appropriately. In particular, they can control their sinful desires. They can control their aggressive speech. They can control the power of their tongue. It will be difficult for the devil to attack these believers because their walls are strong enough.

Counseling Application: A function of ego is to govern and control one's mind and heart. The ego is the master of the world of mind. When the ability to properly coordinate and control multiple desires and numerous conflicts is weakened, it means that the ego is disturbed. In severe cases, it leads to psychosis in which the boundary that differentiates reality from unreality is blurred. In severe cases, a person is vulnerable to demonic attacks, that can lead to demon possession.

Chapter 26 The Foolish and the Lazy

Like snow in summer or rain in harvest, honor is not fitting for a fool (26:1).

Verses 1 through 12 of chapter 26 are a series of proverbs that give specific instruction about the foolish. Verses 13 through 16 are proverbs that characterize the lazy.

Verse 1 is a proverb expressed in metaphor. Snow in the summer or heavy rain in the harvest is not only incompatible, but also not beneficial. Likewise, honor for the foolish is not only incompatible, but also not beneficial. When honor is given to fools, they cannot handle it. Especially, the devil is not worthy of honor and respect. Eternal judgment suits him. Honor befits the wise and the faithful. Honor, glory, and power befit God.

Like a fluttering sparrow or a darting swallow, an undeserved curse does not come to rest (26:2).

Unmerited curses are like sparrows and swallows flying away, meaning that unmerited curses have no effect, even if a person utters them.[410] So if you hear undeserved curses or hurtful words, you don't have to give them any power at all. You can dismiss them as the barking of a dog. It's like watching sparrows and swallows fly away. You see them for a moment, but you don't know to where they are flying, and you don't need to know it.

Verses 1 through 12 are proverbs about the foolish, and only verse 2 does not specify the word "foolish." However, the context suggests that those who curse without reasons are fools. Fools may curse and swear in all kinds of ways, but their words have no effect and power. They themselves are foolish.

---

[410] Bridges nicely put it that the curse of Goliath to David and the curse of Shimei to David were curses scattered to the winds. Bridges, *Proverbs*, 485.

People with schizophrenia often swear and curse to themselves through auditory hallucinations. These words have no effect. They don't come true.

One of the typical symptoms of the demon possessed in the region of Gerasa was the behavior of shouting "night and day among the tombs and in the hills" and cutting himself with stones (Mark 5:5). The content of his crying out day and night must have been curses. He would curse at the top of his voice without realizing what he was saying. His tongue would move as the demon commanded, and he would utter unwanted curses. But the sounds had no effect; they only vibrated the air around the tombs and in the hills where he was staying. He was a poor fool and a foolish man. Finally, Jesus came to heal him and made him whole. Amazingly, he became the first Gentile missionary.

To curse a person who bears the image of God is demonic, for it does not edify the hearer. It is destructive speech that wounds the other person's heart.

Originally, curses belong to God. God has the authority and power to bless and curse. Idols cannot bless, nor can they curse. There are no consequences even if they curse, for they have no life or power. Likewise, the curses of those who curse unjustly and without reasons can cause no consequences. So there is no need to give them power and become bound by them. There is no need at all to listen to the negative warnings of a soothsayer or fortune teller. These are just words to frighten you into compulsive bondage. Those who believe in Jesus have been set free in the truth. We are the Lord's children whether we live or die.

Counseling Application: Some clients are those who have been suffering from the traumatizing effects of being cursed by a parent or someone close to them growing up. When they experience difficulties or low self-esteem, the words of the curse are recalled and reinforced. They have foolishly internalized the curse and digested it as part of who they are. Christian counselors must neutralize the power of these curses in the counseling process. By identifying the sound, content, and facial expression of the internalized objects, that is, curses, and redefining them as "the barking of a mad dog," the counselor can neutralize and "exorcise" them. The counselor must identify the curse as a problem of the cursing person, not the cursed person. The client needs to recognize that the curse has become a "foothold" for the devil to exploit him or her.

A whip for the horse, a bridle for the donkey, and a rod for the backs of fools! (26:3).[411]

The devices used to control horses and donkeys are the bridle and the whip. The bridle acts as a brake and the whip as an accelerator. Horses are much smarter than fools. The fool needs the bridle and whip even more.

Do not answer a fool according to his folly, or you yourself will be just like him (26:4).

The foolish speak foolishly because they are foolish. They say hurtful things because they don't empathize with the other person. They don't know how to speak wisely and empathetically.

If you respond to the words of a fool one by one, the conversation is bound to go sideways. It is foolish to argue with fools by giving meaning or power to their words. If you continue to argue with them, you become foolish like them.

Abigail, the wise wife of Nabal whose name meant "a fool," did not speak to or discuss anything with him in the crisis situation. She resolved the crisis by going directly to David and doing and saying things that helped David's heart to be soothed. If she had tried to persuade Nabal, who was in a drunken stupor, the conversation would not have worked. After reconciling with David, she was wise enough to tell her husband the next morning what she had been holding back. She was in a conjugal relationship

---

[411] Fox rightly points out that the second half of this verse and the second half of 10:13 and the second half of 19:29 are almost identical: "A rod is for the back of one who has no sense" (10:13b); "Beatings for the backs of fools" (19:29b). Fox, *Proverbs 10-31*, 792.

with Nabal but she was not in the least affected by his foolishness. It is too bad that the foolish Nabal was so little influenced by his wise wife.[412]

Answer a fool according to his folly, or he will be wise in his own eyes (26:5).

This proverb has the opposite meaning of verse 4. It tells us to answer fools according to their levels of foolishness. For children, children's level of communication is appropriate. To fools, we must answer at the level of fools for them to understand.

Jesus said, "Do not give dogs what is sacred; do not throw your pearls to pigs. If you do, they may trample them under their feet, and turn and tear you to pieces" (Matt. 7:6). Dogs and pigs are happy when we give them food. If we give them something holy or precious, they will ignore it and attack us because they don't know it's valuable and because we did not give what they want. When we understand them at the level of dogs or pigs, their behavior is natural, because all they need is food.

Counseling Application: In Transactional Analysis (TA), the ego is understood in three parts. They are Parent, Adult, and Child parts. In interpersonal relationships, when one person speaks at the Child part, there are three possibilities for the other person to respond: at the Parent part, at the Adult part, or at the Child part. Which response will be appropriate depends on the appropriateness of the interacting situation. For example, when you speak at a Child level, you may want the other person to respond at a Parent level. In some cases, you may want him or her to respond objectively and wisely at an Adult level. In other cases, you may just want him or her to laugh and enjoy with you at a Child level. If we apply this understanding to the proverb of verse 5, a response at

---

[412] Nabal is very much like Mr. Badman, the main character in John Bunyan's devotional novel *Journey to Hell*. His wife was a very pious person who died before him. But he died later without digesting her religious influences and ended up going to hell.

a Child level would be the only acceptable response for fools. If we respond from a Parent part or an Adult part, they're likely to get annoyed or angry.

Sending a message by the hands of a fool is like cutting off one's feet or drinking poison [drinking violence] (26:6). See also 25:13.

Choosing a childlike fool as a messenger and entrusting him or her with a mission is a "self-defeating behavior," like cutting off one's own arm or foot.[413] The problem is not with the fool, but with the one who entrusts the fool. If a king sends a foolish person as a messenger, the king is even more foolish than the foolish messenger.

It goes without saying that an ambassador or messenger who carries a king's message must be wise. He or she must convey the king's intentions to the other king or nation with precision and wisdom.[414] Such a person will refresh the king's spirit (see 25:13b).

Paul was a faithful messenger, called by Jesus Christ to be an apostle to the Gentiles. He was an apostle and messenger who was well-versed in the Old Testament law and had an accurate knowledge and faith in the truth of the gospel. He was a man who refreshed Jesus' heart.

Like the useless legs of one who is lame [Like a lame man's legs that hang limp] is a proverb in the mouth of a fool. Like tying a

---

[413] When young children are running errands for their parents, they often don't remember everything their parents have asked them to do, which leads to poorly executed errands. This is understandable. Children are vulnerable to anxiety and have a limited memory. It's their psychological traits that if they see something that distracts them in the way to do an errand, they forget about their errands.

[414] If the king's chosen messengers change what he wants to convey, or if they tampered with the message, they will cause the king fatal harm. Such people are wicked messengers.

stone in a sling is the giving of honor to a fool. Like a thornbush in a drunkard's hand is a proverb in the mouth of a fool (26:7-9).

Verses 7, 8, and 9 are interconnected proverbs. Verses 7 and 9 use different metaphors to describe the proverbs that come out of the mouth of the foolish. Verses 7 and 9 form a sentence structure that wraps around verse 8.

In verse 8, Solomon describes giving honor to the foolish as being like tying a stone to a sling (see verse 1). But the meaning of verse 8 is not clear. One possible interpretation is that honor and foolishness soon become irrelevant, just as a stone in a sling quickly flies away and is no longer visible. Verse 8 in *Darby Bible Translation* is translated that "As a bag of gems in a stoneheap, so is he that gives honor to a fool."

The foolish may think they are wise, so they may speak their own philosophies and proverbs of life. But these are a senseless and rubbish philosophy. They are actually foolish words. The problem is that they think their senseless and rubbish philosophies are nice ones.

The thoughts and words of philosophers and wise people of the world are senseless and rubbish before the wisdom of God. Their thoughts are as weak as "useless legs" (7a). The so-called proverbs that come from the mouth of the foolish are like the ramblings of a drunkard. When drunkards sober up, they don't remember what they said in drunkenness. They just pretended to be smart for a while. In drunkenness, they say things they can't say when they are sober. In the worst cases, the drunkard will take a thornbush in his hand and swing it wildly to hurt their family (9a). There are some fathers who drink late at night, come home drunk, and wake up their children, who are already sleeping, and give them long speeches as if they want to admonish them. These admonitions are not proverbs. They are words that only hurt their children's hearts. Their repetitive words only torture their children.

In fact, the mouth of a fool and proverbs do not go together. You cannot expect fools to speak wise words. They should know this reality, but they don't.

Like an archer who wounds at random is one who hires a fool
or any passer-by(26:10).

Hiring a fool or a passerby is like shooting arrows at random. A
random arrow seldom hits the target. It's not impossible to hire a
good, if not great, employee by asking a passerby to be your
employee. But it's a foolish move with a lot of risk. It's a gamble to
take a chance on some persons without references, without
knowing their personalities, and without knowing their
backgrounds.

Despite the meaning of this proverb, the kingdom of God is not
like the kingdoms of the world in that it calls and hires the foolish,
the crippled, the sick, the poor, those without backgrounds, the
strangers, and those workers employed late in the marketplace. In
the world, it is common sense and wisdom to hire people who have
a clear identity, good credentials, and skills. But the kingdom of
God is very paradoxical. It is a kingdom that gives grace to those
who are sinful, broken, unskilled, and unattractive, and calls them
to be born again and serve God with passion. This was exemplified
in the way Jesus called the people of Galilee to be his apostles.

As a dog returns to its vomit, so fools repeat their folly (26:11).[415]

This proverb is quoted in part from 2 Peter 2:22, which says "Of
them the proverbs are true: 'A dog returns to its vomit,' and, 'A
sow that is washed returns to her wallowing in the mud'." The
foolish are those who "have escaped the corruption of the world
by knowing our Lord and Savior Jesus Christ and are again
entangled in it and are overcome" and who "are worse off at the
end than they were at the beginning" (2 Pet. 2:20).

Not all dogs eat what they vomit. Some untrained dogs eat their

---

[415] Fox mentions that this proverb is linked to 23:35: "When will I wake up so I can find
another drink?" Fox, *Proverbs 10-31*, 796.

own vomit again. Some dogs, so-called "biscuit eaters," may even eat their own feces. This is because they've experienced a wrong learning. However, there are some dogs that are wiser than fools. They are loyal, disciplined, and even empathize with their owners.

The dogs in the text are likened compatibly to fools. These dongs foolishly eat back the disgusting things they have vomited up. The same is true of the foolish. They are foolish in the sense that they repeat foolish behaviors.

Poor behaviors can be associated to what psychologists call "abnormal behaviors." People with personality disorders are psychologically underdeveloped. In that sense, they are immature and foolish to some extent. The main characteristic of personality disorders is that they exhibit a repetitive and predictable pattern of behaviors and relationships. The fact that a foolish person does the same foolish thing over and over again indicates that foolishness has been ingrained in his or her personality (11b). So they predictably repeat the same mistakes and errors against their will.

Do you see a person wise in their own eyes? There is more hope for a fool than for them (26:12).

This proverb compares those who think they are wise to those who are foolish. In reality, those who consider themselves wise are also foolish. This is because they do not have the eyes to see themselves objectively. There is still some hope for a fool in comparison with those who think themselves that they are wise (12b). In reality, the foolish are not likely to change, so those who consider themselves wise are even more hopeless.[416]

The literary technique of this proverb ties in with Jesus' literary description of the cities where he did many miracles: "And you, Capernaum, will you be lifted to the heavens? No, you will go down to Hades. For if the miracles that were performed in you had been performed in Sodom, it would have remained to this day" (Matt. 11:23). The core issue with the people of Capernaum was

---

[416] Fox well points out that the same literary technique is found in 29:20: "Do you see someone who speaks in haste? There is more hope for a fool than for them." Fox, *Proverbs 10-31*, 797.

pride. They witnessed many of Jesus' wonders, but they did not repent. They were foolish people who thought they were wise.

The people of Sodom and Gomorrah were destroyed because they did not have ten righteous persons. They were proud and violent. It is very likely that they would not have repented if Jesus preached the gospel to them because they were proud and self-centered. They were the ones who responded to Lot's counsel by saying, "This fellow came here as a foreigner, and now he wants to play the judge! We'll treat you worse than them" (Gen. 19:9). Thus Jesus was making the point by comparison that the people of Capernaum were much more stubborn than the people of Sodom. In reality, both Sodom and Capernaum were hopelessly unable to repent.

So we can see that Solomon's point is that both the foolish and those who consider themselves wise are without hope. But from a gospel perspective, there is still hope because all who have come to faith in Jesus were once foolish and thought themselves wise. Therefore, we still need to have hope for the foolish and those who think they are wise. The people of Israel were also foolish, more foolish than the ox or the donkey, and yet God did not give up on them completely (see Is. 1:3).

A sluggard says, "There's a lion in the road, a fierce lion roaming the streets!" (26:13).

Now verses 13 through 15 are about the lazy. This proverb is almost identical to the one in 22:13: "The sluggard says, There is a lion outside! I'll be killed in the public square!" You can see that excuses and rationalizations are the main defense mechanisms used by the lazy.

As a door turns on its hinges, as a sluggard turns on his bed. A sluggard buries his hand in the dish; he is too lazy to bring it back to his mouth (26:14-15). See 19:24.

Verse 14 describes a lazy person who rolls over in bed and doesn't get up. As expressed in other proverbs, the sluggard's motto in life is "A little sleep, a little slumber, a little folding of the hands to rest" (6:10). Children and adolescents who don't get out of bed until well past the time they are supposed to get up in the morning are difficult to diagnose as slothful because their ego is still in a developing stage. However, if some adults sleep late most days, they are slothful.

If the level of laziness is such that even eating food oneself is troublesome, one's problem is serious. Such persons will want others to scoop food into their mouth and later will be bothered to chew the food themselves.

Counseling Application: When people are depressed, they can't help but be lazy. They don't have the energy to go about their daily lives. If they are housewives, they can't cook, wash clothes, and clean properly. It's hard to take care of themselves. They don't shower or even brush their teeth. If they're Christians, they don't have the energy to sing or pray. They can't concentrate when they read the Bible.

However, depression can be reframed as a creative experience in a Christian's journey of life. Christian life does not always mean living a life full of energy and full of the Holy Spirit. For every uphill climb, there are also downs (see Eccl. 3:1-8).

For those who have been too busy, depression can be an unwanted brake that forces them to take stock of themselves. It helps them take a breath by putting a pause in their lives. It gives them a chance to reflect on themselves at nights they can't sleep. It also gives them a chance to distance themselves from eating, sleeping, and having fun unintentionally. This depression should be distinguished from laziness.

A sluggard is wiser in his own eyes than seven people who answer discreetly (26:16).

This proverbs is connected to verse 12, which says that there is hope for the foolish than for those who consider themselves wise.

The fool has energy for life. They can be zealous and diligent. But the lazy are unmotivated or less motivated. They may think but do not act. They build great walls with their thoughts. They even may have the illusion that the world will go their way (16b).

If some persons think they are wiser than "seven people who answer discreetly," they absolutely have a severe narcissistic personality disorder. Seven is a perfect number. If they think they're smarter and wiser than all the objectively wise and articulate people in the world, they're probably delusional. Persons with severe narcissistic personality disorder have a greatly inflated sense of self, like an overinflated balloon. People with narcissistic personality disorder and laziness are not directly related, but some lazy people have narcissistic personality disorder.

Like one who grabs a stray dog [a dog] by the ears is someone who rushes into a quarrel not their own (26:17).

This proverb does not endorse an individualism. Righteous persons who step in to stop a fight when one side is being beaten or threatened, even though it has nothing to do with them, are praised in society. They are praised because they have the courage and righteous indignation to intervene. If they intervene in an assault because they feel sympathy or anger at the sight of it, it is an act of love for their neighbor in need.[417]

"A passer-by" is an expression that also appeared in verse 10. The proverb in verse 10 warned of the foolishness of bringing in and hiring a passer-by, but this proverb warns of the foolishness of a passer-by intervening in a quarrel where there is no need for him or her to intervene. The analogy is grabbing a stray dog by the ears. It is foolish to intervene in a fight even when quarrelers are not

---

[417] When the Good Samaritan saw a Jew who had nothing to do with him mugged off and nearly killed, he didn't just pass by. He risked his life to help and save the man in need. Jesus called him a neighbor to the robbed man. In case of Moses, out of his righteous indignation he killed an Egyptian who was badly beating a Hebrew. He had to flee because of this incident and lived as an unknown shepherd for forty years before he was called by God.

asking for help and the quarrel is not serious. If you try to grab a stray dog by the ears, you are very likely to get bitten. Similarly, it's foolish to get involved in any fight without discernment. We need wisdom and knowledge enough to make a good association with and make a differentiation well in our daily activity and relationship.

Like a maniac shooting flaming arrows of death is one who deceives their neighbor and says, "I was only joking!" (26:18-19).

This proverb says that a person who deceives a neighbor and is caught saying, "I was just joking," is like a mad person who shoots a deadly arrow. It's like the behavior of a person with antisocial personality disorder who spreads an unsubstantiated rumor and then diminishes its meaning by saying, "I was just trying to be funny!" when exposed.

When persons with mental retardation or schizophrenia kill a person, there are limitations to holding them accountable for the crime of murder. Living around some people with a severe mental illness will make you nervous because you never know when they may do something wrong to you.[418] And if they do, it's hard to hold them accountable.

The problem is that there are real evil people who do evil act intentionally. They make up excuses to rationalize their evil behaviors. When they are caught, they say things that diminish their responsibility for their actions. Their father is the devil. The devil lies at will and takes no responsibility for his lies. He does not take responsibility for his lies because he will be judged in hell anyway.

---

[418] In the United States, there are cases of people who shoot indiscriminately because they cannot distinguish between their hallucinatory world and the real world. They may say they were trying to hunt an animal after shooting and killing a person. It is incredibly frustrating for the victims or their families to hear that they saw passers-by as wild animals.

Without wood a fire goes out; without a gossip a quarrel dies down (26:20).

If you don't add more wood to a fire, it will grow weaker until it finally goes out. Similarly, arguments and misunderstandings tend to diminish when there is no more gossips and rumors. So it is wise to wait patiently when there is an argument or misunderstanding. If you get impatient and start talking to resolve the misunderstanding, you may make a mistake and spread the flames.

However, it's not always wise to do so. In some cases, active intervention is the only way to clear up misunderstandings and defuse arguments. It is wisdom to discern when to intervene and when to wait.

As charcoal to embers and as wood to fire, so is a quarrelsome person for kindling strife (26:21).

This proverb has the same message with verse 20. Whereas verse 20 illustrates that not adding wood to a fire will put it out, this verse illustrates that adding wood to a fire will add fuel to the fire. If someone or the other person in an argument is a argumentative person, it's likely that the argument will turn into a big fight. Quarrelsome people start a big fire with just a small ember. You should be wary of such people.

James diagnosed the problem of a quarrelsome person as being in the tongue. Of course, the problem with the tongue is the problem with the heart. He expressed the destructive power of the tongue well: "The tongue is a small part of the body, but it makes great boasts. Consider what a great forest is set on fire by a small spark. The tongue also is a fire, a world of evil among the parts of the body. It corrupts the whole body, set the whole course of one's life on fire, and is itself set on fire by hell" (James 3:5-6).

The devil loves to quarrel, and he delights in destroying relationships by increasing strife and conflict. James points to the devil as the source of the tongue that causes contention: "But if you harbor bitter envy and selfish ambition in your hearts, do not boast about it or deny the truth. Such 'wisdom' does not come down from heaven but is earthly, unspiritual, demonic. For where you have envy and selfish ambition, there you find disorder and every evil practice" (James 3:14-16).

The words of a gossip are like choice morsels; they go down to the inmost parts (26:22). See also 18:8.

Solomon compares gossip to a delicious delicacy. If you eat something every day, you don't remember what you ate. But if it's special or delicious, the taste, smell, and even the circumstances of the meal are remembered for a long time. Similarly, words of rumor or gossip are easily entered into the mind and remembered for a long time (22b). Especially negative gossips stick in people's minds. We should be very careful about gossiping, recognizing that it can cause people to have misconceptions, prejudices, and preconceived notions for a long time.

It is irresponsible and anti-social to speak unnecessary words or unwarranted words. Furthermore, it is a devilish behavior that destroys people and relationships.

Whoever hears or spreads gossip that seems to be delicious like a delicacy is a fool. Moreover, those who preach heretical teachings that are like delicacies will be accursed, and people who listen to them and follow them are indeed fools.[419] Anything that is not truth and upright instruction should not be heard, even if it is tasted like a delicacy.

---

[419] Instead of listening to what they ought to hear, people in the last days prefer to listen to and follow myths: "For the time will come when people will not put up with sound doctrine. Instead, to suit their own desires, they will gather around them a great number of teachers to say what their itching ears want to hear. They will turn their ears away from the truth and turn aside to myths" (2 Tim. 4:3-4).

Like a coating of silver dross on earthenware are fervent lips with an evil heart (26:23).

It is deceitful to conceal an evil heart and soften words on the outside. It is like putting cheap silver on earthenware. The earthenware is better as it is, but if you put cheap silver on it, it is worth less than the earthenware.[420]

Enemies disguise themselves with their lips, but in their hearts they harbor deceit. Though their speech is charming, do not believe them, for seven abominations fill their hearts (26:24-25).

This proverb is connected with the previous verse 23. Solomon again cautions us to beware of lying lips. We need to beware of deceitful lips and deceitful words, for the hearts of the lying persons man are not like their lips.[421] Moreover, there are seven abominations in their hearts, that is, "all" kinds of abominable lies. And the seven deadly sins are in their hearts: pride, envy, anger, greed, gluttony, lust, wrath, and sloth. If we hear their lying words that sound charming, we are fools. Christians must live in this world as innocent as doves and as shrewd as snakes (see Matt. 10:16).[422]

If Hezekiah had taken this proverb to heart, he would not have failed. He failed to read the minds of the Babylonian envoys who came to congratulate him on his healing. In his excitement, he gave

---

[420] Bridges mentioned that this proverb is related to 10:20: "The tongue of the righteous is choice silver, but the heart of the wicked is of little value" Bridges, *Proverbs*, 497.

[421] Bridges well commented that Absalom's sitting at the gate of the city and stealing the hearts of the peoples is connected to this proverb. Bridges, *Proverbs*, 497. Fox connects this proverb to Ps. 55:21: "His talk is smooth as butter, yet war is in his heart; his words are more soothing than oil, yet they are drawn swords." Fox, *Proverbs 10-31*, 800.

[422] Bridges mentioned this lesson of Jesus in his application of this proverb. Bridges, *Proverbs*, 497.

away the nation's most important secrets. In the end, he became a foolish king who hastened Judah's destruction.

Their malice may be concealed by deception, but their wickedness will be exposed in the assembly (26:26).

People can hide and deceive evil thoughts and hearts from individuals. But they cannot deceive in the presence of the community. Therefore, discerning the evil one cannot be done alone. Falsehood and deception can only be exposed when discerned by a group of people. That's why we need a church community. We are much less likely to be deceived spiritually and relationally when we are involved with a congregation that has mentors and leaders who can counsel and advise us.

The advantage of being married is that you have a spouse to give you feedback so that you are less likely to be deceived. Your spouse's discernment can help you avoid being deceived. This can be connected to the proverb, "Though one may be overpowered, two can defend themselves. A cord of three strands is not quickly broken" (Eccl. 4:12).

Whoever digs a pit will fall into it; if someone rolls a stone, it will roll back on them (26:27).[423]

Evil people fall into a trap they set for themselves. Both the trap digger and the stone roller in this proverb are people with antisocial personality disorder. They want to harm others.

It's possible to gain short-term benefits from antisocial behaviors. In the moment, the behaviors or methods may seem to work. But

---

[423] Fox connected this proverb to Ps. 7:15-16: "Whoever digs a hole and scoops it out falls into the pit they have made. The trouble they cause recoils on them; their violence comes down on their own heads." Fox, *Proverbs 10-31*, 801.

such people are quickly destroyed. There comes a time when they fall into the trap they have set for themselves. For God, who watches over, judges them.

Haman set a trap to slaughter all the Jews. In particular, he built a high pole to hang Mordecai. But he soon found himself on the pole. God avenged the wicked actions of Haman.[424]

A lying tongue hates those it hurts, and a flattering mouth works ruin (26:28).[425]

This proverb is connected to verses 23-26. A flattering mouth is a lying mouth. A lying tongue that speaks differently from one's heart hides hatred and aggression (28a). Those who flatter actually have a heart to harm the other person. It is wisdom to be wary of flatterers.

---

[424] "God is a righteous judge, a God who displays his wrath every day. If he does not relent, he will sharpen his sword; he will bend and string his bow. He has prepared his deadly weapons; he makes ready his flaming arrows" (Ps. 7:11-13).

[425] Fox mentions that this proverb is connected to 29:10: "The bloodthirsty hate a person of integrity and seek to kill the upright." Fox, *Proverbs 10-31*, 801.

Chapter 27 Iron Sharpens Iron

Do not boast about tomorrow, for you do not know what a day may bring (27:1).

This proverb expresses an immutable truth that applies to all human beings. God created human beings not to know what will happen tomorrow. Solomon warns us not to be confident about tomorrow.[426]

Jesus warns us that we cannot be confident about tomorrow's life by telling the parable of the rich man who laid up crops enough to last for many years, was satisfied with himself, but died that night. When King Belshazzar was drinking with his nobles, drinking from gold and silver goblets taken from the Jerusalem temple, he saw the fingers of a human hand appear and write on the wall. Nobody read and interpret the meaning and Daniel was called and he read and interpreted it for him. The king was killed "that very night" (Dan. 5:30).

There is no need to boast about tomorrow, nor to be overly anxious about tomorrow. Faithfully living each day "here and now" is the wise life that all Christians should aim for.

Let someone else praise you, and not your own mouth; an outsider, and not your own lips (27:2).[427]

---

[426] Bridges cited James 4:13-14 as a relevant passage: "Why, you do not even know what will happen tomorrow. What is your life? You are a mist that appears for a little while and then vanishes" (4:14). Bridges, *Proverbs*, 500. The text can also be connected to Jesus' statement, "Therefore do not worry about tomorrow, for tomorrow will worry about itself. Each day has enough trouble of its own" (Matt. 6:34).

[427] Fox sees a connection between this proverb and 29:23: "Pride brings a person low, but the lowly in spirit gain honor." Fox, *Proverbs 10-31*, 803.

Bragging about one's appearance or accomplishments is a symptom of histrionic personality disorder. One's personality disorders suggest that he or she has problems in interpersonal relationships with others. To a certain extent, modern people would say that bragging is a good thing or okay, but in reality, it's not. Most people don't like those who are boastful. They feel sorry for them.

It's nice and thankful to be complimented by others naturally. But it's a symptom of histrionic personality disordered and foolishness for one to try to get others to brag about you. It's an embarrassing behavior that lets people know you're psychologically immature.

Stone is heavy and sand a burden, but a fool's provocation is heavier than both. Anger is cruel and fury overwhelming, but who can stand before jealousy? (27:3-4).

Large stones are heavy. A decent amount of sand is also heavy. Heavy things are hard to lift and hard to carry on your shoulders. Solomon describes dealing with the anger of the foolish as being more difficult than carrying heavy stones or heavy sand.

When the wise are angry, they are angry in a wise way. They can control the emotion of anger so it doesn't lead to destructive consequences. But when the foolish or persons with borderline personality disorder get angry, their rage is too much to handle. It hurts deeply. The anger and fury in this proverb are ones that the foolish express. Their consequences are brutal and hard to bear, like flood damages (4a).

The jealousy of the foolish is especially difficult for others to cope with. The envy and jealousy of people with a severe narcissistic personality disorder are murderous. Saul, who was jealous of David, tried to kill him many times. He tried to kill him by throwing spears at him. He even mobilized his army to go on a manhunt. He was, in effect, a fool. He was not able to discern him a loyal servant to him.

Better is open rebuke than hidden love. Wounds from a friend can be trusted, but an enemy multiplies kisses (27:5-6).

Hidden love is a kind of love that is done like relieving in secret. This hidden love is positive. However, open rebuke is better than hidden love (5a). Solomon describes that honest confrontation of one's friend may wound painfully at the moment but is better than hidden love. A friend's honest feedback is ultimately beneficial if digested well because it is based on trust and loyalty (6a).

Frequent kisses by the enemy, on the other hand, is a behavior that hides his or her aggression. When Judas Iscariot came to seize Jesus and kissed him, saying, "Greetings, Rabbi!" It was a signal to seize him, not a genuine kiss.[428]

One who is full loathes honey from the comb, but to the hungry even what is bitter tastes sweet (27:7).

No matter how delicious something is, a person with a full stomach can't eat anymore. But a hungry person enjoys even spoiled food. The prodigal son was hungry and wanted to fill his stomach with the pigs' food. A thirsty person enjoys drinking even dirty water.

We can apply this proverb to the realm of faith. Those who are satisfied and filled with God have the power to abhor the temptations of the world that taste as sweet as honey. They are already satisfied. On the other hand, those who feel lacking or unfulfilled in their relationship with God are unable to give up the temporary sweetness of sins, even though they know in their hearts that the consequences of sin are bitter. Such is the life of a person addicted to sin.

---

[428] Judas's behavior came from a defense mechanism called "reaction formation" to hide his anxiety. Reaction formation is a defense mechanism that involves being overly nice or overly asserting about an issue that one is actually related so that one's own issue may not be disclosed.

Like a bird that flees [strays from] its nest is anyone who flees from [strays from] home (27:8).

Most people have a hometown where they were born and raised. They have a family they belong to. But some people live without a hometown and without a family. Gypsies, wanderers, or strangers live and die without a home or homeland. Beggars or homeless people leave their homes and wander the streets, and then they die alone.

There are people who have a physical hometown or family, but have lost their emotional home. There are many modern people who live with their families under the same roof but are emotionally cut off from them.

Spiritually speaking, all those who live on this earth without a connection to the kingdom of God are the homeless. They have been expelled from the Garden of Eden. They live and die without spiritual roots. They are like birds that have lost their nest, wandering aimlessly and dying.

Heaven is the home and homeland of believers. It is "my home to return to." Soldiers who have a home and homeland to return to can die anytime and anywhere, because they will be buried in their homeland. Heaven is not where we will be buried, but where we will live with God forever. Although we live as strangers and aliens on this earth, the kingdom of God awaits us, where we will live forever as citizens of heaven. Hallelujah!

Perfume and incense bring joy to the heart, and the pleasantness of a friend springs from their heartfelt advice [earnest counsel] (27:9).

Odors stimulate the olfactory sense and trigger pleasant or unpleasant emotions and memories. The smell of delicious food or flowers makes us feel good. So there is a therapy called "scent therapy" or "aromatherapy." On the other hand, the smell of rotting food is even worse than the smell of feces, and it makes us feel disgusted.

This proverb says that earnest advice from a friend is like smelling a pleasant scent. This proverb is connected to verse 6. It's wise to be mindful of the fact that a friend's sincere rebuke and confrontation may be hard to hear and hurtful at first. At the same time, it is wise to remember that a friend's heartfelt counsel will eventually benefit and please you.

Do not forsake your friend or a friend of your family [the friend of your father], and do not go to your relative's [brother's] house when disaster strikes you—better a neighbor nearby than a relative [a brother] far way (27:10).

Friends and father's friends and close neighbors contrast with siblings (relatives) and siblings far away. Many people are closer to their siblings than their friends. This is normal. However, siblings who grow up in dysfunctional families find it difficult to maintain trust and closeness with one another, so they see one another at holidays, but only out of obligation. So a friend or close neighbor may be better than a sibling.

This proverb connects to the proverbs about friends in verses 6 and 9. However, in this verse Solomon counsels his son to maintain "object constancy" with his friends and the king's friends, rather than with his brothers or his relatives (10a). He also instructs his son not to go to his brothers' houses or relatives' houses in a day of calamity (10a). Brother in this text means a brother who lives "far away" or who is emotionally far away (10b). The idea of this proverb is that it is better to rely on a neighbor or friend who is close to us than to rely on a sibling or relative who is emotionally distant.

The sons of a king are often in psychological and political competition with one another, keeping in mind on the possible succession to the throne. Therefore, calling on brothers for help in a day of disaster can be a shortcut for danger. Solomon's exhortation was to be mindful of this possible reality.[429]

Be wise, my son, and bring joy to my heart; then I can answer anyone who treats me with contempt (27:11).[430]

Every parents would be grateful and proud to see their children grow up to be wise and mature in life and let go of the burden of their children. Especially for parents in leadership positions, their wise children will make them confident and honorable in front of people. Solomon would have felt confident and proud to hand over the throne to his son if his son was wise. As it turned out, Rehoboam was not such a son to his father Solomon.

The prudent see danger and take refuge, but the simple keep going and pay the penalty [suffer for it] (27:12). See also 22:3.

Take the garment of one who puts up security for a stranger; hold it in pledge if it is done for an outsider [for a wayward woman] (27:13). See also 20:16.

---

[429] Solomon would have learned this from David's life. One of David's greatest crises and disasters was the rebellion of his son Absalom. If Absalom had succeeded in his rebellion, David and Solomon would have been killed. In the day of calamity, David had good friends. Ittai the Gittite said to him, "As surely as the LORD lives, and as my lord the king lives, wherever my lord the king may be, whether it means life or death, there will your servant be" (2 Sam. 15:21).

[430] Fox connects this proverb with Ps. 127:4-5: "Like arrows in the hands of a warrior are children born in one's youth. Blessed is the man whose quiver is full of them. They will not be put to shame when they contend with their opponents in court." Fox, *Proverbs 10-31*, 808.

If anyone loudly blesses their neighbor early in the morning, it will be taken as a curse (27:14).

Even if the words are blessing, it's how you say them and the context in which you say them that matters. If you bless your neighbor in a loud voice early in the morning, before they're even awake, it's unlikely to be taken as a sincere blessing. It might be perceived as teasing or even cursing. This is how human speech works: even subtle intonation can change the meaning. This is why context matters.

A quarrelsome wife is like the dripping of a leaky roof in a rainstorm [like a constant dripping on a rainy day]; restraining her is like restraining the wind or grasping oil with the hand (27:15-16). See also 19:13.

This proverb also applies to a "quarrelsome husband." There are some people who are highly aggressive and argumentative in their marital relationships. They are like "the dripping of a leaky roof in a rainstorm." It is very difficult to stop the dripping because the roof is leaky in rain. It is impossible to stop argument with a quarrelsome spouse just as it is impossible to control the wind from blowing and to grasp oil with the hand (16).[431]

Argumentative spouses are characterized by aggression and narcissism. They are easily angered and unable to control their anger. Even if the other spouse placates them to stop, they lash out until they are not mad anymore. They don't have a well-developed ego mechanism to control their anger. So when their spouse try to calm them down, it doesn't work very well. And they repeat the behavior.

---

[431] The difficulty of "restraining" an argumentative wife means that it is difficult to "hide" the quarrel from others, Fox noted. The implication is that if you live with a quarrelsome spouse, you will eventually be known and humiliated. Fox, *Proverbs 10-31*, 810.

Therefore, it is important to have the wisdom to recognize and discern whether a person has a quarrelsome personality before marriage. There are many people who hide their aggression before marriage and then reveal it after marriage. This is because they use defense mechanisms. It is wise to observe carefully and reconsider seriously marrying someone with poor impulse control and a high propensity for aggression.

As iron sharpens iron, so one person sharpens another (27:17).

To make a sharp knife, you need a stronger grinder of iron. We grow and experience healing in relationships of sparring with each other, not only with a friend or spouse but even an enemy.

This proverb can be interpreted in conjunction with verse 16. If you live with a quarrelsome spouse and endure it well, you can become mature psychologically and spiritually. On the other hand, you may lose face and live in pain and shame.

Counseling Application: Encountering an effective counselor can help the client's face shine. A depressed, sad, angry, or anxious face will turn into a bright one.

Supervisors can sharpen their supervisees, counselors-in-training. Just as the moon is illuminated by the light of the sun, supervisees can be influenced by their supervisors to be good influencers on their clients.

The one who guards [tends] a fig tree will eat its fruit, and whoever protects [looks after] their master will be honored (27:18).

This proverb captures the truth that you reap what you sow. For those who plant and care for fig trees, they produce delicious fruit. Similarly, servants who faithfully serve their master receives praise and honor. Officials who are loyal to their king are honored by him. Furthermore, Christians who glorify God are recognized by God.

As water reflects the face, so one's life reflects the heart (27:19).

Just as water reflects the face, so the integrity of people is read in their words, between their words, and in their non-verbal behaviors. Even when they try to hide it, it shows through, especially if you're highly intuitive and perceptive, you can read even the subtlest changes in their mind. This is because the state of mind is revealed to some degree through eye movements, subtle twitches in facial muscles, tone of voice, and inconsistencies in verbal and nonverbal expressions. CIA or FBI agents who are specialized in this can identify and interpret them amazingly.

People can read each other's minds in interpersonal relationships to some degree. And they can tell when things are not what they seem. However, being overly sensitive to the other person's mind can be troublesome for them as well as for the other person. We need to be aware that over-sensitivity in relationships can lead to misunderstandings and even paranoia. It's important to read the other person's mind at the right level.

Counseling Application: It is very difficult to achieve self-awareness on our own, but it is possible to become more aware of through the reflection of others. Persons who only see the other person's reflection and are unable to make associations to themselves are using the defense mechanism of "projection." But persons who see the other person's reflection and recognize their own reflection in it are using a more mature defense mechanism, called "projective identification."

Death and Destruction are never satisfied, and neither are human eyes (27:20).[432]

---

[432] Koptak sees a connection between this verse and verses in 30:15-16: "There are three things that are never satisfied, four that never say, 'Enough!': the grave, the barren womb, land, which is never satisfied with water, and fire, which never says, 'Enough!'" Koptak, *Proverbs*, 610.

The NIV Bible translates Sheol and Abaddon as "Death and Destruction." The Hebrews understood Sheol to be the place of the dead. Even when all the people in the world die and come to Sheol, Sheol does not refuse them, saying there is no room for them (20a). Death and Destruction are never satisfied. Most people in Korea are cremated when they die because there is not enough land for them to be buried, but death itself does not reject and refuse no one.

Similarly, seeing is not satisfying enough (20b). The excitement of seeing something so beautiful and wonderful that it causes us to exclaim for a moment soon fades away and is forgotten. The mouth is also unsatisfied. After eating, the mouth asks for another food a few hours later. The same goes for the body. No matter how luxurious a car you drive, once you get used to it, it's not as satisfying as it was at first. No matter how nice a house you buy, once you get used to it, the impression and excitement will soon fade.

This dynamic is the same as that of addiction. Addicts are never satisfied in the long run. For example, a sex addict feels the joy of sex briefly, but soon forgets about it. They seek sexual stimulation again. With repeated experiences, pleasure decreases and tolerance increases.

The crucible for silver and the furnace for gold, but people are tested by their praise [by the praise he receives] (27:21).

There are two opposing environments to train and discipline people. One is like the crucible and the furnace. The other is an environment of empathy and praise and recognition. An empathetic environment is essential for young children. Experiencing the crucible at a young age stunts psychological development. However, grown-up people need experiences of the crucible and the furnace. Without suffering experiences, it is very difficult to achieve true psychological development or faith development as adults. God molds believers by combining these opposing experiences.

Praise is an important nutrient for psychological development. Given the context of the text, this proverb can be interpreted to mean that a steady and consistent praising can lead people to become psychologically mature persons. As family therapist Virginia Satir said, families are factories that manufacture human beings. So children in a praising home environment are more likely to grow up to become "good products" psychologically.

Another meaning of the text is that the way people respond to praises gives us a glimpse into their psychological and spiritual maturity. The NIV Bible translation is closer to this meaning. The way people behave when they receive praise or a favorable feedback reveals their maturity. If some people take praise for granted or become smug when they receive it, it suggests that they may have narcissistic personality disorder.[433] Praise can disclose a person's symptoms of narcissistic personality disorder or histrionic personality disorder that are not normally visible. Conversely, if a some people are too shy and awkward when receiving compliments or good feedback, it shows their lack of self-esteem. You may see this symptom in people with dependent personality disorder and/or avoidant personality disorder.

Though you grind a fool in a mortar, grinding them like grain with a pestle, you will not remove their folly from them (27:22).

If we understand the foolish as those with personality disorders, the meaning of the text becomes clear. If you put grains in a mortar and pound it with a pestle, you can husk the grains. But personality disorder symptoms are not so easy to be husked. This is because the disorder is structured in one's personality and very difficult to

---

[433] Bridges used the example of Herod, who was praised by the people of Tyre and Sidon and died in his pride: "On the appointed day Herod, wearing his royal robes, sat on his throne and delivered a public address to the people. They shouted, 'This is the voice of a god, not of a man.' Immediately, because Herod did not give praise to God, an angel of the Lord struck him down, and he was eaten by worms and died" (Acts 12:21-23). Bridges, *Proverbs*, 520.

change.

Folly also means sinfulness. If sinners are put into a mortar and ground with a pestle, their sinful nature cannot not be removed, just as no amount of soap can remove the spots from a leopard (see Jer. 13:23).

Counseling Application: If you pastor or counsel with an awareness of this dynamic, you will be less exhausted and less angry in your relationships with members or clients who are slow to change. You can pastor or counsel with patience and build long-term relationships with them.

Be sure you know the condition of your flocks, give careful attention to your herds (27:23).

Good shepherds give attention and affection to the sheep under their care. Their hearts are always with their flock. They name each sheep, remember their names, know their conditions, and care for them.

The kings of Israel were shepherds commissioned by God. They shepherded the people God had entrusted to them. David was an exemplary shepherd and king. David was an exceptional shepherd who shepherded and led them "with integrity of heart" and "with skillful hands" (Ps. 78:72).

Solomon, who had watched David from a young age, expected this from his own son. He wanted his son to be a king who understands the situation of his peoples, who empathizes with and cares for them, and who is equipped with wisdom and loving heart. Unfortunately, his son Rehoboam did not empathize with his peoples. Instead, he threatened them with violent words and became a foolish king who divided the nation.

It is a natural wisdom and quality for parents to know their children well and empathize with them in their upbringing process. Knowing and understanding where they are in their development psychologically and spiritually, and what they are going through are a quality of good enough parents. Good parents have the wisdom and knowledge to understand the characteristics of each child and raise them in a way that suits them.

Counseling Application: This proverb applies to anyone in a position of authority. A counselor or counseling supervisor must know and understand the condition of their clients or supervisees in order to provide them with effective counseling or supervision. The same is true for pastors. Pastors who understand and empathize with the hearts of their church members can minister in a spirit of shepherding.

For riches do not endure forever, and a crown is not secure for all generations (27:24).

The NIV Bible links verses 23 and 24. In this way, verse 24 explains why the people, who are likened to a flock of sheep and a herd of cattle, need to be well cared for and led. Solomon is warning that kings and kingdoms that do not take care of their people well will not last long. He is pointing out that the king's wealth and the crown that symbolizes the kingship will not be passed down from generation to generation without a spirit of good shepherding.

This proverb also can be understood as a stand-alone proverb from verse 23. Riches and honor are short-lived. There are many people who go bankrupt and down in their time. The same is true of honor. We are warned to beware that riches and honor are only "temporary objects."

When the hay is removed and new growth appears and the grass from the hills is gathered in, the lambs will provide you with clothing, and the goats with the price of a field. You will have plenty of goats' milk to feed your family and to nourish your female servants (27:25-27).

It is appropriate to understand verses 25 through 27 together. And this text can be interpreted in conjunction with the preceding verses 3 and 24.

One specific act of good care for a flock of sheep or a herd of cattle is to cut and store a lot of hay for the cold winter months. For this effort, the sheep reward the shepherd by providing wool (26a). By selling the goats he raises, the shepherd can buy more land to expand his ranch (26b). And the sheep and cattle provide milk and meat for the shepherd and his family and servants who care for them (27).

Similarly, the people provide everything a king and royal officials and their families need, because they are taken good care by them. However, evil kings exploit the people's resources forcibly to feed their royal family. But the people voluntarily pay taxes and tribute for a good king and a good government.

God rewards the labors of diligent works in such a way that they and those who are related to them may benefit from the labors. The same is true in the realm of faith: "Let us not become weary in doing good, for at the proper time we will reap a harvest if we do not give up" (Gal. 6:9).

Chapter 28 To Show Partiality Is Not Good

The wicked flee though no one pursues, but the righteous are as bold as a lion (28:1).

There is a great difference between the wicked and the righteous in life. The righteous are not insecure or afraid because they are confident. They are free and bold, even if there are those who would accuse them, because they have nothing to be accused of. The wicked and sinners, on the other hand, are always anxious and afraid deep down. Even when there is no one pursuing them, they flee and run (1a).

The righteous are those who are connected to God. No one can accuse those whom God has recognized as righteous. There is no one and nothing that can separate them from his love (see Rom. 8:38-39). Therefore, the righteous can be as bold as a lion (1b).[434]

When a country is rebellious, it has many rulers, but a ruler with discernment and knowledge maintains order (28:2).

In countries where conspiracy and rebellion are common, kings and rulers cannot live long. Regimes change overnight. And you never know when it will happen. Several kings come and go in a short period of time.

However, when persons of wisdom and knowledge becomes kings, they restore order by suppressing conspiracies and rebellions. Their reigns last long, and they leave a good legacy for future kings.

[434] Bridges identified men and women of faith who had lived with lion-like boldness: Moses, who was not afraid of Pharaoh (Heb. 11:27); Joshua and Caleb (Num. 14:6-10); Elijah, who stood before King Ahab (1 Kings 18:10, 17, 18); Nehemiah, who was bold in the face of threats (Neh. 6:11); and Paul, who was bold before King Agrippa (Acts 26:24-29). Bridges, *Proverbs*, 525.

Dysfunctional churches have frequent pastor and staff changes in a relatively short period of time. Among Korean American churches in the United States, there are many churches with short tenures of pastors. This is because there are many immature members who devalue their pastor they initially idealized. A church with a borderline personality disorder dynamic is unlikely to maintain stability and consistency. Nevertheless, if a pastor with wisdom and knowledge and psychological stability is able to keep "object contancy" to unstable members, the individual member and the church community can be restored and become healthy.

A ruler who oppresses the poor is like a driving rain that leaves no crops (28:3).

The Revised Korean Bible translates the first half of this verse as follows: "The poor who oppresses the poor is like a driving rain." However, the meaning is unclear in context.[435] I think that the NIV Bible's translation is appropriate contextually. In the context of chapter 27, beginning with verse 23, which discusses the qualities and code of conduct for kings/leaders, it is natural to interpret this proverb as an exhortation not to oppress the poor, either as a king or as an official.

Officials who ignore the pleas of the poor, the weak, or the orphans and widows are without mercy and compassion. They are evil officials who do not follow the spirit of the law. Their behaviors are like a heavy rain or hailstorm at harvest time. They are merciless, destroying all the hard work that has been done. Such heavy rain or hail is resented. The same is true of evil officials.

Those who forsake instruction praise the wicked, but those who

---

[435] Bridges commented that it refers to the case where a poor person suddenly becomes an official or rises to a high position and forgets his or her former condition and mistreats the poor. Bridges, *Proverbs*, 527.

heed it resist them (28:4).[436]

The meaning of this proverb becomes clear when understood as a proverb connected to verse 3. Officials who oppress the poor and ignore their cries have forsaken the law. This kind of officials praise the wicked and take the side of the wicked. They are unrighteous judges who have no fear of God.

But officials who heed the law of God and fear God resist the wicked even if they have power and wealth. They judge with justice.

Evildoers do not understand what is right, but those who seek the LORD understand it fully (28:5).

In this proverb, evildoers are either wicked officials or wicked kings, depending on the context. It is unfortunate and frightening when an official or king who is supposed to enforce justice fails to discern what is right (5a).

However, an official or king who seeks the LORD and listens to the law of the LORD has discernment to determine who is righteous in a lawsuit. This is because God has made it clear in his law what justice is.

Justice is knowing God's standards and principles and obeying them. It is not justice to rely on one's own subjective ideas and experiences or to favor what the majority thinks is right. Conforming to popular opinions or politicizing and legalizing it, that is, "political correctness" is not biblical justice!

Better the poor whose walk is blameless than the rich whose ways are perverse (28:6). See 19:1.

---

[436] Fox sees a connection between this proverb and 17:15, which says "Acquitting the guilty and condemning the innocent—the LORD detests them both." Fox, *Proverbs 10-31*, 821.

It is a proverb of the form, "A is better than B." People of integrity, even if they are poor, make their lives precious. But those who are rich, but sin and live unrighteously makes their lives foolish because they walk in the ways of the wicked. So, from a Christian viewpoint, those who are poor but live righteously is far better than those who are rich but live unrighteously.

The world supports those who are rich and powerful, even though their ways of life are perverse. The visible world is all they have. The world pays little attention to those who are righteous but live in poverty without power. They even dismiss them as foolish. But blessed are those who trust in the words of this proverb.

A discerning son heeds instruction [He who keeps the law is a discerning son], but a companion of gluttons disgraces his father (28:7). See also 23:19-21.

Those who digest God's law and word and then obey and practice them in their lives are children of discernment (7a). They relieve their parents' anxiety and please them.

But children who befriend gluttons shame their parents (7b). Gluttony is one of the seven deadly sins. They seek short-term pleasure of eating. They don't realize the long-term consequences of their behavior. Even if they do, they will deny the consequences and continue to pursue the pleasures of the moment. If you befriend them, you become like them. Being a glutton doesn't end with the problem of gluttony. It leads to a life of sloth and lust. They have no thirst or hunger for the Word of God. These people grieve their parents, especially parents of faith (7b).

Whoever increases wealth by taking interest or profit from the poor [by exorbitant interest] amasses it for another, who will be kind to the poor (28:8).

463

God explicitly forbade excessive usury in the law, yet there were those in the Israelite community who practiced usury.[437] These did not "heed instruction," as mentioned in verse 7. Their consciences were numbed by gluttony and greed.

Increasing wealth through legitimate endeavors is a virtue praised by Solomon. However, increasing wealth through usury is a vice and a sin. It ignores what the law forbids.

Solomon warns that the wicked will not enjoy the riches they have gathered wickedly (8b). Nabal was a wealthy man, but he had no compassion for David and his men, who were in desperate need of help. In the end, he was unable to enjoy any of his many riches, and his body turned like stone and he died. His wife Abigail, on the other hand, became David's wife and was able to spend all of Nabal's wealth on David and the poor people who followed him. This is a biblical example of this proverb being fulfilled in real life.

If anyone turns a deaf ear to my instruction, even their prayers are detestable (28:9). See also 15:8, 29.

Those who do not "heed instruction" in verse 7 are connected to those who do not keep the law in verse 8, who increase their wealth by exorbitant interest. Verse 9 describes the dual nature of those who do not obey the law. They hear the law, but they don't do it. Or they close their ears and eyes to the law altogether. Such people are wicked. They do as they please. If they pray at all, their prayers are abominable and detestable.

Isaiah cried out against these people, saying "Hear the word of the LORD, you rulers of Sodom; listen to the instruction of our

---

[437] Amos points out their vices and iniquities "Hear this, you who trample the needy and do away with the poor of the land, saying, 'When will the New Moon be over that we may sell grain, and the Sabbath be ended that we may market wheat?'—skimping on the measure, boosting the price and cheating with dishonest scales, buying the poor with silver and the needy for a pair of sandals, selling even the sweepings with the wheat" (Amos 8:4-6).

God, you people of Gomorrah!" (Isa. 1:10). Regarding prayer, he went on to proclaim, "When you spread out your hands in prayer, I hide my eyes from you; even when you offer many prayers, I am not listening" (Isa. 1:15).

It is obedience, not sacrifice, that God desires. God desires and delights in our obedience to his Word. Isaiah specifically suggested obeying the law, saying "Wash and make yourselves clean. Take your evil deeds out of my sight; stop doing wrong. Learn to do right; seek justice. Defend the oppressed. Take up the cause of the fatherless; plead the case of the widow" (Isa. 1:16-17).

Whoever leads the upright along an evil path will fall into their own trap, but the blameless will receive a good inheritance (28:10). See 26:27.

In the text, "the upright" are "the blameless." Even if they are enticed into an evil path, they do not continue on it, because they see that the ones who enticed them are falling into the trap they themselves set. Even the upright may stumble and fall. But they do not fall completely, for God's right hand upholds them and lift them up again. The wicked, on the other hand, once fall or fall into a trap, but they cannot escape. They go to eternal destruction.

Therefore, believers must be alert to avoid associating with the wicked. We should avoid standing in the path of the wicked, and we should avoid sitting in their seats. And even if we do enter their evil paths, we must come to our senses and leave them as soon as possible. The way of the righteous is approved by the LORD, but the way of the wicked leads to destruction (Ps. 1:6).

The rich are wise in their own eyes; one who is poor and discerning sees how deluded they are [a poor man who has discernment sees through him] (28:11).

In this proverb, the rich and the poor are contrasted. Not all the

465

rich consider themselves wise. There are some among the rich who are discerning and self-aware. Likewise, not all the poor are discerning and self-aware. There are even some poor people who are wise in their own eyes.

Solomon warns against the rich who think they are wise. He also encourages and supports those who are poor but wise. Regardless of whether we are rich or poor, it is important to live with discerning mind to examine ourselves.

When the righteous triumph, there is great elation; but when the wicked rise to power, people go into hiding (28:12).[438]

In this proverb, the righteous and the wicked are contrasted. When the righteous are victorious, people are happy and thankful. On the other hand, when the wicked win, people are anxious, sad, and angry and "go into hiding" (12b). Especially gifted people go into hiding and do not speak out.

God allows wicked people to come to power as well as the righteous. In the history of the kingdom of Judah, there were righteous kings who feared the LORD and wicked kings who disregarded him. When a righteous king was crowned, the people had great joy and peace. There were joy and great elation in the city. On the other hand, when a wicked king was crowned, the people were troubled and suffered. The city was filled with violence and the righteous people were killed or forced to hide.[439]

When the wicked prevail, it is the active stance of Christians to remain in their place and live righteous lives according to God's

[438] Fox notes that the proverbs related to this proverb are mentioned in a row in chapters 28 and 29: 28:28, 29:2, 29:16. Fox, *Proverbs 10-31*, 825.

[439] Such was the case in the days of King Ahab of the northern Israel. He killed the prophets who feared the LORD. Some of the prophets took refuge in caves and survived. Obadiah, who was in charge of Ahab's royal court, was "a devout believer in the LORD" (1 Kings 18:3). He was a righteous man who accomplished God's will by persevering instead of hiding in the midst of evil times. He risked his life to take a hundred of prophets out of Ahab's hands and sheltered them in two caves, fifty in each and provided them with bread and water.

will. However, there is also wisdom in hiding when the wicked prevail and avoiding them when they should be avoided. This is an area that requires individual discernment and decision.

Whoever conceals their sins does not prosper, but the one who confesses and renounces them finds mercy (28:13).[440]

How we deal with sin determines the outcome. It is much easier to deny and hide sin than to admit and confess it, because it takes courage and determination to do it. This is a difficult path, but it is the path to experience God's mercy and compassion. It is a path to prosperity (13a).

The problem with those who conceal their sins is not just that they hide them. The context suggests that they do not turn away from their sins, but sin over and over again. They do not give up their sinful behaviors. They cannot prosper (13a). They may temporarily avoid shame and suffering. But in the long run, their repeated sins lead them to shame and destruction.

When Adam and Eve sinned, they tried to hide from God's face. They tried to cover their shame by making skirts of fig leaves. That was not enough for them. They were quick to defend themselves rather than confess and repent of their sin. With their methods, they could never prosper. But by God's exclusive grace, they experienced compassion and mercy. God clothed them with garments made of skins that could only be made by shedding the blood of animals. They experienced grace.

Likewise, every human being since Adam can receive mercy and grace through the cross of Jesus when they confess their sins and repent before God. Without the grace of the cross, there is no forgiveness of sins.

Counseling Application: Clients who continue to use defense mechanisms to hide their sins or brokenness in counseling cannot be prosperous to change and healing. However, clients who are willing to talk about and vent their sins or shameful narratives to

---

[440] Fox notes that this proverb is unique in that it is the only proverb that speaks of repentance, forgiveness, and mercy. Fox, *Proverbs 10-31*, 826.

the counselor can experience therapeutic change and growth. They experience mercy and compassion from God through the counselor.

Blessed is the one who always trembles before God [fears the LORD], but whoever hardens their heart falls into trouble (28:14).

Those who always fear God confess their sins and turn away from sins. They are blessed (14a). But those who harden their heart do not fear God. They do not recognize and confess their sins. They don't turn away from their sins. They finally fall into trouble and perish (14b).

Like a roaring lion[441] or a charging bear is a wicked ruler over a helpless people (28:15).

When a lion or a bear sees prey, it pounces. In the same way, wicked officials or evil kings see the poor or "helpless people" as prey. They don't recognize that they are rulers or kings "for the people."

The rulers of northern Israel including kings, priests, and prophets were narcissistic and antisocial persons who fed only themselves but ruled the people with violence, as God pointed out through the prophet Ezekiel (see Ezek. 34). They did not strengthen the weak, heal the sick, bring back the strays, or search for the lost. God told them, "I am against the shepherds and will hold them accountable for my flock I will remove them from tending the flock so that the shepherds can no longer feed themselves" (Ezek. 34:10).

Rehoboam, who heard this proverb from his father Solomon, became a wicked king who refused to listen to the pleas of his people, who had already grown weary of labor during Solomon's

---

[441] This contrasts with the bold lion-like figure of the righteous in 28:1.

time. When he vowed to deal more harshly with the people than his father Solomon had done, the people of the ten tribes soon left his kingdom and became independent from his kingdom.

A tyrannical ruler practices extortion [lacks judgment], but one who hates ill-gotten gain will enjoy a long reign (28:16).

Verse 16 can be seen as a proverb that connects to verse 15. Thus, verses 15 and 16 are proverbs that warn against evil officials and tyrannical rulers.

Lack of judgment indicates psychological immaturity. Then tyrannical rulers are understood as ones with personality disorders. In particular, narcissistic personality disorder and antisocial personality disorder are found among them. Kings and officials with these personality disorders are very likely to use threats, manipulation, gaslighting, and violence to govern (16a). They are also likely to be greedy and engage in corruption. These officials and kings are unlikely to last long (16b).

But kings or officials who abhor greed and bribery retain their position for a long time. They enjoy not only the blessing of physical longevity but also political longevity (16b), because God recognizes and delights in them.

Anyone tormented by the guilt of murder will seek refuge in the grave [will be a fugitive till death]; let no one hold them back [let no one support him] (28:17).

God gives the murderer a lifetime of guilt, shame, and anxiety. He explicitly gave the commandment, "You shall not murder" because he well knows the struggle and suffering murderers experience.[442]

---

[442] After Cain killed his brother Abel, he was told by God, "You will be a restless wanderer on the earth" (Gen. 4:12). When he heard this, he replied to God, "My

Murderers with a functioning conscience or who fear God suffer from guilt for the rest of their lives.[443] However, psychopathic murderers are very self-centered and have little superego, so they don't suffer much. Some of them don't even feel any guilt and shame.

It is not advisable to empathize with or support these men. It is not also advisable to do so for the grieving family of the victim. They do not need to be rescued if they fall into a trap and die. However, this does not mean that we do not need to share the gospel with them.

The one whose walk is blameless is kept safe, but the one whose ways are perverse will fall into the pit [will suddenly fall] (28:18).[444] See 28:6.

This proverb is not an endorsement of salvation by works. Those who are without major blame are confident and free. The paths of those who strive to live righteously before God are safe and secure (18a). But those who take crooked paths will "suddenly" fall and fall into the pit (18b).

God is watching to see who is walking in the way of righteousness and who is walking in the way of rebellion. In due time he will intervene and judge. Those who continue to walk in their rebellious ways to the end but enjoy healthy and peaceful lives are actually people whom God has neglected and abandoned. They have no hope of salvation. Blessed is the prodigal who walks crooked paths, but returns to God in the face of an existential crisis or hardship.

---

punishment is more than I can bear" (Gen. 4:13) and expressed his fear by saying, "Whoever finds me will kill me" (Gen. 4:14).

[443] God gave a law of cities of refuge for those who killed unintentionally so that they might flee from the avenger. See Num. 35:1-34.

[444] Fox sees the connection between this proverb and 27:26 and 28:10. Fox, *Proverbs 10-31*, 828.

Those who work their land will have abundant food, but those who chase fantasies will have their fill of poverty (28:19). See also 12:11.

People who spare no labor to cultivate their land are those whose sense of reality is in good working order. God's principle is based on the truth that we reap what we sow. Therefore, it is both realistic and gratifying that those who labor earnestly will reap an abundant harvest.

God is gracious to give fruit to those who labor and sweat. This is evidenced in the Psalmist's praise, "Those who sow with tears will reap with songs of joy. Those who go out weeping, carrying seed to sow, will return with songs of joy, carrying sheaves with them" (Ps. 126:5-6).

But people who follow illusions hope to reap a harvest without having to labor at all. They dream of unearned income. They are psychologically and spiritually very immature. Such people have no capacity to give to others. They can't even take care of themselves. They can only live as parasites on others.

A faithful person will be richly blessed, but one eager to get rich will not go unpunished (28:20).

Verses 20 connects to the preceding verse 19. In this proverb, the "faithful" are contrasted with the ones "eager to get rich."

The faithful and conscientious diligently tend and cultivate their fields. They are faithful to the work entrusted to them. Joseph was faithful to the work entrusted by his master Potiphar. He trusted him enough to entrust him with everything but his own food. Rich blessing is the product for such a person (20a).

In contrast, people who have only a fantasy of becoming rich without endeavoring will not only be destitute but will be punished (20b). This is a typical symptom and life outcome of persons with

471

antisocial personality disorder. The lack of rich blessing is itself a punishment. Those who strive to get rich quickly will overstep the boundaries of the law and end up being socially criticized or in jail. This is the case with those who manipulate the price of stocks and end up in being handcuffed. Those who try to get rich by embezzling public funds or taking bribes will end up in disgrace and in jail.

To show partiality is not good—yet a person will do wrong for a piece of bread (28:21).

The NIV Bible understands the second half as an explanation of the first half of the verse. Then this proverb means that it is not good to show partiality, but people may sin for a piece of bread.[445] This proverb, then, can be understood as a proverb that helps us see the reality of human life. God forbids siding with the poor or the rich in court. In that sense, the first half of the proverb is a proverb that reaffirms the law. The second half of the proverb, however, is a proverb about human frailty. Then we need to be generous with the vulnerability of those who are poor and hungry and may steal a piece of bread if they have nothing to eat.

The stingy are eager to get rich and are unaware that poverty awaits them (28:22).

This proverb can be understood in conjunction with verse 19. In verse 19, Solomon expressed that people who chase after fantasies will become poor. And this proverb says that the stingy eager to get rich don't recognize that poverty awaits them.

This proverb also connects to verse 20. Verse 20 indicated that people who seek to get rich quickly are likely to be punished. This proverb says that neediness and poverty await such people.

---

[445] Fox also takes this translation and interprets it. Fox, *Proverbs 10-31*, 829.

Therefore, we can interpret that poverty and destitution are the punishment for those who try to get rich quickly.

Saving to the point of stinginess is not the same as making money. Human effort is limited. The wealth that is saved can be lost in a day if God blows it away. A life of stinginess is not pleasing to God. Stingy people are too attached with money and not able to be generous to people and God. One of the characteristics of obsessive-compulsive disorder is stinginess.

Whoever rebukes a person will in the end gain favor rather than one who has a flattering tongue (28:23). See 27:6.

This proverb contrasts a rebuking tongue with a flattering tongue. Flattering words may sound nice at first, but they don't last long. The truth of flattery is soon revealed. A rebuke, on the other hand, can be unpleasant to hear at first. It may even hurt the listener. But it won't be long before the listener realizes that the confrontation was sincere and loving, and becomes grateful.

A society of flattering tongues is far from truth. People are unable to move beyond superficial relationships, living in a state of deceiving and being deceived. Relationships and society in the last days are characterized by these symptoms (see 2 Tim. 3:1-7, 4:3-4).

Whoever robs their father or mother and says, "It's not wrong," is partner to one who destroys (28:24).[446]

Those who believe that stealing from a parent is not a sin are

---

[446] Fox sees this proverb and 19:26 as related verses: "Whoever robs their father and drives out their mother is a child who brings shame and disgrace." Fox, *Proverbs 10-31*, 831. He insightfully notes that the rationalizing behavior of the person mentioned in verse 24 is similar to the rationalization of an adulterous woman in 30:20: "This is the way of an adulterous woman: She eats and wipes her mouth and say, 'I've done nothing wrong'." Fox, *Proverbs, 10-31*, 831.

using the defense mechanism of rationalization. There are some children who reach into their parents' pockets without their permission, thinking that they can spend the pocket money that their parents give them anyway. They are sticky-fingered children with undeveloped superego and little developed conscience.

When you catch your child stealing, you should use a spanking to teach them that their behavior is wrong. Otherwise, you run the risk of them taking their stealing behavior outside the home.

Some children who are not financially independent when they reach adulthood sneak money from their parents, or come home drunk, go on a rampage, and ask for money. The Bible calls such persons "wicked." This proverb diagnoses them as partners with the destroyer (24b). The destroyer is the devil. Therefore, these people have joined hands with the devil. If they do not repent, they will perish with the devil.

Jesus pointed out the sin of passive stealing. Pharisees taught that if one says, "*Corban*," which means that the money or gift that one is supposed to give to his or her parents will be given to God, he or she does not sin even when he or she does not give it to the parents. They were violating the words of this proverb (see Mark 7:10-13).

A greedy man stirs up conflict [dissension], but those who trust in the LORD will prosper (28:25).

Those who trust in the LORD are not greedy. They believe and trust that God is in control of their lives and provides them with what they need. They are also content and thankful for their daily bread. In the long run, such believers are happy and prosper.

But the greedy seek to control their insecure and fearful lives themselves. They believe that their future will be secure in their accumulation of money. They feel anxious and ungrateful even when they have wealth, so they become greedy for more. As a result, they are not good with others (25a). They seek only their own benefit. They become stingy, as the proverb in verse 22 says. They are greedy but end up poor, especially in the heart. Even though they may have a lot of money, they become poor in interpersonal relationships as well as in their relationship with God.

Those who trust in themselves are fools, but those who walk in wisdom are kept safe (28:26).

This proverb is connected to verse 25. In contrast to those who trust in God in verse 25, people who trust in themselves are foolish (26a). In connection with verse 25, these people are greedy because their trust lies in the wealth they have amassed. They think they are wise, but in reality they are fools.[447]

All modern people who do not believe in God and try to make it in this world on their own are fools. The problem is that they don't realize they are fools.

But believers who trust in God alone are wise people. They believe and rely on the power of the Word of God and they are kept safe (26b).

Those who give to the poor will lack nothing, but those who close their eyes to them receive many curses (28:27).

This proverb can be interpreted in conjunction with verses 25 and 26. Those who trust in God give relief to the poor. They acknowledge that their resources came from above. They recognize that their wealth does not belong to them. They know the joy of giving because they experienced that joy when he gave to people in need and they know that they have not lacked.

But those who rely on their wealth turn away when they see the poor. They close their eyes and ears. They pretend not to see. They

---

[447] Nabal, who trusted in his riches, was a fool, as his name implied. The rich man who stored grain for many years and consoled himself with the words, "Take life easy; eat, drink and be merry," was also a fool who didn't expect to die that night (Luke 12:19).

think that if they share with the poor, their wealth will decrease and their future will be insecure. These people are stingy by nature. Their sense of control with money is too strong to give.

They will not be recognized and respected by others. In severe cases, they are cursed by others, especially people in need (27b). Furthermore, they do not realize that God, who hears the cries of the poor, will curse them. As a result, they are cursed, impoverished, and defeated.

When the wicked rise to power, people go into hiding; but when the wicked perish, the righteous thrive (28:28).

This proverb connects to verse 12. The first half of this proverb is same with the second half of verse 12: "When the wicked rise to power, people go into hiding." But when the righteous thrive, the wicked will perish (28b). When a righteous king appears, all the wicked and their servants will be destroyed. When Jesus the righteous Judge comes back, the righteous believers will be praised but the wicked will be condemned eternally.

Chapter 29 Discipline Your Children

Whoever remains stiff-necked after many rebukes will suddenly be destroyed—without remedy (29:1).

This proverb warns of the devastating consequences that will befall the proud who remain "stiff-necked" despite being rebuked and warned many times and still have no change in their life. Those who remain "stiff-necked" are the proud. They have learned very little. They are like King Pharaoh. They will suffer a fatal illness or great crisis that they did not expect, or sudden death (1b). At that point, it is useless to regret.

When the righteous thrive, the people rejoice; when the wicked rule, the people groan (29:2). See also 28:12, 28.

The people benefit or suffer depending on the king. When a wicked king comes to power, the people groan and suffer. But when a good king comes to power, the people cheer and rejoice.

The same goes for families. Children who grow up with dysfunctional parents lament without realizing it. They lament their life and lack a sense of self-worth. Children with healthy, good parents, on the other hand, have a relatively happy childhood experience. They have a stable sense of self-worth.

A man who loves wisdom brings joy to his father, but a companion of prostitutes squanders his wealth (29:3). See also 10:1, 15:20, 23:15, 24, 25, 27:11.

Those who seek prostitutes are fools. Those who spend their money on prostitution are foolish. Those who indulge in gambling are also foolish. They have no discernment. They will lose all their wealth as a result of their profligate life (3b). Not only do they lose themselves, but they become children who cause sorrow to their parents. Or they become a parent who hurts their children and spouse.

Parents whose children stay away from infidelity, gambling, or alcohol are relieved. Children who actively love wisdom and God are the pride and joy of parents of faith (3a).

Solomon, a man of wisdom, was so pleasing to God that God gave him the name Jedidiah. He was a son who was a delight to his father David, but in his later years he became a foolish man who loved foreign women and gave himself over to idolatry and debauchery rather than to wisdom. He caused God grief and anger. The fact that he fell into debauchery despite being a wise man and having written many proverbs of wisdom well demonstrates how tempting lust can be. The wise are warned by Solomon's life and strive to follow the path of righteousness to the end.

By justice a king gives a country stability, but those who are greedy for bribes tear it down (29:4).

A just nation is like a person with a "cohesive self" structure. It has the strength to withstand whatever difficulties and trials come its way without falling apart. Israel was able to be a strong nation as long as it was obedient to God's laws and regulations.

But a nation ruled by a king who compels to pay bribes is likened to a person with a "fragile self" structure. Such a king brings down his own kingdom (4b). This proverb connects to verse 2, which says that when the wicked becomes the king, the people lament and suffer. A country with a king and officials who love to take bribes will cause the people to lament. A nation whose people lament will collapse in on itself. A nation whose people increasingly want to leave their country will fall apart. When enemies invade, no one is willing to risk their lives to defend their country. It is only a matter of time before it is destroyed.

478

Those who flatter their neighbors are spreading nets for their feet (29:5).

When people flatter their neighbors, it's because they have ulterior motives.[448] There is no flattery without a reason. People flatter to win the other person's favor, or to disarm his or her defenses. In this proverb, those who flatter their neighbors flatter to hide their aggression. They flatter in order to cast a net over their feet and capture them, like baiting a fish to catch it.

Therefore, it is wise to recognize flatterers and stay away from them. It is wisdom to recognize the aggression behind flattery and not to be fooled by it.

Evildoers are snared by their own sin, but the righteous shout for joy and are glad (29:6). See 26:27.

This proverb can be interpreted in conjunction with verse 5. "Net" and "snare" are connected. Flattery by someone with evil intentions is an act of casting a net. It is sinful to use a trick to trap another person.

The wicked will fall into the trap of their own devices (6a). The righteous, not falling into the trap with them, will sing for thanksgiving (6b).

This proverb was fulfilled in the relationship between Haman and Mordecai. Haman's elaborate plan to kill Mordecai and all the Jews ended with him being hanged on a long pole he had built. The entire Jewish people celebrated Purim to commemorate the defeat of Haman and those who were with him, and their own freedom from death. Purim became a holiday characterized by joy and gratitude.

---

[448] Fox points to other texts in Proverbs that warn against flattery: 2:16, 7:5, 26:28, 28:23. Fox, *Proverbs 10-31*, 835.

479

The righteous care about justice for the poor, but the wicked have no such concern (29:7).

The poor include the weak or those in lowly positions. The wicked are characterized by little interest in and lack of empathy for these people (7b). The behaviors and attitudes of the wicked are consistent with the symptoms of narcissistic personality disorder. People with narcissistic personality disorder generally have little or no empathy for others. Especially, those who are lower than them, poor, unskilled, or ordinary are not of interest to them. In severe cases of explicit narcissism, they have a condescending attitude.

But the righteous empathize with the poor (7a). They identify with the weak. They aim to love their neighbor as themselves. They strive to live out the spirit of the law.

Mockers stir up a city, but the wise turn away anger (29:8).

To stir up a city means to stir up anger, which connects to the second half of the verse. The words and actions of the arrogant stir up the anger of all the people in the city. It's like pouring oil on a fire.[449]

But the words and deeds of the wise appease anger (8b). In this respect, the arrogant and the wise contrast. The arrogant think they are wise, but in reality they are foolish and foolhardy.

A community that a lot of them think they're better than others is prone to conflict and strife. But a community with many humble people is less conflicted because they are able to recognize their own shortcomings, and they are wise enough to understand and reach out to others. There's a saying that goes, "Too many cooks spoil the broth." a community with a lot of arrogant people, that is, people with narcissistic personality disorder, is full of conflicts and disputes due to their self-importance and self-grandiosity.

---

[449] Fox points out that this proverb is connected to 26:21: "As charcoal to embers and as wood to fire, so is a quarrelsome person for kindling strife." Fox, *Proverbs 10-31*, 836.

The arrogant becoming leaders of the church is a discipline or curse from God. It is also God's curse for arrogant people to become denominational leaders. Such a church or denomination will never be at peace. Anger builds up in the hearts of the members. Conversely, a church or denomination with humble and wise leaders brings joy and pride to its members and pastors.

If a wise person goes to court with a fool, the fool rages and scoffs, and there is no peace (29:9).

This proverb connects to the preceding verse 8. In verse 8, the arrogant come first, but in verse 9, the wise come first and the foolish come next in the order. As mentioned in verse 8, the arrogant are fools without wisdom. The arrogant know how to provoke anger, but they don't know how to control it. They never admit when they are wrong.

Therefore, if the wise are involved in a lawsuit with the foolish and arrogant, the arrogant will be enraged and scoff at the wise. The arrogant who believe they have done nothing wrong, will be narcissistically wounded by the very fact that a lawsuit has been brought against them and will lash out. It is unthinkable that they would ever admit wrongdoing or ask for forgiveness. Therefore, it is wise to litigate with such a person with the knowledge that the case may never end. You're better off losing money. They will try to defend themselves by unyielding stubbornly until the end.

Knowing and coping with your opponent is the way to win. To lose to the foolish or the arrogant is to win. Good overcomes evil. It is not only a waste of money to litigate with someone who does not deserve to be litigated, but it is also a life-consuming folly. It is wise to leave it to God, the righteous judge, and take some losses.

The bloodthirsty hate a person of integrity and seek to kill the upright (29:10). See 29:27.

481

If we connect this verse to verses 8 and 9, the bloodthirsty have the characteristics of the foolish and arrogant, as well as the characteristics of antisocial people. They are psychopaths, not just with narcissistic personality disorder, but with antisocial personality disorder.

These people dislike those who are psychologically and spiritually mature (10a). They experience disgust and jealousy. They hate them because they are the exact opposite of themselves. This dynamic is exemplified in the fact that when Jesus, the perfect light, came to earth and shone his light, those who were in darkness, especially the Pharisees and scribes, hated him and tried to kill him on several occasions. They finally took the lead in crucifying him. As the text puts it, they were eager to end the life of the righteous Jesus (10b).

Those who stoned to death the righteous prophets sent by God were also people who delighted in the shedding of blood. They were psychopaths who felt no remorse for their evil deeds. Rather they thought they did righteous actions that pleased God.

Evil systems love to scapegoat good and functional members. They are characterized by marginalizing or eliminating members for not fitting in with other pathological members. Those who work for evil systems eliminate functional members without conflict or even guilt. Such was the case with Doeg under King Saul, who carried out the massacre of innocent priests and all their families without any fear of God.

Fools give full vent to their rage, but the wise bring calm in the end (29:11). See 12:16.

This proverb can be understood in conjunction with verse 9. Verse 9 says that the foolish, or arrogant, are angry when they are involved in a legal case. Verse 11 addresses the level of anger. The air conditioning system in an automobile has a device that allows you to adjust the strength of the airflow. If you keep the air conditioner running at full blast, it puts a strain on the engine. In the same way, frequent peak levels of anger harm one's health.

People with a malfunctioning anger control system are fools. They don't even realize it's broken because they don't have insight and self-awareness.

It's murderous to rage with an intensity that the other person can't cope with. A personality disorder characterized by rage at the highest possible level is borderline personality disorder. With an immature and unstable psychological structure, people with borderline personality disorder are overwhelmed by intense anger and frequently hurt those around them.

The wise who have attained a certain degree of psychological maturity, have "ego strength" to control and express anger appropriately (11b). They have stable interpersonal relationships with others.

If a ruler listens to lies, all his officials become wicked (29:12).

In this text, a ruler refers to a king. When a king listens to lies or flattery, only wicked officials remain (12). This is because those who tell the truth leave the king or the king throws them out.

Those who blind a king's eyes and ears are wicked officials. They do not give honest feedback to the king for their own good. The king is primarily responsible for this. It is also the responsibility of his officials. Loyalists risk their lives to speak out against those who blind the king's eyes and ears.[450] In reality, however, it is very difficult to do so. It is almost certain to cost them their lives. They need discernment whether to associate with or differentiate from a king whose ears are deaf with the lies of dishonest officials.

The poor and the oppressor have this in common: The LORD

---

[450] King Herod was a wicked man, and he committed the evil of taking his brother's wife, Herodias, as his wife. None of Herod's officials spoke out against this evil behavior. But John the Baptist spoke up against Herod's behavior as evil before God and was thrown into prison. Finally, through the machination of Herodias, he was beheaded.

gives sight to the eyes of both (29:13). See also 22:2.

God extends common grace to the poor, the rich, the oppressor, and the oppressed alike. This proverb connects to Jesus' words: "He causes his sun to rise on the evil and the good, and sends rain on the righteous and the unrighteous" (Matt. 5:45). God is a generous God who gives even the wicked air to breathe, water to drink, and good health to live.

If a king judges the poor with fairness, his throne will be established forever [always be secure] (29:14).[451]

This proverb can be interpreted in conjunction with verse 4a, "By justice a king gives a country stability." Just kings rule without bias in the cases of the poor and the weak. They do not allow the phrase "One law for the rich and another for the poor" to be spoken among the people. The people will respect the king who judges without partiality.

A kingdom whose people support the king is stable and unshakable (14b). Its enemies cannot invade it.

God does not take sides. He does not favor the poor or ignore the rich. He doesn't look down on the weak. He values the thought and value of a child the same as an adult. He identifies with the cries of orphans and widows. He judges with equity and justice, without bias to the right or left. God is a king of discernment, judgment, and fairness. God is an eternal king and his kingdom is forever.

A rod and a reprimand [The rod of correction] impart wisdom, but a child left undisciplined [left to himself] disgraces its mother (29:15). See also 19:29; 20:30; 22:15; 23:13, 14.

---

[451] Fox points out a few proverbs that parallel the second half of this proverb: 16:12b, 20:28b, 25:5b. Fox, *Proverbs 10-31*, 839.

When the wicked thrive, so does sin, but the righteous will see their downfall (29:16).

When the wicked prosper, their sins will naturally abound (16a). They will continue to sin as long as they are well and healthy in the world. This was the case with the people in Noah's day. Sin abounded in the world, but they continued to do evil. So it was with the people of Sodom and Gomorrah. Suddenly, one day, they were destroyed.

The world exhibits a phenomenon called entropy, in which the wicked become more numerous as the end draws near. Paul well pointed out the symptoms of wickedness that people in the last days will exhibit (see 2 Tim. 3:1-5). "Evildoers and impostors will go from bad to worse, deceiving and being deceived" (2 Tim. 3:13).

Solomon warns that the wicked may temporarily prosper, but will suddenly be destroyed (16b). That warning will surely be fulfilled.[452]

Discipline your children, and they will give you peace; they will bring you the delights you desire [the delight to your soul] (29:17). See 29:15.

Where there is no revelation, people cast off restraint; but blessed is the one who heeds wisdom's instruction [who keeps

---

[452] David poetically expressed the same meaning as this proverb: "Do not fret because of those who are evil or be envious of those who do wrong; for like the grass they will soon wither, like green plants they will soon die away" (Ps. 37:1-2); "I have seen a wicked and ruthless man flourishing like a luxuriant native tree, but he soon passed away and was no more; though I looked for him, he could not be found" (Ps. 37:35-36).

the law] (29:18).

"Revelation" in this proverb refers to the law or "wisdom's instruction." Without the law, it is difficult to discern what is right or wrong. The period of Judges was characterized by the Israelites' repeated breaking of the law. So they did as they saw fit (Judg. 21:25). The writer of Judges characterized the reason as "Israel had no king," but the real reason was that they did not honor their true king, God, and his law.[453]

Modern people who live with deaf ears to God's Word are those who cast off restraint (18a). There is no blessing for them, but curse and judgment (see 18b). In an age when many people interpret and distort the Bible according to their own will, those who believe, obey, and live according to the Word are blessed to have life (18b).

Servants cannot be corrected by mere words; though they understand, they will not respond (29:19).

One of the characteristics of servants (slaves) is passivity. Servants work tactfully. They are dependent on their master. The psychology of servants is similar to that of children. Solomon emphasizes the benefits of disciplining servants at the right time and in the right way (19a).

But servants don't always have to be ruled with a rod. For among servants there are some wise servants. Joseph was sold into Potiphar's house as a slave, but he was not a slave to be ruled with a rod. He was trusted by his master and became the head of the household, in charge of the entire household. Eliezer, whom Abraham sent to find a prospective wife for Isaac, was also a faithful and wise servant. These are the kind of servants who can become mentors or co-workers to their master. Therefore, masters

---

[453] Subjectivity is the hallmark of postmodern society, which does not accept absolute standards. Subjectivity means that each person's opinion can be right. It is a characteristic of an era that does not recognize God as king.

who harshly rule over their servants are foolish.

However, if servants are involuntary, tricky, and damaging to the master, it's necessary to correct their behaviors with a rod. If they are not punished, they won't obey their master. Passive-aggressive servants sabotage by procrastinating. They express their aggression by doing things that don't please their master. If you neglect this type of servants, they will pretend to be the master, especially when you're not looking. And they will treat other servants as if they were the master.

Counseling Application: Addicts are slaves to their addictions. They are unable to live on their own terms. It is difficult to change their lives by simply talking to them. Even when they know they are addicted, they continue to repeat the addictive behavior. Sometimes they need to be beaten. A traumatic experience, such as a serious health crisis, forced hospitalization, or imprisonment, can be a wake-up call.

Do you see someone who speaks in haste? There is more hope for a fool than for them (29:20). See 26:12.

To be hasty in speech means to speak impulsively. Solomon compares an impulsive speaker to a foolish one and says that there is hope for the foolish. The foolish are not without hope. The fact that impulsive speakers are more hopeless than the foolish means that impulsivity is hardwired into their personality and is very difficult to change.

There's a saying, "A man's word is as good as a bond." It means that a man's word should be prudent. It emphasizes the importance of being careful with our speaking.

A word can be the fuse that ignites a war. A single word can completely tear a couple apart. Like an arrow that leaves bowstring, words spoken are very difficult to take back. Words spoken impulsively and without thinking can cause serious damage to the speaker as well as to the listener.

A servant pampered from youth will turn out to be insolent [If a man pampers his servant from youth, he will bring grief in the end] (29:21).

This proverb can be interpreted in connection with verse 19. After the proverb about rebuking only verbally a servant, who is unlikely to be corrected, Solomon gives a lesson on how to treat young servants. Children born to a servant may be cute and lovable because they are young children. But if they are pampered from youth, they may act as if they were their master's children (21b).

How does this proverb apply in most modern countries where slavery no longer exist? This can be applied to the process of raising children. If you pamper your child too much because you love him or her, it is very likely that he or she will grow up to be a person with narcissistic personality disorder who ignores you and cares only for himself or herself. This kind of love is foolish.

An angry person stirs up conflict [dissension], and a hot-tempered person commits many sins (29:22). See also 15:18, 28:25.

The first half of the verse, "An angry person stirs up conflict," can be connected to the first half of verse 8, "Mockers stir up a city." Thus, the angry and mockers can be paired. Mockers are self-centered and prone to anger. And there is a risk that they will continue to be angry until the other person admits wrongdoing. They don't admit their faults. So they only cause strife (22a).

Hot-tempered people are people whose anger has been structured into their personality. They are easily provoked by the slightest offense, and they hurt those around them. They repeatedly commit sins that disobey the spirit of the law, which is to love their neighbors as themselves. They have little insight and do not feel much guilt or responsibility for their hot temper.

Pride brings a person low, but the lowly in spirit gain honor (29:23).

This proverb can be connected to verse 1. In verse 1, the "stiff-necked" are the proud, and the day will come when their neck will be broken and they will be brought down (23a). In contrast, those who humble themselves will be praised and honored by God and people (23b).

The accomplices of thieves are their own enemies; they are put under oath and dare not testify (29:24).

Those who become accomplices to thieves are fools who harm themselves (24a). They will end up in court. They may not dare to testify in court who they were that stole with them (24b). This is because they are afraid of the consequences of their testimony. They may feel foolish enough to be the only ones in jail while the real thieves are not caught.

Fear of man will prove to be a snare, but whoever trusts in the LORD is kept safe (29:25).

This proverb can be understood in connection with the preceding verse 24. Those who are threatened by psychopathic thieves and are forced to participate in the theft will find themselves in a double bind. They become losers.

If they fear psychopathic thieves who threaten and manipulate, they will fall into a snare. But if they trust in God, who is in control of their life and death, they can boldly testify against the thieves and honestly confess their own mistakes. Then they are free from a snare. It is foolish to give in to the manipulation and threats of psychopaths in order to avoid them in the first place, as it will only lead them deeper into the trap.

Many seek an audience with a ruler, but it is from the LORD that one gets justice (29:26).[454]

This proverb describes a reality in which many people seek to have their grievances addressed directly to the ruler. There are people who go directly to the ruler or petition him because they think their case is important. However, Solomon encourages us to look to the invisible God rather than to rely on visible authorities (26b).

The righteous detest the dishonest; the wicked detest the upright (29:27).

The righteous and the unrighteous cannot mingle. They hate each other. God abhors idols and idolatry. Idols are completely incompatible with God. It's like light and darkness cannot be together. Paul makes this point well:

> Do not be yoked together with unbelievers. For what do righteousness and wickedness have in common? Or what fellowship can light have with darkness? What harmony is there between Christ and Belial? Or what does a believer have in common with an unbeliever? What agreement is there between the temple of God and idols? For we are the temple of the living God (2 Cor. 6:14-16).

The righteous must hate the unrighteous. In fact, they hate injustice more than people. The righteous should not be afraid to do righteousness, knowing that they will be hated by the wicked.

---

[454] Fox sees that the first half of this proverb is connected to the first half of 19:6: "Many curry favor with a ruler." Fox, *Proverbs 10-31*, 847.

Chapter 30 Give Me Neither Poverty Nor Riches

The saying of Agur son of Jakeh—an inspired utterance [an oracle]. This man's utterance to Ithiel [This man declared to Ithiel, to Ithiel and to Ucal]: "I am weary, God, but I can prevail" (30:1).

The proverbs of chapter 30 are distinct from the proverbs of Solomon. Chapter 30 is presented as a proverb with multiple verses addressing a single topic rather than a single, stand-alone proverb. Verses 7-9 are characterized by their form of prayer. The author identifies Agur as the son of Jakeh, but it is not clear who Agur is. It's also unclear who Ithiel and Ucal are.

Surely I am only a brute, not a man [I am the most ignorant of men]; I do not have human understanding. I have not learned wisdom, nor have I attained to [have I] the knowledge of the Holy One (30:2-3).

Agur, the author of chapter 30, takes a self-devaluing stance of humility. He introduces himself as the most ignorant of men, a man who has no human understanding, no learning of wisdom, and no knowledge of the Holy One. His introduction can be seen as an expression of humbling himself in order to exalt wisdom and the Holy One.

Who has gone up to heaven and come down? Whose hands have gathered up the wind [Who has gathered up the wind in the hollow of his hands]? Who has wrapped up the waters in a cloak? Who has established all the ends of the earth? What is his name, and what is the name of his son? Surely you know [Tell me if you know]! (30:4).

Agur asks five questions in quick succession. These questions are reminiscent of God's responses to Job's questions: "Who shut up the sea behind doors when it burst forth from the womb, when I made the clouds its garment and wrapped it in thick darkness, when I fixed limits for it and sets its doors and bars in place" (Job 38:8-10). These questions show that Agur is by no means the unintelligent man he is portrayed to be. He is clearly a man of knowledge who knows the holy God.

Every word of God is flawless; he is a shield to those who take refuge in him (30:5).

All of God's words are flawless and without error. The written revelation, the Bible, was inspired by the Holy Spirit and is infallible. God is faithful and not deceitful. Accordingly, God's word is faithful and not deceitful. Accordingly, we can fully trust and rely on his word. God and all his words are a shield and a fortress to those who trust in them.

Do not add to his words, or he will rebuke you and prove you a liar (30:6).

Adding to the Word of God is a blasphemous sin. It is devilish behavior because Satan added to the Word of God from the beginning. Heresies are also characterized by the addition of revelation other than the written Word of God.

Anyone who adds to the message of the gospel of Jesus Christ is a heretic. Teaching that one must keep the Old Testament laws in addition to the redemption of Jesus on the cross to be saved is a different gospel that tears at the very foundation of the gospel. It is a false gospel. Paul speaks sternly against such people: "As we have already said, so now I say again: If anybody is preaching to you a gospel other than what you accepted, let them be under God's curse!" (Gal. 1:9). Not surprisingly, God will rebuke and judge such people (6b).

Two things I ask of you, LORD; do not refuse me before I die: Keep falsehood and lies far from me; give me neither poverty nor riches but give me only my daily bread. Otherwise, I may have too much and disown you and say, "Who is the LORD?" Or I may become poor and steal, and so dishonor the name of my God (30:7-9).

This is a proverb in the form of a prayer. There are two key prayer requests that Agur makes. The first is a prayer for protection from "falsehoods and lies." He doesn't say why he's praying this prayer. It can be understood as a prayer for protection as he confesses his own weaknesses that might lead him to lie to avoid some difficulties.

The second is a prayer for economic safety. Agur prays for God's provision of daily bread. He makes his reason for this second prayer clear. He is afraid that wealth will make him forget God. And he is also afraid that poverty will cause him to go hungry and steal. He fears that by committing the sin of stealing, which is as serious as lying, he will be the one to defile God's name.

The prayer of Agur provides a direction for the life of believers. One is to seek truth and hate falsehood. The second is to seek a non-anxious life, fully trusting that God is the one who provides our daily bread. Instead of worrying about what to eat, what to drink, and what to wear, we seek first the kingdom of God. Then we can strive to actively live for the glory of God.

Do not slander a servant to their master, or they will curse you, and you will pay for it (30:10).

A didactic proverb make a brief appearance in Agur's proverbs in this verse. The proverbs before and after verse 10 are more of a wise statement than a proverb.

Agur cautions against speaking negatively of other's servants to their master. To speak ill of them nosily, even though the master has not asked for a feedback, is likely to be taken as slandering the master. The master will respond, "Mind your own business," or worse, curse you. You may be sued for libel (10b).

Respecting boundaries in relationships is very important. Problems of a servant fall under the master's jurisdiction. They are within the boundary of the master. It's foolish to intervene unnecessarily and then be insulted. So it's wise to avoid impulsively intervening in other people's business or domestic affairs.

There are those who curse their fathers and do not bless their mothers (30:11).

In verses 11 through 14, Agur uses the sentence structure "There are those who..." to describe four types of groups. The first group is those who show aggression toward their parents. Cursing a father and not blessing a mother are the same thing.

This proverb states that there are people who curse their parents. They curse their parents because they are unable to control their anger, even though the law says that those who curse their parents should be stoned to death (see Ex. 21:17).

Adult children who treat their elderly parent who is weak physically or financially with disrespect are those who do not fear the LORD. This proverb from Agur can be understood in connection with the proverb of Solomon: "Whoever robs their father and drives out their mother is a child who brings shame and disgrace" (19:26).

Those who are pure in their own eyes and yet are not cleansed of their filth (30:12).

The second group are those who consider themselves clean and deceive themselves.[455] They are unaware that they are unclean, even though they are in a state of uncleanness. Their defense mechanisms of denial and repression prevent them from being self-aware. As a result, they don't feel any need to be redeemed from their sins. Even if they are told to, they will question why they need to.

Most people who do not accept the gospel consider themselves moral and ethical. They do not understand and accept the gospel that diagnoses them as sinners. They are unable to accept the biblical truth that they were born with a sinful nature from the womb. They don't realize that their state of separation from God and themselves is itself sin. They are not aware that there are sinfulness and evil in their unconscious realm. Therefore, they do not accept the gospel of salvation by being washed in the blood of Jesus Christ.

Laodicean church members had this dynamic, which led to Jesus' stern diagnosis: "You say, 'I am rich; I have acquired wealth and do not need a thing.' But you do not realize that you are wretched, pitiful, poor, blind and naked" (Rev. 3:17).

Counseling Application: Some counselors who lack self-awareness fool themselves into thinking they are almost healed. They are foolish. Christian counselors who reflect on themselves in the light of Scripture recognize their brokenness and dirtiness and continue to ask for the Holy Spirit's help. And they continue to work to change those areas.

---

[455] Fox connects this proverb to the proverb of Solomon: "All a person's ways seem pure to them, but motives are weighed by the LORD" (16:2). Fox, *Proverbs 10-31*, 866.

Those whose eyes are ever so haughty, whose glances are so disdainful (30:13).

The third group are those whose eyes are so haughty and disdainful. Typically, these are people with narcissistic personality disorder. Narcissistic personality disorder is characterized by a pattern of interpersonal relationships that are exploitative, not empathetic, self-elevating.

Especially in case of people with "overt" narcissism, their pride is visible in their eyes. They look down on and belittle most people. They have little concern for the weak.

The first of the six or seven sins that God hates is "haughty eyes" (see 6:17). Verse 13 can also be connected to verse 12. People with prideful eyes see themselves as problem-free. They think they have done nothing wrong. So they never apologize, and they defend their righteousness to the end.

People with narcissistic personality disorder fix their eyes on people who are higher than them. They identify with them and very much want to be in their position. They don't care about or empathize with people below them.

Those whose teeth are swords and whose jaws are set with knives to devour the poor from the earth and the needy from among mankind (30:14).

The fourth group are those who display antisociality and aggression to the fullest. These are psychopaths. Their teeth are like swords and knives. They hurt, deceive, threaten, and steal for their own benefit. They chew and "devour" with their incisors and molars, especially the poor and those in need, instead of helping them.

They "devour" the land of orphans and widows. They take what belongs to the powerless by force. They lend at usury and devour everything that belongs to others in need. They do not feel sorry, sad, or ashamed because their conscience is seared. They are the people Isaiah referred to. They are the psychopaths who exploit to

496

fill their own bellies: "Woe to you who add house to house and join field to field till no space is left and you live alone in the land" (Isa. 5:8).

To summarize the four groups of people, the group in verses 11 and 14 are people dominated by antisocial personality disorder. The group in verses 12 and 13 are people primarily characterized by narcissistic personality disorder. In many cases, people with antisocial personality disorder are likely to also have narcissistic personality disorder.

The leech has two daughters. "Give! Give!" they cry. There are three things that are never satisfied, four that never say, "Enough!": the grave, the barren womb, land which is never satisfied with water, and fire, which never says, "Enough!" (30:15-16).

Leeches attach themselves to the skin and suck blood. They continue to suck blood even when their own body is filled with blood. It's like they're saying "Give, give." What does it mean that the leech has two daughters? Fox interestingly comments that the two daughters are twins, because they have the same name "Give" and they both speak "Give!"[456]

Agur gives four examples of things in the world that keep asking "Give, give." First, death. Death doesn't say, "it's enough, no more death." It takes all lives who are alive without exception. Second, the womb, which cannot bear a baby. No matter how much man's semen the womb receives, some wombs cannot conceive. Third, a land that cannot be filled by water. Even if it rains a lot, rainwater soon soaks into the ground. The ground does not refuse the rain. Fourth, fire. Fire is insatiable in that it burns whatever it comes across and reduces everything to ashes unless there is intervention. The same is true of sin and addiction. Sin is never enough. The addict is never satisfied.

---

[456] Fox, *Proverbs 10-31*, 867.

497

The eye that mocks a father, that scorns an aged mother, will be pecked out by the ravens of the valley, will be eaten by the vultures (30:17). See verse 11.

This proverb is connected to verse 11. Whereas verse 11 merely states that there are those who "curse their fathers and do not bless their mothers," this proverb warns of the consequences that will befall them. The eyes that mock the father and scorns the mother are the eyes that God hates. This proverb warns in strong tones that such people will be stoned to death, and the eyes in their bodies will be eaten by the crows and vultures that dwell in the valley (17b).[457]

There are three things that are too amazing for me, four that I do not understand: the way of an eagle in the sky, the way of a snake on a rock, the way of a ship on the high seas, and the way of a man with a young woman. This is the way of an adulterous woman: She eats and wipes her mouth and says, "I've done nothing wrong" (30:18-20).

There are so many amazing things in the world. The providence of God's creation is amazingly wonderful. The course of the stars and the vastness of the universe are so mysterious and incomprehensible. Agur gives three or four examples of amazing phenomena.

In the modern age of advanced technology, there is a way to track an eagle. We can do this by attaching a small camera to the eagle's leg. Now sea paths and sky paths are identified. The track of a man and a women also leaves traces. You can find out who was there through bodily fluids or fingerprints.

---

[457] It will be difficult to gouge out the eyes of the living. The implication is that when the crows and vultures eat the bodies of those who have been stoned to death for cursing and mocking their parents, they will also peck out their eyes.

However, in the context of the Old Testament era, all of this was unverifiable and unsearchable. Agur describes fornication as "eating" (20b). Fornication is like washing the mouth after eating and then saying, "I didn't eat it." It is difficult to find evidence of adultery because it usually leaves no trace. But God sees and knows the way of the eagle, the way of the serpent, the path of a ship, and the track of one's adultery. Therefore, God will judge as the witness of all hidden sins.

Under three things the earth trembles, under four it cannot bear up: a servant who becomes king, a godless fool who gets plenty to eat, a contemptible woman [an unloved woman] who gets married, and a servant [a maidservant] who displaces her mistress (30:21-23).

This is the third group of the structure, "there are three or four things…" Agur criticizes the world for not having common sense, even though it is a fallen world. He cites three or four examples of unusual situations that don't make sense. The first is a servant becoming king. The order of the world is completely reversed. The second is the foolish enjoying an abundance of food. Solomon repeatedly said that the foolish become poor and lazy, so it is an abnormal situation when such a person is given an abundant life. The third is a woman who has never received attention from men getting married. This will be a surprise to the world.[458] The fourth is a maidservant displacing her mistress. This is similar to the first case.[459]

---

[458] From a perspective of belief, this woman is favored by God. The world hates this, but in God it is possible. It was an amazing providence of God that Leah, who was not given Jacob's favor, took Rachel's place and married Jacob.

[459] Abraham did not hesitate to have offspring through Sarah's maidservant Hagar, so he slept with her. When Hagar became pregnant, she despised her mistress, Sarah. When she tried to take charge, she was rebuked by Sarah. Her son Ishmael harassed his mistress Sarah's son Isaac and was eventually cast out of Abraham's house along with his mother Hagar.

Four things on earth are small, yet they are extremely wise: Ants are creatures of little strength, yet they store up their food in the summer; hyraxes are creatures of little power, yet they make their home in the crags; locusts have no king, yet they advance together in ranks; a lizard can be caught with the hand, yet it is found in kings' palaces (30:24-28).

Agul goes on to list three or four examples of the fourth group, in which they are the smallest animals but the wisest. The first is the weak ants, that are simply stepped on and killed, but that have wisdom to store up their food. The second is the hyrax, that is also a weak animal, but it has the wisdom to build its home in the rocks. The third is the locusts, that travel together in ranks despite having no king over that. Locusts were also used as God's army.[460] The fourth is the lizard, that can be caught with your bare hands. Snakes are not easy to catch and can be poisonous. However, lizards are small and weak reptiles. Lizards are known to be very diverse. Despite their small size, they're characterized by their agility. One of their wisdoms is their ability to land on walls, which they do by adjusting the angle of their tail.

Man is greater, more powerful, wiser, and more beautifully created than these four creatures, but there are many who are less wise and more foolish than these four creatures. These four creatures teach such people a lesson. As Solomon said, the lazy should go to the ants and learn from them.

There are three things that are stately in their stride, four that move with stately bearing: a lion,mighty among beasts, who

---

[460] "I will repay you for the years the locusts have eaten— the great locust and the young locust, and the other locusts, and the locust swarm—my great army that I sent among you" (Joel 2:25).

retreats before nothing; a strutting rooster, a he-goat, and a king secure against revolt (30:29-31).

This is the fifth one of the structure, "There are three or four things…." Agur points out that among the animals God created, there are three that are majestic in their walk. The first is the lion. In the case of the lion, Agur adds characterizing modifiers. It is "strong" enough to be called the king of animals and "does not back down" before any beast. The second is the strutting rooster. The third is a he-goat. The fourth is not really an animal, but a king escorted by an army.

God created humans as beings with authority and power to rule and care for all animals and all of the natural world. Humans are made in the image of God and are meant to be majestic beings. However, all human beings who are fallen by original sin fall short of God's image. Humans should learn from the lion, the rooster, or the he-goat. Those who are afraid of death and are slaves to the devil can be transformed into beings who are not afraid of death if they believe in Jesus Christ and are armed with faith of resurrection. They can live boldly and courageously in this world as beings in the image of God.

If you play the fool and exalt yourself, or if you plan evil, clap your hand over your mouth! (30:32).

Verses 32 and 33 are so typical of the general nature of proverbs that it almost feels like they are from Solomon. Most people unknowingly speak foolishly at times. We inadvertently say things that boast ourselves. No one is perfect. When we do, we should say, "Oops!" and clap our hand over our lips (32b). If we are self-aware and watch ourselves, others will understand and say, "Those things are bound happen!" and be forgiving.

When we have an evil thought, we need to realize it and repent. As Luther said, a bird's poo may fall on our head when it is flying, but we must not allow it to build a nest on our head. It is wise to recognize our sinful nature and repent and turn away from evil thoughts.

For as churning cream produces butter, and as twisting the nose produces blood, so stirring up anger produces strife (30:33).

It's interesting that the last proverb of Agur is about anger. When we stir up anger, we run the risk of escalating disputes and arguments in our relationships. It's like stirring milk over and over again. Its predictable result is butter or cheese. Or if we keep twisting our nose, the natural outcome is a nosebleed. In the same way, if one provokes the other person's anger, quarrels will arise, and even murder will occur. Between nations, wars will break out.

Thinking ahead to foreseeable situations will help us avoid catastrophic outcomes. It is wise to control our anger before it reaches dangerous levels.

Chapter 31 Speak up for the Poor and Needy

The sayings of King Lemuel—an inspired utterance [an oracle] his mother taught him (31:1).

This proverb is attributed to King Lemuel, but it was actually taught to him by his mother. He internalized and digested the proverbs his mother had taught him. It is unclear who King Lemuel is. While Solomon's proverbs were written by a father to his son, chapter 31 is unique in that it is written by a mother to her son, a king.

Listen, my son! Listen, son of my womb! Listen, my son, the answer to my prayers! [O my son, O son of my womb, O son of my vows] Do not spend your strength on women, your vigor on those who ruin kings (31:2-3).

Repetitive calling of her son is an expression of a mother's earnestness and affection as she teaches the next lesson.[461] What she says first is very important expresses her prioritized concern. Verse 3 has the feel of a mother making a will to her son. She cautions her son king not to use his strength on women. Kings who are infatuated with women will not be able to lead their country wisely. Kings who spend their strength on women are doomed.[462]
The latter years of Solomon's life were against this proverb. Many

---

[461] This expression is reminiscent of what David said when Absalom died: "O my son Absalom! My son, my son Absalom! If only I had died instead of you-- O Absalom, my son, my son!" (2 Sam. 18:33). Anders suggests that the phrase "my son, the answer to my prayers!" suggests that King Lemuel's mother might have offered him to God, just as Hannah offered her vowed son Samuel to God. Anders, *Proverbs*, 360.

[462] Moses already pointed out this danger: "He must take many wives, or his heart will be led astray" (Deut. 17:17a).

kings have failed because of lust. King Lemuel's mother counsels against sexual depravity as the first danger for his son king. Sexual immoralilty has brought down many leaders and statesmen including Christian leaders. It's the same for men and women.

It is not for kings, Lemuel—it is not for kings to drink wine, not for rulers to crave beer, lest they drink and forget what has been decreed, and deprive all the oppressed of their rights. Let beer be for those who are perishing, wine for those who are in anguish! Let them drink and forget their poverty and remember their misery no more (31:4-7).

The second will-like lesson is about alcohol. King Lemuel's mother, who called him "my son" three times in verse 2, warns him three times not to drink.

No king's feast is complete without alcohol. But for a king to indulge to the point of addiction is just as destructive as his use of strength over women.[463]

King Lemuel's mother lays out the destructive effects of alcohol on the king beginning in verse 5. When he is drunk, he cannot remember the specifics of the law of the land and the law of God. Ant then he cannot judge the petitions of the innocent with discernment.[464] Lives depend on the king's word, and no one can stop him if he judges drunk. The result is just as deadly as driving drunk.

King Lemuel's mother says that alcohol can be helpful for those who are perishing or dying, and for those whose hearts are troubled. Alcohol has the effect of making the poor forget, even temporarily, their sorrows and circumstances (7). The conclusion

[463] One of the reasons King Xerxes was so frivolous and deposed the queen was because the king was drunk at the feast: "When King Xerxes was in high spirits with wine, he commanded the seven eunuchs who served him" (Esth. 1:10).

[464] Alcohol affects the brain, elevating the mood, impairing the judgment and, in severe cases, causing the black out drunk.

of this proverb is to beware of women and beware of alcohol.

Speak up for those who cannot speak for themselves, for the rights of all who are destitute. Speak up and judge fairly; defend the rights of the poor and needy (31:8-9).

This proverb is connected with the preceding warning about wine. King Lemuel's mother adds a positive admonition to the negative admonition not to get drunk and misjudge. She exhorts him to defend those who are not in a position to defend themselves, to advocate for the poor, and to be on the side of the weak. It is easy for the person with power to side with the strong. She teaches her son to defend the rights of the poor and needy.[465] The king must advocate for them, but judge them fairly.

A wife of noble character who can find? She is worth far more than rubies (31:10).[466]

Whereas the proverb in verse 3 was a counsel not to use the king's strength to women, verse 10 is an active exhortation to take a wise woman as his wife. The rest of the instruction, up to verse 31, consists of specific references to the characteristics of a wife of noble character. Considering the length of this section, we can see that King Lemuel's mother's primary concern is to ensure that the king takes a woman of wisdom and nobleness as his wife.[467]

---

[465] From this text, we see that King Lemuel's mother was a woman of wisdom and empathy for systemic issues that went beyond the individual. She was not only a woman of the royal family, but also a woman who cared about and empathized with the people in need.

[466] Fox notes that there are several allegorical interpretations of "a wife of noble character," including that she symbolizes wisdom, that she symbolizes the church, or that she symbolizes the heart. Fox, *Proverbs 10-31*, 907.

[467] Bridges suggested 19:14 as a proverb that relates to this proverb: "Houses and wealth

A wife with wisdom and integrity inspires confidence and trust to her husband (11a). She has "object constancy," the ability to be consistent and stable in her marital relationship with him no matter what the circumstances.

"She is worth far more than rubies" can be interpreted to mean that it is difficult to find a wife with noble character. It is difficult to find a mature wife or a mature husband as a spouse, especially in the Korean context. It is nothing short of a miracle that young adults in a generation that grew up in a competitive educational environment where getting into a prestigious college is the biggest goal in life are able to marry at a psychologically mature stage.

In a general sense, I can say that mature personality and character are developed through a marriage relationship. The development and growth of personality is limited when a person remains unmarried to old age. When an incomplete husband and wife experience growth by refining each other through the ups and downs of marriage relationship, they are able to mature into a noble husband and a noble wife. However, marriage relationship does not guarantee growth and maturation of one's personality. It is also a reality that many couples end their relationship with divorce. Therefore, it is important to find a mature person as a spouse, but it is more important for each young adult to strive to become such a person. When a couple matures together, the children growing up under them will benefit.

Her husband has full confidence in her and lacks nothing of value (31:11).

When a husband and wife have a trusting relationship each other, the work of their hands is productive. God blesses the hands of such a couple. He will not let them suffer in their economy. He docs not allow the children of the righteous to be beggars.[468]

---

are inherited from parents, but a prudent wife is from the LORD." Bridges, *Proverbs*, 620.

[468] Of course, this doesn't mean that poor couples become poor because they have a problematic relationship necessarily.

Having full trust in spouse is crucial to maintaining family stability. When mistrust becomes severe, it can lead to pathological symptoms such as paranoia. If you are not entrusted with money by your spouse, you are unable to make decisions on your own. You will experience frequent anxiety from being watched or being controlled.

Some people are impulsive buyers and prone to overspending. They can't balance their income and expenses and get into debt easily. A spouse who has a borderline personality disorder dynamic with poor impulse control are predictably more likely to suffer financially. In that sense, a wife of noble character in the text is not an impulsive woman and well manages her household.

She brings him good, not harm, all the days of her life (31:12).

A wife of noble character is basically good in her husband. She knows how to be happy and how to do good in life (see Eccl. 3:12). She is not the "quarrelsome wife" that Solomon warned against several times in Proverbs.

Although this proverbs refers to a wife, it can be applied to a husband as well. Persons of mature character know how to empower their spouse. They are empathetic and considerate of their spouse. They don't abuse verbally or physically their spouse. In this proverb, "a wife of noble character" is someone who is psychologically mature.

On the other hand, psychologically immature persons are more self-centered and unable to empathize with their spouse. They are more likely to do more harm than good.

There are many people who are a lifelong burden to their spouses and hurt them. For those who are married to their spouse with issues such as alcoholism or domestic violence, their marriage is like hell, and their life is like the slavery life of the Israelites in Egypt. There are many people in this world who cannot abandon their "enemy" spouse and live with resignation and sighs. There are also many Christian families who live in such a co-dependent relationship. This is a sad reality.

507

She selects wool and flax and works with eager hands. She is like the merchant ships, bring her food from afar. She gets up while it is still night; she provides food for her family and portions for her female servants. She considers a field and buys it; out of her earnings she plants a vineyard. She sets about her work vigorously; her arms are strong for her tasks. She sees that her trading is profitable, and her lamp does not go out at night. In her hand she holds the distaff and grasps the spindle with her fingers. She opens her arms to the poor and extends her hands to the needy (31:13-20).

In this paragraph, King Lemuel's mother describes specific aspects of the life of a wife of noble character. First, she is industrious with her hands. She has the skill and diligence to gather wool and flax to make clothes for her family.

Second, she has the ability and wisdom to get food for the entire family from the outside world, just as merchants trade goods on the ship. She is active in the economic and social spheres.

Third, she wakes up early in the morning and starts working. She never sleeps late. She has a sense of responsibility as a mistress who prepares breakfast for her household and assigns tasks to her maids. As a supervisor, she has the administrative skills to coordinate the work and relationships of her servants.

Fourth, she has the judgment and independence to look after the fields herself and buy good fields.

Fifth, she buys, clears, and cultivates vineyards with her own money, not her husband's.

Sixth, she works as hard as men and takes care of the field with her own hands. She ties her waists and strengthens her arms so that she can work with a healthy body.

Seventh, she has the wisdom to invest in and profit from her business.

Eighth, she gets up at dawn and works by the light of day.

Ninth, she grasps the spindle with her fingers.
Tenth, she provides relief for the needy and the poor.[469]

When it snows, she has no fear for her household; for all of them are clothed in scarlet. She makes coverings for her bed; she is clothed in fine linen and purple (31:21-22).

[469] The ten descriptions of a wise wife and wise mother thus far are idealized images of the "perfect mom." In reality, very few women are able to be good in all areas and relationships to their husbands, to their children, to their in-laws, to those around them, and to themselves. Such a wife is so rare that it is said, "A wife of noble character who can find? She is worth far more than rubies." Expensive pearls are rare. Even more precious and rare than that pearl is a wife or husband of noble character. Generally speaking, mothers have high expectations for their sons, so they will be rarely satisfied with their prospective daughter-in-law. Likewise, fathers have high expectations of their daughters, so they will be rarely satisfied with their prospective son-in-law. It is conceivable that King Lemuel's mother may have high expectations for her son similar to this dynamic, leading to perfectionist expectations. Personally, I felt suffocated when I read this text. I realized how hard it must be for a woman to live a life like this, and how suffocating it must be for her husband and her children including her servants in the household. Fox notes that such a woman may be rare, but she is a real possibility. Fox, *Proverbs 10-31*, 912. However, the image of the wise woman described in this proverb should be understood as a goal for a husband or wife to strive for. Humans are not capable of doing it all. Human beings are sinful and limited. We need at least five to six hours of sleep a night. No human being can be perfect in all areas. If we do, we would be manic. And God doesn't give one person everything. He even allowed the Apostle Paul to experience a painful thorn in the flesh to keep him from becoming arrogant. When speaking of the gifts given to the church, he asked, "Are all apostles? Are all prophets? Are all teachers? Do all work miracles? Do all have gifts of healing? Do all speak in tongue? Do all interpret?" (1 Cor. 12:29-30). Just as the body has many parts, some more precious and some less beautiful, so every person has strengths and weaknesses. If we understand the woman of noble character as described in the text with modern eyes, her behaviors are parallel with symptoms of a workaholic. She is hardly the "weaker partner" that the apostle Peter described (see 1 Pet. 3:7). It would be almost impossible to marry if one is looking for a woman who fits the descriptions of a wife of noble character. Age-wise, it is also very difficult to find a woman in her twenties or thirties who possesses the qualities and abilities of this wise woman.

Eleventh, she ensures every person in her household enjoys the benefits from her. They are all dressed in fine clothes and treated as such. "When it snows," that is, in times of crisis, she is not afraid, because her household is financially secure.

Twelfth, she is devoted to others, but also has time to take care of herself. She makes beautiful quilts for her bed and wears in fine line and purple. Purple colored clothing was very expensive in the Old Testament time. However, she affords to wear expensive clothes.

Her husband is respected at the city gate, where he takes his seat among the elders of the land (31:23).

Thirteenth, she supports her husband and places him in a position of social honor. He has the status enough to sit at the gate with the elders of the city. She is indeed the "queen of assisting her husband." And her husband receives the recognition and respect he deserves. Status is not the only thing that people recognize. Her husband's integrity and abilities are also proven.

She makes linen garments and sells them, and supplies the merchants with sashes. She is clothed with strength and dignity; she can laugh at the days to come (31:24-25).

Fourteenth, she has the skill to make linen garments herself. She also sells them or trades with merchants.

Fifteenth, she not only adorns herself outwardly with linen and purple garments, but also adorns herself inwardly by wearing her inner garments with strength and honor.[470]

___

[470] We can connect this with Peter's exhortation to women: "Your beauty should not come from outward adornment, such as elaborate hairstyles and the wearing of gold

Sixteenth, she has the ability to laugh about the future. She has the faith and psychological space to write her future narrative positively, not just the present. Even if there are some difficulties in the present, she does not get frustrated or discouraged.

She speaks with wisdom, and faithful instruction is on her tongue. She watches over the affairs of her household and does not eat the bread of idleness. Her children arise and call her blessed; her husband also, and he praises her: "Many women do noble things, but you surpass them all" (31:26-29).

Seventeenth, when she opens her mouth, words of wisdom flow from her heart. She teaches and nurtures her children with wisdom. Her mouth is that of a counselor.

In the phrase, "She speaks with wisdom," I see the importance of wise communication between a husband and wife. A healthy couple has the ability to communicate by using all wisdom and knowledge and empathizing with each other. They have the wisdom to recognize when to speak and when not to speak.

Eighteenth, she cares about the affairs of her entire household, just as Joseph faithfully served in charge of Potiphar's household.

Nineteenth, she does not live in idleness. She also does not fill her house with unrighteous gains. She does not take advantage of her husband's social position to accept bribes.

Twentieth, she earns the respect from her children. She has good enough object relations with her children.

Finally, she receives praise and recognition from her husband, who is closest to her. She is praised for being more virtuous than other women.

In summary, the picture of a wife of noble character with her twenty-one virtues and talents is the picture of the wise person's life that Christians should aspire to. Being as industrious as an ant,

jewelry or fine clothes. Rather, it should be that of your inner self, the unfading beauty of a gentle and quiet spirit, which is of great worth in God's sight" (1 Pet. 3:3-4).

serving the poor with compassion, speaking wise words, neither seeking nor accepting bribes, raising a happy family, and being a good influence on the people and communities around us are God's will for us to be done on earth as it is in heaven.

Christologically speaking, many virtues and strengths of a wife of noble character remind us of Jesus Christ. He is worth far more than rubies (10b). God the Father has full confidence in him (11a). She brings God the Father and us good, not harm, all the days of his life (12a). He worked diligently and faithfully with his hands in his ministry in the world (13b). He brought food of life from afar and became the bread of life from above for us (14b). He got up while it was still night and prayed in solitude and provided spiritual food of God's word for his disciples and followers (15). He set about his work rigorously; his arms were strong for his tasks and his speech was authoritative (17). He opened his arms to the poor and extended his hand to the needy and many people with illnesses (20). His clothes became dazzling white, whiter than anyone in the world could bleach them and he was glorified (22b, Mk. 9:3). He was clothed with strength and dignity and could laugh at the days to come and took cross for us (25). He spoke with wisdom and faithful instruction was on his tongue. (26). He had watched over the affairs of his household before he officially started his ministry (27). He did not eat the bread of idleness (27b). His brothers and sisters in Christ arise and call him blessed and worship him (28a). God the Father glorified him (28b). He surpass all noble men and women (29). We honor him for all that his hand have done (31a). Blessed is a man who finds his wife of noble character. Much more blessed are those who accept Jesus Christ as their bridegroom.

Charm is deceptive, and beauty is fleeting; but a woman who fears the LORD is to be praised. Honor her for all that her hands have done, and let her works bring her praise at the city gate (31:30-31).

This is the last proverb in the book of Proverbs. In particular, the wording of verse 30 suggests that King Lemuel may be Solomon. The declaration that "Charm is deceptive, and beauty if fleeting" is consistent with the central theme of Ecclesiastes: "'Meaningless! Meaningless!' says the Teacher. 'Utterly meaningless! Everything is meaningless'" (Eccl. 1:2). Solomon goes on to ask: "What do people gain from all their labors at which they toil under the sun?" (Eccl. 1:3). In connection with Solomon's statement and question, the qualities of a wife of noble character can be summarized as "charming" and "beautiful. Solomon's pessimistic diagnosis of a human life can be interpreted as a declaration that even if a man finds and lives with an idealized, perfect wife, if she is not a woman who "fears the LORD" (30b), it is all in vain.

The key message of the entire book of Proverbs is that the fear of the LORD is paramount. It is important to be wise and discerning in our interpersonal relationships, but if we do not fear the LORD vertically, our lives are vain and meaningless. This is the conclusion of Proverbs. At the end of Ecclesiastes, Solomon makes this clear: "Now all has been heard; here is the conclusion of the matter: Fear God and keep his commandments, for this is the duty of all mankind" (Eccl. 12:13).

It seems that verse 31 is somehow incomplete and unfinished as the final verse of the entire book of Proverbs. The wise woman is promised that she will reap the fruit of her life. She is also promised that she will receive praise and recognition from the elders at the gates of the city and from the people "for all that her hands have done.[471] Like her, those who fear the LORD will be praised and honored in this world as well as in the final kingdom of God.

---

[471] From an eschatological perspective, we may interpret that a wife of noble character is a metaphor of Christians, the bride of Christ. When we are sincere and diligent in our God-fearing faith in all areas of life, we will hear the praise of the Triune God at the gates of heaven: "Well done, good and faithful servant! You have been faithful with a few things; I will put you in charge of many things. Come and share your master's happiness!" (Matt. 25:21, 23).

References

Kim, Jung Woo (2007). *Bible Commentary: Proverbs.* Korean Christian Books Publisher. (Korean book).

Anders, Max (2005). *Proverbs: The Holman Old Testament Commentary.* Nashville, TN: Broadman & Holman Publishers.

Bridges, Charles (1977). *Proverbs.* rpt. Carslie, PA: The Banner of Truth Trust.

Bunyan, John (1999). *Journey to Hell.* Whitaker House.

Bunyan, John (2001). *The Holy War.* Whitaker House.

Clifford, Richard (1999). *Proverbs.* Louisville, KY: Westminster John Knox Press.

Coogan, Michael (Ed.) (2001). *The New Oxford Annotated Bible.* 3rd Edition. Oxford University Press.

Erickson, Millard (1998). *Christian Theology.* 2nd Ed. Grand Rapids, MI: Baker Books.

Fox, Michael (2009). *Proverbs 10-31.* New Haven, MA: Yale University
  Press.

Fox, Michael (2000). *Proverbs 1-9.* New York: Doubleday.

Hamilton, N. Gregory (1992). *Self and Others: Object Relations Theory in Practice.* Northvale, NJ: Jason Aronson.

Horne, Milton (2003). *Proverbs-Ecclesiastes.* Smith & Helwys Bible Commentary. Macon, GA: Smyth & Helwys.

Jones, David (1994). *Biblical Christian Ethics.* Grand Rapids, MI:

Baker Books.

Koptak, Paul (2003). *Proverbs: The NIV Application Commentary*. Grand Rapids, MI: Zondervan.

Lockyer, Herbert (Ed.) (1986). *Nelson's Illustrated Bible Dictionary*. Nashville: Thomas Nelson Publishers.

Lucas, Ernest (2015). *Proverbs*. Grand Rapids. MI: William B. Eerdmans Publishing Company.

McKane, William (1970). *Proverbs: A New Approach*. Philadelphia: Westminster Press. 1970

Murphy, Roland (1998). *Proverbs: Word Biblical Commentary*. Nelson Reference & Electronic.

Phillips, John (1996). *Exploring Proverbs: An Expository Commentary*. Vol.2. Grand Rapids, MI: Kregel Publications.

Phillips, John (1995). *Exploring Proverbs: An Expository Commentary*. Vol. 1. Grand Rapids, MI: Kregel Publications.

Southard, Samuel (1989). *Theology & Therapy: The Wisdom of God in a Context of Friendship*. Dallas, TX: Word Publishing.

Made in the USA
Columbia, SC
26 October 2024

7c8f3da7-2b9a-4bc0-af95-95a349d64e1aR01